Allah's name with I begin, who is the Most Merciful & Most Beneficent.
Peace and Blessings be upon our Noble Master Prophet Mohammad, his family &
companions

Under the guidance of Renowned Islamic Scholar and Profound leader of the
Naqshbandī Ṣūfī Order

Ḥaḍrat ʿAllāmah Pīr Alāudīn Ṣiddīqī Ṣaḥib (late)

The Tears,

The English Translation of

Al-ʿAbarāt

Musṭafā Luṭfī Al-Manfalūṭī

Including the Arabic text

Translated by

Majid Khan Malik Saddiqui

Edition 1

The Tears, The English Translation of Al-ʿAbarāt

Mustafa Lutfi Al-Manfaluti; Including the Arabic text,

Translated by Majid Khan Malik Saddiqui.

Copyright © 2017. Majid Khan Malik. All rights reserved. First edition Published on the 26th June 2017.

ISBN 978-0-9930730-3-8

British Library Cataloguing in Publication Data.

A catalogue record for this book is available from the British Library.

No part of this publication may be reproduced, distributed, or transmitted in any form or by any means, including photocopying, or other electronic or mechanical methods, without the prior written permission of the publisher, except in the case of brief quotations embodied in critical reviews and certain other non-commercial uses permitted by copyright law.

Published by:

Noor Alam publications

Malik Cloth House

122–126 Lumb lane

Bradford

West Yorkshire

BD8 7RS

United Kingdom

07969608551

majidmalik@hotmail.co.uk

www.hajisclothhouse.co.uk

Allah's name with I begin, who is the Most Merciful & Most Beneficent. Peace and Blessings be upon our Noble Master Prophet Mohammad, his companions, the mothers of the believers and his family.

Introductory Sermon

All praises belong to Allah ﷻ, we praise Him, we seek His assistance and we seek His forgiveness, and to Him we turn. We seek protection in Allah ﷻ from the evil in ourselves and from the evil of our actions. Whoever Allah ﷻ guides, none can misguide, and whoever Allah ﷻ misguides, for him there is no guide. I testify that there is none worthy of worship but Allah ﷻ, and that He is alone and has no partners with him. I also testify that Mohammad ﷺ is His slave and Messenger, whom Allah ﷻ has sent with guidance and with the Religion of Truth.

The most truthful speech is the book of Allah ﷻ and the best guidance is the guidance of Prophet Mohammad ﷺ. The worst of matters are the evil innovated matters in religion. Every bad innovation is misguidance and leads to the fire of hell. We seek refuge with Allah ﷻ from making any lawful act unlawful and likewise making any unlawful act lawful. Those things which have been forbidden by Allah ﷻ and his Messenger ﷺ are unlawful and those things which have been classified lawful by Allah ﷻ and his Messenger ﷺ are lawful.

We also acknowledge, as permissible voluntary practice, those things which have not been mentioned, provided that if they fit in within the framework of Islam.

We testify that our beloved master Prophet Mohammad ﷺ was the first creation of Allah ﷻ, in the form of a blessed light (Nūr) which was then transported from the loin of Prophet Adam (Peace of Allah ﷻ be upon him), through countless centuries, to the womb of dear mother Āminah (Rd). This is when the Prophet's blessed light/Nūr was combined with his blessed body and he ﷺ was born in Mecca, Saudia Arabia. Therefore, we acknowledge that the Holy Prophet Mohammad

ﷺ is the possessor of two states: He was made out of light as well as possessing a human body. This is inevitably the view, belief and the doctrine of the **Mainstream Orthodox Islamic world.** The holy Prophet Mohammad ﷺ is the best of all creation, more prestigious, remarkable and supreme than any other creation.

We further acknowledge that the best man after all the Prophets is the blessed companion Ḥaḍrat Abū Bakr Siddīq (Rd), the first Caliph of the Muslim nation. Following him, Ḥaḍrat ʿUmar bin Khaṭṭāb (Rd), known as Farūq the great who became the second Caliph of the Muslim nation. Then, Ḥaḍrat ʿUthmān Bin ʿAffān (Rd), famously known as ʿUthman-e-Ghanī dhi-n-nūrayn, the third Caliph of the Muslim nation. Following him, Ḥaḍrat ʿAli Bin Abī Tālib (Rd) known as Ḥaydar-e-Qarrār, the son-in-law and the cousin of our beloved master Prophet Mohammed ﷺ, and also the fourth Caliph. These great Caliphs hold their degrees of excellence according to their order of succession.

May Allah ﷻ and his beloved Messenger ﷺ accept this book in their courts through the supplications of my beloved Shaykh, Shaykhu-l-Islām ʿAllāmah Pīr Alāudīn Siddīqī Sāhib (Rh), the supplications of my beloved Parents and of my respected teachers, Āmīn.

Acknowledgments

The Tears, has been written by Muṣṭafā Luṭfī Al-Manfalūṭī and translated into English by Majid Khan Malik Saddiqui. The English translation has been produced with help from the following people. Their tireless efforts have been paramount to the success of this book. May Allah ﷻ reward their efforts, both in this life and the hereafter, Amīn.

- **Qiblah Ḥaḏrat Shaykh ʿAllāmah Pīr Alāudīn Ṣiddīqī Ṣāḥib (late) (Rh)**. Their knowledge and guidance during my study of this book has been greatly appreciated. A couple of paragraphs are assigned to Qiblah Pīr Ṣāḥib in the upcoming dedication section.

- ʿAllāmah Qāḍhī Sājid Ẓafar Ṣāḥib (Birmingham, UK). Many thanks for his teaching expertise. A man with the following qualities: -
  - A profound cleric, scholar and minister of Islam.
  - Master of Islamic Jurisprudence and liberal Arts.
  - Former Judge of Azad Kashmir.
  - Awarded a Gold medal for his intermediate exams from former Prime Minister of Azad Kashmir Sardar Muhammad Abdul Qayyum Khan.

- Allāmah Qārī Ḥāfiẓ Shawwāl Aḥmad Hāshmī Ṣāḥib (Bradford, UK). Many thanks for enhancing my analytical skills in Arabic literature.

- Sobea Hussain BA (Joint Hons) -English Literature & Theology (Bradford, UK). Many thanks for proof reading this book several times, for mentoring my work and closely guiding the compilation throughout.

- Umme Abid (BA Hons) – Combined studies, Postgraduate Certificate Research Methods (Bradford UK). Many appreciations for proof reading this book numerous times.

Teachers

In conjunction with the teachers acknowledged, the following respected authorities have also had a great part in shaping and developing my understanding of the Arabic language and of the Islamic knowledge, through the mercy of Allah ﷻ and His Messenger Mohammad ﷺ. May Allah Almighty bless them all: -

- Late Mowlānā Bas͟hīr A͟hmad Siyālwī (Birmingham, UK) (R͟h)
- ʿAllāmah Rasūl Ba͟k͟hs͟h Saʿīdī (Birmingham, UK)
- Late ʿAllāmah Saʿīd A͟hmad Bandyālwī (Birmingham, UK) (R͟h)
- Mowlānā Professor ͟Hāfi͟z Amīn Madanī (Birmingham, UK)
- Muftī ʿAbdu-r-Rusūl Mansūr Alazharī (Redditch, UK)
- Mowlānā ͟Hāfi͟z Qārī As͟hraf Qādrī (Bradford, UK)
- ʿAllāmah Pirzada Imdad Hussain (Jamiatu-l-Karam – Retford UK)
- Ha͟drat Pīr Sayyid Maʿrūf ͟Hussayn S͟hah ʿĀrif Nows͟hāhī Qādrī (Bradford, UK) (Dba)
- ʿAllāmah S͟hayk͟hu-l-͟Hadīth Pīr Irfān S͟hah Mas͟hhadī (Bradford, UK)
- Muftī Fā͟dil Bandyālwī (Bradford, UK)
- Muftī Aslam Bandyālwī (Bradford, UK)
- Professor ͟Khalīfah ʿĀrif (Nelson, UK)
- ͟Hāfi͟z Qārī Alāudīn (Bradford, UK)
- Mowlānā S͟hazād (Nottingham, UK)
- Late Mowlānā Firdowsī As͟hraf S͟hah (Bradford, UK)

- ʿAllāmah Anwāru-l-Muṣṭafā Hamdamī (Bradford, UK)
- Pīr Nūru-l-ʿĀrifīn Ṣaḥib Naqshbandī (Dba) (Aston, Birmingham)
- Pīr Sulṭānu-l-ʿĀrifīn Ṣaḥib (Dba) (Neyriyā Sharīf, AK, Pakistan)
- Mowlānā Zayd Hussayn (Bradford, UK)
- Beloved colleague Mowlānā Ḥamzah Raḥīm ʿAlī (Bradford UK)
- Mowlānā Shafīqu-r-Raḥmān (Walsall UK)
- Mowlānā Usman Shah (Heckmondwike UK)
- Mowlānā Saḥibzāda Ẓahīru-d-Dīn (Birmingham, UK)
- Mowlānā Ḥafiẓ Zulfiqār (Birmingham, UK)
- Mowlānā Muḥammad Suleymān (Birmingham, UK)
- ʿAllāmah Saʿīd Asad Naqshbandī (Fayslabād, Pakistan)
- Amjad Bashīr (Aylesbury UK)
- Kadir Bashir (Reading UK)
- Ṣūfī Anṣar Raḥmān (Keighley UK)

Dedication

All praise is for Allah the Lord of the entire universe. Peace and Blessings be upon our most noble and beloved Master Prophet Mohammad, his blessed wives the mothers of the believers, his family, his progeny and all of his companions.

I have translated this book with the supplications of my most respected Shaykh ʿAllāmah Pīr Alāudīn Ṣiddīqī Ṣāhib (Rh). I am also a student who has benefitted from the knowledge of various sciences under the supervision of my beloved

Shaykh in his Islamic academy, Jamia-Mohiuddin Saddiquia Birmingham UK. This is where my Shaykh has provided Islamic knowledge to myself and my other colleagues for eight years, out of his own expense. Therefore, if as a reader, student or scholar, you do benefit from this book, it is my Shaykh who is entitled to the credit, and not myself. I pray for my Shaykh from the depth of my heart as he was the person who gave me inspiration and motivation. His blessed attention to a sinful being like myself is the biggest gift in my life, and I am dedicating this book to him. A few paragraphs giving a brief account of his works are followed shortly below. I make the supplication to Allah ﷻ that He ﷻ accepts this work in his glorified courts with the medium of the Holy Prophet Mohammad ﷺ.

Also, my work has benefitted greatly from the prayers and patronage of my parents, Ḥāji ʿAbdul Mālik and Ḥājan Nasīm Akhtar Kalsūm Bī, who have invested a lot of wealth towards my Islamic education. I request all readers to make a special supplication for them. They have supported me with great compassion throughout my life, and still continue to support me and my family, both financially and morally. May Allah ﷻ always keep them under his shade, making both their worldly life and hereafter fruitful and blissful, and let no calamity or misfortune ever befall them, Āmīn.

Throughout the process of this book, I have continually received the patience and support of my wife Shamim Ara, and all other family members and friends. I pray to Allah Almighty to safeguard them, and all their dearest, from calamity and misfortune, and give them every legitimate happiness, both in this life and the hereafter, Āmīn.

I implore all readers to make a special supplication for my best friend Imran Iqbal, who has supported me since childhood, through good times and bad. I also request the readers to make supplications for all my friends and all my loved ones. Please make a supplication for my friends Molana Hamza Rahim Ali, Zafir Bashir, Safeer Bashir, Haroon Awan and Nadeem Rahim, all from Bradford, UK. May Allah ﷻ make their world and hereafter blissful, and always keep them steadfast in Faith, Āmīn.

Through Allah's ﷻ mercy and the medium of our beloved Rasūl ﷺ, the final version of this book has been accomplished. **The Tears, The English Translation of Al-'Abarāt**, by Majid Khan Malik Saddiqui, is the product of tireless support, prayers and commitment from all individuals mentioned in both the Acknowledgments and Dedication. May Allah ﷻ always keep them, and myself, under His ﷻ shade in both worlds, away from satanic influences, and in the height of faith at all times, Āmīn.

Respected S̲h̲ayk̲h̲ ʿAllāmah Pīr Alāudīn S̲iddīqī S̲āh̲ib
(Late) (Rh̲)

S̲h̲ayk̲h̲ ʿAllāmah Pīr Alāudīn S̲iddīqī S̲āh̲ib (Rh̲) was a remarkable and renowned Sunni scholar of Islam. He was also a prominent Sūfī Master of the Naqs̲h̲bandī Sūfī order and made the successor of the Naqs̲h̲bandī Sūfī order by his father, Pīr ʿAllāmah Muh̲yu-d-dīn G̲h̲aznawī (Rh̲). His remarkable character and profound personality was respected by all. Furthermore, he was followed by millions due to his spiritual and intellectual teachings and countless worldwide projects relating to charity, education, health and welfare. He was the founder and the chairman of Sky channel 812, Noor TV, which is televised in over 160 countries. He was the chancellor for the Islamic Mohiuddin University (A.J.K) and Medical College Mirpur (P.K). He also launched The **Sūfī Academy** in April 2009 with Hazel Blears (former secretary of state for local government) and Sion Simon (former education minister) at Westminster in the Houses of Parliament, UK.

My respected S̲h̲ayk̲h̲ is known for translating and commentating on **Math̲nawī**, the works of **Mowlānā Jalāludīn Rūmī** (Rh̲) on Noor TV. He is also known for making large contributions towards charity. In 2014 he raised a sum of £180,000 to donate towards the Palestinians in the Gaza appeal. In October 2005 he provided substantial aid and money towards the tragedy of the 17th largest world earthquake, which appeared in Kashmir, Pakistan. Child sponsorship is also a recognised merit of Pīr S̲āh̲ib's works. He also took projects to provide clean and fresh water in remote locations benefitting, 70-80 thousand residents at places such as Dera Ghazi Khan (D.G khan), Pakistan.

Furthermore, he annually organised the biggest Milādu-n-Nabī ﷺ gatherings ever organised in European history at Aston Park, Birmingham, UK, in which Islamic scholars, people from all other faiths and politicians had taken part.

My beloved Pīr Sāhib also spearheaded the diplomatic campaign against the defamation of Islam and of the holy Prophet Mohammad in 2012 as the head of the British Muslim Alliance. Protests and meetings were conducted inside and outside of the houses of Parliament at Westminster. He conducted a meeting with the British Prime Minister David Cameron about the matter at 10 Downing Street. A filed petition signed by over 170,000 people, collected by ʿAllāmah Pīr Alāudīn Siddīqī Sāhib (Rh) was then given to the British Parliament in support of passing the bill to protect all faith symbols. In March 2013, this matter was discussed further in the European Parliament in Brussels, Belgium.

Shaykhu-l-Islām ʿAllāmah Pīr Alāudīn Siddīqī Sāhib (Rh) can be found on Facebook, twitter, YouTube, www.mohiudintrust.com, www.thenoortv.tv, aftab@mohiudddintrust.com. and at www.baharemadinah.com. Further reading of ʿAllāmah Pīr Alāudīn Siddīqī Sāhib (Rh) life and works can be obtained from the book, As-Siddīqiyatu-l-Kāmil, ISBN: 978-0-9930730-0-7.

Author's note: -

There is a concise version of this book available in paperback, English only, as a general read, ISBN: - 978-0-9930730-1-4. The same book is also available as an EBook, ISBN: - 978-0-9930730-2-1.

This book has been read exhaustively and checked limitless times. All efforts and scrutiny have been used to ensure that it is free from any errors, discrepancies and deficiencies. However, as a reader or critic, if you do find a mistake, we would be grateful if you could inform us, so we can remove or rectify in the next edition. To do this, please email - majidmalik@hotmail.co.uk

Arabic to English Transcription

The Arabic Alphabet

Twenty-nine characters of the Arabic alphabet are illustrated in **Fig 1**. All these letters are consonants with the exception of the letter Alif.

Fig 1.

Tr.	Name		Letter	Tr.	Name		Letter
T	طا	Tā	ط	-	ألف	Alif	ا
Z	ظا	Zā	ظ	B	با	Bā	ب
ʿ	عين	ʿAyn	ع	T	تا	Tā	ت
Gh	غين	Ghayn	غ	**Th**	ثا	Thā	ث
F	فا	Fā	ف	J	جيم	Jīm	ج
Q	قاف	Qāf	ق	**H**	حا	Hā	ح
K	كاف	Kāf	ك	**Kh**	خا	Khā	خ
L	لام	Lām	ل	D	دال	Dāl	د
M	ميم	Mīm	م	**Dh**	ذال	Dhāl	ذ
N	نون	Nūn	ن	R	را	Rā	ر
H	ها	Hā	ه	Z	زا	Zā	ز
W	واو	Wāw	و	S	سين	Sīn	س
A	همزة	Hamzah	ء	**Sh**	شين	Shīn	ش
Y	يا	Yā	ي	**S**	صاد	Sād	ص
				D	ضاد	Dād	ض

Tr. = Transcription

The short vowels in the Arabic language are expressed through diacritical marks. These vowels are transcribed below in **Fig 2**.

Fig 2.

Name	Diacritical Mark	Tr.
Dammah	ُ (Above letter)	u
Fathah	َ (Above letter)	a
Kasrah	ِ (Below letter)	e/i

The long vowels in the Arabic language are proceeded after the Hurūf-e-Maddah. These are three, (1) Wāw (2) Alif (3) Yā. These vowels are transcribed below in **Fig 3**.

Fig 3.

Name	Tr.
Wāw Maddah	Ū
Alif Maddah	Ā
Yā maddah	Ī

A Vowel-less letter

In the Arabic language, at times they are consonants which contain neither a **Fathah,** a **Dammah** or a **Kasrah**. In this case they would be considered as a consonant with no vowel upon it. In Arabic the consonant which is vowel-less is called a **Sākin** and it is represented by a **small circle** which is placed directly above that consonant. That specific circle is called a **Sukūn**.

The Contents Page

- About the Author; Mustafā Lutfī Al-Manfalūtī — Page xiii
- About Al-ʿAbarāt — Page xvi
- About the Translation in English — Page xvii
- Note regarding the name of Allah ﷻ — Page xviii

- The Orphan - Al-Yatīm — Page 1
- The Martyrs - Ash-Shuhadā — Page 23
- The Veil - Al-Hijāb — Page 57
- The Remembrance - Adh-Dhikrā — Page 85
- The Abyss - Al-Hāwiyyah — Page 115
- The Reward - Al-Jazā — Page 137
- The Punishment - Al-ʿIqāb — Page 163

- The Victim – Ad-Dahiyyah – The Story — Page 197
- The Victim – Ad-Dahiyyah – Margaret's Diary — Page 255
- The Victim – Ad-Dahiyyah – Prudence's Diary — Page 303

- Crediting of the Merits — Page 314
- References — Page 317
- Glossary — Page 318

About the Author; Muṣṭafā Luṭfī Al-Manfalūṭī

The early and the late nineteenth century witnessed many prominent writers. These writers took great inspiration from their time and surroundings, making a huge contribution to literary heritage.

Such talented writers include British Novelists such as Mohammad Marmaduke Pickthal or Charles Dickens, and Dr Sir Mohammad Iqbal from the Indian Sub-continent. Also history cannot deny another distinguished Arabic litterateur, who was born in Egypt on the 30th December 1876, in a town called Manfalūt, belonging to the province of Asyūt. This man was called Muṣṭafā Luṭfī Al-Manfalūṭī. The title of 'Al-Manfalūṭī' is suffixed to his name to represent his place of birth. This town of Manfalūt is about two hundred and thirty miles south of Cairo itself.

Muṣṭafā Luṭfī Al-Manfalūṭī is prestigiously enlisted as one of the most talented and prolific writers/novelists of his time. He was predominantly known for translating many plays and French novels into the Arabic language. His ethnicity was a mix of Arab and Turkish decedents. His father was of Arab origin and his mother was part Turkish. Their family tree went back to the Ḥussaynī lineage and the holy Prophet Mohammad ﷺ.

The atmosphere of his household centred around education and knowledge. To be precise, in Islamic Jurisprudence and Tasawwuf. Muṣṭafā Luṭfī Al-Manfalūṭī's father practiced law, as he was a qualified Judge/Qāḍhī, who used to offer his services to a Muslim Court.

Until the age of eleven, Muṣṭafā Luṭfī Al-Manfalūṭī attained his primary education from a local school, cross learning the Quran at the same time in the mosque. The Mosque and the school were connected to one another. This was the norm of the society. It was during this time when Muṣṭafā Luṭfī Al-Manfalūṭī memorised the holy Quran by heart.

From then onwards, in 1888, Muṣṭafā Luṭfī Al-Manfalūṭī was enrolled by his father at the Al-Azhar University, Cairo, in order to maintain the family legacy. Within the span of ten years, Muṣṭafā Luṭfī Al-Manfalūṭī acquired religious, traditional and scientific knowledge, and was also educated in literature and linguistics. He studied exegesis of the holy Quran, and Arts in Eloquence. He motivated his entire attention towards the department of linguistics, language and literature.

Muṣṭafā Luṭfī Al-Manfalūṭī's passion for memorising poetry and poetic quotes led him to write poems and articles, which made him popular within his circle. Mohammad Abduhu was drawn to him, He was a lecturer at the Al-Azhar University, and also an Egyptian Islamic Jurist, who helped Muṣṭafā Luṭfī to refine his linguistic skills. Both men became close friends.

It would be no exaggeration to call Muṣṭafā Luṭfī Al-Manfalūṭī a reviver of language. He clearly demonstrated a new side and style of language, which was revolutionary for that time. Without a shadow of doubt he was a genius, and one of a kind. He had the ability to touch the emotions of people in depth through poetic structure, metaphorical language and sophisticated, eloquent imagery. During his time, he was an innovator of writing and a pioneer of modern Arabic Prose. Despite being unfamiliar with any European languages, or ever leaving Egypt, his talent and work transcends all cultural and social boundaries.

In his era, old literature was not admired but new literature was in demand and welcomed. He covered social, nostalgic and environmental values alongside portraying varied and complex sentiments within the framework of his literature. He is profoundly recognised for his work *'Al-'Abarāt,'* translated as *'The Tears,'* the book which we have selected to translate into English. His readers have identified with the characters of his novels instantly and sympathised with the moral message of the text.

He was a predominant translator of his time. There is a dispute amongst people about whether Muṣṭafā Luṭfī Al-Manfalūṭī was an author or solely a translator. Some say he had modified other adaptions which belonged to Western fiction, and merged them into Arabic. However, this is only partly true, and to call him a mere translator would be incorrect. Muṣṭafā Luṭfī Al-Manfalūṭī also authored his own works. As he himself could not speak, read, neither write any European languages, his friends dictated and narrated for him various plays to Arabic which he then composed and structured into novels. Using his uniquely sensitive, talented and emotive style within the stories, he incorporated his own style of melancholy and sentimentality.

Muṣṭafā Luṭfī Al-Manfalūṭī did have many ups and down in his life and underwent many different phases. At the early stages of his life, for a period of six months, he was imprisoned for publishing a poem. This poem was considered an insult to Mohammad Ali, Tewfik Pasha and Abbas Hilmi Pasha, who ruled Egypt and Sudan at that time, under the movement Khedive Abbas of the Ottoman Empire. Surprisingly, Muṣṭafā Luṭfī Al-Manfalūṭī later twice became a reporter in the Ministry of Education, under Sayyad Pasha, and remained there until his death. After Muṣṭafā Luṭfī Al-Manfalūṭī had served his six-month term, he was deeply saddened to learn about the death of Mohammad Abduhu when he returned home in 1924. Muṣṭafā Luṭfī Al-Manfalūṭī gained fame in 1907.

Muṣṭafā Luṭfī Al-Manfalūṭī had published many works. The first was in 1910 called *'Al-Naẓrāt'* translated as *'The Looks.'* One volume out of three encompassed stories, criticisms and other writings from *'Al-Mu'ayyad,'* a weekly newspaper, regarded as the voice of the Khadive Abbas, which Muṣṭafā Luṭfī Al-Manfalūṭī contributed towards previously. The book *'Al-Naẓrāt'* was also known as *'Al-Usbu'iyāt.'* In 1912 Muṣṭafā Luṭfī Al-Manfalūṭī published *'Magdulin/Mājdawlīn,'* in which he translated the emotional novel *'Sous les Tilleuls'* belonging to Alphonse Karr. In 1912 *'Mukhtārāt'* was also composed which was the collection of the poems of Muṣṭafā Luṭfī Al-Manfalūṭī.

In year 1915, Muṣṭafā Luṭfī Al-Manfalūṭī's book *'Al-'Abarāt'* which translated as *'The Tears'* was published. This book contains his authored stories in conjunction with other short stories. Approximately a hundred years after, Allah ﷻ has now given us the opportunity to translate this book into English.

Progressing forth, in 1920 Muṣṭafā Luṭfī Al-Manfalūṭī published *'Fī Sabīli-t-Tāj'* translated as *'For the sake of the Crown,'* in which he adapted Francois Coppee's play *'Pour la Couronne'.'* In 1921 he converted Edmond Rostand's play *'Cyrano de Bergerac'* into a novel and published it as *'Ash-Shā'ir.'* In 1923 he reproduced Bernardin de Saint Pierr's adaption *'Paul et Virginie'* and named it *'Al-Faḍīlah.'*

Muṣtafā Luṭfī Al-Manfalūtī lived up to the age of 48 and passed away on the 25th July 1924. At that time, he was currently working as a reporter in the Ministry of Education, under Sayyad Pasha, for the welfare of the state.

About Al-'Abarāt – The Tears

The book *Al-'Abarāt* which is authored by Muṣtafā Luṭfī Al-Manfalūtī is inclusive of eight short stories in total. Four short stories from amongst them are the authors very own production, which are; Al-Yatīm/The Orphan, Al-Ḥijāb/The Veil, Al-Hāwiyyah/The Abyss and Al-'Iqāb/The Punishment. The remaining four are translations of the works of others. These are; Ash-Shuhadā/The Martyrs, Adh-Dhikrā/The Remembrance, Al-Jazā/The Reward and Ad-Daḥiyyah/The Victim. Adding to this note, it has been said that the story 'Al-'Iqāb/The punishment,' is based on an American story called 'The cry of the Grave.'

Amongst the four translated stories, two are the writings of Chateavbriand, who was a French Diplomat and a writer. 'Ash-Shuhadā/The Martyrs,' is a revised account of the French play *'Atala'* which was initiated in 1801. 'Adh-Dhikrā/The Remembrance' is a rendered version of the French play *'Les aventures du dernier Abencerage'* which was written in 1826. Furthermore, 'Ad-Daḥiyyah/The Victim' is reproduced from Alexandre Dumas Fils's *'La dame aux camelias'* (1848). This story is the longest in the collection and it appears at the end. Concerning the story 'Al-Jazā/The Reward,' it is said that this has also been revised from a French adaption.

These stories emphasise certain themes, messages and sentiments which the readers could draw at their discretion. For example, the story 'Adh-Dhikrā/The Remembrance, has some historical significance, as it is set around the era of the collapsing of the Mohammadan ﷺ Rule in Spain.

All the stories invite discussion, upon topics such as how the author/translator felt towards them, how he incorporated Western values and how he represented different cultures. Due to this work, Muṣtafā Luṭfī Al-Manfalūtī gained a high degree of popularity in the twentieth century. His book *Al-'Abarāt*, in conjunction with his other works still lives and is highlighted within the Arab world even today.

Al-ʿAbarāt holds significance even today, in leading educational institutions of the Arab peninsula and beyond. In Cairo at the Al-Azhar University this particular book plays a very important and a crucial part in terms of teaching students Arabic at a higher tier/level. Certain sections are selected and taught in order to build a platform for the students.

About the Translation in English

As mentioned earlier, this book is the English translation of the Arabic book *Al-ʿAbarāt* which means **'The Tears,'** authored by an Egyptian scholar Muṣtafā Luṭfī Al-Manfalūṭī. The Arabic Text of the original book has also been included in conjunction with the English translation. This has been done in order to aid students in analysing the English and the Arabic text simultaneously.

All attempts have been made in order to accurately translate this classical Arabic into English. However, a direct word to word translation has not been carried out. This is because the formalities and conventions of the English language differ from the Arabic language. Certain vocabulary has been substituted to aid consistency and ease of understanding. A direct word for word translation of the whole text would have been difficult for the reader to comprehend.

Adding to that, at some places we have only used the meanings, the connotations of the Arabic text drawn from collective sentences and then translated them into the English language with its best counterpart. This has only been done to avoid confusion and to bring the translated text into the correct alignment with current linguistic conventions.

We have also referred to an Urdu translated version of this book, by Muḥammad Amīn Khokhar and Mowlānā Akhyārullah, composed and edited by Yasin Kasuri. The details of this book are enlisted in the reference section.

For each story, we have not provided a brief introduction. This has been included in the Urdu translated version but not in the original Arabic version. This was because we did not want to spoil the novel for the readers. We want to maintain the suspense throughout.

Note regarding the name of Allah ﷻ in the English translation

This book predominantly contains stories belonging to the Christian background and not Islam. Hence, reference is made to God on numerous accounts. Regardless, whenever reference will be made to God, we will use the name of Allah ﷻ specifically instead of God in the English translation. This is because of the following two reasons.

Firstly, the author Mustafā Lutfī Al-Manfalūtī has himself used the name of Allah ﷻ in his works; As we are translating from his text, it would be accurate to stick with the name of Allah ﷻ not God.

Secondly, Muslims believe in the same God as Christians and Jews. In other words, Allah ﷻ is the God of Moses, the God of Jesus and God of Prophet Mohammad (Peace be upon them all) as well as the God of all creation. Therefore, as He ﷻ is the same divine being, it is correct to utilise the name of Allah ﷻ in the English translation.

"Remember us, for we too have lived, loved and laughed."

(Quote taken from; **Shutter Island, 19/12/10 Hollywood Motion Picture.** *A close up shot of the Hospital Cemetery stating this quote on a plaque).*

The Orphan / Al-Yatīm (Composed)

Some time ago, in a neighbouring high flat, there lived a boy, who was aged between nineteen or twenty. I presumed that he was a student, from the town's college or university.

I used to observe him regularly, through the window of my library, which was directly opposite his flat. Before me, I witnessed a paled faced, distressed and weak young man, sitting soulfully besides a kindled lamp in one corner of his room.

Sometimes, the young man was studying a book, or writing, at other times he was revising from a piece of paper. I never had paid attention or was bothered with a thing from his affairs until the night I returned to my house after midnight. The night was extremely cold. It was one of cold nights of the winter. I entered my library to work. I took a look at that young man and caught him sitting in his place besides his lamp. He was leaning with his head facing down upon the opened book before him. I presumed that he was either suffering from being awake or tiredness from revising. His eyes were heavy under the weight of sleep. Finally retiring for the night, while going to his bed, he fell down.

Before I had moved from my place, the young man raised his head and I discovered that his eyes were full of tears. He was weeping upon his book, tears had soaked the pages and erased the text, making the ink spread across the pages. After a while that young man gathered himself together, cleaned his pen and returned to his former state of studying.

It distressed me that I had seen this troubled, poor young man, who was all alone in a cold empty room in the dark night. He did not have a blanket or a fire which could protect him from the bitter coldness. He was grieving over the stresses of life, or he had fallen into the calamities of life before he had reached the age of stresses and calamities. He was in such a state, and had no one to share his feelings to, nor any helper. I thought to myself, that most certainly there must be a man with a broken heart behind this distressing scene, who's heart was rapidly melting away between his ribs, and his body was going to collapse like the way a deteriorated building would collapse. I stayed standing in my place, not moving until I saw him folding away his book and taken refuge in his bed. Then, I turned towards my bedroom.

اليتيم
(موضوعة)

سكن الغرفة العليا من المنزل المجاور لمنزلي من عهدٍ قريبٍ فتًى في التاسعة عشر أو العشرين من عمره، وأحسب أنه طالب من طلبة المدارس العليا أو الوسطى في مصر،

فقد كنت أراه من نافذة غرفة مكتبي، وكانت على كثبٍ من بعض نوافذ غرفته فأرى أمامي فتًى شاحباً نحيلاً منقبضاً جالساً إلى مصباح منيرٍ في إحدى زوايا الغرفة،

ينظر في كتابٍ أو يكتب في دفترٍ أو يستظهر قطعةً أو يعيد درساً، فلم أكن أحفل بشيءٍ من أمره، حتى عدت إلى منزلي منذ أيام بعد منتصف ليلة قرةٍ من ليالي الشتاء، فدخلت غرفة مكتبي لبعض الشؤون، فأشرفت عليه فإذا هو جالس جلسته تلك أمام مصباحه، وقد أكب بوجهه على دفترٍ منشورٍ بين يديه على مكتبه فظننت أنه لما ألم به من تعب الدرس وآلام السهر قد عبثت بجفنيه سنة من النوم، فأعجلته من الذهاب إلى فراشه وسقطت به مكانه؛

فما رمت مكاني حتى رفع رأسه، فإذا عيناه مخضلتان من البكاء، وإذا صفحة دفتره التي كان مكباً عليها قد جرى دمعه فوقها فمحا من كلماتها ما محا، ومشى ببعض مدادها إلى بعض، ثم لم يلبث أن عاد إلى نفسه فتناول قلمه ورجع إلى شأنه الذي كان فيه.

فأحزنني أن أرى في ظلمة ذلك الليل وسكونه هذا الفتى البائس المسكين منفرداً بنفسه في غرفةٍ عاريةٍ باردة لا يتقي فيها عادية البرد بدثارٍ ولا نارٍ، يشكو هماً من هموم الحياة أو رزءٍ من أرزائها قبل أن يبلغ سن الهموم والأحزان من حيث لا يجد بجانبه مواسياً ولا معيناً، وقلت لا بد أن يكون وراء هذا المنظر الضارع الشاحب نفس قريحة معذبة تذوب بين أضلاعه ذوباً فيتهافت لها جسمه تهافت الخباء المقوض، فلم أزل واقفاً مكاني لا أبرحه حتى رأيته قد طوى كتابه وفارق مجلسه وأوى إلى فراشه فانصرفت إلى مخدعي،

The night passed with the exception of a little remaining. Only a small portion of darkness remained on the page of the horizon, near where the tongue of the morning would advance and lick it off.

After that, I continued to look at him during most nights. Either he was crying, or leaning forward, hitting his head on his chest. Sometimes he was wrapped up in bed sobbing like a distressed mother, who has lost her child, or walking up and down his room touching the walls in a distressed state until tiredness took over him. Then he would fall down on his chair, crying and screaming. I became emotionally moved and cried when I saw him cry, wishing I had the power to remove his calamities like a true friend. I wanted to discover his secret, so that I could participate in his sorrows. However, I disliked interfering, to discover the hidden secret of his heart as this would invade his privacy.

Yesterday, after a slight portion of the night had passed, I saw that his silent room was darkened. Initially I presumed that he had gone out for some matter, but after a while I heard from the midst of the room a constant low sound of wailing. I became worried, as I felt his calling came out from the bottom of his heart. I thought that this young man is ill, and does not have anyone who could care for him. I became increasingly concerned for his wretched state, and went to check on him.

My servant guided me with his lamp until I reached his house. Upon reaching the front door, I felt a dreadful fear, like one who is standing upon the door of a grave, to say his last farewell to its resident.

I entered and he opened his eyes when he felt my presence. In the dim lamp light, I saw the dazed look of amazement on his face. He stared at me for a while without talking and neither moving. I drew near to his bed and sat down next to him, declaring "I am your neighbour. For a while I have been listening to you, and have gathered that you require prompt medical attention. I know you are alone in this room. Are you ill? I am sorry for your condition and have come to help you as best as I can." He raised his hand slowly and placed it on his forehead, I too placed my hand on his head on top and I felt he was extremely feverish.

His fever seemed to have passed through his body. He writhed and struggled in his loose leather shirt. I instructed my servant to bring the appropriate medicine from my home, and gave him a few drops.

Upon drinking, he regained some consciousness and said "Thank you" with the same look of amazement.

وقد مضى الليل إلا أقله، ولم يبق من سواده في صفحة هذا الوجود إلا بقايا أسطرٍ يوشك أن يمتد إليها لسان الصباح فيأتي عليها.

ثم لم أزل أراه بعد ذلك في كثيرٍ من الليالي إما باكياً، أو مطرقاً أو ضارباً برأسه على صدره، أو منطوياً على نفسه في فراشه يئن أنين الوالهة الثكل، أو هائماً في غرفته يذرع أرضها، ويمسح جدرانها حتى إذا نال منه الجهد سقط على كرسيه باكياً منتحباً، فأتوجع له وأبكي لبكائه وأتمنى لو استطعت أن أداخله مداخلة الصديق لصديقه، أستبثه ذات نفسه وأشركه في همه لولا أنني كرهت أن أفجأه بما لا يحب، وأن أهجم منه على سر ربما كان يؤثر الإبقاء عليه في صدره، وأن يكاتمه الناس جميعاً،

حتى أشرفت عليه ليلة أمس بعد هدأةٍ من الليل، فرأيت غرفته مظلمة ساكنةً فظننت أنه خرج لبعض شأنه، ثم لم ألبث أن سمعت في جوف الغرفة أنّةً ضعيفةً مستطيلةً فأزعجني مسمعها وخيل إلي، وهي صادرة من أعماق نفسه، كأنني أسمع رنينها في أعماق قلبي، وقلت إن الفتى مريض ولا يوجد بجانبه من يقوم بشأنه، وقد بلغ الأمر مبلغ الجد فلا بد لي من المصير إليه،

فتقدمت إلى خادمي أن يتقدمني بمصباح حتى بلغت منزله وصعدت إلى باب غرفته فأدركني من الوحشة عند دخولها ما يدرك الواقف على باب قبرٍ يحاول أن يهبطه ليودع ساكنه الوداع الأخير،

ثم دخلت ففتح عينيه عندما أحس بي، وكأنما كان ذاهلاً أو مستغرقاً، فأدهشه أن يرى بين يديه مصباحاً ضئيلاً ورجلاً لا يعرفه، فلبث شاخصاً إلي هنيهةً لا ينطق ولا يطرف، فاقتربت من فراشه وجلست بجانبه، وقلت أنا جارك القاطن هذا المنزل، وقد سمعتك الساعة تعالج نفسك علاجاً شديداً، وعلمت أنك وحدك في هذه الغرفة فعناني أمرك، فجئتك علني أستطيع أن أكون لك عوناً على شأنك، فهل أنت مريض؟ فرفع يده ببطءٍ ووضعها على جبهته، فوضعت يدي حيث وضعها، فشعرت برأسه يلتهب التهاباً فعلمت أنه محموم،

ثم أمررت نظري على جسمه فإذا خيال سار لا يكاد يتبينه رائيه، وإذا قميص فضفاض من الجلد يموج فيه بدنه موجاً، فأمرت الخادم أن يأتيني بشرابٍ كان عندي من أشربة الحمى، فجرعته منه بعض قطراتٍ،

فاستفاق قليلاً ونظر إلي نظرةً عذبةً صافيةً وقال شكراً لك،

I asked "What is your pain O brother?"

He replied "I have no problem."

I then asked "How long have you been in this sorrowful state?"

He replied "I do not know."

I said "Do you require a doctor? Can I call him for you so that he may examine you?"

He let out a long sigh, looked at me sadly and said "Verily the one who gives preference to life over death is the one who needs a doctor." Then he closed his eyes and returned to his unconscious state.

I did not have any other alternative but to call a doctor, whether he wanted one or not. I sent for him, and he arrived in an angered state, complaining and sighing loudly because I had disturbed his bedrest I made him come through small, dark alleyways on a cold night. I apologized, but did not care about his complaints as I would pay him well. He felt the pulse of the patient and whispered in my ear "O sir your patient is hovering upon danger, I am presuming that he will not stay alive for much longer, only Allah ﷻ knows and we do not know." He sat in a corner and began to write a prescription and his bill. Satisfied with my apologies, he then left. I brought the prescribed medicine and spent the entire night on the patient's side, like the way a lost star in the night of the sky. I continued his medication throughout the night, and cried for his wretched state until the early hours of the morning.

He gained consciousness, and turned his eyes around his bed until he saw me, asking "Are you still here?"

I replied "Yes, and I hope that you are feeling better than before."

He sighed "If only I hoped that was the case."

I asked "Dear brother, can I ask who you are? Why are you alone in this house? Are you a stranger in this town, or are you from its residents? Are you suffering from a physical illness, or an internal pain?"

He replied "I am suffering both."

I said "Could you tell me about your condition and your pain, the way a friend opens up to a friend? I have become concerned for you."

فقلت ما شكاتك أيها الأخ؟

قال: لا أشكو شيئاً؛

فقلت: فهل مر بك زمن طويل على حالك هذه؟

قال: لا أعلم؛

قلت: أنت في حاجة إلى الطبيب فهل تأذن لي أن أدعوه إليك لينظر في أمرك؟

فتنهد طويلاً ونظر إلي نظرةً دامعةً وقال إنما يبغي الطبيب من يؤثر الحياة على الموت، ثم أغمض عينيه وعاد إلى ذهوله واستغراقه،

فلم أجد بدأ من دعاء الطبيب رضي أم أبى، فدعوته فجاء متأففاً متذمراً يشكو- من حيث يعلم أني أسمع شكواه- إزعاجه من مرقده وتجشيمه خوض الأزقة المظلمة في الليالي الباردة؛ فلم أحفل بتعريضه أنني أعلم طريق الاعتذار إليه؛ فجس نبض المريض، وهمس في أذني قائلاً: إن عليلك يا سيدي مشرف على الخطر، ولا أحسب أن حياته تطول كثيراً إلا إذا كان في علم الله ما لا نعلم، وجلس ناحيةً يكتب ذلك الأمر الذي يصدره الأطباء إلى عمالهم الصيادلة أن يتقاضوا من عبيدهم المرضى ضريبة الحياة، ثم انصرف لشأنه بعد ما اعتذرت إليه ذلك الاعتذار الذي يؤثره ويرضاه، فأحضرت الدواء وقضيت بجانب المريض ليلةً ليلاء، ذاهلة النجم، بعيدة ما بين الطرفين، أسقيه الدواء مرةً وأبكي عليه أخرى، حتى انبثق نور الفجر؛

فاستفاق ودار بعينيه حول فراشه حتى رآني فقال: أنت هنا؟

قلت: نعم، وأرجو أن تكون أحسن حالاً من ذي قبل،

قال: أرجو أن أكون كذلك،

قلت: هل تأذن لي يا سيدي أن أسألك من أنت؟ وما مقامك وحدك في هذا المكان؟ وهل أنت غريب في هذا البلد أو أنت من أهليه، وهل تشكو داءً ظاهراً أو هماً باطناً؟

قال: أشكو هما معاً،

قلت: فهل لك أن تحدثني بشأنك وتفضي إلي بهمك كما يفضي الصديق إلى صديقه، فقد أصبحت معنياً بأمرك عنايتك بنفسك؟

He said, "Do you promise me to hide my secret if Allah ﷻ grants me life, and safeguard my will if I die?"

I replied "Yes."

He said "I have trusted your promise, because the one who holds a heart as honourable as yours, could not be a liar nor a deceiver. I am the son of so and so, my father passed away a very long time ago, leaving me poor and alone at the age of six. I had no wealth so my paternal uncle took guardianship of me. He was the most noble from all uncles, extremely good and kind, the best in love and generosity. He loved me as much as he loved his small daughter. She was my age or a little younger than me. It gave him great happiness to see by her side a brother, which he had wished from Allah ﷻ for a very long time.

Hence he favoured me the way he favoured her. He enrolled us to school on the same day. I loved my new sister very much. I found happiness and memorable moments in her companionship, which took away my problems and the pain of losing my parents. People would always see us both going to school or returning, playing in the porch or the garden. We used to be studying in the library or talking to one another in the bedroom, until she came of age, wore a veil and stayed indoors. I continued with my studies in the outside world.

Our hearts became knotted in a timeless love. I only found the taste of life in her company and the light of chastity in the morning of her smiles. I would have gladly sacrificed all the happiness in the world for each moment I spent with her. She was a young lady of great calibre, chastity, forbearance, mercy, purity and humility.

Our happy childhood days were the great white wings which shaded and distanced me from my earlier darkness, sorrows and the calamities. Our souls sparkled like sparkling drinks in tall glasses.

I can still see that flowered garden which inhabited our happiness, dreams and wishes, as if it is in front of me, with its water shining and pebbles glittering. Branches and multi-coloured flowers radiated a beautiful fragrance, as we both sat on the bench in the morning and evening, passing the time in merriment and delightful discussions. Sometimes we would prepare a bouquet of flowers, muse over the pages of a book, even compete with one another in drawing. I clearly remember the low-lying green bushes, under which we would peacefully rest after we had raced and become tired, like baby chicks find security in the comfort of their mother's wings.

قال: هل تعدني بكتمان أمري إن قسم الله لي الحياة، وبإمضاء وصيتي إن كانت الأخرى؟

قلت نعم،

قال: قد وثقت بوعدك، فإن من يحمل في صدره قلباً شريفاً مثل قلبك، لا يكون كاذباً ولا غادراً. أنا فلان بن فلان، مات أبي منذ عهدٍ بعيدٍ؛ وتركني في السادسة من عمري فقيراً معدماً لا أملك من متاع الدنيا شيئاً، فكفلني عمي فلان فكان خير الأعمام وأكرمهم وأوسعهم براً وإحساناً وأكثرهم عطفاً وحناناً، فقد أنزلني من نفسه منزلةً لم ينزلها أحداً من قبلي غير ابنته الصغيرة، وكانت في عمري أو أصغر مني قليلاً، وكأنما سره أن يرى لها بجانبها أخاً بعد ما تمنى على الله ذلك زمناً طويلاً،

فلم يدرك أمنيته فعني به عنايته بها، وأدخلنا المدرسة في يومٍ واحدٍ، فأنست بها أنس الأخ بأخته، وأحببتها حباً شديداً، ووجدت في عشرتها من السعادة والغبطة ما ذهب بتلك الغضاضة التي كانت لا تزال تعاود نفسي بعد فقد أبوي من حينٍ إلى حين، فكان لا يرانا الرائي إلا ذاهبين إلى المدرسة أو عائدين منها، أو لاعبين في فناء المنزل أو مرتاضين في حديقته، أو مجتمعين في غرفة المذاكرة أو متحدثين في غرفة النوم، حتى جاء يوم حجابها فلزمت خدرها واستمررت في دراستي.

ولقد عقد الود بين قلبي وقلبها عقداً لا يحله إلا ريب المنون، فكنت لا أرى لذة العيش إلا بجوارها، ولا أرى نور السعادة إلا في فجر ابتساماتها، ولا أؤثر على ساعةٍ أقضيها بجانبها جميع لذات العيش ومسرات الحياة، وما كنت أشاء أن أرى خصلةً من خصال الخير في فتاةٍ من أدبٍ أو ذكاءٍ أو حلمٍ أو رحمةٍ أو عفةٍ أو شرفٍ أو وفاءٍ إلا وجدتها فيها.

وأني أستطيع، وأنا في هذه الظلمة الحالكة من الهموم والأحزان أن أرى على البعد تلك الأجنحة النورانية البيضاء من السعادة التي كانت تظللنا معاً أيام طفولتنا فتشرق لها نفسانا إشراق الراح في كأسها،

وأن أرى تلك الحديقة الغناء التي كانت مراح لذاتنا ومسرح آمالنا وأحلامنا، كأنها حاضرة بين يدي أرى لألاء مائها، ولمعان حصبائها، وأفانين أشجارها، وألوان أزهارها، وتلك القاعدة الحجرية التي كنا نقتعدها منها طرفي النهار فنجتمع على حديثٍ نتجاذبه أو طاقة تؤلف بين أزهارها أو كتاب نقلب صفحاته، أو رسم نتبارى في إتقانه، وتلك الخمائل الخضراء التي كنا نلجأ إلى ظلالها كلما فرغنا من شوطٍ من أشواط المسابقة فتشعر بما تشعر به أفراخ الطيور اللاجئة إلى أحضان أمهاتها،

I can remember that we used sticks to make small holes in the ground, which we declared as the edges of canals and reservoirs. We would fill them up with water and sit around pretending to fish, even putting the fish in the water ourselves. The moment we used to capture a fish, we were overwhelmed by happiness, as if we had captured some great booty. I still remember the strange golden cages in which we used to raise sparrows and different kind of birds, enjoying their company for long periods. They brought us great joy, and we named them and cared for them, watching them drink water and peck seeds. When we called them, they would respond by whistling and chirping.

In reality, I had become unsure whether my love was merely brotherly or a lover's infatuation. However, what I did know very clearly was that our love was doomed, as I had withheld my feelings, and never told her that I loved her. This was because she was my uncle's daughter and my childhood friend. So, how could I be the one to hurt her feelings? Also I did not have the nerve nor the power to join our lives as one. I knew that her parents would not approve of the likes of me, a poor person of straitened circumstances, as suitable match for their daughter's marriage and welfare. I always considered her superior to me and never wanted to be embarrassed in this way before her. Furthermore, I never dwelled into the secrets of her heart, and clarify whether she loved me as a brother or as a lover. If it was the latter, then I might even have pressed her parents for their daughter's hand. However, the reality of my love for her was like that of a secluded priest, who in a church worships the statue of virgin Mary and does not look at her with any wrong intention.

We both continued living our innocent lives, until my uncle became extremely ill. Unable to recover he left this world as Allah ﷻ claimed his soul. On his death bed, he declared in his last words to his wife that he had always loved me dearly and held me in high esteem. He requested her to continue my upbringing and nurturing, which death had not allowed him to complete. He also bid her to be like a loving and caring mother to me just like he had been a loving and caring father. This way, I would not suffer from his loss.

The days of mourning were not even over yet, when I began to see the faces, eyes and circumstances changing. Before this, I had never encountered such animosity in my uncle's house. I was grieved, and felt at despair from life. For the first time ever, I felt like a stranger in the household, despised and rejected.

وتلك الحفائر الصغيرة التي نحتفرها ببعض الأعواد على شاطىء الجداول والغدران فنملؤها ماء، ثم نجلس حولها لنصطاد أسماكها التي ألقيناها فيها بأيدينا فنطرب إن ظفرنا بشيءٍ منها كأنا قد ظفرنا بغنم عظيم، وتلك الأقفاص البديعة الذهبية التي كنا نربي فيها عصافيرنا وطيورنا، ثم نقضي الساعات الطوال بجانبها نعجب بمنظرها ومنظر مناقيرها الخضراء، وهي تحسو الماء مرةً وتلتقط الحب أخرى، ونناديها بأسمائها التي سميناها بها، فإذا سمعنا صفيرها وتغريدها ظننا أنها تلبي نداءنا،

ولا أعلم هل كان ما كنت أضمره في نفسي لابنة عمي وداً وإخاءً، أو حباً وغراماً، ولكنني أعلم أنه كان بلا أمل، ولا رجاء، فما قلت لها يوماً إني أحبها لأني كنت أضن بها- وهي ابنة عمي ورفيقة صباي- أن أكون أول فاتح لهذا الجرح الأليم في قلبها، ولا قدرت في نفسي يوماً من الأيام أن أصل أسباب حياتي بأسباب حياتها؛ لأني كنت أعلم أن أبويها لا يسخوان بمثلها على فتًى بائس فقير مثلي، ولا حاولت في ساعةٍ من الساعات أن أتسقط منها ما يطمع في مثله المحبون المتسقطون، لأني كنت أجلها عن أن أنزل بها إلى مثل ذلك، ولا فكرت يوماً أن أستشف من وراء نظراتها خبيئة نفسها لأعلم أي المنزلتين أنزلها من قلبها، أمنزلة الأخ فأقنع منها بذلك، أم منزلة الحبيب، فأستعين بإرادتها على إرادة أبويها؟ بل كان حبي لها حب الراهب المتبتل صورة العذراء الماثلة بين يديه في صومعته يعبدها ولا يتطلع إليها.

ولم يزل هذا شأني وشأنها حتى نزلت بعمي نازلة من المرض لم تنشب أن ذهبت به إلى جوار ربه، وكان آخر ما نطق به في آخر ساعات حياته أن قال لزوجته، وكان يحسن بها ظناً (لقد أعجلني الموت عن النظر في شأن هذا الغلام فكوني له أماً كما كنت له أباً، وأوصيك أن لا يفقد مني بعد موتي إلا شخصي).

فما مرت أيام الحداد حتى رأيت وجوهاً غير الوجوه ونظراتٍ غير النظرات، وحالاً غريبةً لا عهد لي بمثلها من قبل، فتداخلني ألهم واليأس ووقع في نفسي للمرة الأولى في حياتي أنني قد أصبحت في هذا المنزل غريباً، وفي هذا العالم طريداً.

One morning, when I was sitting in my room, the house maid entered: She was an extremely chaste and a sincere woman and discreetly said 'The Lady (my aunt) has a request. She would like to get her daughter married soon as she has no father now, and it is inappropriate for you both to stay together like this, now you are adults. Your current life together will send wrong connotations to her future fiancé. Consequently, she would like you to move out, so she can turn your room into an abode for the new couple. All your requirements will be taken care of, you will not even feel that you have separated.'

I felt like the maiden had stuck a sharp arrow in my liver. Quickly composing I said, 'Very soon with the will of Allah ﷻ I will do just that, I accept this decision.' When she had left, I shed a stream of tears in loneliness. To leave this house now was the decree of Allah the Almighty.

When the night-fall came, I packed my bag with my clothes and books. My heart was heavy. All the fortunes of life rested with the one I loved, through her I had learned also to love myself. There was now a veil between us, so I had no regrets after this. I sneaked out from the house very quietly so no one would find out. Before I departed, I took one last look at my uncle's daughter behind the curtain: She was sleeping. This the last time I ever set eyes on her.

> ***I swear by your life, I did not leave Baghdad in happiness.***
>
> ***Only if I could have found an alternative way not to leave.***
>
> ***How grievous it was, that I did not have the power to say my farewells.***
>
> ***And I was unable to speak to its loving residents.***

Like this, I parted from the house which I had spent many happy days, similar to the way Prophet Adam (Peace and blessings of Allah be upon him) was taken out from Paradise. I was surprised, despised and afflicted with love. Sorrows and hardships were hovering upon me once again. Knowing also that I would be separated from my childhood companion, I was destitute with no authority or friend. I entered poverty and found no well-wisher or helper from amongst the people.

فإني لجالس في غرفتي صبيحة يوم إذ دخلت علي الخادم، وكانت امرأةً من النساء الصالحات المخلصات، فتقدمت نحوي خجلةً متعثرة، وقالت: قد أمرتني سيدتي أن أقول لك يا سيدي إنها قد عزمت على تزويج ابنتها في عهدٍ قريبٍ. وإنها ترى أن بقاءك بجانبها بعد موت أبيها وبلوغكما هذه السن التي بلغتماها ربما يريبها عند خطيبها، وإنها تريد أن تتخذ للزوجين مسكناً هذا الجناح الذي تسكنه من القصر، فهي تريد أن تتحول إلى منزلٍ آخر تختاره لنفسك من بين منازلها على أن تقوم لك فيه بجميع شأنك، وكأنك لم تفارقها.

فكأنما عمدت إلى سهمٍ رائشٍ فأصمت به كبدي، إلا أنني تماسكت قليلاً ريثما قلت لها: سأفعل إن شاء الله ولا أحب إلي من ذلك. فانصرفت لشأنها فخلوت بنفسي ساعةً أطلقت فيها السبيل لعبراتي ما شاء الله أن أطلقها.

حتى جاء الليل فعمدت إلى حقيبتي فأودعتها ثيابي وكتبي، وقلت في نفسي: (قد كان كل ما أسعد به في هذه الحياة أن أعيش بجانب ذلك الإنسان الذي أحببته وأحببت نفسي من أجله، وقد حيل بيني وبينه فلا آسف على شيءٍ بعده). ثم انسللت من المنزل انسلالاً من حيث لا يشعر أحد بما كان، ولم أتزود من ابنة عمي قبل الرحيل غير نظرةٍ واحدةٍ ألقيتها عليها من خلال كلتها وهي نائمة في سريرها فكانت آخر عهدي بها.

لعمرك ما فارقت بغداد عن قِلَى

لو أنا وجدنا من فراقٍ لها بدا

كفى حزناً أن رحت لم أستطع لها

وداعاً ولم أحدث بساكنها عهدا

وهكذا فارقت المنزل الذي سعدت فيه حقبةً من الزمان فراق آدم جنته، وخرجت منه شريداً طريداً حائراً ملتاعاً قد اصطلحت على الهموم والأحزان، فراق لا لقاء بعده، وفقر لا ساد لخلته، وغربة لا أجد عليها من أحدٍ من الناس مواسياً، ولا معيناً.

Despite everything, I had some money remaining from the good times which were long gone. With it, I rented this room, as I did not have the power to stay at my old residence even for a moment. I intended to journey the open land belonging to Allah ﷻ, so that I could cure myself from the tribulations and afflictions which had befallen me. I undertook a long journey for several months, traveling from one city to the other, spending sunrise somewhere and sunset somewhere else. Finally, my heart gained peace when my tears rested in my eye sockets, neither had they shed nor did they become dry.

I became content with my lot. The school's annual term was commencing soon, so I returned. I solemnly pledged to live alone on this earth, even if I am in a community, I will be absent from its affairs and dealings. I will forget everything other than my love, and seek the power to continue my life without her. Thus, I became bound to my room and my school, and I never parted from them. Time helped me to conceal all traces of her memory. Rarely when my past did resurface, I shed a few tears for her, but revealed nothing to anyone. Only Allah ﷻ knew of my pain, and this fact cooled my heart.

Stubbornly I remained in this state until yesterday, when I directed my attention to my remaining money and I saw that soon it would be expire. In order to continue with life and also to pay for my schooling, these funds were crucial. In this city, schools are very expensive workshops, which do not give credit. Knowledge is an asset only for the rich, acquired through wealth. No one is ready to bestow knowledge for free.

This troubled me as I could not see any means to acquire my livelihood. In desperation, I took all my extra books to the book market. Despite spending all day there, I found no one who was even ready to give a quarter of the price of the books. I left in despair, despising my unfortunate luck.

When I arrived home, at the door step, I saw a woman who was enquiring about me from the residents. When I took a closer look at her I realised that she was the maid from my uncle's house who used to take care of me.

'You?' I asked.

She replied, 'Yes.'

I enquired 'What brings you here?'

She answered 'If you permit me I would like to speak to you.'

وكانت معي صبابة من مالٍ قد بقيت في يدي من آثار تلك النعمة الذاهبة، فاتخذت هذه الحجرة العارية في هذه الطبقة العليا مسكناً، فلم أستطع البقاء فيها ساعةً واحدةً، فأزمعت الرحيل إلى حيث أجد في فضاء الله ومنفسح آفاقه علاج نفسي من همومها وأحزانها، فرحلت رحلةً طويلةً قضيت فيها بضعة أشهرٍ لا أهبط بلدةً حتى تنازعني نفسي إلى أخرى، ولا تطلع علي الشمس في مكانٍ حتى تغرب عني في غيره، حتى شعرت في آخر الأمر بسكونٍ في نفسي يشبه سكون الدمع المعلق في محجر العين لا يفيض، ولا يغيض.

فقنعت بذلك، وكان ميعاد الدراسة السنوية قد حان فعدت، وقد استقر في نفسي أن أعيش في هذا العالم منفرداً كمجتمع وغائباً كحاضرٍ وبعيداً كقريب، وأن ألهو بشأن نفسي عن كل شأنٍ سواه. وأن أستعين عليَّ نسيان الماضي باجتناب موطنه ومظاهره، فلزمت غرفتي ومدرستي، أداول بينهما لا أفارقهما، ولم يبق لذلك العهد القديم في نفسي إلا نزوات تعاود قلبي من حينٍ إلى حينٍ فأستعين عليها بقطرات من الدمع أسكبها من جفني في خلوتي من حيث لا يعلم إلا الله ما بي فأجد برد الراحة في صدري.

لبثت على ذلك برهةً من الزمان حتى عدت بالأمس إلى تلك الفضلة التي كانت في يدي من المال فإذا هي ناضبة أو موشكة، وكنت مأخوذاً بأن أهيء لنفسي عيشاً مستقلاً، وأن أؤدي للمدرسة قسطاً من أقساطها، والمدرسة في هذا البلد حانوت قاسٍ لا تباع فيه السلعة نسيئة، والعلم في هذه الأمة مرتزق يرتزق منه المرتزقون لا منحة يمنحها المحسنون.

فأهمتني نفسي، وعلمت أني مشرف على الخطر، ولا أعرف سبيلاً إلى القوت بوجه ولا حيلة، فعمدت إلى كتبي فاستبقيت منها ما لا غنى لي عنه وحملت سائرها إلى سوق الوراقين فعرضته هناك يوماً كاملاً فلم أجد من يبلغ به في المساومة ربع ثمنه، فعدت به حزيناً منكسراً، وما على وجه الأرض أحد أذل مني ولا أشقى.

فلما بلغت باب المنزل رأيت في فنائه امرأةً تسائل أهل البيت عني فتبينتها فإذا هي الخادم التي كانت تخدمني في منزل عمي،

فقلت: فلانة؟

قالت: نعم،

قلت: ماذا تريدين؟

قالت: لي إليك كلمة فائذن لي،

I took her to my room, when we were alone I requested her 'Now tell me.'

She said, 'It has been three days since I have been finding you but I could not seek your address, finally I have located you.'

After this, she burst out crying loudly. Her crying troubled me, and I feared some calamity had befallen upon the house which I had loved so dearly. I asked 'Why are you crying?'

She replied, 'Do you not know anything about your uncle's house?'

I said 'No, what is the matter?'

She moved her hand towards her veil and from it she took out an enveloped letter. I took the letter from her and slit off its seal, knowing immediately it was from my cousin, my uncle's daughter. The words imprinted on it are seared in my memory until this day. It read,

'You parted from me, without even saying goodbye, but I still forgive you. Now I have reached the door of my grave. If you do not come now, I will never forgive you. Are you not going to come to me for the last time to say your farewells?'

I threw the letter from my hands and advanced towards the door rapidly. The maid restrained me and asked 'Where are you going?'

I said 'She is ill and I have to be with her, it is important.'

For a moment, she became silent and motionless, and in a trembling low voice said 'You do not need to do so, dear. Before you get to her, you will discover that she has already passed away, and has met her Lord.'

When I heard this, it felt like that my heart had moved from its place to another. The earth started spinning, in a daze I fell down to the ground, having no sense of what was happening around me. I gained consciousness after a long time. When I opened my eyes, I discovered it was night. I saw the maid sitting beside me screaming and crying. I drew closer to her and asked her, 'O woman. Is it true what you say?'

She replied 'Yes.'

I requested 'Tell me everything.' She began…

فصعدت معها إلى غرفتي، فلما خلونا قلت: هات،

قالت: مرت بي ثلاثة أيام وأنا أفتش عنك في كل مكان فلم أجد من يدلني عليك حتى وجدتك اليوم بعد اليأس منك،

ثم انفجرت باكيةً بصوتٍ عالٍ؛ فراعني بكاؤها وخفت أن يكون قد حل بالبيت الذي أحبه بأس، فقلت: ما بكاؤك؟

قالت: أما تعلم شيئاً من أخبار بيت عمك؟

قلت: لا، فما أخباره؟

فمدت يدها إلى ردائها وأخرجت من أضعافه كتاباً مغلقاً فتناولته منها ففضضت غلافه فإذا هو بخط ابنة عمي فقرأت فيه هذه الكلمة التي لا أزال أحفظها حتى الساعة:

(إنك فارقتني ولم تودعني فاغتفرت لك ذلك، فأما اليوم وقد أصبحت على باب القبر فلا أغتفر لك ألا تأتي إليّ لتودعني الوداع الأخير).

فألقيت الكتاب من يدي وابتدرت الباب مسرعاً فتعلقت الخادم بثوبي وقالت: أين تريد يا سيدي؟

قلت: إنها مريضة ولا بد لي من المصير إليها.

فصمتت لحظةً ثم قالت بصوتٍ خافتٍ مرتعش: لا تفعل يا سيدي فقد سبقك القضاء إليها.

هنالك شعرت أن قلبي قد فارق موضعه إلى حيث لا أعلم له مكاناً، ثم دارت بي الأرض الفضاء دورةً سقطت على أثرها في مكاني لا أشعر بشيءٍ مما حولي، فلم أفق إلا بعد حين؛ ففتحت عيني فإذا الليل قد أظللني وإذا الخادم لا تزال بجانبي تبكي وتنتحب، فدنوت منها وقلت: أيتها المرأة أحق ما تقولين؟

قالت: نعم،

قلت: قصي عليّ كل شيءٍ فأنشأت تقول:

'O sir, verily your uncle's daughter, could not contain her grief after you left. She enquired after the reason for your departure. I had told her about that message which your aunty instructed me to convey. To this her only reply was 'What will happen to him now? A poor man in such dire circumstances?! They do not know anything about me and him.' After this, she never spoke of you again, either good or bad. Nevertheless, news of your departure seared her heart deeply, and she endured the terrible pain in silence for a few days, until she became ill. Her beauty withered, and her smile dried up. She became bed bound and worsened still. Her mother became fearful for her health. She stopped discussing marriages and grooms with her in case she grew worse, despite it being the only subject she seemed to revel in day and night. In her desperation to cure her daughter, she consulted every doctor and herbalist, but no one could do anything for her, as she slowly and gradually headed towards her grave.

It was during this time that I stayed awake for a few nights at her bedside. She gestured me to move closer, so promptly I drew near to her. She indicated that I hold her hand. I did so, and helped her to sit upright. Weakly she asked me, 'What part of the night are we in?'

I replied 'A small portion of the night still remains.'

She asked, 'Are you alone here?'

I replied, 'Yes, all the people of this house are sleeping.'

She enquired 'Do you know the abode of my cousin?'

I was surprised by her question, as I had never before heard from her tongue anything relating to this matter. I replied, 'Certainly dear, I know of his place.' Even though I had no idea of it. I felt sorry for her, and desired that the last remaining thread of hope which she had of finding you, did not break.

Then she said to me 'Are you going to help me by delivering my letter to him?'

I replied, 'My respectable Lady, I will love to do this.'

Again through her gestures she indicated that the ink pot be brought to her. I did so, and with it she wrote the letter which you have just read.

إن ابنة عمك يا سيدي لم تنتفع بنفسها بعد رحيلك فقد سألتني في اليوم الذي رحلت فيه عن سبب رحيلك فحدثتها حديث الرسالة التي حملتها إليك من زوجة عمك، فلم تزد على أن قالت: (وماذا يكون مصير هذا البائس المسكين! إنهم لا يعلمون من أمره ولا من أمري شيئاً). ثم لم يجر ذكرك بعد ذلك على لسانها بخيرٍ ولا بشرٍ، كأنما كانت تعالج في نفسها ألماً ممضاً، وما هي إلا أيام قلائل حتى سرى داء نفسها إلى جسمها فاستحالت حالها، وغاض ماء جمالها، وانطفأت تلك الابتسامات العذبة التي كانت لا تفارق ثغرها ثم سقطت على فراشها مريضةً لا تبل يوماً حتى تنتكس أياماً، فراع أمها أمرها، وورد عليها ما قطعها عن ذكر العرس والعروس، والخطبة والخطيب، وكانت لا تزال تهتف بذلك نهارها وليلها، فلم تدع طبيباً ولا عائداً إلا فزعت إليه أمرها، فما أغنى العائد ولا الطبيب، وأصبحت الفتاة تدنو من القبر رويداً رويداً.

فبينا أنا ساهرة بجانب فراشها منذ ليال إذ شعرت بها تتحرك في مضجعها، فدنوت منها، فأشارت إلي أن آخذ بيدها ففعلت، فاستوت جالسة وقالت: في أي ساعة نحن من الليل؟

قلت: في الهزيع الأخير منه،

قالت: أأنت وحدك هنا؟

قلت: نعم فقد هجع أهل البيت جميعاً،

قالت: ألا تعلمين أين مكان ابن عمي الآن؟

فعجبت لكلمةٍ لم أسمعها منها قبل اليوم وقلت: بلى يا سيدتي أعلم مكانه، وما كنت أعلم شيئاً، ولكني أشفقت على هذا الخيط الرقيق الباقي في يدها من الأمل أن ينقطع فينقطع بانقطاعه آخر خيطٍ من خيوط أجلها،

فقالت: ألا تستطيعين أن تحملي إليه رسالة مني من حيث لا يعلم أحد بشأني؟

قلت: لا أحب إلي من ذلك يا سيدتي...

فأشارت أن آتيها بمحبرتها، فجئتها بها، فكتبت إليك هذا الكتاب الذي تراه.

When morning commenced, I left the house, enquiring your address from one place to the other. I was observing faces of people passing by, hoping that I may see you or that I may find one who may guide me to you. Despite all my efforts, I was unsuccessful. As the sun set, I returned home, finding that some part of the night had already passed: Fearfully I heard mourning and crying, and sadly realised that the arrow of death had hit its mark once again. Our home had lost its rose, the fresh rose which used to bless this world with its beauty. Its last petal had just fallen. I was grieving like the way a mother would grieve for the death of her only child. Other than this day, I had never before witnessed a day of such grief and bereavement.

The greatest sadness for me was the fact that she wanted to see you in her last moments of life, but was unfortunate not to do so. She passed away before she could be granted her wish. After her death, I secretly safeguarded her letter and continued to look for you until this day.'

I thanked her for this favour, and permitted her request to leave my home. When I was left alone, I felt that a black cloud was rising steadily towards my eyes until everything in front of me was hidden. I do not remember anything after until I saw you."

He stopped talking and took a warm breath. Through his sighs I felt that his liver was coming out piece by piece. I drew near him and asked him, "What has happened to you?"

He replied, "I want to shed a tear so that I can lessen my sorrow but I am unable to do so."

For a while he remained in silence. I felt that he was whispering something. When I listened closely, I discovered, he was saying,

"O Allah ﷻ, you know that I am a traveller upon this earth: I have no one who can take care of me, nor any helper. I am a dependant, I am not the owner of the necessities of life. I cannot help myself. I am helpless and weak. I do not see a way towards any door from the doors of livelihood and neither am I capable of devising a plan for my welfare. Certainly the wound which has afflicted me, has ground my heart to pieces. Thus, nothing remains from it other than the ruins of my spirit. Verily I feel shame when I take my hands towards my soul, which you have placed with your hands. I want to strip it out from its place and throw it in your courts, so that you are disappointed with it and be ready to punish it. Therefore, command my soul back to you. Take back your possession and call it towards your pure house. No doubt, the best house is your house and the best neighbours are your neighbours."

فلما أصبح الصباح خرجت أسائل الناس عنك في كل مكانٍ، وأتصفح وجوه الغادين والرائحين، علني أراك وأرى من يهديني إليك، فلم أظفر بطائلٍ، حتى انحدرت الشمس إلى مغربها، فعدت إلى المنزل وقد مضى شطر من الليل فما بلغته حتى سمعت الناعية، فعلمت أن السهم قد بلغ المقتل، وأن تلك الوردة الناضرة التي كانت تملأ الدنيا جمالاً وبهاء قد سقطت آخر ورقةٍ من ورقاتها؛ فحزنت عليها حزن الثاكل على وحيدها، وما رئي مثل يومها يوم كان أكثر باكيةً وباكياً.

وكان أكبر ما أهمني من أمرها أن كل ما كانت ترجوه في الساعة الأخيرة من ساعات حياتها أن تراك، ففاتها ذلك وسقطت دون أمينتها، فلم أزل كاتمةً أمر الرسالة في نفسي، ولم أزل أتطلب السبيل إليك حتى وجدتك.

فشكرت لها صنيعها وأذنتها بالانصراف فانصرفت... فما انفردت بنفسي حتى شعرت أن سحابةً سوداء تهبط فوق عيني شيئاً فشيئاً حتى احتجب عن ناظري كل شيء، ثم لا أعلم ماذا تم بعد ذلك حتى رأيتك.

وما وصل من حديثه إلى هذا الحد حتى زفر زفرةً خلت أن كبده قد أرفضت وأن هذه أفلاذها. فدنوت منه وقلت: ما بك يا سيدي؟

قال بي أني أطلب دمعةً واحدةً أتفرج بها مما أنا فيه فلا أجدها.

ثم صمت ساعةً طويلةً، فشعرت أنه يهمهم ببعض كلماتٍ فأصغيت إليه فإذا هو يقول :

(اللهم إنك تعلم أني غريب في هذه الدنيا لا سند لي فيها ولا عضد، وأني فقير لا أملك من متاع الحياة ما أعود به على نفسي، وأني عاجز مستضعف لا أعرف السبيل إلى بابٍ من أبواب الرزق بوجهٍ ولا حيلة، وأن الضربة التي أصابت قلبي قد سحقته سحقاً فلم يبق فيه حتى الذماء وإني أستحييك أن أمد يدي إلى هذه النفس التي أودعتها بيدك بين جنبي فأنتزعها من مكانها وألقي بها في وجهك ساخطاً ناقماً، فتول أنت أمرها بيدك واسترد وديعتك إليك وانقلها إلى دار كرامتك، فنعم الدار دارك، ونعم الجوار جوارك).

Then he held his head with his hand as if he was stopping it from escaping. In a weak silent voice, he said, "My head is burning severely and my heart is melting away. I guess that I will not remain for long upon this wretched earth." In these final moments, he turned to me in desperation, imploring "If Allah ﷻ grants me death like He did to her, please promise to place my grave next to hers, and also bury this letter with me."

I replied "Yes but I pray to Allah ﷻ for your speedy recovery and health."

He said "Now I can die peacefully, not worrying about a thing." Then he took one shivering fit and died.

***

No doubt, I severely grieved the death of this troubled young man. I had the power to fulfil his dying wish, and buried him with his cousin and the letter also. Her letter had called him, and he could only respond to her through his death.

In this way, two loyal friends were united. The world and castle above them had become too tight to accommodate their love and companionship. Despite this, after their death, the ditches of their grave had created enough space to contain them both, finally sealing their union.

ثم أمسك رأسه بيده كأنما يحاول أن يحبسه عن الفرار وقال بصوتٍ ضعيفٍ خافت: أشعر برأسي يحترق احتراقاً وقلبي يذوب ذوباً، لا أحسبني باقياً على هذا، فهل تعدني أن تدفنني معها في قبرها وتدفن معي كتابها إن قضى الله في قضاءه؟

قلت: نعم، وأسأل الله لك السلامة،

قال: الآن أموت طيب النفس عن كل شيء. ثم انتفض انتفاضةً فاضت نفسه فيها.

***

لقد هون وجدي على هذا البائس المسكين أني استطعت إمضاء وصيته كما أراد، فسعيت في دفنه مع ابنة عمه، ودفنت معه تلك الرسالة التي دعته فيها أن يوافيها فعجز عن أن يلبي نداءها حياً فلباها ميتاً.

وهكذا اجتمع تحت سقفٍ واحدٍ ذانك الصديقان الوفيان الذان ضاق بهما في حياتهما فضاء القصر، فوسعتهما بعد موتهما حفرة القبر.

The Martyrs / A<u>sh</u>-<u>Sh</u>uhadā (Translation)

After the death of her husband and her parents, nothing remained for her, other than her small son whom she loved, and a caring brother. She also had a little wealth, with which it she could pass by the remaining days of her life.

However now, that remaining wealth had also come to pass. Her brother had been afflicted by the harmful events of society, the society had snatched away his wealth and everything. Due to this, he had left and went far away, and his whereabouts were unknown. After this, she had become needy and support less.

This unfortunate woman went through so much pain and so many tribulations, which hardly any mankind could bear, in search for livelihood. She stitched clothes until her eyesight became extremely weak, she washed so many clothes that her hands became dry. She made so many trips to the factories until she became helpless. Nevertheless, she and her son managed to stay alive.

A woman like this should not be permitted to live. However, Allah ﷻ favoured her by taking away her prosperity and equipped her with the wealth of patience. Thus, when the night of misfortunes unlit her surroundings and her life darkened in front of her, then far in the horizon, she used to see an outburst of three rays due to the mercy of Allah ﷻ. Hence, these three rays used to penetrate in her heart which then filled her with patience and peace. One ray was of the love that she had for her son, the other ray was of the hope that she had of her brother returning, and the third ray was of the happiness that her self-respect and dignity was still safeguarded.

The days kept passing by conventionally, eventually she grew old and her son became a young adult. The pain of hardship transported from her heart into the young man's heart. Now it was crucial for him to stay alive in order to think of the welfare of his mother like the way she had always thought of the welfare of her son. Hence, he embarked on a search for his livelihood at all roads, and stopped at every spring in search for provisions. Eventually luck took him towards the faculty of painting/drawing. He became content with this profession, and gave his full attention towards it. As time went on, he mastered this art.

الشهداء

(مترجمة)

لم يبق لها بعد موت زوجها وأبويها إلا ولد صغير يؤنسها، وأخ شفيق يحنو عليها، وصبابة من المال تترشف الرزق منها ترشفاً مصانعةً للدهر فيها.

أما الصبابة فقد نضبت، وأما الأخ فقد ضمه الدهر ضمةً ذهبت بماله وبجميع ما تملك يده، فهاجر هجرةً بعيدةً لا تعرف مصيره فيها، فأصبحت من بعده لا تملك مالاً، و لا عضداً.

لقد لقيت هذه المرأة المسكينة من الشقاء في طلب العيش ما لا يستطيع أن يحتمله بشر، فخاطت الملابس حتى عشى بصرها، وغسلت الثياب حتى يبست أطرافها، ودخلت المصانع حتى كلت، وخدمت في المنازل حتى ذلت، ولكنها استطاعت أن تحيا ويحيا ولدها بجانبها.

ما كان لمثلها أن يحيا على مثل ذلك، ولكن الله كان أرحم بها من أن يسلبها السعادة ويسلبها العزاء عنها معاً، فقد كانت إذا دجا ليل الحوادث حولها، وأظلمت الحياة أمام عينيها، رأت في الأفق البعيد ثلاثة أشعةٍ تنبعث من سماء الرحمة الإلهية حتى تتلاقى في فؤادها فتملأه عزاءً وصبراً؛ شعاع الأنس بولدها، وشعاع الرجاء في أخيها، وشعاع السرور بما وفقت إليه من صيانة عرضها.

دارت الأيام دورتها فاكتهلت الأم وشب الولد وانتقل هم قلبها إلى قلبه، وكان لا بد له أن يعيش، وأن يحسن إلى تلك التي طالما أحسنت إليه، فمشى يتصفح وجوه الرزق وجهاً وجهاً، ويرد مناهله منهلاً منهلاً، حتى وقف به حظه على مهنة الرسم، فأنس بها، وما زال يعطيها من نفسه وجده حتى مهر فيها،

However, time does not highlight the qualities of a person, it is the person himself who through his wisdom and understanding highlights his qualities. Unfortunately, this young man did not possess this attribute and neither did he know of a way to promote himself, therefore he was left unknown. Through this profession, he gained his provision, drop by drop. Although for his mother, he could not give her complete prosperity, he by all means, was able to obtain the essentials and the necessities of life. Thus, his mother sufficed upon this and started to stay at home as she felt the coolness of tranquillity in her heart.

However, when she remembered her separated brother, she longed for him like the way an old mother cow yearns for its lost calf. She was highly grieved over the fact that she had not seen him for fifteen years and that no letter had come from him. Since ten years till this day, she had no place of refuge where she could take her pain and sorrows to. She used to cry in seclusion until her grief was satisfied, then she used to come out to greet her son in a jovial state of happiness as if she had not cried before.

One day her son entered her room when she was alone. Thus, he saw her crying while she was holding a picture in her hand. When he observed the picture closely, he discovered that it was the picture of his maternal uncle. At that point he felt that hidden pain in his mother's heart and he withheld his flowing tears in his lashes. It was very difficult for him to control his emotions. He advanced towards his mother and placed his hand upon her shoulder and said "O mother, just have a little more patience, soon you will find out about your lost brother."

Her face out of happiness began to twinkle and she said "How is that?"

He said "It has come to my attention, that after a few months in Washington, which is the capital of America, there is going to be an Art exhibition in which there have allocated small and big prizes for the contestants. One of my friends has promised me that he will help me with the travel expenses, so that perhaps I may become recognised through this Art exhibition, and can save myself and you from this unfortunate life of calamity and hardship. Over there I will search for your lost brother. I will keep on searching for him until I find him or obtain convincing and definite news about him."

والمهارة لا تدل على صاحبها وحدها، بل هو الذي يدل عليها بحيلته ورفقته، وما كان الفتى يملك أداة ذلك، ولا يعرف السبيل إليه، فاستمر خاملاً مغموراً لا تدر له مهنته إلا القطرة بعد القطرة في الفينة بعد الفينة فلم يستطع أن يسعد أمه، ولكنه استطاع أن يسد خلتها فقنعت منه بذلك ولزمت منزلها، ووجدت برد الراحة في صدرها.

إلا أنها كانت إذا ذكرت ذلك الغائب النائي عنها حنت إليه حنين النيب إلى فصالها، وأحزنها أنها لم تره منذ خمسة عشر عاماً، ولم تر منه كتاباً منذ عشرة أعوامٍ حتى اليوم، فلا تجد لها بداً كلما هاجها الوجد إليه إلا أن تلجأ إلى ذلك الملجأ الوحيد الذي يفزع إليه جميع البائسين والمحزونين في بأسائهم و ضرائهم، خلوتها ودموعها، فتبكي ما شاء الله أن تفعل، ثم تخرج لاستقبال ولدها باشةً باسمةً كأن لم تكن باكيةً قبل ذلك.

دخل عليها ولدها يوماً في خلوتها فرآها تبكي، ورأى في يدها صورةً فتبينها فإذا هي صورة خاله بسريرة نفسها وأمسك بين أهداب عينيه دمعةً مترقرقةً ما تكاد تتماسك، فمشى إليها حتى وضع يده على عاتقها، وقال: رفهي عن نفسك يا أماه فستعلمين خبر غائبك عما قليل،

فتطلق وجهها وأضاء، وقالت: وكيف السبيل إلى ذلك؟

قال: قد علمت أن معرضاً سيقام للرسم في واشنطون حاضرة أمريكا، بعد بضعة شهور، وأنهم قدروا له جوائز مختلفة صغرى وكبرى، وقد وعدني بعض أصدقائي أن يساعدني على الشخوص إليه علني أستطيع أن أنال ما أقيم به وجهي، وأنقذ به نفسي ونفسك من هذا الشقاء، وهنالك أفتش عن غائبك حتى أجده أو أجد منقطع أثره،

Her twinkling face drooped and she said "O son do not do this, because by seeing you besides me, I do not find myself to be unfortunate, and neither are you unfortunate. Are you not content with the distribution of Allah ﷻ? If you were to do this, then upon the face of the earth there would not be a more sorrowful and unfortunate woman than me. If I have cried once for my brother, then upon your separation I will cry a thousand times. Whenever I remember him, I take a look at your face in which I then find patience and peace. So how can I possibly gain patience if both of you be away from my eyes?"

Despite her reluctance, he kept on persuading her, kept on urging, until finally he had convinced her. She became tender and agreed to entrust his affair with Allah ﷻ.

After a few days, destiny struck with adversities. The mother was left all alone in France without a friend and neither a helper. Her son became a stranger, helpless and without any support in America.

The young man managed to reach the Art exhibition and presented his pictures. Amongst them was a drawing of the shore and the ocean where his mother was saying her farewells. This was an extremely emotional sight, and very beautifully sketched. People were highly impressed with it and liked it a great deal. They agreed to fix a prize for his efforts the way he had been expecting. When that prize reached his hands, he felt that he was one of the greatest people on the face of this Earth. This was his first day where he had been recognised. It was as if before this moment, he had never tasted the bitterness of life and neither had he seen the face of calamities.

Like this, life plays with a human being, and it makes him taste the flavours of both joy and adversity. It makes a person face different hardships and difficulties until he is desolate and doubtful. At that point his heart becomes full of rage and anger. After that, life sparkles a false hope of light in the dark sky, then with his free will and pleasure, man returns to his abode like a non-understanding animal heading towards his place of slaughter with the greed of eating grass and hay. How man, through the hands of life, can become fortunate and likewise unfortunate?

فاستسر بشرها الذي كان متلألئاً وقالت: لا تفعل يا بني فما أنا بشقيةٍ ما رأيتك بجانبي، وما أنت بشقيٍ ما قنعتَ بما قسم الله لك، ولئن فعلت لا تكونن امرأة على وجه الأرض أعظم مني لوعةً ولا أشقى، ولئن بكيت لفراق أخي مرةً فسأبكي لفراقك ألف مرة، وإني كلما ذكرته وجدت في وجهك العزاء عنه، فمن لي بالعزاء عنكما إن فقدت وجهيكما معاً.

فما زال يروضها ويمسحها ويمنيها في رحلته الأماني العذاب حتى أسلست وهدأت وأسلمت إلى الله أمرها.

وما هي إلا أيام قلائل حتى ضرب الدهر بينهما بضرباته فإذا الأم وحيدةً في فرنسا لا مؤنس لها، وإذا الولد غريب في أمريكا لا يعرف له سنداً؛ ولا عضداً.

وصل الفتى إلى معرض الرسم فعرض رسمه هناك، وكان يمثل فيه موقف الوداع الذي جرى بينه وبين أمه على شاطىء البحر يوم رحيله، وكان موقفاً محزناً فأحسن تمثيله، فأعجب القوم بجماله، وأثر في نفوسهم منظره فقضوا له بالجائزة التي كان يمني نفسه بها. فما حصلت في يده حتى خيل إليه أنه أسعد أهل الأرض طراً، وأن هذا اليوم هو أول يومٍ هبط فيه عالم الوجود، وأنه ما ذاق قبل الساعة مرارة العيش، ولا رأى صورة الشقاء!

وكذلك يعبث الدهر بالإنسان ما يعبث، ويذيقه ما يذيقه من صنوف الشقاء وألوان الآلام حتى إذا علم أنه قد أوحشه وأرابه وملأ قلبه غيظاً وحنقاً أطلع له في تلك السماء المظلمة المدلهمة بارقةً واحدةً من بوارق الأمل الكاذب فاسترده بها إلى حظيرته راضياً مغتبطاً كما تقاد السائمة البلهاء بأعواد الكلأ إلى مصرعها، فما أسعد الدهر بالإنسان وما أشقى الإنسان به.

That young man sent some money to his mother and kept some for himself. He wrote to his mother saying, 'Until I do not fulfil my promise I will remain here.' He progressed in search for his maternal uncle from one town to the other. He enquired about him from every resident and every immigrant he met. He finally met someone who told him that his last meeting with his uncle was a couple of years ago. He told him that his uncle was in the process of embarking upon an expedition towards the southern islands in search of brass mines. As soon as he heard this, he commenced his journey towards where he was told, in order to get to his maternal uncle.

He finally reached a wasted land, an island which was extremely frightful. Its towns were still shadowed with the old dark traditions and customs. He passed by a Negro tribe who dwelled behind an isolated mountain. When they saw him, hatred and enmity arose within their hearts against him, and their animosity against white people awoke. They even hated the shining sun and the lighted stars. Thus, they had surrounded him, raided him and then arrested him and took him towards their dwelling. Over there they detained him in an underground tunnel, they used to call this the prison of retribution.

***

Here, he realised that the fortune, prosperity and hope sparkling in the sky on the day of the exhibition, was nothing other than the deception of life. The happiness which he had thought to be his future destiny, perished yesterday, and he had become the corroded pages of an old manuscript.

He had the ability to overcome the hardship which he had fallen into, and bear his suffering. However, one adversity which was too heavy and difficult for him, was that another soul was participating in his misfortune. His shoulders were burdened with the problems and responsibility of his mother.

أرسل الفتى إلى أمه بعض المال واستبقى لنفسه بعضاً، وكتب إليها أنه لن يبرح هذه الأرض حتى يفي لها بما عاهدها عليه، ومشى في طريقه يفتش عن خاله في أنحاء البلاد، ويسائل عنه كل من لقيه من القاطنين والطارئين حتى حدثه بعضهم أن آخر عهدهم به رحلةٌ رحلها عنهم من بضع سنواتٍ إلى بعض الجزر الجنوبية في التفتيش عن معدن نحاسٍ هناك ثم لم يعد بعد ذلك.

فمشى في الطريق التي علم أنه سلكها حتى وصل إلى جزيرةٍ موحشةٍ مقفرة، وكانت لا تزال تغشي سماء تلك البلاد بقية من ظلمات العصور الأولى، فمر بقبيلةٍ من قبائل الزنج نازلةٍ هناك وراء بعض الجبال المنقطعة، فما رأوه حتى هاجت في صدورهم أحقاد تلك العداوة اللونية التي لا يزال يضمرها هؤلاء القوم لكل شيءٍ أبيض حتى للشمس المشرقة، والكواكب الزاهرة؛ فداروا به دورةً سقط من بعدها أسيراً في أيديهم، فاحتملوه حتى وصلوا به إلى ديارهم فاحتبسوه هناك في نفقٍ تحت الأرض كانوا يسمونه (سجن الانتقام).

***

هنالك علم أن تلك البارقة التي لاحت له في سماء السعادة من الأمل يوم المعرض إنما هي خدعة من خدع الدهر وأكذوبة من أكاذيبه، وأن ما كان يقدره لنفسه من سعادةٍ وهناءٍ في مستقبل أيامه قد ذهب بذهاب أمس الدابر، وأصبح صحيفةً باليةً في كتاب الدهر الغابر.

ولقد كان في استطاعته أن يخلد للنازلة التي نزلت به ويستمسك لها لو أنه استقل بحملها، ولكن الذي آده وأثقله أن هناك إنساناً آخر كريماً عليه يقاسمه إياها، فقد أصبح يحمل مصيبته و مصيبة أمه فيه على عاتقٍ واحد.

They descended him into a prison cell and tied him up with a heavy chain with enormous links. Then they closed the door on him, leaving him all alone. In his loneliness, he opened his eyes, and could not see anything in front of him. He was not able to distinguish whether he had become blind, or whether he was in pitch black darkness, which hid everything from his eyes. He, himself was in the state of shock until the night had elapsed, and through a small crack from the wall of the prison cell, he saw a small ray of the sun entering as a thin thread of whiteness. He stood before this stranger and became attached to it, like a traveller becomes attached to his companion. He thanked the sun which had sent him a messenger to console him in his loneliness. His eyes continued following that sun beam as if dependent upon it. Wherever that sunbeam went, his eyes shifted towards it. Eventually, he could see, that ray of sun shrinking and gradually departing. Then it ascended back from that crack within the wall where it had descended from and went back to the sky where it had come from. He grieved its separation and parting the way a loyal friend feels pain when he is separated from his companion.

He looked around his surroundings and discovered that the pieces of darkness were gathering around him and that they were merging into one another. He realised that he was also a dark fragment from the fragments of darkness which were turning in on him. He was disturbed, perplexed like the spirit is within the darkness of the grave. He did not know of his whereabouts or location. He began to walk in that tight space, touching with his hand, struggling to find himself, until he heard the sound of the chain which was cuffed to his feet, and found himself. He was tired from walking. Thus, he fell down crying.

Like this, the connection of this poor man was cut-off from the rest of the world. There remained no link good or bad, for this man and the outside world, other than that bright sunbeam which used to come every morning in order to greet him, or that gatekeeper who used to knock on his door every evening.

نزلوا به إلى المحبس وقادوه إلى سلسلةٍ غليظةٍ الحلقات فسلكوه فيها ثم أغلقوا الباب من دونه و تركوه و شأنه؛ فما انفرد بنفسه حتى فتح عينيه فلم ير أمامه شيئا، فلم يعلم هل كف بصره أم اشتدت الظلمة أمام عينيه فحجبت عن ناظره كل شيءٍ حتى نفسها؟ فلم يزل في حيرته حتى انقضى الليل، فانحدر إليه من ثقبٍ صغيرٍ في حائط المحبس خيط دقيق أبيض من شعاع الشمس حتى استقر بين يديه فأنس به أنس الغريب بالغريب، وشكر للشمس رسولها الذي أرسلته إليه ليؤنسه في وحدته، واستمر بصره عالقاً به لا يفارقه أينما سار وحيثما انتقل حتى رآه يتقبض شيئاً فشيئاً، ويتراجع قليلاً قليلاً، ثم علا إلى ثقبه الذي انحدر منه، ثم طار إلى سمائه التي هبط منها، فحزن لفراقه حزن العشير لفراق عشيره،

ودار بعينيه حول نفسه فإذا قطعٌ سوداء مظلمة تتدجى وتتكاثف من حوله ويملس بعضها في أحشاء بعض. وإذا هو نفسه قطعة من تلك القطع هائمة بينها هيمان الروح الحائر في ظلمات القبور، فما كاد يعرف مكانه منها، فمشى في ذلك المعترك المائج يفتش عن نفسه ويتلمسها بيده تلمساً حتى سمع صلصلة السلسلة الملتفة على قدميه فوجدها، وكان قد أجهده المسير فتساقط على نفسه باكياً منتحباً.

وكذلك انقطع هذا المسكين عن العالم كله خيره وشره، ولم يبق بينه وبينه من صلةٍ إلا ذلك الشعاع الأبيض الذي يزوره كل صباح، وذلك السجان الأسود الذي يطرقه كل مساء.

Not even a complete year had passed. As that man had forgotten himself, he forgot his mother and had forgotten the world that he lived in along with the world that he was currently in. He forgot the day and the night. He failed to distinguish darkness from light. He also failed to acknowledge fortunes from misfortunes. He was standing upon the edge of life and death. He was neither happy nor sad. He did not remember the past and had no hope for the future. He did not know whether in between the nearby stones there was a stone, a fragment of darkness, a moving body, an imagination, a superstition or only a mere non-existing entity.

***

A few years had passed by upon his poor and helpless mother who did not see her son and neither did she find anyone who could direct her towards him. People used to see her on the streets; an old, lost, hunched-back lady who was passionately in love with her son, mourning his separation. In her hand there was a walking stick, with it she walked, and it swivelled in her hand. Her skinny and bent body had torn rags hanging off her. An observer could only speculate that due to them being extremely old, they were pieces of cloth which were dangling from her, or either they were rotten old clothes which the wind was pushing through the air.

Every morning she used to visit places of worship, going to go to the doors of churches, synagogues and mosques in order to beg Allah ﷻ for mercy. She asked food from passers-by. When the sun used to set from the heart of the sky, she walked towards the sea shore and sat on one of the rocks, whispering to the waves and to the particles of sand. She used to look at the circular horizon very carefully, like a fortune-teller would observe the stars in the sky with scrutiny. Whenever there was a gust of breeze in her direction she used to sense the fragrance of her son. Whenever she saw a wave coming in her direction, she acknowledged that it was a message from her son.

وما مرت به على حاله تلك سنة واحدة حتى نسي نفسه، ونسي أمه ونسي العالم الذي كان يعيش فيه، والعالم الذي انتقل إليه، ونسي الليل والنهار والظلمة والنور، والسعادة والشقاء، وأصبح في منزلةٍ بين منزلتي الحياة والموت فلا يفرح ولا يتألم، ولا يذكر الماضي، ولا يرجو المستقبل، ولا يعلم هل هو حجر بين تلك الأحجار أو قطعة بين قطع الظلام، أو جسد يتحرك، أو خيال يسري، أو وهمٌ من الأوهام أو عدمٌ من الأعدام!

***

مرت على تلك الأم المسكينة بضعة أعوامٍ لا ترى ولدها ولا تجد من يدلها عليه، فأصبح من يراها في طريقها يرى عجوزاً حدباء والهةً متسلبة مذهوباً بها قد توكأت على عصاها ما تزال تضطرب في يدها، وأسبلت فوق جسمها الناحل المحقوقف أهداماً خلقاناً يحسبها الناظر إليها لكثرة ما نالت يد البلى عنها أهداباً متلاصقة أو مزقا متطايرة،

تقف صدر النهار بأبواب المعابد والكنائس تسأل الله أن يرحمها، والناس أن يطعموها، حتى إذا زالت الشمس عن كبد السماء أخذت سمتها إلى شاطىء البحر، وجلست فوق بعض صخوره تناجي أمواجه ورماله، وترقب أفقه البعيد كما يرقب المنجم كوكبه في أفق السماء، فإذا سرت إليها نسمة وجدت ريح ولدها فيها، وإذا أقبلت عليها موجة ظنت أنها رسول منه إليها،

Whenever she saw a ship on the surface of the ocean, she presumed that it was that ship which was bringing back her son. Her eyes used to rest upon it, until the ship's anchor was casted. She stood in the paths of the passengers, identifying them and very closely monitoring their behaviour and screaming her son's name as loud as possible. She stood saying "O the people of Allah ﷻ, who can tell me about my son? Who can find him for me on the face of this earth? I have lost him a long time ago, after him the world has afflicted me with calamities, I cannot forget him nor can I find him in any possible way." She continued saying "At least through guesswork, for the sake of Allah ﷻ, please tell me, has he returned with you or was he unable to come with you? Is he going to come after you, or has the world finished him off so that after today, I keep no hope of him returning?" Not even a single soul paid any attention to her, nor could they understand her plea. Very rarely if anyone did pay any attention to her, they presumed that she was insane, and out of pity and compassion for her they gave her some money.

She remained in this state and station, until she saw the mothers, sisters and young ladies departing towards their houses with their children, brothers and fathers. The people passing by the sea shore had gone, and that other than her there was no one remaining. She then took her walking stick and with the aid of it, came home slowly.

Now she used to spend her time next to the corner of a grave which she dug in the ground with her own hands, calling it her son's grave. Most times she used to cry over it and murmur over it. She used to say "O my son, which land has taken you in its bosom? Where is your abode? Under which star was your place of death? Where is your place of residence in the ocean? In which wild-cattle's stomach is your dwelling? If that bird who tore up your intestines, or that wild-cattle who stained its paws with your blood, or that grave which has hidden you inside itself, or that ocean which has took you in its belly only knew, that behind you there is an old, poor and a helpless mother which is going to cry over you, then certainly they would have been compassionate towards you because of me.

وإذا تراءت لها سفينة ماخرة على سطح الماء حسبتها السفينة التي تحمله، فلا يزال بصرها عالقاً بها لا يفارقها حتى ترسو على الشاطىء فتقف في طريق ركبانها تتصفح الوجوه وتتفرس الشمائل وتهتف باسم ولدها صارخةً معولةً وتقول: عباد الله، من يدلني على ولدي أو ينشده لي في معالم الأرض ومجاهلها فقد أضللته منذ عهدٍ بعيدٍ فحار بي الدهر من بعده، فلا أنا سالية عنه ولا واجدة إليه سبيلاً فاحتسبوها يداً عند الله وحدثوني عنه هل عاد معكم، أو تخلف عنكم ليأتي على أثركم، أو انقطع الدهر به فلا أمل فيه بعد اليوم؟ فلا يلتفت إليها أحد ولا يفهم أحد ما تقول، وربما لمحها بعض الناس فظنها امرأةً ملتاثة فرثى لها أو سائلة فتصدق عليها.

ولا يزال هذا شأنها في موقفها هذا حتى ترى الأمهات والأخوات والفتيات قد عدن بأولادهن وإخوانهن وآبائهن إلى منازلهن ولم يبق على شاطىء البحر من غادٍ ولا رائحٍ سواها. فتتناول عصاها وتعود أدراجها إلى بيتها،

فتأخذ مجلسها من حافة قبرٍ كانت قد احتفرته بيدها في أرض قاعتها وتوهمته مدفناً لولدها فتظل تبكي و تقول: في أي بطنٍ من بطون الأرض مضجعك يا بني، وتحت أي نجمٍ من نجوم السماء مصرعك، وفي أي قاع من قيعان البحر مثواك، وفي أي جوفٍ من أجواف الوحوش الضارية مأواك؟ لو يعلم الطير الذي مزق جثتك، أو الوحش الذي ولغ دمك، أو القبر الذي ضمك إلى أحشائه، أو البحر الذي طواك في جوفه، أن وراءك أماً مسكينة تبكي عليك من بعدك لرحموك من أجلي؟

O son please come back, whether you are poor, disabled or even blind, for me it is sufficient enough that whenever I depart from this world, I can give you a last farewell kiss. And I will take a pledge from you to visit my grave day and night, so that through your visits, any hardships of the grave become light for me. Through your radiant face becomes illuminated that extreme darkness. How fortunate and lucky are those mothers who go to their graves before their children and how unfortunate are those mothers whose children go to their graves first. However, the most unfortunate and helpless mother is that one who is slowly crawling towards her death and she does not know whether she has left her son behind or that she will find him in the next life."

Like this, her state remained from morning to night. She used to cry over her son like how Prophet Jacob used to cry over his son (Prophet Joseph), until, like Prophet Jacob her sight had perished, but she still could not endure having patience and hope for her son's return. (Peace and blessings of Allah be upon all the Prophets).

***

One night, the prison guard came close to the young man, he drew his hands towards the chain which was connected to the wall and pulled it towards himself. The prisoner did not say anything to him nor did he even speculate in his heart that today may be the time of his release or whether it was the time of his death. The gatekeeper brought him out from the prison cell and fastened his chain to a rock which was near the central meeting place for the tribal villagers. After the gatekeeper had done this, he left.

The man then opened his eyes and discovered his location was changed. He learned that he had entered into another setting than his previous scene. He acknowledged that he was under a different sky and on top of another land. His senses were slowly and gradually coming back to him until he gained full awareness. He began to ponder and familiarise himself with his surroundings.

عد إلي يا بني فقيراً أو مقعداً أو كفيفاً فحسبي منك أن أراك بجانبي في الساعة التي أفارق فيها هذه الحياة لأقبلك قبلة الوداع وأعهد إليك بزيارة مضجعي مطلع كل شمسٍ ومغربها لتخف بزورتك عني ضمة القبر، وتستنير بوجهك الوضاء ظلماته الحالكة. ما أسعد الأمهات اللواتي يسبقن أولادهن إلى القبور، وما أشقى الأمهات اللواتي يسبقهن أولادهن إليها، وأشقى منهن تلك الأم المسكينة التي تدب إلى الموت دبيباً وهي لا تعلم هل تركت ولدها وراءها، أو أنها ستجده أمامها؟

وهكذا كان شأنها صباحها ومساءها، فلم تزل تبكي ولدها بكاء يعقوب ولده، حتى ذهب بصرها ذهاب بصره، ولكنها لم تستطع عن يوسفها صبراً.

***

دخل السجان على الفتى عشية ليلةٍ في محبسه، فاقترب منه ومد يده إلى سلسلته المثبتة في الجدار، فانتزعها من مكانها فلم يقل شيئاً ولم يسائل نفسه هل هي ساعة نجاته أو ساعة حمامه، ثم قاده إلى خارج المحبس حتى وصل به إلى صخرةٍ جاثمةٍ على مقربةٍ من مجتمع القبيلة، فشد سلسلته إليها وتركه مكانه ومضى،

ففتح عينيه فرأى مكاناً غير مكانه، ومنظراً غير منظره، وسماءً وأرضاً غير سمائه وأرضه، فبدأ شعوره يعود إليه شيئاً فشيئاً، حتى استفاق فتذكر ما كان فيه ورأى ما صار إليه.

Here, he remembered the fortunes and the misfortunes of his migration and his home land. He recollected the prison cell, the darkness within and those chains along with their weight. Then his memories powered through, and, crossing the ocean, he remembered his mother. His lengthy departure would surely have afflicted her with unimaginable grief. Her separation was terrible for him. During this recollection, his eyes shed one tear, this was the first tear which he shed from the dark times of his adversities. From then onwards, he cried and cried uncontrollably until one portion of the night had passed. All the people went to their abodes and slept on their beds peacefully. He inclined his head upon his knees and allowed his thoughts to travel wherever he had pleased for them to go.

He was in such a state that tiredness and sleep was hovering upon his eyes. At once, he felt the touch of a hand upon his shoulder. He raised his head and saw a bright and a white body standing before him. He thought that it was a shining angel who had descended from the highest points of the skies in order to save him from his hardships. When he observed closely, he realised that it was a very beautiful, white, young lady, who he never seen before. In her whiteness, there was a very fine brownish colour mixed with it, like fine, brownish, wheat coloured cloud, which is mixed with the sunlight at forenoon.

He asked her "Who are you?"

She replied "I am a girl belonging to this tribe, I felt sorry for you seeing you in this state. Learning that you are an unfortunate man, I have come over to sympathise with you and to release you from your shackle so that you become free and go wherever you please. On the Day of Judgment, a person cannot offer a bigger gift to his Lord other than showing that he has counselled and helped a troubled person, and removed his worldly calamities." The man was amazed that a pagan and a barbaric white Negro woman, would have so much love and affection in her heart for the troubled and hopeless. He presumed in his heart that certainly there must have been some catastrophe that she had gone through. He pondered upon this excessively, and her love upon his heart became firm. He forgot all of the affairs of life, with the exception of her, as only she remained in his thoughts.

For a short time, he remained silent and did not say anything, then he spoke "Dear Lady, please mind your way, I do not seek salvation." She realised that despair was gradually dominating him. She drew near him and put her hand on his shoulder and said,

هنا تذكر السعادة والشقاء، والغربة والوطن، والسجن وظلمته، والقيد ووطأته، ثم طار بخياله إلى ما وراء البحار فذكر أمه وشقاءها من بعده، وحنينها، ويأسها من لقائه، فذرفت عيناه دمعةً كانت هي أول دمعةٍ أرسلها من جفنيه من تاريخ شقائه. وما زال يرسل العبرة إثر العبرة لا يهدأ ولا يستفيق حتى مضى شطر من الليل، وهدأ الناس جميعاً في مضاجعهم، فأسلم رأسه إلى ركبتيه وذهب بخياله إلى حيث شاء أن يذهب.

فإنه لكذلك وقد رنقت في عينيه سنة من النوم إذا شعر بيدٍ تلمس كتفيه فرفع رأسه فإذا شبح أبيض قائم فوق رأسه، فخيل إليه أن ملكاً نورانياً نزل إليه عن علياء السماء لينقذه من شقائه، فتبينه، فإذا فتاة جميلة بيضاء ما التفت الأزر على مثلها حسناً وبهاء، تتمشى في بياضها سمرة رقيقة كسمرة السحاب الرهو الذي يخالط وجه الشمس في ضحوة النهار.

فسألها: من أنت؟

قالت: أنا فتاة من فتيات هذا الحي، وقد ألممت بشيءٍ من أمرك فعلمت أنك شقي فرحمتك مما أنت فيه فجئتك أطلق وثاقك لتذهب حيث تشاء، فلا مثوبة يقدمها المرء بين يدي ربه يوم جزائه أفضل من مواساة البائس وتفريج كربة المكروب، فعجب لزنجيةٍ بيضاء ووثنيةٍ تعبد الله، وبربريةٍ تحمل بين جنبيها قلباً يعطف على البؤساء والمنكوبين، وقال في نفسه: ما لهذه الفتاة بد من شأن، وورد عليه من أمرها ما ذهب بلبه، وملك عليه نفسه وهواه، وأنساه كل شأنٍ في الحياة إلا شأنها،

فلبث صامتاً واجماً لا ينطق وقال لها: اذهبي لشأنك يا سيدتي فإنني لا أريد النجاة، فعلمت أنها ثورة من ثوارت اليأس، فدنت منه ووضعت يدها على عاتقه وقالت:

"Do not give way to despair in your heart, O young man save your life from the hands of death, because there is no distance remaining between you and death. If you are still here when the veil upon the face of the night is removed, then the sharp edges of swords will slice your meat. Do not frighten your heart with the thought of death, neither grieve this sad, poor woman who is standing in front of you. I will be extremely saddened to see you slaughtered through the hands of a butcher, or become a morsel entering the mouths of people."

He said to her "You cannot release me."

She replied "I do not understand what you are talking about, because I know for what reason and why I have come here."

He said "Prior to this I was tied up in a bond. Now, you are the relationship which I am bound to. If you were to open the chains of my feet, how are you possibly going to open the bond of my heart?" She understood and realised what his heart contained.

In pain she raised her head towards the sky for a moment. Then he also raised his head towards her and observed her like how an artist would observe his masterpiece. He witnessed a warm tear drop flow from her eye and fall in front of him. Her tears fell heavily on his cheeks, a single tear rolled from his eye and met her tear, they mixed and became one.

He stretched out his hand towards her coverlet and pulled it towards himself saying, "O my respectable lady you have been standing up for a while now, please sit with me so that we may talk about things." She sat next to him as he said "At this stage, my tear joining with your tear means that, whether living or dead we will never part from one another. If you are intending to release me now, how possibly can I take freedom other than with you?"

She said "Only if I had the power to do that O dear."

He said "What is prohibiting you from doing this O lady?"

She looked at him with eyes full of tears and said "I fear that I will start loving you."

He said "And why would you fear?"

لا تجعل لليأس إلى قلبك أيها الفتى سبيلا، وانج بحياتك من يد الموت فليس بينك وبينه إن بقيت هنا إلا أن ينحدر عن وجهك قناع هذا الليل فإذا أنت فلذٌ طائرةٌ مع شفرات السيوف، فلا تفجع نفسك في نفسك، ولا تفجع هذه المسكينة الواقفة بين يديك فإن شديداً علي جداً أن أراك بعد قليلٍ ذبيحةً في يد الذابح، أو مضغةً في فم الآكل،

قال: إنك لا تستطيعين نجاتي.

قالت: لا أفهم ما تقول فإنني ما جئتك إلا وأنا عالمة ماذا أصنع،

قال: قد كنت قبل اليوم موثقاً بوثاقٍ واحدٍ فأصبحت موثقاً بوثاقين فإن استطعت أن تحلي وثاق قدمي فإنك لا تستطيعين أن تحلي وثاق قلبي، فألمت بسريرة نفسه.

فرفعت وجهها إلى السماء ولبثت شاخصةً إليها ساعةً، فرفع رأسه إليها ولبث شاخصاً إلى وجهها نظر المصور الماهر إلى تمثاله البديع حتى شعر بدمعةٍ حارةٍ قد سقطت من جفنها على وجهه، فجرت في مجرى الدموع من خده فانحدرت من جفنه دمعة مثلها فالتقت بدمعتها فامتزجتا معاً،

فمد يده إلى ردائها فاجتذبها إليه وقال: قد طال وقوفك يا سيدتي فاجلسي بجانبي نتحدث قليلاً، فجلست على مقربةٍ منه فقال لها: إن امتزاج دمعي بدمعك في هذه الساعة قد دلني على أننا لن نفترق بعد اليوم أحياءً أو أمواتاً، فإن كنت تريدين لي النجاة فإنني لا أنجو إلا بك،

قالت: ليتني أستطيع ذلك يا سيدي،

قال: وما يمنعك منه؟

فنظرت إليه نظرةً دامعةً وقالت: أخاف أن أحبك.

قال: ولم تخافين؟

She said "I do not know."

He said "I will not ask you about that which you are hiding in your heart, however only a request which is to leave my affair in the hands of destiny, and let it decide for me. Verily I had feared death before I had met you, however now I am reassured that your glance of mercy will overcome the bitterness of death when you will look at my place of slaughter, and is sufficient for me that tear which you will drop on my grave after my death."

She welcomed his conversation. Her cheeks dampened with flowing tears, like scattered pearls from a broken necklace. Then, she advanced her hands towards the chains and broke them fiercely. She said "Come on, I will come with you, let the decree of Allah ﷻ be in our favour."

Both of them set off, passing through jungles, crossing rivers and lakes, enduring the hot and cold weather, drinking sour and sweet water, eating dry and ripe fruits. When a shade of a tree, or a river bank approached, or if they saw a ravine, they rested for a while and then advanced. Ever since the girl had left her native country, a shade of bleakness had shown upon her face like the shade of a cloud which never dispersed.

Whenever they camped at a place they used to make their beds from its soil and its stones. Hence she used to get up from her sleep after resting for some night, and then she used to advance to some corner where she could not be found. There she used to place her hand on her chest and then she used to take out a small cross which she kissed and then mumbled some words. She used to behave in a strange manner, whispering to an invisible man and seeking forgiveness for her sins. From him, she used to seek help on her journey, for which the outcome was unknown. She remained on this state until dawn break. Then, she returned where she slept. Whenever the man wanted to enquire of her affair, she avoided it, and would stop him, until he felt shame asking her again. Thus he left her in her state. He himself was bearing and hiding such a big calamity in his heart, bigger than hers by many times.

After thirty days, the pair had drawn closer to some population. They were excited. At this point, they were convinced that they had left all their troubles and misfortunes behind them. Both of them came close to a small lake. On its bank, they sat under some thick trees and started talking. This was the first time they had indulged in conversation.

قالت: لا أعلم،

قال: أنا لا أسألك عما تكتمين في صدرك من الأسرار، ولكني أسألك أن تتركيني وشأني في يد القدر يفعل بي ما يشاء، فقد كنت أخاف الموت قبل أن أراك، أما اليوم فحسبي عزاء عما ألاقيه من غصصه وآلامه نظرة رحمةٍ تلقينها علي في مصرعي، ودمعة حزنٍ تسكبينها من بعدي على تربتي...

فما استقبلته إلا بدموعها تنحدر على خديها كالعقد وهي سلكة فانتثر، ثم مدت يدها إلى قيده فعالجته حتى انصدع، وقالت: إني ذاهبة معك و ليقض الله في وفيك قضاءه.

مشيا يطويان القفار، ويعبران الأنهار ويضحيان مرة ويخصران أخري، ويردان آجن المياه وصفوها، ويقتاتان يابس الثمار ورطبها، فإذا لاح لهما ظل شجرةٍ أو شاطىء غديرٍ أو سفح جبلٍ أويا إليه فاستراحا بجانبه قليلاً ثم عادا إلى شأنهما. وكانت لا تزال تغشى وجه الفتاة مذ فارقت موطنها سحابة سوداء من الحزن ما تكاد تنقشع عنه.

وكانا إذا نزلا منزلاً وأخذا مضجعهما من تربه وأحجاره نهضت من مرقدها بعد هدأةٍ من الليل وانتحت ناحيةً من حيث تظن أنه لا يشعر بمكانها، ومدت يدها إلى صدرها فتناولت صليباً صغيراً فقبلته، ثم أنشأت تهمهم بكلامٍ خفيٍ كأنها تناجي به شخصاً غائباً عنها فتستغفره من ذنبٍ جنته إليه مرة وتطلب معونته على أمر لا تعرف مصيره،، ولا تعلم وجه الصواب فيه أخرى حتى ينبثق نور الفجر فتعود إلى مرقدها، وكان كلما سألها عن شأنها عن شأنه التوت عليه ودافعته عنها حتى تلوم أن يعاودها فتركها وشأنها، وقد أصبح يحمل في صدره من الهم فوق ما تحمل من هم نفسها،

حتى أشرفا بعد مسير ثلاثين يوماً على سواء العمران فاستبشرا وعلما أنهما قد أصبحا في الساعة الأخيرة من ساعات الشقاء. وكانا قد وصلا إلى نهر صغير هناك، فجلسا بجانبه تحت شجرةٍ مورقةٍ يتحدثان، وهي أول مرةٍ جلسا فيها للحديث.

The young man said "See, how Allah ﷻ safeguarded us in this long journey, which was through the barren and frightening jungle. Allah ﷻ has done this, because He ﷻ has written in the destiny, in the divine tablet for us a fortune. This is such a fortune that was not probably even prescribed for his pious people in Paradise."

She said "When has this life ever been an abode or a station of fortunes, and when has ever its residents been successful, that we may also become successful like them?" She continued to say "And if happiness in this life is difficult to obtain, then to find happiness, a human being should live satisfied with the belief that no one is happy in the world, only then can he pass his days of destiny peacefully and with satisfaction. This way, no false wish or hope can hinder his joy of life."

He said "Prosperity is in front of us, between it and us is only the distance of this desolate ground. If we wish to pass it, it should not be a big deal. We will take refuge in the first house, whichever one it should be from the houses of Allah ﷻ. For a short while in front of the place of slaughter, we will bend down on our knees, then after that, we will come out as a flourishing couple as there will be no obstacle standing in between us and neither would a second environment be the means of unpleasantness."

For a moment the girl put her head down and then she raised it. On her cheek, a clear tear was rolling down. The young man said, "O dear why are you crying?"

She said "Do you remember the night of escape when you invited me to runoff with you, as I told you if I were to run away with you, I will fall in love with you."

He said "Yes."

The girl said "Woe! Today it has happened what I feared." Then she started to scream out aloud and said "O mother what have you done?" She fell down face front. The man drew near to her and held her in his arms. He saw that her body parts were shaking extremely and that she was feverish. So, he broke off some twigs from the tree in order to kindle a fire. From afar he saw a cottage.

In search of a spark to kindle the twigs, he advanced towards the cottage. When he had reached at the door of that small house, he met an old dignified priest. He offered the priest his greetings. The priest replied to his greetings in a very respectable manner and asked him "O son what is the matter?"

فقال لها: ما حفظ الله حياتنا في هذه السفرة الطويلة في هذه القفرة الجرداء الموحشة إلا وقد كتب لنا في لوح مقاديره سعادةً لا أحسب أنه قد أعد خيراً منها لعباده المتقين في جنات النعيم،

قالت: ومتى كانت هذه الحياة موطناً للسعادة أو مستقراً لها؟ ومتى سعد أبناؤها بها فنسعد مثلهم كما سعدوا؟ وإن كان لا بد من سعادةٍ في هذه الحياة فسعادتها أن يعيش المرء فيها معتقداً أن لا سعادة له فيها ليستطيع أن يقضي أيامه المقدرة له على ظهرها هادىء القلب ساكن النفس لا يكدر عليه عيشه أمل كاذب، ولا رجاء خائب.

قال: إن السعادة حاضرة بين أيدينا، وليس بيننا وبينها إلا أن نطوي هذه المرحلة الباقية من هذا القفر فنلجأ إلى أول بيتٍ نلقاه في طريقنا من بيوت الله فنجثو أمام مذبحه ساعةً نخرج من بعدها زوجين سعيدين لا يحول بيننا حائل، ولا يكدر صفونا مكدر،

فأطرقت هنيهةً، ثم رفعت رأسها فإذا دمعة صافية تنحدر على خدها. فقال: ما بكاؤك يا سيدتي؟

فقالت: أتذكر ليلة النجاة إذ دعوتني إلى الفرار معك، فقلت لك إني أخاف إن فررت أن أحبك؟

قال: نعم.

قالت: واأسفاه لقد وقع اليوم ما كنت منه أخاف.. ثم صرخت صرخةً عاليةً وقالت: ماذا يا أماه.. وسقطت مكبة على وجهها، فدنا منها وأمسك بيدها فإذا رعدة شديدة تتمشى في أعضائها، فعلم أنها البرداء، وعمد إلى بعض الأشجار فاقتطع منها بضعة أعوادٍ،

ومشى يفتش عن الناس في كوخٍ كان يتراءى له على البعد حتى بلغه، فوجد على بابه كاهناً شيخاً جليل المنظر، فدنا منه وحياه تحية حي بأحسن منها وقال له: ما شأنك يا بني؟

He replied "I have left a poor girl at the river bank who is shivering with cold. Do you have a spark, so that I could take it to light a fire?"

The priest gave him a spark and said "Allah ﷻ has prescribed for you and for your patient wellbeing and good health. You carry on and I will follow behind you."

The young man ran fast until he reached the river bank. To his amazement he saw the girl sitting down comfortably. She was not complaining of any cold or pain. With a smile he approached her and said "As days are passing by, perhaps the pain of parting from your home and from your community is slowly but gradually departing."

In response she said "I have no such thing in my heart."

Then she said "Please sit down, I will tell you the entire story, because time has come now that I reveal my secret to you." He sat next to her.

She said "I am also a foreigner like you. I do not know anyone from these villages nor do I know this land. Other than myself, I only know about a grave whose signs have also perished and its resident decayed due to being buried for a long time. My mother gave me birth on a bed belonging to a man with white complexion. This man was from your end and came here about twenty years ago. He passed through here and met my mother. Both starting loving each other and ran away behind this desolated land. My mother had accepted his religion and then got married with him. Then they gave birth to me. For a term we lived a life of peace and prosperity.

The people belonging to my mother's tribe were always in search for us, until one dark night, they raided us. They took us all to their homeland and at that time I was close to turning ten years old. In front of me and my mother, they killed my father. That sight, I can still picture today and it still does not part from my vision. This extreme sadness started to draw my mother closer to her grave until her time also came. A devotee of Jesus Christ (Peace and blessings of Allah be upon him) at that time was present, whom sometimes used to come and go there. My mother had brought me in front of him and said to me 'O daughter, my mother had given me birth to face tribulations in this world, I fear that I have likewise given you birth for the same reason. It is sufficient for you that you also do not become a means of this misfortune after me, like virgin mother Mary (Peace and blessings of Allah be upon her) you also take a pledge of not marrying, which then only death can solve.' In front of the priest I accepted this order and made him a witness over this account. Then, after that, my mother's face starting sparkling with happiness and joy as then she raised her glance towards the sky and said 'O Roneal I am coming behind you' as her soul departed."

قال: إن بجانب ذلك النهر فتاةً مسكينةً تركتها ورائي تشكو البرد فهل أجد عندك جذوة نارٍ أعود بها إليها لتصطلي بها؟

فمكنه من طلبه، وقال له: (كتب الله ولعليلتك السلامة يا بني فاذهب فإني على أثرك).

فعدا الفتى عدواً شديداً حتى بلغ النهر فأدهشه أن رأى الفتاة هادئةً ساكنةً طيبة النفس لا تشكو برداً ولا ألماً، فأقبل عليها متهللاً، وقال لها: لعل ما كان يخالط نفسك من الألم لذكر أهلك ووطنك قد ذهب بذهاب الأيام،

قالت: ما كان يخالط نفسي من ذلك شيء فاجلس أحدثك حديثي فقد آن أن أفضي به إليك، فجلس بجانبها فأنشأت تحدثه،

وتقول: أنا فتاة غريبة مثلك عن هذه الديار لا أعرف من ساكنيها غير نفسي، ولا من أرضها غير قبرٍ قد زال اليوم رسمه وبلي مع الأيام دفينه، فقد ولدتني أمي على فراش رجلٍ أبيض وفد من دياركم منذ عشرين عاماً فالتقى بها عند مروره بحيها فأحبها وأحبته، ثم فرت معه إلى ما وراء هذه الصحراء فدانت بدينه، ثم تزوجها فولداني وعشنا جميعاً حقبةً من الدهر عيش السعداء الآمنين،

وكان رجال قبيلة أمي لا يزالون يتطلبون السبيل إلينا حتى سقطوا علينا في جنح ليلةٍ من ليالي الظلام فاقتادونا جميعاً إلى أرضهم، وكنت إذ ذاك لم أسلخ العاشرة من عمري، فقتلوا أبي أمامي وأمام أمي قتلةً لا يزال منظرها حاضراً بين يدي حتى الساعة لا يفارقني، فحزنت أمي عليه حزناً شديداً، ما زال يدنو بها من القبر شيئاً فشيئاً، حتى جاءت ساعتها فحضر موتها رسول من رسل المسيح كان لا يزال يختلف إليها من حينٍ إلى حين، فدعتني إليها أمامه وقالت لي: يا بنية إن أمي قد ولدتني للشقاء في هذا العالم، وأحسب أني قد ولدتك له كذلك فحسبنا ذلك، ولا تكوني سبباً في شقاء أحدٍ من بعدك، وانذري نفسك للعذراء نذراً لا يحله إلا الموت. فأذعنت لأمرها وأشهدت الكاهن على نذري فتلألأ وجهها بشراً وسروراً، ثم نظرت نظرةً في السماء وقالت: ها أنذا على أثرك يا رافائيل، ثم فاضت روحها.

The young man, upon hearing this name, startled and said "Do you know about your father's country and his family?"

She said "Yes."

When she had clarified and explained it the young man jumped up in joy and said, "O Allah ﷻ! Thank you, I have found my lost thing."

The girl was surprised and said "Which lost thing?"

The young man said "Do you remember the night we met, and our tears joined together and I said to you that our connection is unbreakable until death?

She replied "Yes."

He said, "Before this day I only loved you, now I am even closer to you. From today onwards you are my love and also my maternal uncle's daughter."

In a low voice she starting saying, "O Allah ﷻ! Thank you, in this delicate moment I have found besides me a brother." Her body in a very severe state starting shaking and her face slowly but gradually started to become fatigued.

The young man become scared and inclined towards her and said "What am I seeing?"

She said "Do not be worried, put your ear next to me so that I can tell you my remaining story which you have not heard fully as yet." She continued her story saying, "Ever since I have safeguarded my mother's will and entrusted my life towards virgin mother Mary (Peace and blessings of Allah be upon her), now it was inevitable for me to find a place of refuge for that day when my temptations overpower my religion. For this reason, I have always kept this small glass bottle with me. Now that day has arrived which I had feared. I have taken refuge in this and I have entrusted you towards Allah ﷻ."

The young man started to look at that direction which the girl had pointed to. He discovered that a bottle was placed behind him. He picked it up only to find that it was empty and that only a few yellow drops were remaining in its vessel. From there, he understood everything.

فاضطرب الفتى عند سماع هذا الاسم وقال لها: هل تعرفين وطن أبيك وأسرته؟

قالت نعم،

وسمتهما له فاستطير فرحاً وسروراً وقال: أحمدك اللهم فقد وجدت ضالتي، فعجبت لأمره، وقالت: وأي ضالةٍ تريد؟

قال: أتذكرين ليلة اللقاء إذا امتزجت دمعتانا معاً فقلت لك إنها صلة بيني وبينك لا يقطعها إلا الموت؟

قالت: نعم.

قال: قد كنت أمت إليك قبل اليوم بحرمة الحب وحدها فأصبحت أمت إليك بحرمة الحب والقربى، فأنت اليوم حبيبتي وابنة خالي معاً.

فقالت بصوتٍ خافت: أحمد الله فقد وجدت لي في هذه الساعة العصيبة أخاً، وأخذ جسمها يضطرب اضطراباً شديداً، ووجهها يربد شيئاً فشيئاً،

فذعر الفتى وارتاع وحنا عليها وقال: ماذا أرى؟

قالت: لا ترع فأصغ إلي فإن لحديثي بقية لم تسمعها، إنني منذ حفظت وصية أمي ووهبت العذراء نفسي، كان لا بد لي أن أتخذ لي ملجأ أفزع إليه في اليوم الذي أخاف أن يغلبني فيه هواي على ديني، فكنت لا أزال أحمل تلك القارورة معي حتى جاء اليوم الذي خفته فلجأت إليها فنجوت، وأستودعك الله.

فنظر الفتى حيث أشارت فرأى قارورةً مطرحة وراءها فتناولها فإذا هي فارغة إلا من بقيةٍ صفراء في قرارتها ففهم كل شيء.

The young man felt as if a fragment of his heart had broken off and was trapped in his ribs, and as if a bird had spread out his wings and through his head, had flown away in the sky's atmosphere. Thus, he fell down in his state, unconscious. He did not feel anything around him after that. After a while, he gained consciousness and opened his eyes, only to find the girl besides him had become cold. He saw there standing in front of her the same priest from the cottage, holding food which he had brought for both of them in his hand. He was looking at her with a glance of amazement and shock, he could not believe what he was seeing. The young man rushed and stood in front of him, he started to stare at him like a person taking blood retribution would look at a murderer. The priest had become dumfounded.

The young man started mumbling in a low voice. "O person, do you know why has this girl died? She died because she had pledged her life to virgin mother Mary (Peace and blessings of Allah be upon her). Then after that, love had become a barrier in her way. She could not see any escape from her heart and from her religion, other than committing suicide. O the contractors of religion, these are your sins which you commit on the face of the earth. Was it not sufficient for you that already you had restricted marriages with your own hands? You make matrimony permissible for whom you chose, but then for others you make marriage inaccessible, like an unpayable loan. Without a doubt, that Supreme Being who has created us, the one who has moulded our spirits into our bodies; He is also the one who has created for us this heart and has created for us love. He orders us to love and live in this world with affection and prosperity. What right do you have to interfere between a person and his Lord, and between a person and his heart?"

He continued saying "Verily Allah ﷻ is far and very high up in the skies. Our sight is constrained and it cannot reach there and neither can our senses meet with His ﷻ senses. We do not have any method to see Him ﷻ in His ﷻ manifest beauty and magnificence, nor can we discuss Him ﷻ through strange gesticulations other than observing His ﷻ creation and loving them.

If you want us to live in this world without love, then take our throbbing hearts away from us. Only after that you can demand whatever you want from us. This is because we cannot stop loving until our hearts are beating."

Advancing further, he said, "O people! Do you think that we were created in this world only to be transferred from the darkness of the womb in to the blackness of a monastery, and then from the duskiness of the monastery into the darkness of the grave? If so, then how bad is our life and how immoral is our birth? This world contains no other virtue than the sanctification of love. We do not have any place of refuge where we can escape to from the sorrows and tribulations of life. So, before you sanction love itself, find and invent for us another place of refuge first."

هنالك شعر كأن شعبةً من شعاب قلبه قد هوت بين أضلاعه، وكأن طائراً قد نفض جناحيه، ثم طار عن رأسه إلى جو السماء، فصعق في مكانه صعقةً لم يشعر بعدها بشيءٍ مما حوله، فلم يستفق إلا بعد حينٍ، ففتح عينيه فإذا الفتاة بجانبه جثةً باردة، وإذا الكاهن صاحب الكوخ واقفاً أمامه يحمل على كفه طعاماً كان قد جاء به إليهما ويقلب نظره حائراً لا يفهم مما يرى شيئاً، فوثب الفتى إليه حتى صار أمامه وجهاً لوجه، ونظر إليه نظرةً شزراء كتلك النظرة التي يلقيها الموتور على وجه واتره، وكأن قد خولط في عقله.

فأخذ يهذي ويقول: أتدري أيها الرجل لم ماتت هذه الفتاة؟ لأنها وهبت نفسها للعذراء، ثم عرض لها الحب في طريقها فوقفت حائرةً بين قلبها ودينها، فلم تجد لها سبيلاً إلى الخلاص إلا سبيل الانتحار فانتحرت. تلك جرائمكم يا رجال الأديان التي تقترفونها على وجه الأرض، ما كفاكم أن جعلتم أمر الزواج في أيديكم تحلون منه ما تحلون، وتربطون ما تربطون، حتى قضيتم بتحريمه قضاءً مبرماً لا يقبل أخذاً، ولا رداً؟ إن الذي خلقنا وبث أرواحنا في أجسامنا هو الذي خلق لنا هذه القلوب وخلق لنا فيها الحب، فهو يأمرنا أن نحب، وأن نعيش في هذا العالم سعداء هانئين، فما شأنكم والدخول بين المرء وربه، والمرء وقلبه؟

إن الله بعيد في علياء سمائه عن أن تتناوله أنظارنا، وتتصل به حواسنا، ولا سبيل لنا أن نراه إلا في جمال مصنوعاته وبدائع آياته، فلا بد لنا من أن نراها ونحبها لنستطيع أن نراه ونحبه.

إن كنتم تريدون أن نعيش على وجه الأرض بلا حب فانتزعوا من بين جنوبنا هذه القلوب الخفاقة ثم اطلبوا منا بعد ذلك ما تشاؤون؟ فإننا لا نستطيع أن نعيش بلا حب ما دامت لنا أفئدة خافقة.

أتظنون أيها القوم أننا ما خلقنا في هذه الدنيا إلا لننتقل فيها من ظلمة الرحم إلى ظلمة الدير، ومن ظلمة الدير إلى ظلمة القبر؟ بئست الحياة حياتنا إذن، وبئس الخلق خلقنا، إننا لا نملك في هذه الدنيا سعادةً نحيا بها غير سعادة الحب، ولا نعرف لنا ملجأ نلجأ إليه من هموم العيش وأرزائه سواها، فتفتشوا لنا عن سعادةٍ غيرها قبل أن تطلبوا منا أن نتنازل لكم عنها.

Unrelenting, he said, "These birds which are singing in their nests, in reality they are humming the songs of love. This wind which is passing the atmosphere, this also is carrying the messages of love in its curves. These stars of the sky, these planets in orbit, flowers in their gardens, the greenery of the pastures and the bloom of the meadows, as well as animals and the insects of burrows, all of these, are living through the blessing of love. O hard hearted people, these dumb animals and the silent raw materials are more exalted than speaking human beings, and through the mercy of love they have more right to live than us. They are fortunate that whatever you say they do not understand and whatever you tell they cannot hear. This way, they are safe from misery, tribulations and everlasting misfortune."

Continuing his cry, he said, "O people, we do not know you neither do we recognise your religion. We do not want to overpower our bodies and our souls with your visions. We do not want to look at your faces neither would we like to listen to your voices. Therefore, hide yourselves from us and enter into your places of worship and caves because neither can we follow you nor can we live with you. Behind us there are delicate hearted women and weak minded men, we fear that your wickedness might reach them also. It is imperative that we become a barrier in your way, so that we can separate you from them, and that you cannot reach them in terms of brainwashing their lingering hearts and minds."

He added "We do not worship anyone other than Allah ﷻ, He ﷻ is one and we do not associate any partners with Him ﷻ. It is through our own capability that we find our path towards Him ﷻ, alone, without the guidance of people like you, so we do not require your help. Our book and signs of Allah ﷻ, as well as the sweet says of nature, are sufficient for our belief. We do not require your articles of faith. The beauty of the heavens and the earth, the splendour of those who speak and those who are silent, and the loveliness of the stationary and the moving, all these are a crystal clear mirror in which we see the supreme majesty of Allah ﷻ being illuminated. In front of Allah ﷻ we fall in prostration, and then with full consciousness we motivate ourselves to Him ﷻ so that we can listen to His ﷻ command. Allah ﷻ says, 'O people! I have created splendour and beauty only for you to enjoy, so enjoy it, and you were created to give life to beauty, so give life to it.' This is the command of Allah ﷻ which we hear and obey beyond everything else."

هذه الطيور التي تغرد في أفنائها إنما تغرد بنغمات الحب، وهذا النسيم الذي يتردد في أجوائه إنما يحمل في أعطافه رسائل الحب، وهذه الكواكب في سمائها، والشموس في أفلاكها، والأزهار في رياضها، والأعشاب في مروجها والسوائم في مراتعها، والسوارب في أحجارها.. وإنما تعيش جميعاً بنعمة الحب. فمتى كان الحيوان الأعجم والجماد الصامت أيها القساة المستبدون أرفع شأناً من الإنسان الناطق وأحق منه بنعمة الحب والحياة؟ فهنيئاً لها جميعها أنها لا تعقل عنكم ما تقولون، ولا تمسح منكم ما تنطقون، فقد نجت بذلك من شرٍ عظيمٍ، وشقاءٍ مقيمٍ.

إننا لا نعرفكم أيها القوم ولا ندين بكم، ولا نعترف لكم بسلطانٍ على أجسامنا أو أرواحنا، ولا نريد أن نرى وجوهكم أو نسمع أصواتكم، فتواروا عنا واذهبوا وحدكم إلى معابدكم أو مغاوركم، فإنا لا نستطيع أن نتبعكم إليها، ولا أن نعيش معكم فيها. إن وراءنا نساءً ضعاف القلوب ورجالاً ضعاف العقول ونحن نخافكم عليهم أن يمتد شركم إليهم.. فلا بد لنا أن نقف في وجوهكم ونعترض سبيلكم لنذودكم عنهم حتى لا تصلوا إليهم فتفسدوا عليهم البقية الباقية من قلوبهم وعقولهم.

إنا لا نعبد إلا الله وحده، ولا نشرك به غيره، وفي استطاعتنا أن نعرف الطريق إليه وحدنا بدون دليلٍ يدلنا عليه، فلا حاجة لنا بكم ولا بوساطتكم. كتاب الكون يغنينا عن كتابكم، وآيات الله تغنينا عن آياتكم، وأناشيد الطبيعة ونغماتها تغنينا عن أناشيدكم ونغماتكم.. هذا الجمال المترقرق في سماء الكون وأرضه، وناطقه وصامته ومتحركه وساكنه، إنما هو مرآة نقية صافية تنظر فيها فنرى وجه الله الكريم مشرقاً متلألئاً فنخر بين يديه ساجدين، ثم نصغي إليه لنستمع وحيه فنسمعه يقول لنا: (أيها الناس إنما خلق الجمال متعة لكم فتمتعوا به، وإنما خلقتم حياة للجمال فأحيوه). ذلك أمر الله الذي نسمعه ولا نسمع أمراً سواه.

At this point in his speech, his tongue became heavy, his courage gave up on him and his joints started to tremble. He fell down in his station and started taking severe warm sighs, complaining and lamenting. The old priest drew near him and, putting his hand on his forehead, said, "Son, have some patience and assurance, you are not the first on the face of this earth who is wounded with pain and sorrows, and neither was your beloved friend the first to depart from this world. The one who endures patience upon the blessing and the will of Allah ﷻ, for him is reassurance, and for the pious there is a reward."

The young man took hold of his hands and kissed them. He said "O Father, forgive me my sin, I am from amongst the unjust."

The priest said "May Allah ﷻ forgive you O son, verily the door of mercy is not closed, neither is there a barrier nor anything preventing it from closing."

The young man said to the priest, "O father, this girl was all alone on the face of this earth. Besides me she had no one. She died because of me and for me. Do you permit me to go near her and give her a farewell kiss in these last moments?"

The priest said "You do this O son." Hence, he rose upon his knees and crawled to her, upon reaching her he gave her a very tight hug. Then, placing his face upon her face, for the first time ever in his life, he gave her a kiss. With it, his soul had also departed.

***

These two martyrs were buried at the same time under the green, luscious tree which was next to the flowing river. Meanwhile, faraway an old neighbour went to visit the young man's mother, next to the open grave she used to sit and cry next to. This time, the mother was not present. She drew nearer to the ditch, only to find her enveloped in her sheet of cloth, stained with soil, without sense or motion; lying dead. Sighing, she filled up that five hand span gap of the grave with soil. That gap was the distinction between life and death. Then she shed one tear upon her grave, the overall lot which the dying lady had gained from this world.

وما وصل إلى حديثه إلى هذا الحد حتى ثقل لسانه، ووهنت عزيمته، وارتعدت مفاصله، فسقط في مكانه يزفر زفيراً شديداً، ويئن أنيناً محزناً، فاقترب منه الشيخ ووضع يده على رأسه وقال له: ارفق بنفسك يا بني، فما أنت بأول ثاكلٍ على وجه الأرض، ولا فقيدك بأول راحلٍ عنها، وإن في رحمة الله ورضوانه عزاءً للصابرين وجزاءً للمحسنين،

فأهوى الفتى على يده وأخذ يقبلها ويقول: اغفر لي ذنبي يا أبت، فقد كنت من الظالمين،

قال: غفر الله لك يا بني فما دون رحمة الله باب موصد ولا رتاج معترض،

قال له: يا أبت إن هذه الفتاة غريبة عن هذه الأرض وليس لها فيها أحد سواي، وقد ماتت من أجلي وفي سبيلي؛ فهل تأذن لي أن أدنوا منها لأقبلها قبلة الوداع في آخر ساعةٍ من ساعاتها على وجه الأرض؟

قال: افعل يا بني، فزحف على ركبتيه حتى بلغ مكانها فضمها إليه ضمةً شديدةً وأهوى بفمه على فمها فقبلها لأول مرةٍ في حياته قبلةً فاضت روحه فيها.

***

في الساعة التي دفن فيها هذان الشهيدان تحت تلك الشجرة المورقة على شاطىء ذلك النهر الجاري مرت بكوخ العجوز امرأة من جاراتها كانت تعتادها الزيارة من حينٍ إلى حين، فنظرت إلى مكانها الذي اعتادت أن تتخذه من حافة ذلك القبر المفتوح فرأته خالياً، فأشرفت على الحفرة فوجدتها مترديةً فيها معفرةً بترابها لا حراك بها، فملأت بالتراب الذي كان مجتمعاً حول الحفرة تلك الأشبار الخمسة التي هي مسافة ما بين الحياة والموت، ثم أسبلت فوق تربتها دمعةً كانت هي كل نصيبها من الدنيا.

The Veil / Al-Hijāb (Composed)

A man went to Europe, who had no bad habits. He stayed there for a few years and then returned. We could not recognize his good characteristics anymore, those which we used to see in him, they had perished.

He went with a face of humility, as if he was a lady on the first night of her wedding, and when he returned, his face was like the soft particles on soil of a rainy night. When he went, he went with a clean heart which was inclined towards forgiveness and compassion. However, when he returned, he had a hollow heart which was bitter against the land and its residents, full of mistrustfulness and jealousy. He was displeased and aggrieved with the heavens and their creator. When he went, he went with a freshly blooming heart, a soul full of humility, he saw everyone above himself. Nevertheless, when he returned, he returned with a sour personality and did not see anyone above himself.

He did not look at anyone with humility anymore. He went with a head which was full of wisdom and shrewdness. However, when he came back, his head resembled the sculpture of a punctured skulled, which was not full of anything other than deteriorated conjectures. He departed as if he did not consider anything on earth more beloved to him than his religion and his patriotism for his country. Though, when he had come back those things felt the most inferior to him on the planet.

I used to see the strange faces which weak young men used to bring back to their countries from these nations. Verily those colours of the West which colour their bodies, only last until the sun of the East declines. The Western colour extinguishes and its particles are flown away in the sky's atmosphere. For them, they consider foreign countries like a mirror for their faces. Whenever the face is turned from it, the reflection finishes within. I did not like to leave this friend alone. I had covered his faults for the sake of previous loyalty. I had tolerated him and hoped for him to leave his foolishness, his superstitions, his void perceptions and his strange ways. A person like me cannot endure this kind of behaviour, but I did, until he came to me at the beginning of one night in a stressful state with a severe problem.

الحجاب

(موضوعة)

ذهب فلان إلى أوروبا وما ننكر من أمره شيئاً، فلبث فيها بضع سنين. ثم عاد وما بقي مما كنا نعرفه منه شيء.

ذهب بوجهٍ كوجه العذراء ليلة عرسها، وعاد بوجهٍ كوجه الصخرة الملساء تحت الليلة الماطرة؛ وذهب بقلبٍ نقيٍ طاهرٍ يأنس بالعفو ويستريح إلى العذر، وعاد بقلبٍ ملففٍ مدخولٍ لا يفارقه السخط على الأرض وساكنها، والنقمة على السماء وخالقها؛ وذهب بنفسٍ غضةٍ خاشعةٍ ترى كل نفسٍ فوقها، وعاد بنفس ذهابٍ نزاعةٍ لا ترى شيئاً فوقها،

ولا تلقي نظرةً واحدةً على ما تحتها؛ وذهب برأسٍ مملوءةٍ حكماً ورأياً، وعاد برأس كرأس التمثال المثقب لا يملؤها.. إلا الهواء المتردد؛ وذهب وما على وجه الأرض أحب إليه من دينه ووطنه، وعاد وما على وجهها أصغر في عينيه منهما.

وكنت أرى أن هذه الصورة الغريبة التي يتراءى فيها هؤلاء الضعفاء من الفتيان العائدين من تلك الديار إلى أوطانهم إنما هي أصباغ مفرغة على أجسامهم إفراغاً لا تلبث أن تطلع عليها شمس المشرق حتى تتصل وتتطاير ذراتها في أجواء السماء، وأن مكان المدينة الغريبة من نفوسهم مكان الوجه من المرآة؛ إذا انحرف عنها زال خياله منها، فلم أشأ أن أفارق ذلك الصديق، ولبسته على علاته وفاءً بعهده السابق ورجاءً لغده المنتظر، محتملاً في سبيل ذلك من حمقة ووسواسه وفساد تصوراته وغرابة أطواره، ما لا طاقة لمثلي باحتمال مثله، حتى جاءني ذات ليلةٍ بداهية الدواهي ومصيبة المصائب، فكانت آخر عهدي به.

In our meeting, I noticed that he was quiet and distressed. I offered my greetings to him and he replied with a gesture. I then asked him "What is the matter?"

He replied "Since last night, I have been upset with this woman over a matter which I cannot obtain redemption from. The decision which I have made in this matter, I see no fate in it."

I asked "Which woman are you talking about?"

He said "It is that woman whom the people address as my wife and I consider her to be a very big obstruction in the way of my desires and motives."

I said "Verily you have numerous desires O friend, which desire are you talking about?"

He said "I have only one desire in my life, which is that, I close my eyes and then open them to see that no woman in this town ever wears a veil covering her face."

I said "This, you do not have neither power nor opinion over."

He said "A lot of people share a similar view and desire to mine concerning the veil. There is only one barrier to them unveiling, revealing themselves and freely mixing with consenting men. This is the humility, weakness and fear which has always existed, typical of people of the East. Whenever courageous people attempt making a move for this modern change, they are stopped by old traditions. I see myself hastening to destroy these old customary foundations which are standing in between notional success and fortunes for a very long time. I see myself as a revolutionary, propagating the liberation and freedom of women, a task yet unfulfilled.

Thus, I presented this scenario to my wife, she esteemed it and considered it a valuable task. However, at the same time she acknowledged that I will be the one bringing upon her big trials, catastrophes and troubles.

She said 'If I reveal myself and start mixing in with the men, then I will not be able to socialize with the women after this anymore on the basis of shame and modesty.'

دخلت عليه فرأيته واجماً مكتئباً، فحييته فأومأ إلي بالتحية إيماءً، فسألته ما باله؟

فقال: ما زلت منذ الليلة من هذه المرأة في عناءٍ لا أعرف السبيل إلى الخلاص منه، ولا أدري مصير أمري فيه،

قلت: وأي امرأة تريد؟

قال: تلك التي يسميها الناس زوجتي، وأسميها الصخرة العاتية في طريق مطالبي وآمالي.

قلت: إنك كثير الآمال يا سيدي فعن أي آمالك تحدث؟

قال: ليس لي في الحياة إلا أمل واحد هو أن أغمض عيني ثم أفتحهما فلا أرى برقعاً على وجه امرأةٍ في هذا البلد،

قلت: ذلك ما لا تملكه ولا رأي لك فيه،

قال: إن كثيراً من الناس يرون في الحجاب رأيي، ويتمنون في أمره ما أتمنى، ولا يحول بينهم وبين نزعه عن وجوه نسائهم وإبرازهن إلى الرجال يجالسنهم كما يجلس بعضهن إلى بعض إلا العجز والضعف والهيبة التي لا تزال تلم بنفس الشرقي كلما حاول الإقدام على أمرٍ جديد، فرأيت أن أكون أول هادم لهذا البناء العادي القديم الذي وقف سداً دون سعادة الأمة وارتقائها دهراً طويلاً، وأن يتم على يدي ما لم يتم على يد أحدٍ غيري من دعاة الحرية وأشياعها،

فعرضت الأمر على زوجتي فأكبرته وأعظمته وخيل إليها أنني جئتها بإحدى النكبات العظام والرزايا الجسام،

وزعمت أنها إن برزت إلى الرجال فإنها لا تستطيع أن تبرز إلى النساء بعد ذلك حياءً منهن وخجلاً،

I say, in fact, here there is no humility and shame, but only immobility, death and a disgrace which Allah ﷻ strikes upon the women of this country, who are forced to live in the darkness's of their graves within their veils and scarves. In death, they are then only transported from their worldly grave to that of the hereafter. Thus, it is crucial for me to materialise and complete my task, my desire. I will cure this head strong stubbornness or else break it in two."

From his conversation, my heart filled with sadness and sorrow. I looked at him, with eyes full of mercy. I said to him "O friend, do you know what you are talking about?"

He replied "Yes, I am speaking the truth in which I have firm belief, this is my perception, which is apparent in yourself and in the hearts of many people as well."

I said "Do you grant me permission, so I can say something to you? You have spent a long time living between a nation where there is no veil between men and women. Can your heart recall any day where you had wished for a woman whom you had no right over, and you were successful in obtaining her and yet her guardian was unaware?"

He said "That happened many times, but what are you getting at?"

I said "What I would like to say is that, I fear that people do not also tarnish your reputation the way you have blemished theirs, through the actions which you have committed."

He said "Certainly a modest woman has the power to live amongst men, and yet still safeguard her modesty and her chastity in a well-fortified fortress, so no seducer can present his desires."

Thus, he interposed me and I could not bear him, I said, "O you weak people, this is Satan's deception, penetrating through the corners of your heads, dismantling your brains and senses. Regarding modesty, this is not but a word, which has no room in linguistics and in dictionaries. Hence, if we try to investigate it from the hearts and through the sentiments of people, it is very rare that we will find it. The heart of mankind is like a stationary reservoir which is always extremely clean, however when a stone falls into it, it becomes tumultuous. Chastity is also a colour from the colours of the soul whose true essence is an essence within itself. It is very rare that these colours could endure the beams of a static sun."

ولا خجل هناك ولا حياء، ولكنه الموت والجمود والذل الذي ضربه الله على هؤلاء النساء في هذا البلد أن يعشن في قبورٍ مظلمةٍ من خدورهن وخمرهن حتى يأتيهن الموت فينتقلن من مقبرة الدنيا إلى مقبرة الآخرة، فلا بد لي أن أبلغ أمنيتي، وأن أعالج هذا الرأس القاسي المتحجر علاجاً ينتهي بإحدى الحسنيين إما بكسره أو بشفائه.

فورد علي من حديثه ما ملأ نفسي هماً وحزناً، ونظرت إليه نظرة الراحم الراثي وقلت: أعالم أنت أيها الصديق ما تقول؟

قال: نعم أقول الحقيقة التي أعتقدها وأدين نفسي بها واقعة من نفسك ونفوس الناس جميعاً حيث وقعت،

قلت: هل تأذن لي أن أقول لك إنك عشت فترةً طويلةً في ديار قوم لا حجاب بين رجالهم ونسائهم، فهل تذكر أن نفسك حدثتك يوماً من الأيام وأنت فيهم بالطمع في شيء مما لا تملك يمينك من أعراض نسائهم فنلت ما تطمع فيه من حيث لا يشعر مالكه؟

قال: ربما وقع لي شيء من ذلك وفماذا تريد؟

قلت: أريد أن أقول لك إني أخاف على عرضك أن يلم به من الناس ما ألم بأعراض الناس منك،

قال: إن المرأة الشريفة تستطيع أن تعيش بين الرجال من شرفها وعفتها في حصنٍ حصينٍ لا تمتد إليه المطامع،

فتداخلني ما لم أملك معه وقلت له: تلك هي الخدعة التي يخدعكم بها الشيطان أيها الضعفاء، والثلمة التي يعثر بها في زوايا رؤوسكم فينحدر منها إلى عقولكم ومداركم فيفسدها عليكم، فالشرف كلمة لا وجود لها في قواميس اللغة ومعاجمها، فإن أردنا أن نفتش عنها في قلوب الناس وأفئدتهم قلما نجدها، والنفس الإنسانية كالغدير الراكد لا يزال صافياً رائقاً حتى يسقط فيه حجر فإذا هو مستنقع كدر، والعفة لون من ألوان النفس لا جوهر من جواهرها، وقلما تثبت الألوان على أشعة الشمس المتساقطة،

He said "Do you deny the existence of modesty between people?"

I replied "I do not deny it, because I know that it does superficially exist, but only between the foolish and the weak. However, I do deny its existence, between the shrewd, capable men and the modern, skilful women who sit in seclusion with one another without a veil."

I further added "Which environment from this town would you like to expose your women and men in? Once, when an educated man was asked, 'Why have you not married?' His reply was that 'All the women of this town are my wives.' Amongst students, there are those who, for the sake of their modesty, hide their faces from the eyes of their friends. However, everyday, in their school bags are carrying pictures and letters from their lovers and admirers.

Amongst the rough and common people, a lot of them enter a house as despised servants, but leave as honoured son in-laws without marriage.

Thus after all of this, why are you still so stubborn about the subject of women? Why are you so passionate about discussing them, and veiling or their unveiling? What is so alarming about women obtaining freedom or being a captive? Have you fulfilled all the rights and the obligations of the nation which were demanded by you, that now you have decided to deluge others with these blessings?

Before you can teach any manners and etiquettes to the women, you must first turn the men into fine, noble gentlemen. Hence, if you are unable to do so, then without question you are unable to do anything for the women.

In front of you they are many doors of worthy causes, you can knock on any. However, leave this door closed. Verily if you were to open this door, you will bring upon yourself great devastation and everlasting catastrophe.

Show me one man from amongst you, who has the power to withstand his desires when he is in front of a woman he admires? Then I will believe that a woman can control herself in front of a man whom she admires.

You want to create hardships for women, those which you do not even have the power to carry out. You are demanding from them that which you do not even find and recognise in yourself. Thus, you are endangering them in the combat field of a menacing life. You do not know whether women will benefit or be at a mere loss. I think that you are amongst the losers.

قال: أتنكر وجود العفة بين الناس؟

قلت: لا أنكرها لأني أعلم أنها موجودة بين البله الضعفاء والمتكلفين؛ ولكني أنكر وجودها عند الرجل القادر المختلب والمرأة الحاذقة المترفقة إذا سقط بينهما الحجاب وخلا وجه كل منهما لصاحبه.

في أي جو من أجواء هذا البلد تريدون أن تبرز نساؤكم لرجالكم؟ أفي جو المتعلمين وفيهم من سئل مرةً: لم لم يتزوج؟ فأجاب: نساء البلد جميعاً نسائي. أم في جو الطلبة وفيهم من يتوارى عن أعين خلانه وأترابه وخجلاً إن خلت محفظته يوماً من الأيام من صور عشيقاته وخليلاته أو أقفرت من رسائل الحب والغرام؟

أم في جو الرعاع والغوغاء وكثير منهم يدخل البيت خادماً ذليلاً، ويخرج منه صهراً كريماً؟

وبعد: فما هذا الولع بقصة المرأة، والتمطق بحديثها، والقيام والقعود بأمرها وأمر حجابها وسفورها، وحريتها وأسرها، كأنما قد قمتم بكل واجب للأمة عليكم في أنفسكم، فلم يبق إلا أن تفيضوا من تلك النعم على غيركم.

هذبوا رجالكم قبل أن تهذبوا نساءكم، فإن عجزتم عن الرجال فأنتم عن النساء أعجز.

أبواب الفخر أمامكم كثيرة، فاطرقوا أيها شئتم، ودعوا هذا الباب موصداً؛ فإنكم إن فتحتموه فتحتم على أنفسكم ويلاً عظيماً وشقاءً طويلاً.

أروني رجلاً واحداً منكم يستطيع أن يزعم في نفسه أنه يمتلك هواءً بين يدي امرأة يرضاها؛ فأصدق أن امرأة تستطيع أن تملك هواها بين يدي رجلٍ ترضاه.

إنكم تكلفون المرأة ما تعلمون أنكم تعجزون عنه، وتطلبون عندها ما لا تعرفونه عند أنفسكم، فأنتم تخاطرون بها في معركة الحياة مخاطرةً لا تعلمون أتربحونها من بعدها أم تخسرونها، وما أحسبكم إلا خاسرين.

A woman has never come up to you with a complaint of injustice, neither has she demanded you to open her shackles and to release her from her captivity, so why do you then interfere between her and her affairs? Why do you discuss their issues so passionately, day and night?

Certainly they do not complain about your curiosities and your absurd behaviour, the annoyance which you create for them when you stand in front of them wherever they go and wherever they stand. You make the atmosphere very uncomfortable for them. Hence, they see no option but to confine themselves in their houses, regardless of the wishes of their household. They close the doors and close the curtains. They have become fed up of you and want to escape your prying. It is amazing that with your own hands you have imprisoned them. Then, you go and stand upon the door of their prison and cry and sympathise over their misfortunes?

You do not have any mercy for them, but you have mercy for yourself. You do not cry for them, but you cry over those gratifying days which you spent in your town, where there was unveiled beauty on display and the environment was full of immodesty and the drift of shamelessness. If it was up to you, you would cut off your nose in order to win back that immoral life which you have left behind. Verily in that life of yours, purity was contained in a water skin, veiled and closed. You continued puncturing its corners every day and purity, drop by drop, kept on dripping until the water skin became dry and shrivelled up. This was still not sufficient for you, as today you have come in order to open its knot only to discover that there is not even one drop of purity remaining in the water skin.

For a long time, The Egyptian women lived with peace and satisfaction in their houses. They were content with themselves and with their lives. They considered it a complete blessing, either in fulfilling their obligations, or to stand in front of their Lord, or to look at their children with affection, or to have a conversation with the neighbouring lady about herself and sharing her feelings and her secrets with her.

A woman saw the best piety out of all pieties to show humility to her father and to obey her husband and to keep him happy, this was considered a complete act of modesty. She understood the meaning of love and was unaware of the meaning of amatory and lustful love. Thus, she loved her husband because he was her husband the way she loved her child because it was her child. Other women considered love being the foundation of wedlock, but she thought that wedlock was the foundation of love.

ما شكت المرأة إليكم ظلماً، ولا تقدمت إليكم في أن تحلوا قيدها وتطلقوها من أسرها، فما ذخولكم بينها وبين نفسها؟ وما تمضغكم ليلكم ونهاركم بقصصها وأحاديثها؟

إنها لا تشكو إلا فضولكم وإسفافكم، ومضايقتكم لها ووقوفكم في وجهها حيثما سارت وأينما حلت، حتى ضاق بها وجه الفضاء فلم تجد لها سبيلاً إلا أن تسجن نفسها بنفسها في بيتها فوق ما سجنها أهلها فأوصدت من دونها بابها، وأسبلت أستارها، تبرماً بكم وفراراً من فضولكم، فواعجباً لكم تسجنونها بأيديكم ثم تقفون على باب سجنها تبكونها وتندبون شقاءها!

إنكم لا ترثون لها، بل ترثون لأنفسكم، ولا تبكون عليها، بل على أيامٍ قضيتموها في ديارٍ يسيل جوها تبرجاً وسفوراً، ويتدفق خلاعةً واستهتاراً، وتودون بجدع الأنف لو ظفرتم هنا بذلك العيش الذي خلفتموه هناك. لقد كنا وكانت العفة في سقاءٍ من الحجاب موكوء فما زلتم به تثقبون في جوانبه كل يومٍ ثقباً، والعفة تتسلل منه قطرة قطرة حتى تقبض، وتكرش ثم لم يكفكم ذلك منه حتى جئتم اليوم تريدون أن تحلوا وكاءه حتى لا تبقى فيه قطرة واحدة.

عاشت المرأة المصرية حقبةً من دهرها هادئةً مطمئنةً في بيتها، راضيةً عن نفسها وعن عيشها، ترى السعادة كل السعادة في واجبٍ تؤديه لنفسها، أو وقفةٍ تقفها بين يدي ربها، أو عطفةٍ تعطفها على ولدها، أو جلسةٍ تجلسها إلى جارتها تبثها ذات نفسها وتستبثها سريرة قلبها،

وترى الشرف كل الشرف في خضوعها لأبيها وائتمارها بأمر زوجها، ونزولها عند رضاهما، وكانت تفهم معنى الحب وتجهل معنى الغرام، فتحب زوجها لأنه زوجها، كما تحب ولدها لأنه ولدها، فإن رأى غيرها من النساء أن الحب أساس الزواج رأت هي أن الزواج أساس الحب،

Then, you came along, and said to them 'Those people of your house who overpower you with commands, they are not more intellectual than you, neither their opinion is superior to yours. They cannot watch out your welfare better than you. Therefore, they have no right and neither any authority to govern you the way they think they can.'

Due to your words, the woman now considers her father to be dishonourable, and has started rebelling against her husband. As a result, the house which yesterday was blooming with happiness and laughter like that of a wedding night, has become a dwelling of death, whose flames never extinguished or perished.

You said to her, 'It is inevitable for you that you select your husband yourself, so that your family cannot deceive and neither deprive you from your future fortune.' Hence, she made a bad selection for herself, which her family did not choose for her. Such a marriage prospers only for one day and one night, then it is followed by long hardships, and humiliating punishment after.

Then you said to her 'Certainly the basis of a marriage is love.' Thus, she started rolling, elevating and directing her eyes upon the faces of men until love affiliated with wedlock. Thus, this is how she took care of this matter.

Then you said to her 'Verily the prosperity in the life of a woman is that her husband must be her previous boyfriend and her lover.' Before this, she did not know anything other than a husband's love. Due to this, she went out in search for a new husband every day in order to revive the grieving love which had died with the old husband. Hence like this, she lost her old husband and could not benefit from a new one.

You said to her, 'It is vital for you to learn, so that you can educate your children beautifully and at the same time manage the system of the house.' Hence, she learnt everything, but failed in the upbringing of her children and the management of the household.

You said to her 'We only get married to the women who we love and the ones we are pleased with, making sure that our taste corresponds with theirs and that our feelings match their emotions.' Thus, she saw that certainly for her it was necessary to recognise the station of your desires and to work out what glitters in your eyes, so that she could adorn herself according to what you love. Hence, she examined the index of your life, page by page. She did not see in it anything other than the names of vulgar, shameless women, for pleasure and entertainment. The men praised their intelligence and their mesmerising looks.

فقلتم لها إن هؤلاء الذين يستبدون بأمرك من أهلك ليسوا بأوفر منك عقلاً ولا أفضل رأياً، ولا أقدر على النظر لك من نظرك لنفسك، فلا حق لهم في هذا السلطان الذي يزعمونه لأنفسهم عليك،

فازدرت أباها؛ وتمردت على زوجها وأصبح البيت الذي كان بالأمس عرساً من الأعراس الضاحكة مناحةً قائمةً لا تهدأ نارها، ولا يخبو أوارها.

وقلتم لها: لا بد لك أن تختاري زوجك بنفسك حتى لا يخدعك أهلك عن سعادة مستقبلك فاختارت لنفسها أسوأ مما اختار لها أهلها، فلم يزد عمر سعادتها على يومٍ وليلةٍ ثم الشقاء الطويل بعد ذلك والعذاب الأليم.

وقلتم لها: إن الحب أساس الزواج، فما زالت تقلب عينيها في وجوه الرجال مصعدةً مصوبةً حتى شغلها الحب عن الزواج فعنيت به عنه.

وقلتم لها: إن سعادة المرأة في حياتها أن يكون زوجها عشيقها، وما كانت تعرف إلا أن الزوج غير العشيق. فأصبحت تطلب في كل يوم زوجاً جديداً يحيي من لوعة الحب ما أمات الزوج القديم، فلا قديماً استبقت ولا جديداً أفادت.

وقلتم لها: لا بد أن تتعلمي لتحسني تربية ولدك، والقيام على شؤون بيتك، فتعلمت كل شيءٍ إلا تربية ولدها، والقيام على شؤون بيتها.

وقلتم لها: نحن لا نتزوج من النساء إلا من نحبها ونرضاها ويلائم ذوقها ذوقنا، وشعورها شعورنا، فرأت أن لا بد لها أن تعرف مواقع أهوائكم، ومباهج أنظاركم لتتجمل لكم بما تحبون، فراجعت فهرس حياتكم صفحةً صفحةً، فلم تر فيه غير أسماء الخليعات المستهترات، والضاحكات اللاعبات والإعجاب بهن والثناء على ذكائهن وفطنتهن،

From this, she became unashamed and obscene as well in order to obtain your satisfaction and desire. Then she walked towards you, wearing very fine, thin transparent clothing, presenting herself to you the way a concubine would present herself in the market of slaves. When you saw this behaviour, you disliked and refrained from her. Saying, 'We men do not marry roguish and immoral women who have a bad character.' You did not care whether the entire nation of women becomes indecent, as long as your wives remain pure and sound. Thus, she returned with a broken and despaired heart, as now lecherous people do not like them and decent people refrain from them. Hence, she found in front of her a tumbling door, and fell in it.

In this way, doubt circulated in the hearts of the entire nation, and men and women started to have ill assumptions about each other. Both became desolate from each other and the atmosphere darkened between them. Their houses became like monasteries and a spectator could not see but men as priests and women as nuns.

O people of mercy! This is the reality of your cries, your mourning and your sympathising for the women!

Like you, we know that indeed women need education. Hence their fathers or brothers must teach them etiquettes because manners are more beneficial to them than knowledge. If she requires an honest and merciful husband, then her father should seek for his daughters a good husband. If the husband requires a good wife, then he should take good care of her and to take her out towards clean and fresh air in order to rejuvenate her and to enjoy the blessing of life. Thus, her guardians should give her the permission for this, along with allowing her companion to accompany her for her recreation activities at mornings and at evenings, the way a shepherd escorts his sheep due to the fear of wolves. If, however, we are unable to take a father, a brother or a husband to do this, then we should wash our hands away from the entire nation of men and women. This is because a woman does not have the capability of self-controlling her righteousness the way a man has the competence to reform her.

It is amazing that you have learned everything apart from this thing, which was near your understanding. This is vital for you to learn before everything. Certainly for every green land there is a specific grass which it cultivates, and that grass grows at exclusive times, this is when its progress and the green land becomes lush.

فتخلعت واستهترت لتبلغ رضاكم، وتنزل عند محبتكم، ثم مشت إليكم بهذا الثوب الرقيق الشفاف تعرض نفسها عليكم عرضاً، كما تعرض الأمة نفسها في سوق الرقيق، فأعرضتم عنها ونبوتم بها، وقلتم لها: إنا لا نتزوج النساء العاهرات، كأنكم لا تبالون أن يكون نساء الأمة جميعاً ساقطاتٍ إذا سلمت لكم نساؤكم، فرجعت أدراجها خائبةً منكسرةً وقد أباها الخليع، وترفع عنها المحتشم، فلم تجد بين يديها غير باب السقوط فسقطت.

وكذلك انتشرت الريبة في نفوس الأمة جميعاً، وتمشت الظنون بين رجالها ونسائها، فتعاجز الفريقان وأظلم الفضاء بينهما، وأصبحت البيوت كالأديرة لا يرى فيها الرائي إلا رجالاً مترهبين ونساءً عانسات.

ذلك بكاؤكم على المرأة أيها الراحمون، وهذا رثاؤكم لها وعطفكم عليها!

نحن نعلم كما تعلمون أن المرأة في حاجةٍ إلى العلم، فليهذبها أبوها أو أخوها، فالتهذيب أنفع لها من العلم؛ وإلى اختيار الزوج العادل الرحيم، فليحسن الآباء اختيار الأزواج لبناتهم وليجمل الأزواج عشرة نسائهم. وإلى النور والهواء تبرز إليهما وتتمتع فيهما بنعمة الحياة، فليأذن لها أولياؤها بذلك، وليرافقها رفيق منهم في غدواتها وروحاتها كما يرافق الشاة راعيها خوفاً عليها من الذئاب، فإن عجزنا عن أن نأخذ الآباء والإخوة والأزواج بذلك فلننفض أيدينا من الأمة جميعاً: نسائها ورجالها، فليست المرأة بأقدر على إصلاح نفسها من الرجل على إصلاحها.

أعجب ما أعجب له في شؤونكم أنكم تعلمتم كل شيءٍ إلا شيئاً واحداً هو أدنى إلى مداركهم أن تعلموه قبل كل شيءٍ، وهو أن لكل تربةٍ نباتاً ينبت فيها، ولكل نباتٍ زمناً يمنو فيه!

You have seen the scholars in Europe who indulge in the study/progress of sciences between their nations. Verily they are self-indulgent from all their needs. You have also become indulgent like them, enforcing their ideals on a nation whose majority do not even know the letters of the alphabet.

You have seen the philosophers there. Through their ill-founded intellect and etiquettes, they are propagating the philosophy of rejecting God between the branches of disbelief. This could deprive some from their faith. You have also started propagating the same element to a nation who are weak and simple, but unfortunately you cannot deprive them from their faith, even if there was something there to withdraw them from their belief.

You have seen a European man who is absolutely free, he does what he pleases, and lives the way he wants. This is because he has the power to look after himself and to watch his footsteps at a time when he knows that he has reached the boundary of freedom which he has specifically chosen for himself. He is careful not to transgress it. However, you intend to bestow this liberty to the one who is weak in his intentions and has scrawny objectives? A non-westerner is living his life with good conduct at the peak of a slanting, slippery rock. If his feet slip once, he will tumble in such a way that he will not have the ability to stop until he will fall into a ditch, and would deteriorate in its penetration.

You have seen a European husband whose dignity has been extinguished by the environment. The humility and modesty of his heart have been perished. He has the capacity to see another man put his hand around his wife's waist, whoever she is happy with. He is happy with her befriending whomever she wills and chooses to be alone with. Her husband will remain stationary, motionless and unaffected. Would you like that a high esteemed, simple Eastern man also stand back and withhold his honour the way this European man does?

Furthermore, have you seen a European wife? She is full of audacity and bravery. She can stand up in all situations with the men, and safeguard herself and her esteem. Do you think that such safeguarding is appropriate amongst the simple, naive and weak women of Egypt?

Every type of vegetation which is cultivated in a land other than its land or that it is planted in a time other than its time, is either rejected by the land or destroyed by it.

رأيتم العلماء في أوروبا يشتغلون بكماليات العلوم بين أممٍ قد فرغت من ضرورياتها، فاشتغلتم بها مثلهم في أمةٍ لا يزال سوادها الأعظم في حاجةٍ إلى معرفة حروف الهجاء.

ورأيتم الفلاسفة فيها ينشرون الكفر بين شعوبٍ ملحدةٍ، لها من عقولها وآدابها ما يغنيها بعض الغناء عن أيمانها، فاشتغلتم بنشرها بين أمةٍ ضعيفةٍ ساذجةٍ لا يغنيها عن أيمانها شيءٌ إن كان هناك ما يغنى عنه.

ورأيتم الرجل الأوروبي حراً مطلقاً، يفعل ما يشاء ويعيش كما يريد، لأنه يستطيع أن يملك نفسه وخطواته في الساعة التي يعلم فيها أنه قد وصل إلى حدود الحرية التي رسمها لنفسه، فلا يتخطاها، فأردتم أن تمنحوا هذه الحرية نفسها رجلاً ضعيف الإرادة والعزيمة يعيش من حياته الأدبية في رأسِ منحدرٍ زلقٍ، إن زلت به قدمه مرةً تدهور من حيث لا يستطيع أن يستمسك حتى يبلغ الهوة ويتردى في قرارتها.

ورأيتم الزوج الأوروبي الذي أطفأت البيئة غيرته، وأزالت خشونة نفسه وحرشتها، يستطيع أن يرى زوجته تخاصر من يشاء، وتصاحب من تشاء، وتخلو بمن تشاء؛ فيقف أمام ذلك المشهد موقف الجامد المتبلد، فأردتم الرجل الشرقي الغيور الملتهى أن يقف موقفه، ويستمسك استمساكه.

ورأيتم المرأة الأوروبية الجريئة المتفتية في كثيرٍ من مواقفها مع الرجال أن تحتفظ بنفسها وكرامتها، فأردتم من المرأة المصرية الضعيفة الساذجة أن تبرز للرجال بروزها، وتحتفظ بنفسها احتفاظها!

وكل نباتٍ يزرع في أرضٍ غير أرضه، أو في ساعةٍ غير ساعته، إما أن تأباه الأرض فتلفظه، وإما أن ينشب فيها فيفسدها.

We are requesting you, for the sake of the country's honour and secrecy of religion, that you leave the remaining women alone who are living in their houses peacefully. Do not torment them with your dreams and wishes the way you have tormented women previously. For every wound there is an ointment other than wounded modesty. If you cannot refrain from doing this, then just wait a while, you will see that time will eventually strip away from your hearts that modesty and that integrity which you have inherited from your forefathers, and then you will live your new lives in baseless prosperity and in peace."

***

After I had explained everything, a sarcastic and hallucinating smile appeared on his young face. He started saying, "We have not come here but only to cure our foolish actions, hence we will be patient upon this until Allah ﷻ decrees a verdict between us and them."

Thus, I said to him "You have the authority upon yourself and your household, thus do with them as you please. Permit me to say this, that after today I will not have the power to come and go to your house anymore, preserving you and myself, because I know the moment you will have the veil removed from your house and from the face of your wife, I will die out of shame and humiliation." Then I departed, creating separation between me and him.

Not even a few days passing by, I heard from people that, he had removed the veil between the men and women in his house. His house is always crowded with friends and upon his door there is always the noise of pounding shoes. Thus, my eyes shed a tear, I did not know that whether this was a tear of destroyed integrity, or a tear of grief for a lost friend?

This incident occurred three years ago, I did not go to meet him in his house and neither did he come to see me. I did meet him at times when crossing paths, I offered him greetings like how a stranger would to a stranger and then I carried on. During this time nothing was discussed, as then I left walking on that path altogether.

Yesterday I was returning home, the first part of the night had elapsed. Unexpectedly, I saw him coming out from his house and he appeared confused and perplexed. With him was a constable who was from the police department. It seemed like the police constable was supervising him, or that he was driving him out. Thus, I grieved and felt sorry for him in his dilemma. I drew near him and enquired about his affair.

إنا نضرع إليكم باسم الشرف الوطني والحرمة الدينية أن تتركوا تلك البقية الباقية من نساء الأمة مطمئناتٍ في بيوتهن، ولا تزعجوهن بأحلامكم وآمالكم كما أزعجتم من قبلهن، فكل جرح من جروح الأمة له دواء إلا جرح الشرف، فإن أبيتم إلا أن تفعلوا فانتظروا بأنفسكم قليلاً ريثما تنتزع الأيام من صدوركم هذه الغيرة التي ورثتموها عن آبائكم وأجدادكم لتستطيعوا أن تعيشوا في حياتكم الجديدة سعداء آمنين.

***

فما زاد الفتى على أن ابتسم في وجهي ابتسامة الهزء والسخرية، وقال: تلك حماقات ما جئنا إلا لمعالجتها فلنصطبر عليها حتى يقضي الله بيننا وبينها،

فقلت له: لك أمرك في نفسك وفي أهلك، فاصنع بهما ما تشاء، وائذن لي أن أقول لك إني لا أستطيع أن أختلف إلى بيتك بعد اليوم إبقاءً عليك وعلى نفسي، لأني أعلم أن الساعة التي ينفرج لي فيها جانب سترٍ من أستار بيتك عن وجه امرأةٍ من أهلك تقتلني حياءً وخجلاً. ثم انصرفت. وكان هذا فراق ما بيني وبينه.

وما هي إلا أيام قلائل حتى سمعت الناس يتحدثون أن فلاناً هتك الستر في منزله بين نسائه ورجاله، وأن بيته أصبح مغشياً لا تزال النعال خافقةً ببابه، فذرفت عيني دمعةً لا أعلم هل هي دمعة الغيرة على العرض المذال، أو الحزن على الصديق المفقود؟

مرت على تلك الحادثة ثلاثة أعوامٍ لا أزوره فيها، ولا يزورني، ولا ألقاه في طريقه إلا قليلاً، فأحييه تحية الغريب للغريب من حيث لا يجري لما كان بيننا ذكر، ثم أنطلق في سبيلي.

فإني لعائد إلى منزلي ليلة أمس، وقد مضى الشطر الأول من الليل، إذ رأيته خارجاً من منزله يمشي مشية الذاهل الحائر، وبجانبه جندي من جنود الشرطة، كأنما هو يحرسه أو يقتاده، فأهمني أمره، ودنوت منه فسألته عن شأنه.

Hence, he replied "I do not know anything other than that this constable has come now and knocked on my door to take me to the police station. I cannot find or work out the reason for this demand. I am neither a culprit nor am I a suspect. O dear friend, would it be possible for me to hope that you will spend this night in my company, despite that there is a friction between me and you, it might be that I may require some help from you if any matter was to arise?"

I said, "I will love to come with you." I walked with him silently, I did not talk to him and neither did he say anything to me. Despite our silence, I felt that he held something in his heart which he wanted to share with me, but shame and shyness hindered him.

Opening up the conversation, I asked, "Are you able to tell me what the reason for this call is?"

He looked at me with amazement and said "I fear that some event has happened with my wife tonight. I am in doubt about her because she has not returned home yet and this has never happened with her before."

I said "Was there anyone with her?"

He replied "No."

"Do you know where she had gone?"

"No."

"Over which thing are you fearful?"

He said "I do not fear of anything other than that I know she is a passionate and foolish woman, perhaps some people tried messing around with her on the way, then she must have quarrelled with them aggressively, and thus some incident must have occurred, because of which, the matter has reached the police station."

By now we had arrived at the police station. The police constable took us to the commanding police officer, and we stood before him. He gestured to the constable in front of us, giving a signal, which we did not understand. Then he requested the young man to come near, and said to him "Dear sir, I am sorry to inform you that indeed tonight the police men found a man and a woman from a suspicious location in improper circumstances and have brought them both to the police station. The woman has revealed her relationship to you, this is why you were called, so that you can disclose her matter to us. If she is truthful we will permit her to go with you, honouring and protecting your respect, and your humility will stay intact. Otherwise she is an adulteress woman who will have no escape and will be subject to being penalised for her crime. Both of them are now behind you, so look at them. The constable has brought them both from the other room."

فقال: لا علم لي بشيءٍ سوى أن هذا الجندي قد طرق الساعة بابي يدعوني إلى مخفر الشرطة، ولا أعلم لمثل هذه الدعوة في مثل هذه الساعة سبباً، وما أنا بالرجل المذنب، ولا المريب، فهل أستطيع أن أرجوك يا صديقي بعد الذي كان بيني وبينك أن تصحبني الليلة في وجهي هذا علني أحتاج إلى بعض المعونة فيما قد يعرض لي هناك من الشؤون؟

قلت: لا أحب إلي من ذلك، ومشيت معه صامتاً لا أحدثه، ويقول لي شيئاً، ثم شعرت كأنه يزور في نفسه كلاماً يريد أن يفضي به إلي فيمنعه الخجل والحياء،

ففاتحته الحديث وقلت له: ألا تستطيع أن تتذكر لهذه الدعوة سبباً؟

فنظر إلي نظرةً حائرةً، وقال: إن أخوف ما أخافه أن يكون قد حدث لزوجتي الليلة حادث، فقد رابني من أمرها أنها لم تعد إلى المنزل حتى الساعة، وما كان ذلك شأنها من قبل.

قلت: أما كان يصحبها أحد؟

قال: لا.

قلت: ألا تعلم المكان الذي ذهبت إليه؟

قال: لا.

قلت: ومم تخاف عليها؟

قال: لا أخاف شيئاً سوى أني أعلم أنها امرأة غيور حمقاء، فلعل بعض الناس حاول العبث بها في طريقها فشرست عليه، فوقعت بينهما واقعة انتهى أمرها إلى مخفر الشرطة،

وكنا قد وصلنا إلى المخفر، فاقتادنا الجندي إلى قاعة المأمور فوقفنا بين يديه. فأشار إلى جندي أمامه إشارةً لم نفهمها، ثم استدنى الفتى إليه، وقال له: يسوؤني في أن أقول لك يا سيدي إن رجال الشرطة قد عثروا الليلة في مكانٍ من أمكنة الريبة برجلٍ وامرأة، في حالٍ غير صالحةٍ، فاقتادوهما إلى المخفر، فزعمت المرأة أن لها بك صلةً، فدعوناك لتكشف لنا الحقيقة في أمرها. فإن كانت صادقةً أذنا لها بالانصراف معك إكراماً لك وإبقاءً على شرفك، وإلا فهي امرأة عاهرة لا نجاة لها من عقاب الفاجرات، وها هما وراءك فانظرهما، وكان الجندي قد جاء بهما من غرفةٍ أخرى،

My estranged friend looked and discovered that it was his wife, and the man with her, was one of his friends. Hence, he screamed so loudly that the walls of police station shook, the doors and windows turned into eyes and ears. Then he fell down in his place unconscious. I requested the police inspector to send the woman to her father's house. He did this, and let her friend go.

Then we took the young man in the car to his house and called a doctor for him. He was diagnosed with having a very severe brain fever. The doctor stayed awake next to him for the remaining night, treating him until morning drew near. He departed, saying that he will return whenever called, and made me responsible for his care. I sat next to my friend, feeling sorry for his condition. I awaited the decree of Allah ﷻ in his matter, until I saw that he was making a movement in his bed.

He opened his eyes and saw me. He stared at me for a while, as if he wanted to say something but did not have the power to do so. Thus I drew near to him and said, "Do you require anything, dear?"

He replied with a low, weak voice "My requirement is that no one from the people should come in to see me."

I said "No one shall come in to see you other than who you want."

For a short while he looked down, and then he raised his head, as his eyes were saturated with tears.

I asked "Why are you crying dear?"

He asked "Do you know where my wife is now?"

"What do you want from her?"

"Nothing other than to say to her that verily I have forgiven her."

"She is in her father's house."

He said "May Allah ﷻ shower his mercy upon her, her father and upon her clan. Certainly before they had established a relationship with me, they were highly noble and glorified. However, ever since they tied a connection with me I did nothing other than dress them up in a garment of nudity, which the time and destiny will not be able to eliminate.

فالتفت وراءه، فإذا المرأة زوجته، وإذا الرجل أحد أصدقائه، فصرخ صرخةً رجفت لها جوانب المخفر وملأت نوافذه وأبوابه عيوناً وآذاناً، ثم سقط في مكانه مغشياً عليه، فأشرت على المأمور أن يرسل المرأة إلى منزل أبيها ففعل، وأطلق سبيل صاحبها،

ثم حملنا الفتى في مركبةٍ إلى منزله، ودعونا له الطبيب فقرر أنه مصاب بحمى دماغية شديدة، ولبث ساهراً بجانبه بقية الليل يعالجه حتى دنا الصبح فانصرف على أن يعود متى دعوناه، وعهد إلي بأمره، فلبثت بجانبه أرثي لحاله، وأنتظر قضاء الله فيه، حتى رأيته يتحرك في مضجعه،

ثم فتح عينيه فرآني، فلبث شاخصاً إلي هنيهةً كأنما يحاول أن يقول لي شيئاً فلا يستطيعه، فدنوت منه وقلت له: هل من حاجةٍ يا سيدي؟

فأجاب بصوت ضعيفٍ خافت: حاجتي أن لا يدخل علي من الناس أحد،

قلت: لن يدخل عليك إلا من تريد،

فأطرق هنيهة، ثم رفع رأسه، فإذا عيناه مخضلتان بالدموع،

فقلت: ما بكاؤك يا سيدي؟

قال: أتعلم أين زوجتي الآن؟

قلت: وماذا تريد منها؟

قال: لا شيء سوى أن أقول لها إني قد عفوت عنها،

قلت: إنها في بيت أبيها،

قال: وارحمتاه لها ولأبيها ولجميع قومها، فقد كانوا قبل أن يتصلوا بي شرفاء أمجاداً، فألبستهم مذ عرفوني ثوباً من العار لا تبلوه الأيام.

Who is there for me to take this message to all of them? I am a patient who is near death. I fear that when I meet Allah ﷻ, I will meet Him with their blood. Therefore, I am begging them to pardon me and to forgive me for my going astray before death overtakes me.

Indeed, I made a pledge with her father the day she was given to me that I will safeguard her respect the way I protect my life, that I will keep her protected from everything which I protect myself from. I was unable to keep my promise. So will he forgive me my sin so that Allah ﷻ would forgive me through his pardoning?

Yes, indeed she is the one who has killed me. However, I was the one who placed that knife in her hand which she has pierced in my chest. Hence, no one should question her for my sin.

The house was my house, the wife was my wife and the friend was my friend. I was the one who opened the door of my house for my friend to reach to my wife. There is no one else to blame other than myself."

Then, after a short while, he stopped talking. I looked at him and saw a black cloud hovering upon his forehead, which gradually covered his face. He took such a warm sigh that I presumed that the curtain of his heart had burned. Then he said,

"Woe, how severe is the darkness in front of my eyes and how narrow is this world upon me. In this room, upon the sofa, under this roof, I used to see them two siting and talking to one another. My heart used to fill with joy and happiness, praising Allah ﷻ that he has bestowed me a friend who socialises with my wife in her loneliness, and a kind, generous wife who respects my friend when I am not there. Thus, announce to all mankind, that verily this man, who yesterday used to boast about his cleverness and his wisdom, and labelled himself superior than all in intelligence and shrewdness, today declares in his dying breaths that he is the highest of fools, and that there is no degree of imprudence beyond his. Woe upon me, my mother should have never given birth to me, and my father should have had no sons in his destiny.

Perhaps people knew about my wife's affair. Perhaps, when I passed them, they looked at each other, winked at each other and smiled at one another. Maybe they would stare for a long time at my face in order to see how stupidity looks on the faces of the foolish, and how idiocy prevails on the faces of the idiots.

من لي بمن يبلغهم عني جميعاً أنني مريض مشرف، وأنني أخشى لقاء الله إن لقيته بدمائهم، وأنني أضرع إليهم أن يصفحوا عني ويغتفروا زلتي، قبل أن يسبق إلي أجلي؟

لقد كنت أقسمت لأبيها يوم اهتديتها أن أصون عرضها صيانتي لحياتي، وأن أمنعها مما أمنع منه نفسي، فحنثت في يميني، فهل يغفر لي ذنبي فيغفر لي الله بغفرانه؟

نعم إنها قتلتني! ولكنني أنا الذي وضعت في يدها الخنجر الذي أغمدته في صدري فلا يسألها أحد عن ذنبي.

البيت بيتي، والزوجة زوجتي، والصديق صديقي، وأنا الذي فتحت باب بيتي لصديقي إلى زوجتي، فلم يذنب إلي أحد سواي.

ثم أمسك عن الكلام هنيهة، فنظرت إليه فإذا سحابة سوداء تنتشر فوق جبينه شيئاً فشيئاً، حتى لبست وجهه، فزفر زفرةً، خلت أنها خرقت حجاب قلبه، ثم أنشأ يقول:

آه ما أشد الظلام أمام عيني! وما أضيق الدنيا في وجهي! في هذه الغرفة، على هذا المقعد، تحت هذا السقف كنت أراهما جالسين يتحدثان فتملأ نفسي غبطةً وسروراً، وأحمد الله على أن رزقني بصديقٍ وفيٍ يؤنس زوجتي في وحدتها، وزوجةٍ سمحةٍ كريمةٍ تكرم صديقي في غيبتي، فقولوا للناس جميعاً: إن ذلك الرجل الذي كان يفخر بالأمس بذكائه وفطنته ويزعم أنه أكيس الناس وأحزمهم قد أصبح يعترف اليوم أنه أبله إلى الغاية من البلاهة، وغبي إلى الغاية التي لا غاية وراءها. والهفاً على أمٍ لم تلدني وأبٍ عاقرٍ لا نصيب له في البنين.

لعل الناس كانوا يعلمون من أمري ما كنت أجهل، ولعلهم كانوا إذا مررت بهم يتناظرون ويتغامزون ويبتسم بعضهم إلى بعض، أو يحدقون إلي ويطيلون النظر في وجهي ليروا كيف تتمثل البلاهة في وجوه البله، والغباوة في وجوه الأغبياء!

Perhaps those people, who loved me and made me their friend, only did so because of my wife and not because of me. Maybe those people addressed me as a pimp amongst themselves and considered my wife as a prostitute and my house as a brothel. I used to consider myself as the noblest from the people, and most respected.

May the Lord have mercy on me if I were to stay alive on this earth for another moment after today. Woe be upon the nook of the solitary in the fearful grave which will envelope me and envelope my nakedness with me."

Then he closed his eyes and returned to his slumber and unconscious state. During that moment, a midwife entered, and brought in his child, she placed him next to his bed. She left the child there and departed. The infant crawling besides him climbed up on the chest of his father, he felt him as he opened his eyes to see. He smiled at the toddler and cuddled him upon his chest with love and affection. He drew his face closer to his in order to kiss him.

After that he had a shivering fit, upsetting his happiness. He pushed the infant away severely with his hands, and screamed. "Take him away from me! I do not know him! I do not have a child nor do I have a wife! Ask his mother who is his father and take him to him! I will not bear shame in my life, and I leave him upon this slander forever after my death."

The midwife returned quickly after hearing the screech of the child, she picked him up and took him away with herself. The man heard the child's voice was slowly departing from him. He shouted so she could hear, "Bring him back to me."

The midwife brought him back and he took the child from her hands, observing his face closely, saying, "O son, for the sake of Allah ﷻ, please forgive the inheritance of an orphan given to you from your father and the heritage of disrobe from your mother, pardon us both. Indeed, your mother was a weak woman, she was unable to control her instincts, so she fell. Your father's crime was only to do good and righteousness, however he sinned.

It is the same to me, whether you are my son or the son of your culprit mother through sin. Without doubt, this short time, I am very fortunate and lucky to have you, I will never forget the favour of happiness and the joy which you have given me whether I stay alive or die." Then, he took him in his lap and gave him a kiss on his forehead. I did not know whether this was a kiss from a kind father or a kiss from a generous caring being.

ولعل الذين كانوا يتوددون إلي ويتمسحون بي من أصدقائي إنما كانوا يفعلون ذلك من أجلها لا من أجلي؟ ولعلهم كانوا يسمونني فيما بينهم قواداً ويسمون زوجتي مومساً، وبيتي ماخوراً وأنا عند نفسي أشرف الناس وأنبلهم!

فوارحمتاه لي إن بقيت على ظهر الأرض بعد اليوم ساعةً واحدةً، وواهفاً على زاويةٍ منفردةٍ في قبرٍ موحشٍ يطويني ويطوي عاري معي.

ثم أغمض عينيه وعاد إلى ذهوله واستغراقه. وهنا دخلت الحجرة مرضع ولده تحمله على يدها حتى وضعته بجانب فراشه ثم تركته وانصرفت، فما زال الطفل يدب على أطرافه حتى علا صدر أبيه فأحس به، ففتح عينيه فرآه فابتسم لمرآه وضمه إلى صدره ضمة الرفق والحنان، وأدنى فمه من وجهه ليقبله،

ثم انتفض فجأةً واستسر بشره، ودفعه عنه بيده دفعةً شديدةً وأخذ يصيح: أبعدوه عني لا أعرفه، ليس لي أولاد ولا نساء، سلوا أمه عن أبيه من هو واذهبوا به إليه؟ لا ألبس العار في حياتي وأتركه أثراً خالداً ورائي بعد مماتي؛

وكانت المرضع قد سمعت صياح الطفل فعادت إليه وحملته وذهبت به؛ فسمع صوته وهو يبتعد عنه شيئاً فشيئاً، فأنصت إليه واستعبر باكياً وصاح: أرجعوه إلي؛

فعادت به المرضع فتناوله من يدها وأنشأ يقلب نظره في وجهه ويقول: في سبيل الله يا بني ما خلف لك أبوك من اليتم، وما خلفت لك أمك من العار، فاغفر لهما ذنبهما إليك، فلقد كانت أمك امرأةً ضعيفةً فعجزت عن احتمال صدمة القضاء فسقطت، وكان أبوك حسن في جريمته التي اجترمها، فأساء من حيث أراد الإحسان.

سواء أكنت ولدي يا بني أم ولد الجريمة فإني قد سعدت بك حقبةً من الدهر، فلا أنسى يدك عندي حياً أو ميتاً! ثم احتضنه إليه، وقبله في جبينه قبلةً لا أعلم هل هي قبلة الأب الرحيم أو المحسن الكريم؟

His state got better, but then his fever returned and his head started burning severely. Slowly and gradually his state became heavier. I feared that his time had drawn near so I sent someone to call the doctor. Hence, the doctor came and cast a long eye upon him. Then, in despair, the doctor removed the disheartened and sorrowful sight away from him.

The young man took his last breath and started sighing aloud, which was fearful. Every eye which saw became tearful, crying for his recovery.

We were sat beside him and indeed the dark curtains of death were gradually casting over his bed. At once, a woman who was enveloped in a black coverlet entered the room and approached him slowly. She inclined over him, and kissed his hand which was placed over his chest.

Softly, she spoke, "Do not leave this world with doubts about your son. Undeniably his mother acknowledges her fault in front you. You are departing towards your Lord, and I was near committing the sin of fornication but I did not commit it. Please forgive me O the father of my son. I will beg Allah ﷻ that when you stand in front of Him, He joins me with you. This is because there is no good for me in my life after you."

Then she burst out in tears. Hence the man opened his eyes and looked at her with a smile. This was the man's last look in his life before he died.

***

Now, I have returned from the graveyard after I have buried my friend with my hands. I have entrusted this flourishing, radiant and glowing flower in the ditch of the grave. I have sat down now in order to write these lines and cannot gain control over my tears. My sighs, my sorrows and my feelings towards him are still not lessening. However, over this I am content, that indeed this nation was standing in front of a door of extreme danger. This man advanced and jumped into this danger alone. He stormed into it, and died the death of a martyr. Hence, his sorrowful example served as a clear warning to all, and he saved the nation from destruction.

وكان قد بلغ منه الجهد فعاودته الحمى، وغلت نارها في رأسه، وما زال يثقل شيئاً فشيئاً حتى خفت عليه التلف، فأرسلت وراء الطبيب فجاء وألقى عليه نظرةً طويلةً ثم استردها مملوءةً يأساً وحزناً.

ثم بدأ ينزع نزعاً شديداً، ويئن أنيناً مؤلماً، فلم تبق عين من العيون المحيطة به إلا ارفضت عن كل ما تستطيع أن تجود به من مدامعها.

فإنا لجلوس حوله، وقد بدأ الموت يسبل أستاره السوداء على سريره، وإذا امرأة مؤتزرة بإزارٍ أسود قد دخلت الحجرة وتقدمت نحوه ببطءٍ حتى ركعت بجانبه ثم أكبت على يده الموضوعة فوق صدره فقبلتها وأخذت.

تقول له: لا تخرج من الدنيا وأنت مرتاب في ولدك، فإن أمه تعترف بين يديك وأنت ذاهب إلى ربك، أنها وإن كانت قد دنت من الجريمة ولكنها لم ترتكبها، فاعف عني يا والد ولدي، وأسأل الله عندما تقف بين يديه أن يلحقني بك فلا خير لي في الحياة من بعدك.

ثم انفجرت باكيةً.. ففتح عينيه، وألقى على وجهها نظرةً باسمة، كانت هي آخر عهده بالحياة وقضى.

***

الآن عدت من المقبرة بعد ما دفنت صديقي بيدي، وأودعت حفرة القبر ذلك الشباب الناضر، والروض الزاهر، وجلست لكتابة هذه السطور، وأنا لا أكاد أملك مدامعي وزفراتي، فلا يهون وجدي عليه، إلا أن الأمة كانت على باب خطرٍ عظيمٍ من أخطارها، فتقدم هو أمامها إلى ذلك الخطر وحده، فاقتحمه، فمات شهيداً فنجت بهلاكه.

The Remembrance / A<u>dh</u>-<u>Dh</u>ikrā (Translation)

The last king of Granada, Abu Abdullah, was standing upon the shore of the black sea under Mount Gibraltar in Spain, after losing to the army of King Ferdinand's and Queen Izabal's. He was waiting to embark on a ship which would transport him to Africa. In his surroundings, women, children and the nobles of the tribe of Banū A<u>h</u>mar were standing. He gazed longingly upon the kingdom which he had lost and would not return, his eyes filled with tears. He drew his blanket near his face and cried excessively. He was making a very emotional heart touching sound, and the people who were standing beside him also started to cry. The sea shore became a place of death, which echoed sighs and cries. He was standing at a place where he had forgotten himself and his status. At once he heard a voice calling from the skies above.

He raised his head to discover that it was an old man reclining on a walking stick, standing at the entrance of a mountain cave. The old man began "Certainly O fallen down governor, you should cry upon your kingdom like women, because you could not safeguard your kingdom like men. Verily you were laughing yesterday, so now cry in the same proportion to your laughter. Verily happiness is the day of life and sorrow is its night. After a bright day the darkness of the night is inevitable.

Only if that kingdom that you had lost through your hands had been lost through the troubles of destiny or through a divine decree from the skies, which you had no strategy to overcome, nor command or control over. Verily you have disposed the kingdom with your own hands. You have handed over the kingdom to your enemy with your free will. Hence, cry over this like how a remorseful, shameful being would cry who cannot find any solace or comfort from his misery.

Allah ﷻ does not allow injustice on any one from amongst his people, nor does He ﷻ intend any evil or calamity to afflict them. However, it is the people who refuse, they stand on the corner of a deep ditch and take a deep breath and then their feet slip. It is the people who walk under visible rocks which then collapse upon their heads.

الذكرى

(مترجمة)

وقف أبو عبد الله، آخر ملوك غرناطة بعد انكساره أمام جيوش الملك فرديناند والملكة إيزابيلا، على شاطىء الخليج الرومي تحت ذيل جبل طارق قبل نزوله إلى السفينة المعدة لحمله إلى أفريقيا، وقد وقف حوله نساؤه وأولاده وعظماء قومه من بني الأحمر فألقى على ملكه الذاهب نظرةً طويلةً لم يسترجعها إلا مبللةً بالدمع، ثم أدنى رداءه من وجهه وأنشأ يبكي بكاءً مراً وينشج نشيجاً محزناً حتى بكى من حوله لبكائه، وأصبح شاطىء البحر كأنه مناحةٌ قائمةٌ تتردد فيها الزفرات، ويستبق العبرات، فإنه لواقف موقفه هذا وقد ذهل عن نفسه وموقفه إذا أحس هاتفاً يهتف باسمه بصوتٍ كأنما ينحدر إليه من علياء السماء.

فرفع رأسه، فإذا شيخ ناسك متكىء على عصاه، واقف على باب مغارةٍ من مغارات الجبل المشرف ينظر إليه ويقول: نعم.. لك أن تبكي أيها الملك الساقط على ملكك بكاء النساء فإنك لم تحتفظ به احتفاظ الرجال. إنك ضحكت بالأمس كثيراً، فابك اليوم بمقدار ما ضحكت بالأمس، فالسرور نهار الحياة والحزن ليلها، ولا يلبث النهار الساطع أن يعقبه الليل القاتم.

لو أن ما ذهب من يدك من ملكك ذهب بصدمةٍ من صدمات القدر، أو نازلةٍ من نوازل القضاء، من حيث لا حول لك في ذلك ولا حيلة، لهان أمره عليك، أما وقد أضعته بيدك، وأسلمته إلى عدوك باختيارك، فابك عليه بكاء النادم المتفجع الذي لا يجد له عن مصابه عزاءً ولا سلوى.

لا يظلم الله عبداً من عباده، ولا يريد بأحدٍ من الناس في شأنٍ من الشؤون شراً ولا ضيراً، ولكن الناس يأبون إلا أن يقفوا على حافة الهوة الضعيفة فتزل بهم أقدامهم، ويمشوا تحت الصخرة البارزة المشرفة فتسقط على رؤوسهم.

You were not content with the division of Allah ﷻ which he had ordained for you from his provisions. You rejected it as you were only interested in the country and the kingdom. Hence, you quarrelled with your paternal uncle, then you sought help against him from your mutual enemy. Thus your enemy kept on pounding your heads together, making you fight with one another until a well of blood flowed under both of your feet, and both of you drowned within.

O Banū Aḥmar, I have been waiting upon this mountain for seven years now, just to see the outcome of your foolish journey. I have been waiting for this moment to see such a leader leave, with no hope of return. This is because I know that when a guardian of a kingdom is a fool and illiterate, then there is inevitably no progress or place for him in his land.

You have made enmity amongst yourselves, and every one of you has become an enemy for his companion. Thus, you have dragged out the Muslims towards the battlefields, they are killing each other while your enemy is kneeling down behind you and observing this, awaiting your loss in delight. The enemy saw every one of you as a commanding general who is waging a war with their enemy, attempting to exile them from his country. He saw you falling down due to weakness and fatigue, then he plunged into you, he patrolled around you one or two circuits until he obtained victory from you.

Soon you shall stand in front of Allah ﷻ, O the leaders of Islam. Soon you shall be asked about the Islam which you had lost and whose elevated dignity and status you brought down to the dust. You are going to be asked about the Muslims, whom you have entrusted to your enemy with your own hands, so that they can live amongst them in a life of degradation and weakness. Allah ﷻ will ask you about the Islamic civilisations and the cities which your forefathers had bought with their blood and their lives, then they had left them for you so that you can safeguard them and honour them. Thus you stayed constant and still until your enemy overpowered you. Hence you started living a despised life, and they drove you out like strangers and trespassers. So, what would be your answer if tomorrow you are asked about all of these things?

لم تقنع بما قسم الله لك من الرزق، فأبيت إلا الملك والسلطان، فنازعت عمك الأمر واستعنت عليه بعدوك وعدوه، فتناول رأسيكما معاً، وما زال يضرب أحدهما بالآخر حتى سال تحت قدميكما قليب من الدم فغرقتما فيه معاً.

لي فوق هذه الصخرة يا بني الأحمر سبعة أعوام، أنتظر فيها هذا المصير الذي صرتم إليه، وأترقب الساعة التي أرى فيها آخر ملكٍ ملكاً يرحل عن هذه الديار رحلةً لا رجعة من بعدها، لأني أعلم أن الملك الذي يتولى أمره الجاهلون الأغبياء لا دوام له ولا بقاء.

اتخذ بعضكم بعضاً عدواً، وأصبح كل واحدٍ منكم حرباً على صاحبه فسقتم المسلمين إلى ميادين القتال يضرب بعضهم وجوه بعض، والعدو رابض من ورائكم يتربص بكم الدوائر، ويرى أن كلاً منكم قائد من قواده ينبعث بين يديه لقتال أعدائه، والمناضلة على ملكه، حتى رآكم تتهافتون على أنفسكم ضعفاً وهناً، فاقتحمكم، فما هي إلا جولة أو جولتان حتى ظفر بكم معاً.

ستقفون غداً بين يدي الله يا ملوك الإسلام، وسيسألكم عن الإسلام الذي أضعتموه وهبطتم به من علياء مجده حتى ألصقتم أنفه بالرغام. وعن المسلمين الذين أسلمتموهم بأيديكم إلى أعدائهم ليعيشوا بينهم عيش البائسين المستضعفين، عن مدن الإسلام وأمصاره التي اشتراها آباؤكم بدمائهم وأرواحهم ثم تركوها في أيديكم لتذودوا عنها، وتحموا ذمارها، فلم تحركوا في شأنها ساكناً حتى غلبكم أعداؤكم عليها، فأصبحتم تعيشون فيها عيش الإذلاء، وتطردون منها كما يطرد الغرباء، فماذا يكون جوابكم إن سئلتم عن هذا كله غداً؟

Look! The church bells are ringing here upon the minarets instead of the Adhān (call to Muslim prayer). Take a look, the cross bearers' shoes are trampling over the Mosques on the ground where the foreheads of the Muslims used to touch. What kind of Muslims are these who are running from one place to the other with their religion, taking refuge upon the peaks and gates of mountains? They do not have the power to fulfil any religious obligations whatsoever, but they are in a cave similar to the one I am in.

Only if the Muslims lived their lives in their eras without a government, without a country and without a king, the way the homeless live in the corners of the cities. Verily, this was a better option for them than being ruled by men who are like themselves, greedy and unjust. They have put a big shackle on their necks and are dragging themselves towards the place of destruction and loss, defenceless and unable to retaliate against the totalitarianism.

Allah ﷻ will question you, 'O Banū Ahmar! About me and about my children, those who you snatched away from my hands, even though I needed them a great deal. You dragged them towards the battlefields so that they could fight their Muslim brothers. Here, there was no nobleness and honour, yet they all died the death of inferiority and lowliness. Why did you not leave them besides me so that I could have had their company in my loneliness, and I would have requested their help in my senile old age? Why did you not take them towards the battlefield in honour, so that I could have found solace in knowing that they had died as martyrs for their religion or for their country as patriots?

Take a look, I am living all alone after them in this fearful cave on top of this segregated rock, crying over them and asking Allah ﷻ to join me with them. Oh, when is Allah ﷻ going to respond to my supplication?"

Then, because of crying, his throat became asphyxiated. He turned his face away and walked off with the aid of his stick to his cave, disappearing from sight.

ها هي النواقيس ترن في شرفات المآذن بدل الأذان، وها هي المساجد تطأ نعال الصليبيين في تربتها مواقع جباه المسلمين، وها هو المسلم يفر بدينه من مكانٍ إلى مكانٍ، ويلوذ بأكناف الهضاب والشعاب، لا يستطيع أن يؤدي شعيرةً من شعائر دينه إلا في غارٍ كهذا الغار الذي أعيش فيه!

ليت المسلمين عاشوا دهرهم فوضى، لا نظام لهم ولا ملك ولا سلطان، كما يعيش المشردون في آفاق البلاد، فقد كان ذلك خيراً لهم من أن يتولى أمرهم رجال مثلكم، طامعون مستبدون، يلفون على أعناقهم جميعاً غلاً واحداً يسوقونهم به إلى موارد التلف والهلاك من حيث لا يستطيعون ذوداً عن أنفسهم. وما تفعل الفوضى بأمة ما يفعل بها الاستبداد.

يسألكم الله يا بني الأحمر عني وعن أولادي الذين انتزعتموهم من يدي انتزاعاً أحوج ما كنت إليهم، وسقتوهم إلى ميادين القتال ليقاتلوا إخوانهم المسلمين قتالاً لا شرف فيه ولا فخار حتى ماتوا جميعاً موت الأذلاء الأدنياء، فلا أنتم تركتموهم بجانبي آنس بهم في وحشتي، وألجأ إلى معونتهم في شيخوختي، ولا أنتم ذهبتم بهم إلى ميدان قتالٍ شريفٍ فأتعزى عنهم من بعدهم بأنهم ماتوا فداءً عن دينهم ووطنهم.

فها أنذا عائش من بعدهم وحدي في هذا الغار الموحش، فوق هذه الصخرة المنقطعة أبكي عليهم، وأسأل الله أن يلحقني بهم فمتى يستجيب الله دعائي؟

ثم اختنق صوته بالبكاء، فأدار وجهه و مشى بقدمٍ مطمئنةٍ، يتوكأ على عصاه حتى دخل مغارته وغاب عن العيون،

The ruler was astonished with his words, even he was not as sorrowful as this man about losing his kingdom and the collapsing of his throne. Hence, he screamed and said, "This is not a man, verily this is the voice of justice which is scaring me about the future misfortune, which is more severe than the calamities of the past. Allah ﷻ can do what He pleases with me, because justice is with Him and He can do whatever He wills."

Then he progressed towards his ship, and his family followed behind him. Cutting through the waves of the water, the ship set off, carrying them inside it. History had written down this event in its pages, and this was the time that indeed the exile of the Arabs from Andalus Spain, had been complete. The Arabs prior to this had ruled Spain for eight hundred years.

***

Twenty-four years after the incident, not even one soul remained alive from Banū Aḥmar, other than a young man who was twenty years of age. His name was Saeed (Saʿīd). He did not see Granada nor did he see the Qaṣru-l-Ḥamrā. Neither did he see the meadows of Granada nor the Generalife (Jannatu-l-ʿĀrīf). He did not see the Ebro river, the Sierra Navada nor the mountain of snow. However, he always had its vision seared in his memory, memorised through the songs of Andalus which the ladies of his nation used to sing in his childhood, besides his cradle. In those songs there was mention of his father, his grandfather, of their works, and the honour of their Kingdom which existed in their army. He also remembered the painful song, upon which the poets of Andalus had cried. That is, fallen dignity and wasted kingdom. Thus, whenever he was alone, he hummed the tune of these old folksongs, glorifying the traditions of his ancestors. He used to sing them with a lot of passion, a great depth of feeling, which inflamed his pain and tears. Sometimes, he used to cry and scream so much that he used to draw close to his death.

For himself, he never desired anything from Allah ﷻ the way other people did, other than that he wanted to see Granada only once in his lifetime, so that he could be satisfied and consoled. After that, he wanted to leave his affairs to the discretion of destiny, which will choose for him whatever it wills.

فنالت كلماته من نفس الأمير ما لم ينل منها ضياع ملكه وسقوط عرشه، فصاح: ما هذا بشراً إنما هو صوت العدل الإلهي ينذرني بشقاء المستقبل فوق شقاء الماضي، فليصنع الله بي ما يشاء فعدلٌ منه كل ما صنع.

ثم انحدر إلى سفينته، وانحدر أهله وراءه، فسارت السفينة بهم تشق عباب الماء شقاً، فسجل التاريخ في تلك الساعة: أنه قد تم جلاء العرب عن الأندلس بعد ما عمروها ثمانمائة عام.

***

بعد مرور أربعة وعشرين عاماً على تلك الحوادث لم يبق في إفريقية حي من بني الأحمر إلا فتى في العشرين من عمره اسمه (سعيد) لم ير غرناطة ولا قصر الحمراء ولا المرج ولا جنة العريف ولا نهر شنيل ولا عين الدمع ولا جبل الثلج ولكنه ما زال يحفظ في ذاكرته من عهد الطفولة تلك الأناشيد الأندلسية البديعة التي كان يترنم بها نساء قومه حول مهده، ويرددن فيها ذكر آبائه وأجداده وآثار أيديهم وعزة سلطانهم في تلك البقاع، وتلك المراثي المحزنة المؤثرة التي بكى فيها شعراء الأندلس ذلك المجد الساقط والملك المضاع، فكان كلما خلا إلى نفسه ردد تلك المراثي بنغمة شجيةٍ محزنةٍ تستثير عبرته، و تهيج أشجانه، فلا يزال يبكي وينتحب حتى يشرف على التلف.

فكان لا يتمنى على الله من كل ما يتمنى امرؤ على ربه في حياته إلا أن يرى غرناطة ساعةً من زمانٍ يشفي بها غلة نفسه، ثم ليصنع الدهر به بعد ذلك ما يشاء.

Whenever he intended to go to Granada, he ended up sitting back down with the thought of leaving an old woman behind him, who was from his family. He did not have the power to leave her nor did he find anyone who he could trust to look after her if he was to go. Eventually, her time also came, and she met her Lord.

Hence, he embarked on a journey through the ocean from the Sabie River in Africa, all the way to the corner of Mula, Spain. Then, he advanced towards Granada disguised in an Arab Doctors dress, appearing to be seeking herbals upon the mountains of Andalus. He finally reached outside the town at evening time. He ascended upon the peak of an icy mountain. Here, he saw the water which was descending very peacefully as if its sparkling and glittering surface had a luminous shirt over it, or that it was a dome made out of crystal. When this water reached the ravine, it appeared like white, frightened snakes that scattered everywhere, as if trying to save themselves, escaping through a brook and hiding themselves within.

Then he turned his attention towards the city. From far, he saw some burgundy towers. High, prestigious domes and tall minarets, which were talking to the sky. Thus, he became stationary in front of this astonishing sight, in full humility and respect. He put his hand over the other, and placing them above his chest, as if he is standing in front of a mihraab (mi<u>h</u>rāb), offering his prayer and remained in that position for a while.

Then, he announced in a very loud voice which echoed all over the woodlands and the jungle.

"This is the inheritance of my father and my grandfather. There is nothing remaining for me from this heritage other than this separation. This separation is similar to the agony of a devastated mother when she parts from her son. These are their beds in which now their enemies sleep in. However, in reality, the bedding of the enemy was nothing other than the sand of the desert upon small rocks at night.

وكان كلما هم بالذهاب إليها قعد به عن ذلك أن وراءه عجوزاً من أهله مريضة، وما كان يستطيع أن يتركها، ولا يجد من يعتمد عليه في القيام بشأنها حتى وافاها أجلها،

فركب البحر من سبتة إلى شاطىء ملقة، ثم انحدر منها إلى غرناطة متنكراً في ثوبِ طبيبٍ عربيٍ من أطباء الأعشاب يتبقل في جبال الأندلس وسهولها حتى بلغ ضاحيتها ساعة الأصيل، فوقف على هضبةٍ من هضاب جبل الثلج فرأى الأمواه تنزلق عنه في هدوءٍ وسكونٍ كأنها فوق سطحه اللامع المتلألىء قميص من النور، أو قبة من البلور، حتى تصل إلى سفحه فإذا هي حيات بيضاء مذعورة تنبعث ههنا وههنا لا يهم إلا النجاة من يد مطاردها حتى تعثر بجدول ماءٍ في طريقها فتدغم فيه وتنساب في أحشائه.

ثم التفت إلى المدينة فرأى على البعد أبراجها العقيقية الحمراء وقبابها العالية الشماء، ومآذنها الذاهبة في جو السماء، فوقف أمام هذا المنظر الجليل المهيب موقف الخاشع المتخضع، وضم إحدى يديه إلى الأخرى ووضعها على صدره كأنما هو قائم أمام المحراب يؤدي صلاته، ولبث على ذلك برهةً،

ثم صاح بصوتٍ عالٍ رددته الغابات والحرجات يقول:

هذا ميراث آبائي وأجدادي لم يبق لي منه إلا وقفة بين يديه كوقفة الثاكل المفجوع بين أيدي الأطلال البوالي والآثار الدوارس. هذه مضاجعهم ينام فيها أعداؤهم، وهم لا مضاجع لهم إلا رمال الصحراء وكثبان الفلوات.

These are their castles which are looking at the open atmosphere of the land. Their windows are the eyes which are looking at them in such a way that they appear in wait hoping that they will return and dwell again. However, they will not do this.

These are their domes and minarets which raise their heads towards the sky day and night, supplicating to Allah ﷻ imploring, 'Bring back their carers and guardians', but their beseeching is not accepted.

It is these gardens in which they used to rest. Under these shades they used to sleep. Upon these river banks they used to spend their days and nights. However, today, there is no one from amongst them who could do his morning here neither anyone to do the night. Under this sky there is no one who is coming or going."

Then he looked towards the horizon, he saw the sun setting from the West, he saw that the army of night was empowering the defeated army of day, and dispersing through the sky. He fell to the ground, head first, and starting saying,

"Like this the governments change and like this the crowns fall. It is like this that darkness prevails in places of light. It is like this that the clouds of death scatter over the faces of life."

Then he turned with the aid of his hand, and fell into deep sleep above the bed of the earth and under the roof of the sky. He did not wake up until the kingdom of night had passed. Thus, after awaking, he walked towards the flowing river which was under the mountain, and offered his morning prayer.

After that he departed towards the city in order to seek lodgings/ a hotel where he could take shelter. He did not find in his way anyone who could guide him towards where he wanted to go until he reached the Ebro river. Then he walked towards its corner and began searching for seeds and herbals. He remained there in wait for the residents of the city to wake up.

هذه قصورهم تشرف على الأرض الفضاء وتطل من عيون نوافذها كأنما تترقب أن يعودوا إليها فيعمروها كما كانوا فلا يفعلون.

هذه قبابهم وأبراجهم رافعة رأسها ليلها ونهارها إلى السموات العلا تدعو الله أن يعيد إليها بناتها وحماتها فلا يستجاب لها دعاء.

في هذه البساتين كانوا ينعمون، وتحت هذه الظلال كانوا يقيلون؛ وعلى ضفاف هذه الأنهار كانوا يغدون ويروحون، واليوم لا غادٍ منهم ولا رائح، ولا سانح تحت هذه السماء ولا بارح..

ثم نظر إلى الأفق فرأى الشمس تنحدر إلى مغربها، ورأى جيش الليل يطارد فلول جيش النهار فيبددها بين يديه تبديداً فتهافت على نفسه، وهو يقول:

هكذا تدول الدول وتسقط التيجان، وهكذا تحل الظلمات محل الأنوار، وهكذا تنتشر سحب الموت على وجه الحياة.

ثم توسد ذراعه، واستغرق في نومه بين وطاء الأرض وغطاء السماء، فلم يستفق حتى مضت دولة الليل، فمشى إلى نهرٍ جارٍ في سفح الجبل فصلى عنده صلاة الفجر،

ثم انحدر إلى المدينة يفتش عن خانٍ يأوي إليه، فلم يجد في طريقه من يرشده إلى طلبته حتى بلغ نهر شنيل فمشى على ضفته يتفقد البذور ويتلمس الأعشاب وينتظر يقظة المدينة بعد هجعتها.

He was in this state when suddenly before him a large castle door opened. There, he saw a Spanish girl coming out from it. Her face was veiled with a transparent black veil and upon her chest there was a small golden cross hanging off. Behind her there was a boy walking, holding a holy book. Surprised to see him, she glanced at the place where he was standing. She drew closer to him and lifted her veil from her face. She was extremely beautiful, and stunning like the sun in full beam. In a language which comprised of Arabic and non-Arabic she said to him "O young man, are you a stranger in this town?"

He replied "Yes, verily I have come here just now, I do know the way to an inn where tourists can take sanctuary. Neither have I found anyone who could guide me towards it."

The girl sensed modesty and nobleness in his voice, and the signs of happiness and bliss appeared on her face. She became considerate towards him. She gestured towards him and told him to follow her for guidance and direction. They walked side by side until they reached a motel. She gave her regards to him with a smile and in a very honourable way she said to him "O stranger, do not forget your meeting with me, whenever you are in need of anything, just ask." Then she walked towards the church.

***

A human heart is always circulating in between different desires and emotions collectively and individually, until it reaches the age of puberty and the sun of love rises upon him dimming and overpowering in front of him all previous desires and emotions. It is like how the different stars circulate in the sky of a darkened night, lighting up the night's sky, and the bright flame circulates, glowing up its dark corners until the sun rises from the east, and dims the brightness of all previous lights.

وإنه لكذلك إذ انفتح بين يديه باب قصرٍ عظيمٍ، وإذا فتاة إسبانية خارجة منه قد أسبلت على وجهها خماراً أسود شفافاً، وأرسلت على صدرها صليباً ذهبياً صغيراً، ومشى وراءها غلام يحمل على يده الكتاب المقدس، فلمحته في مكانه فأدهشها موقفه فدنت منه ورفعت قناعها عن وجهها فإذا الشمس طالعة حسناً وبهاءً، وقالت له بلسانٍ عربي تخالطه بعض العجمة: أغريب أنت عن هذا البلد أيها الفتى؟

قال: نعم لقد نزلت به الساعة فلم أعرف طريق الخان الذي يأوي إليه الغرباء، ولم أجد في طريقي من يدلني عليه،

فسمعت في صوته رنة الشرف ورأت بين أعطافه مخائل النعمة فأهمها أمره، وأشارت إليه أن يتبعها لتدله على ما يريد، فمشى بجانبها حتى بلغا موضع الخان، فحيته بابتسامةٍ عذبة، وقالت له: لا تنس أن تزورني أيها الغريب كلما عرضت لك حاجة... ثم سارت في طريق كنيستها .

***

كما أن السماء في ظلمة الليل تختلف إليها النجوم فتضيء صفحتها وتمر بها الشهب فتلمع في أرجائها، حتى إذا طلعت الشمس من مشرقها محا ضوؤها جميع تلك النيرات؛ كذلك القلب الإنساني لا تزال تمر به مختلف العواطف وأشتات الأهواء مجتمعةً ومفترقةً، حتى إذا بلغ وأشرقت عليه شمس الحب غربت بجانبها جميع تلك العواطف والأهواء.

Thus, indeed at many instances, the prince looked at Granada from a different perspective than before. In the face of Granada, he saw the face of love after the face of terror. He saw light after darkness and he saw life after death. Hence, he forgot his fear and felt a cool breeze in his heart. The sharpness of his previous anger cooled down, and was steaming between his ribs. Thus, when he passed by a mosque from amongst the mosques of Granada, which were converted to churches now, he stood there for a while so that he may see that Spanish girl from amongst those who entered and came out.

Whenever he saw a cross on top of a minaret he remembered that beautiful gold cross which he saw upon the chest of that Spanish girl on the day they had met. The hatred with which he previously viewed such objects had been replaced with love, as they now reminded him of her, not his past. Whenever he heard the church bells ringing surrounding the atmosphere, he remembered the time when he saw that Spanish girl. This was because he heard the church bells ringing at that time when he had met her. Hence, he became content every time he heard the church bells and his heart became relaxed.

Like this, every morning, that poor gentleman used to go to the river bank of River Ebro for an outing. There he rolled his eyes upon the doors of the big castles, hoping that he may recognise the castle of that Spanish girl, but unfortunately did not. He used to observe the faces of girls who had passed in the mornings and evenings, hoping that he might see her. However, he was unable to do so. When he became hopeless, he returned to the graves of his forefathers which were visible in the town. There, he sat in between them and shed his tears in abundance. He did not know whether these tears were of his devastating past, or the pining of his present love.

***

Two years before this time, great trials and calamities had descended upon Florinda. The pain drawn from this has still not parted from her heart even today. Verily her father was the chancellor and the president of this state, which, for a few years, was in heavy opposition against its administration. Their aim was to give its residents complete liberation to practice their religion and claim their self-identity, despite their religion and identity. They continued this struggle until they became completely exhausted from doing their duty.

فقد أصبح الأمير ينظر إلى غرناطة منذ الساعة بعينٍ غير العين التي كان ينظر بها إليها من قبل، ويرى في وجهها صورة الأنس بعد الوحشة، والنور بعد الظلمة، والحياة بعد الموت، فسكن ثائره وبردت جوانحه، وهدأت نفسه ثورة الغضب التي كانت لا تزال تعتلج بين أضلاعه، فكان إذا مر بمسجدٍ من تلك المساجد التي استحالت إلى كنائس استطاع أن يقف أمامه هنيهةً علّه يرى الفتاة الإسبانية بين الداخلات إليه أو الخارجات منه،

وإذا رأى الصليب مشرفاً على رأس مئذنةٍ ذكر الصليب الذهبي الجميل الذي رآه على صدرها يوم اللقاء فاغتفر منظر هذا لمنظر ذاك، وإذا سمع أصوات النواقيس ترن في أجواز الفضاء ذكر أنه كان يسمع ذلك الصوت الرنان في الساعة التي رآها فيها، فأنس به وسكنت نفسه إليه.

وكذلك أصبح هذا الأمير المسكين ولا هم له إلا أن يتمشى صبيحة كل يومٍ على ضفاف نهر (شنيل) يقلب نظره في أبواب القصور المشرفة على ذلك النهر علّه يعرف قصر الفتاة فلا يعرفه، وفي وجوه الغاديات والرائحات من الفتيات علّه يراها بينهن فلا يراها، حتى إذا نال منه اليأس انكفأ راجعاً إلى مقبرة آبائه في ظاهر المدينة فجلس بين القبور يذرف دموعاً غزاراً، لا يعلم هل هي دموع الذكرى القديمة أو دموع الذكرى الجديدة!

***

نكب الدهر (فلورندا) منذ عامين نكبةً لا تزال لوعتها متصلةً بقلبها حتى اليوم، فقد كان أبوها رئيس جمعية (العصابة المقدسة) التي قامت في وجه الحكومة أعواماً طوالاً تطالبها بالحرية الدينية والشخصية لجميع الشعوب المحكومة على اختلاف مذاهبها وأجناسها حتى أعيا رجال الحكومة أمرها،

A secret conspiracy was devised to assassinate the president under the veil of darkness, and he was executed. After this, his daughter Florinda was devastated. She was also deeply saddened over her mother's death. Her mother had died worrying severely about her husband, who had never parted from her, and stayed with her mornings and nights.

When Florinda became eighteen years of age, she retreated to her castle, living a monastic life. Any onlooker only saw her coming or going to the church with her servant, or standing upon the signs, marks and the customs of the old government. They saw her observing these from every angle and it appeared that she was taking heed of them. Some saw her in the beauty spots and recreation parks of Granada, walking in a melancholy and distressed manner until the darkness veiled the night with its curtains. Then, after that, she returned to her castle. This was the state which she had always remained in. The people of Granada used to address her as the beautiful nun.

One day Florinda was passing by the graves of Banū Ahmar, there at once she saw a young Arab man from a distance. He was facing down kneeling over a grave and it appeared that he was kissing the surface of the grave and was making the soil of the grave wet with his tears. She felt sorry for him and she walked towards him until she drew near. The young man heard her sound and raised his head. He recognised her and she recognised him.

She said "O young man, are you crying over your Kings which existed yesterday? Cry, cry as much as you want because the soil of their graves has become dry as there was no one to cry over them."

That young man said "O dear, are you also upset over them?"

She replied "Yes certainly, indeed they were great people. The period and time has trampled over them. Certainly these people have more right to be cried over than anyone else from amongst the great fallen people."

He said "Thank you very much O respectable lady, this is the first time I have felt the garment of consolation creeping over my heart, ever since I have laid my feet upon this land of yours."

She said "Have you seen their castles and their symbols which they have left behind in this country?"

فدسوا لرئيسها من قتله غيلةً تحت ستار الظلام، فحزنت ابنته عليه وعلى أمها التي ماتت على أثره حزناً شديداً ما كان يفارقها في جميع غدواتها وروحاتها،

فأصبحت وهي لم تسلخ الثامنة من عمرها تعيش في قصرها عيش الزاهدات المتبتلات، فكان لا يراها الرائي إلا ذاهبةً إلى الكنيسة أو عائدةً منها لا يصحبها إلا غلامها، أو واقفةً على أطلال الدولة الماضية ورسومها تقلب فيها نظر العظة والاعتبار، أو هائمةً على وجهها في مروج غرناطة وبساتينها حتى ينزل ستار الليل فتعود إلى قصرها، وكذلك كان شأنها في جميع أيامها حتى سماها أهل غرناطة (الراهبة الجميلة).

فإنها لسائرة يوماً بجانب مقبرة بني الأحمر إذ لمحت على البعد فتًى عربياً مكباً على أحد القبور كأنما يقبل صفائحه ويبل تربته بدموعه، فرثت لحاله ومشت نحوه حتى دنته فأحس بها فرفع رأسه فعرفها وعرفته.

فقالت له: إنك تبكي ملوكك بالأمس أيها الفتى فابكهم كثيراً فقد جف تراب قبورهم لقلة من يبكي عليهم.

قال: أترثين لهم يا سيدتي؟

قالت: نعم، لأنهم كانوا عظماء فنكبهم الدهر وليس أحق بدموع الباكين، من العظماء الساقطين.

قال: شكراً لك يا سيدتي فهذه أول ساعة شعرت فيها ببرد العزاء يدب في صدري مذ وطئت قدماي أرضكم هذه،

قالت: هل زرت قصورهم وآثارهم التي تركوها من بعدهم في هذه الديار؟

The gentleman for a little while put his head down and then he raised his head as there was a drop of tear hovering in his eyes. He said "No O respectable lady, I did intend to go near them but the guards who were guarding the doors threw me out. They are unaware that, from all of the living people, I am the only one individual who has more right to see them."

The lady said "Are you connected to any one from amongst their companions, are you a descendant of theirs, or are you their child?"

He said "No O respectable lady, I am but their freed slave, I was born in their hands, through their mercy. They handcrafted, planted their love in me which I shall never forget till I am alive."

She said "If you meet me here in this place at the same time tomorrow, I will take you wherever you would like to go."

He replied "If you were to do this, then in this world there is never going to be anyone more thankful to you than me." Thus, she offered her greetings and departed. The young man also proceeded to his hotel with mixed emotions of love and hope, which was killing him, and at the same time giving him life.

Florinda fulfilled her promise to her Arab friend, and the next day she came. She showed him some places. Then on the third day she came and showed him more sights. Like this, they kept on meeting and parting every day. Wherever they wanted, they went to see the old landmarks. The people who used to see them never thought badly of them. Whenever they saw them together they presumed that the beautiful nun is intending to guide and incline the Arab gentleman towards her religion.

As time went on, the kindness that she felt in her heart for him turned into burning love. Like this, kindness always becomes the road towards love, or it is the love itself which becomes a garment for the non-clothed. Not even one of them revealed what feelings they had for each other in their hearts, until that day came when the gentleman intended to visit the Qasru-l-Hamrā, as this was the last historical sight which yet remained. After this, both of them never met again for sightseeing.

***

فأطرق قليلاً ثم رفع رأسه فإذا دمعة تترجرج في مقلتيه وقال: لا يا سيدتي، لقد حاولت الدنو منها فطردني عنها الموكلون بأبوابها كأنما هم يجهلون أن ليس بين الأحباء جميعهم في هذا العالم كله من هو أولى بها مني،

قالت: أتمت إلى أحدٍ من أصحابها بنسبٍ أو رحمٍ؟

قال: لا يا سيدتي ولكني عبدهم ومولاهم، وصنيعة أيديهم، وغرس نعمتهم، فلا أنسى ولاءهم ما حييت،

قالت: إن رأيتك غداً في مثل هذه الساعة في هذا المكان ذهبت بك إلى ما تريد منها،

قال: لئن فعلت لا يكونن امرؤ على وجه الأرض أشكر لنعمتك مني، فحيته وانصرفت، ومضى إلى خانه بين صبابةٍ تقيمه وتقعده، وأملٍ يميته ويحييه.

وفت (فلورندا) لصديقها العربي بما وعدته به فجاءته في اليوم الثاني فأزارته بعض الآثار، ثم جاءته في اليوم الثالث فأزارته بعضاً آخر منها، وهكذا، ما زالا يجتمعان كل يومٍ ويفترقان، ويختلفان إلى ما شاءا من الرسوم والآثار لا ينكر الناس من أمرهما شيئاً؟ فقد كانوا إذا رأوهما معاً: إن الراهبة الجميلة تحاول أن تهدي الفتى العربي إلى دينها القويم،

حتى استحال العطف الذي كانت تضمره له في نفسها مع الأيام إلى حب شديد، وكذلك العطف دائماً طريق الحب أو هو الحب نفسه لابساً ثوباً غير ثوبه. إلا أن أحداً منهما لم يجرؤ أن يكاشف صاحبه بما أضمره له في نفسه حتى جاء اليوم الذي عزم فيه على زيارة قصر الحمراء، وهو آخر ما بقي بين أيديهما من الآثار، فلا لقاء بينهما بعد اليوم.

***

The prince stood in front of the Qaṣru-l-Ḥamrā. He saw that the sky was in battle with another sky. One big mountain was colliding with the Gemini sky. One highland was highest amongst all other highlands. The clouds were passing by above other clouds. The mountain was so high, to observe it, eyes became tired, and the intellect failed. There is a castle nearby, which the vicissitudes of time could not remove. The days and years have passed by besides it. He entered and saw a very big city which had gardens and silk in it. He saw huge domes, over which the stars dotted with joy. There were towers there, on whose surfaces destiny had spread its hands over. The floor of the courtyard was made of faint pebbles as if it was a bright garden. The walls were glossy and soft, and became mirrors for everything in front of them. They were clear like a mirror in which reflect the faces of beautiful women. Its walls were full of waves which contained delight in them, like a sheet of glass. He passed by the sights with respect, amazement and awe, humming poetry,

I stood close to the Qaṣru-l-Ḥamrā shedding tears
and taking heed from it,

I was Lamenting, I said "O Qaṣru-l-Ḥamrā is the return possible?"
It replied "Do the dead ever return?"

I kept on weeping at its traces.
Woe upon woe, only if the tears could give some benefit?

As if those who have left their trails behind,
them trails have become the crying women who are crying over the dead.

After this, he reached the biggest courtyard. He saw that the floor of the courtyard was made out of yellow marble, there were tall, slim pillars, upright, and lining all four corners. In the corners of the courtyards, there were rooms with high domes on them. Thus, he understood that these were the rooms of the princes and princesses from amongst his family. Hence, past memories flared up in his heart and he felt it was going to explode due to the pain and agony that he was feeling. He was compelled towards crying, but he withheld his tears in front of Florinda. He left her busy observing some of the architecture, and went towards some other rooms. First he laid his eyes upon one line of writing, which was inscribed upon a door. When he read it he yelled out "O father," and fell in a swoon.

وقف الأمير أمام قصر الحمراء فرأى سماءً تطاول السماء، وطوداً يناطح الجوزاء، وهضبةً تشرف على الهضاب، وسحابةً تمر فوق السحاب، وجبلاً تحسر عن قمته العيون، وتضل في جوانبه الظنون، وحصناً تتقاصر عنه يد الأيام، وتتهافت من حوله السنون والأعوام. ثم دخل فإذا ملك كبير وجنة وحرير، وقباب تفضي إليها النجوم بالأسرار، وأبراج تنزلق عن سطوحها يد الأقدار، وصحون مفروشة بألوان الحصباء، كأنها الرياض الزهراء، وجدران صقيلة ملساء تصف ما بين يديها من الأشياء، كما تصف المرآة وجه الحسناء، وكأن كل جدارٍ منها لجة متلاطمة الأمواج يحبسها عن الجريان لوح من زجاج، فمشى يقلب نظر العظة والاعتبار، بين تلك المشاهد والآثار ويتنغم في نفسه بقول القائل:

وقفت بالحمراء مستعبرا   معتبراً أندب أشتاتا

فقلت يا حمراء هل رجعة   قالت وهل يرجع من ماتا

فلم أزل أبكي على رسمها   هيهات يغني الدمع هيهاتا

كأنما آثار من قد مضوا   نوادب يندبن أمواتا

حتى وصل إلى الساحة الكبرى فرأى صحناً مفروشاً ببساطٍ من المرمر الأصفر قد دارت به في جهاته الأربع أربعة صفوف من الأعمدة النحاف الطوال، وتراءت في جوانبه حجرات متقابلات، تعلوها قباب مشرفات، فعلم أنها حجرات الأمراء والأميرات من أهل بيته، فهاجت في نفسه الذكرى، وشعر أن صدره يحاول أن ينشق عن قلبه حزناً ووجداً، وأحس بحاجته إلى البكاء فاستحيا أن يبكي أمام (فلورندا)، فتركها في مكانها لاهيةً عنه بالنظر إلى بعض النقوش، ومشى إلى بعض تلك القاعات حتى داناها، فكان أول ما تناوله نظره منها سطراً مكتوباً على بابها، فما قرأه حتى صاح صيحةً شديدةً قائلاً: (وا أبتاه) وسقط مغشياً عليه،

After a long time, he gained consciousness. When he opened his eyes he found his head placed in the lap of Florinda and he discovered that she had tears in her eyes. She said "Indeed I knew from before this day that you were hiding something from me, a secret in your heart, and verily I am convinced now that you are neither the slave of Banū Ahmar nor are you their freed slave the way you said, but you are one of the princes'. Indeed, you are in the castle of your grandfather and you are in front of your father's room. O Banū Ahmar, it is amazing to what degree you have been aggrieved. O poor prince, how unfortunate are you?"

After this, the prince did not find any other way to hide his affair. Thus, he began narrating his family's story to her, and what they suffered at the hands of destiny since they were exiled from Andalus, up to the present day. However, when he had finished narrating his story, he gave her melancholy look and said,

"O Florinda, indeed all of them misfortunes which I had received yesterday, are unquestionably smaller than those misfortunes which I shall receive tomorrow."

She said "Which misfortune is it that you are waiting for, is it greater than that misfortune which you are already in?"

He became silent for a while, then he raised his head and said "Verily, I have the power to bear everything in life other than the fear of parting from you, and not ever meeting you again."

She said "O prince do you love me?"

He said "Yes, the way a thirsty dried up flower loves a drop of rainwater."

She said "Do you have the power to love me, a Christian girl who does not belong to your religion?"

He replied "Yes, certainly the path of religion to the heart is different from the path of love. Verily I have found in you those attributes which I love, thus, I love you for them. After this, I will not be dishonoured by anything you believe in."

She said "Do you have love without any expectation?"

He replied "Why not? Love itself is the verge of every happiness in life, if it is destined for us. When we reach the perimeter of love, we obtain the ultimate bliss of life."

فلم يستفق إلا بعد ساعة طويلة، ففتح عينيه فوجد رأسه في حجر (فلورندا)، ووجد في عينيها آثار البكاء، فقالت له: لقد كنت أعلم قبل اليوم أنك تكاتمني شيئاً من أسرار نفسك، والآن عرفت أنك لست عبد بني الأحمر ولا مولاهم كما تقول، ولكنك أحد أمرائهم، وأنك الساعة في قصر جدك وأمام حجرة أبيك. فما أسوأ حظكم يا بني الأحمر! وما أعظم شقائك أيها الأمير المسكين!

فلم يجد سبيلاً بعد ذلك إلى كتمان أمره، فأنشأ يقص عليها قصته وقصة أهل بيته وما صنعت يد الدهر بهم مذ جلوا عن الأندلس حتى اليوم، فلما فرغ من قصته نظر إليها نظرةً منكسرةً وقال لها:

فلورندا؟ إن جميع ما لقيته من الشقاء بلأمس يصغر بجانب الشقاء الذي تدخره لي الأيام غداً.

قالت: وأي شقاءٍ ينتظرك أكثر مما أنت فيه؟

فأطرق هنيهةً ثم رفع رأسه وقال: إنني أستطيع أن أحتمل كل شيءٍ في الحياة إلا أن أفارقك فراقاً لا لقاء من بعده،

قالت: أتحبني أيها الأمير؟

قال: نعم، حب الزهرة الذابلة للقطرة الهاطلة،

قالت: وهل تستطيع أن تحب فتاةً مسيحيةً لا تدين بدينك؟

قال: نعم لأن طريق الدين في القلب غير طريق الحب، ولقد وجدت فيك الصفات التي أحبها فأحببتك لها، ثم لا شأن لي بعد ذلك فيما تعتقدين.

قالت: وهل تستطيع أن تحب بلا أمل؟

قال: ولم لا يكون الحب نفسه غايةً من الغايات التي نجد فيها السعادة إن ظفرنا بها؟ ومتى كان للسعادة في هذه الحياة نهاية محدودة، فلا نجد الراحة إلا إذا وصلنا إلى نهايتها؟

The night verily had become dark. Hence, both of them got up from their station and walked and talked until both reach the place where they parted. Florinda placed her hand in his hand and said "O prince, soon I shall also love you the way you love me and my love for you will be unconditional. If religion has created a distance between our bodies, love will join our hearts together." Then, she left him there and departed.

After this, they became happy together, and enjoyed days filled with contentment and pleasure, making them forget their previous calamities and catastrophes. Above the land of Granada and under its sky, both of them became two beautiful birds which flew wherever they wanted to in the open air. The worlds surface glittered up for them, and they flew, sang and pecked wherever they pleased.

If only the people had ignored them and left them both alone in their world. If only the society had given them respite for a little while, to let them enjoy the bliss of life for a few moments, which they had bought in exchange for an abundance of tears and masses of tribulations. Other than this happiness, neither of them were the possessors of any other happiness. Thus, if they lost this happiness they would lose everything.

One day during this difficult time, both of them were sitting by a stream. Dan Roderick, the son of the governor of Granada passed by them. He saw both of them sitting together and they did not see him. Dan Roderick had seen Florinda before and had adored her. For a few days he kept on coming and going to Florinda's house, declaring his love for her and proposing marriage. Florinda adamantly refused his proposal and said to him "I will never ever marry the son of my father's killer." Swallowing his anger, he had left, and ever since he had been hiding his rage in his heart, until this day. Now, as he saw her sitting down, he speculated in his heart that Florinda had closed the door of her heart for him only because she had opened her heart for the handsome Arab man who was sitting with her. The next day, he went to her castle in order to reveal what he had in his heart for her. Florinda refused to meet him. He left the castle raging and fuming. He had a very callus and cruel idea of revenge in his heart.

وكان الليل قد أظلمها فبرحا مكانهما ومشيا يتحدثان حتى بلغا الموضع الذي اعتادا أن يفترقا فيه، فوضعت (فلورندا) يدها في يده وقالت له: (سأحبك كما أحببتني أيها الأمير، وسيكون حبي لك بلا أملٍ كحبك. ولقد فرق الدين بين جسدينا، فليجمع الحب بين قلبينا) وتركته وانصرفت.

ثم مرت بهما بعد ذلك أيام سعدا فيها بنعمة العيش سعادةً أنستهما جميع ما لقيا في حياتهما الماضية من شقاءٍ وعناءٍ فأصبحا فوق أرض غرناطة وتحت سمائها طائرين جميلين يطيران حيث يصفو لهما وجه السماء، وتترقرق صفحة الهواء ويقعان حيث يطيب لهما التغريد والتنقير،

فليت الدهر ينام عنهما ويتركهما وشأنهما ولا ينفس عليهما هذه الساعات القليلة من السعادة التي ابتاعاها بكثيرٍ من دموعهما وآلامهما والتي لا يملكان من سعادة الحياة سواها، فإن خسراها خسرا كل شيء!

بينما هما جالسان ذات يومٍ على ضفة جدولٍ من جداول عين الدمع إذ مر بهما (الدون رودريك) ابن حاكم مدينة غرناطة، فرآهما في مجلسهما هذا من حيث لا يريانه، وكان قد رأى (فلورندا) قبل اليوم فأحبها، فاختلف إلى منزلها أياماً يتحبب إليها ويدعوها إلى الزواج منه فأبت أن تصغي إليه وقالت له: إنني لا أتزوج ابن قاتل أبي. فانصرف بلوعةٍ لا تزال كامنةً في نفسه حتى اليوم؛ فلما رآها جالسةً مجلسها هذا زعم في نفسه أنها ما أوصدت باب قلبها في وجهه إلا لأنها كانت قد فتحته من قبل لذلك الفتى العربي الجميل الذي يجالسها، فذهب إلى قصرها في اليوم الثاني ليفضي إليها بما وقع في نفسه، فأبت أن تقابله، فخرج غاضباً يحدث نفسه بأفظع أنواع الانتقام.

A few days passed by, the prince, Saeed bin Yusaf, the son of Abu Abdullah, was dragged in front of a court for investigation. This was very humiliating for this progeny of Banū Aḥmar, whom yesterday were the kings and the protectors of this land and its welfare and dignity, the makers and the owners of its castles and gardens. The criminal slander pelted on him was that he was forcing a Christian woman to leave her religion. This was considered the biggest crime one can ever do against the state.

The prince stood in front of the magistrate in order for his case to be analysed. The judge questioned him about the allegation made about him. The gentleman denied this accusation. Nevertheless, the judge did not care about his refuting this contention and said to him "There is no other proof of your innocence other than you leaving your religion and accepting the religion of Christianity." The prince raged with anger, he yelled out aloud, and his voice echoed through the courtroom.

He said "In which book from your books, and which covenant from the covenants of your Prophets and Messengers, is written that the punishment of those who do not adopt a religion like yours, and do not accept your religion is death? From which world under the sky and above the land have you obtained this understanding, that people are forcefully dragged towards religion? Is this how beliefs are spread, like how alcohol and water is drunk?

The day you came to this town, you took an oath, where is that oath? In that oath you pledged that you will give us our democratic right to practice freely our religions and our beliefs. In that oath you vowed not to harm us, wherever our hearts inclined, and also not to harm us in our religious ceremonies.

All this that you are doing today, is this what you promised to do yesterday? This, what you are doing certainly qualifies as the fulfilment of the pact, and a means to safeguard its citizens!

Yes, certainly you people can do whatever you please as verily the town has been emptied for you and you are the people of power and the kingdom is yours. Is this the dignity and respect of the rulers that they cannot fulfil and honour their pledge?

Verily that pledge which is between the powerful and the weak, in reality it is like a powerful sword which amputates the hands of the former and it is a shackle which is chained around the necks of the latter. May Allah ﷻ never pardon the mistakes of the foolish and may He ﷻ never allow ease/coolness for the eyes of the unwise.

وما هي إلا أيام قلائل حتى سيق الأمير سعيد بن يوسف بن أبي عبد الله سليل بني الأحمر ملوك هذه البلاد بالأمس ومؤسسي مجدها وعظمتها، وبناة قلاعها وحصونها، وأصحاب قصورها وبساتينها، ذليلاً مهاناً إلى محكمة التفتيش متهماً بمحاولة إغراء فتاةٍ مسيحيةٍ بترك دينها، وهي عندهم أفظع الجرائم وأهولها.

وقف الأمير أمام قضاة محكمة التفتيش فسأله الرئيس عن تهمته فأنكرها فلم يحفل بإنكاره، وقال له: لا يدل على براءتك إلا أمر واحد، وهو أن تترك دينك وتأخذ بدين المسيح، فطار الغضب في دماغه، وصرخ صرخةً دوت بها أرجاء القاعة وقال:

في أي كتابٍ من كتبكم، وفي أي عهدٍ من عهود أنبيائكم ورسلكم أن سفك الدم عقاب الذين لا يؤمنون بإيمانكم، ولا يدينون بدينكم؟ من أي عالم من عوالم الأرض أو السماء أتيتم بهذه العقول التي تصور لكم أن الشعوب تساق إلى الإيمان سوقاً، وأن العقائد تسقى للناس كما يسقى الماء والخمر؟

أين العهد الذي اتخذتموه على أنفسكم يوم وطئت أقدامكم هذه البلاد أن تتركونا أحراراً في عقائدنا ومذاهبنا وأن لا تؤذونا في عاطفةٍ من عواطف قلوبنا، ولا في شعيرةٍ من شعائر ديننا؟

أهذا الذي تصنعون اليوم، والذي صنعتم بالأمس، هو كل ما عندكم من الوفاء بالعهود والرعي للذمم؟

نعم لكم أن تفعلوا ما تشاءون، فقد خلا لكم وجه البلاد وأصبحتم أصحاب القوة والسلطان فيها، وللسلطان عزة لا تبالي بعهدٍ ولا وفاءٍ.

إن العهود التي تكون بين الأقوياء والضعفاء إنما هي سيفٌ قاطعٌ في يد الأولين، وغلٌّ ملتفٌّ على أعناق الآخرين، فلا أقال الله عثرة البلهاء ولا أقر عيون الأغبياء.

You are the people of power and we are the people of weakness. You are upon clear truth and proof, so you can initiate whatever you want. This is your right which you have obtained through the power which you have been granted. You may spill our blood the way you please and you may strip away our rights the way you want. You can captivate our minds and our intellects so that we do not accept any other religion other than yours, and that we do not go towards any other religion but wherever you intend us to go. Hence-away with you! We are discharged from being amongst the powerful. It is inevitable for us that we have a share from that what the weak people obtain and receive."

Then the Prince tried his best to continue with his words, but the Judge cut him off and ordered that he be taken to the same public square where ten thousand Muslims were massacred and burned before. Thus, he was dragged towards this place of execution. Men and women gathered around his place of slaughter. Before the executioner even raised his sword upon the head of the prince, within the midst of the crowd, people heard the scream of a woman. They quickly looked, but did not recognise where the voice had come from. It only took the twinkling of an eye and the princes' head fell on the ground in front of everyone in a manner that could not be compared to anything else.

***

Even today, when a passer-by walks besides the graveyard of Banū Ahmar in Granada, he sees a beautiful embellished grave which is constructed from a yellow, clean, transparent stone. Under its surface there is a shallow dent, which collects rain water. Thus, the birds take refuge towards this on scorching days in the summer, and drink water from it. On one side of the grave, these lines are inscribed,

This is the final grave of Banū Ahmar
From his loyal friend who fulfilled his pledge until death
(Florinda Philip)

أنتم أقوياء ونحن ضعفاء فأنتم أصحاب الحق الأبلج والحجة القائمة؛ فاصنعوا ما شئتم فهذا حقكم الذي خولتكم إياه قوتكم. اسفكوا من دمائنا ما شئتم، واسلبوا من حقوقنا ما أردتم، واملكو علينا مشاعرنا وعقولنا حتى لا ندين إلا بما تدينون، ولا نذهب إلا حيث تذهبون فقد عجزنا عن أن نكون أقوياء، فلا بد أن ينالنا ما ينال الضعفاء.

ثم حاول الاستمرار في حديثه فقاطعه الرئيس وأمر أن يساق إلى ساحة الموت التي هلك فيها من قبله عشرة آلاف من المسلمين قتلاً أو حرقاً، فسيق إليها واجتمع الناس حول مصرعه رجالاً ونساءً، وما جرد الجلاد سيفه فوق رأسه حتى سمع الناس صرخة امرأةٍ بين الصفوف، فالتفتوا فلم يعرفوا مصدرها، وما هي إلا غمضة وانتباهة أن سقط ذلك الرأس الذي ليس له مثيل.

***

يرى المار اليوم بجانب مقبرة بني الأحمر في ظاهر غرناطة قبراً جميلاً مزخرفاً هو قطعة واحدة من الرخام الأزرق الصافي قد نحتت في سطحها حفرة جوفاء تمتلىء بماء المطر فيهوي إليها الطير في أيام الصيف الحار فيشرب منها، ونقشت على ضلع من أضلاعها هذه السطور:

(هذا قبر آخر بني الأحمر)

(من صديقته الوفية بعهده حتى الموت)

(فلورندا فيليب)

The Abyss / Al-Hāwiyyah (Composed)

To what proportion are the days of life plentiful and to what proportion are they less?

I have spent many years living in this world. However, in reality I have only lived for one year. That year which I had lived passed by me like an ancient star which passes in the sky at night only once, then no one sees it after that ever again.

I spent the first portion of my life in search of a sincere friend. I was looking for a friend who would not look at his friends with an eye of a merchant inspecting his stock. Neither did I want a friend who would observe his friends with an eye of a farmer, who inspects his cattle. I encountered many friendship failures until I met someone whom I had known for eighteen years. In him, I saw great qualities, and characteristics, a good person with good etiquettes, the friend which I had long been seeking.

I did not find these attributes in anyone else except him. Whenever I imagined the face of a man belonging to the most excellent character, his face would sparkle and glitter in my mind. Thus, I held him in high esteem and respect. He made a place in my heart the likes of which no one had ever made before, and our cup of friendship overflowed with brotherly love.

There was nothing which faded away our friendship until, due to some unseen circumstances, I was forced to leave my place of residence, Cairo, and move back to my home town. I was not grieved upon anything except the saddening of the separation of this generous friend. For some time, we wrote to each other. After, his letters started decreasing, eventually they completely stopped.

I became severely upset over this. I started having all kinds of assumptions and concerns about him, though I never doubted his friendship and loyalty. Whenever I intended to travel to him and see how he was doing, my personal circumstances did not allow me to do so.

Thus, I only returned to Cairo after a couple of years. The day I set my foot on the land of Cairo, I had intended first to go and see my friend. I went to his house in the first portion of the night. When I got there I witnessed an atmosphere which even today it is connected to my heart.

الهاوية
(موضوعة)

ما أكثر أيام الحياة وما أقلها؟

لم أعش من تلك الأعوام الطوال التي عشتها في هذا العالم إلا عاماً واحداً مر بي كما يمر النجم الدهري في سماء الدنيا ليلةً واحدةً ثم لا يراه الناس بعد ذلك.

قضيت الشطر الأول من حياتي أفتش عن صديقٍ ينظر إلى أصدقائه بعينٍ غير العين التي ينظر بها التاجر إلى سلعته، والزارع إلى ماشيته، فأعوزني ذلك حتى عرفت (فلاناً) منذ ثماني عشرة عاماً فعرفت امرءاً ما شئت أن أرى خلةً من خلال الخير والمعروف في ثياب رجلٍ إلا وجدتها فيه،

ولا تخيلت صورةً من صور الكمال الإنساني في وجه إنسانٍ إلا أضاءت لي في وجهه، فجلت مكانته عندي، ونزل من نفسي منزلةً لم ينزلها أحد من قبله، وصفت كأس الود بيني وبينه.

لا يكدرها علينا مكدر حتى عرض إلي من حوادث الدهر ما أزعجني من مستقري فهجرت القاهرة إلى مسقط رأسي غير آسفٍ على شيءٍ فيها إلا على فراق ذلك الصديق الكريم، فتراسلنا حقبةً من الزمن ثم فترت عني كتبه ثم انقطعت،

فحزنت لذلك حزناً شديداً وذهبت بي الظنون في شأنه كل مذهب، إلا أن أرتاب في صدقه ووفائه، وكنت كلما هممت بالمسير إليه لتعرف حاله قعد بي عن ذلك هم كان يقعدني عن كل شأنٍ حتى شأن نفسي.

فلم أعد إلى القاهرة إلا بعد أعوامٍ فكان أول همي يوم هبطت أرضها أن أراه، فذهبت إلى منزله في الساعة الأولى من الليل فرأيت ما لا تزال حسرته متصلةً بقلبي حتى اليوم.

When I had left this house, it was like the spirit of a small garden from amongst the highest gardens of Paradise, where people could see all different colours of life shining, and observe the faces of its residents glittering with tranquillity and peace. Today, I have visited the same house only to discover that I am standing in front of a graveyard, frightening and scary, surrounded with silence. There was no voice which was echoing in the house nor in any corner could a human being or a kindling lamp be seen. I presumed that I had mistaken it for another house, or that I was in front of an abandoned house. I was pondering on this matter when I heard the cry of a small baby. I saw a very vivid light coming in through some of the windows of the house.

Consequently, I walked towards the door and knocked. No one answered so I knocked once more. Then I saw some light coming out through a crack of the door. It was not long after that I saw the face of a small boy, who was dressed in old rags. He was holding a lamp in his hand which was fairly bright. When I concentrated upon his face through the light of that lamp, I saw in him the face of his father. I had recognized that certainly he is that beautiful pampered boy whom yesterday was the flower of this house and the star of its sky. I asked him about his father. He gestured to me to come in and he walked in front of me holding his lamp, until he took me to a very unclean hall which was extremely dusty.

In that large room there were deteriorated sofas placed and very old curtains hanging down. Despite the darkness, I recognised some old inscriptions and wall markings which had remained, without them I would have never recognized that certainly this is that same room where we had spent our blissful and fruitful nights for twelve months. Then a brief conversation took place between me and the youth. He had recognized who I was and I also gathered that his father had not returned home as of yet, and that he would be shortly. Then, he left me and went away. He returned briefly to say that his mother would like to talk to me regarding his father. My heart started beating fast out of fear and fright. I felt certain that some calamity had befallen which I had no idea of.

I turned back to discover that there was a woman wrapped in a black blanket standing upon the door step. She greeted me, and I greeted her as well.

She asked me "Do you know that after you had gone what role destiny played with your friend?"

I replied "No" and explained that this was the first day I was returning to this town ever since I had parted seven years ago.

تركت هذا المنزل فردوساً صغيراً من فراديس الجنان تتراءى فيه السعادة في ألوانها المختلفة، وتترقرق وجوه ساكنيه بشراً وسروراً، ثم زرته اليوم فخيل إلي أنني أمام مقبرةٍ موحشةٍ ساكنةٍ لا يهتف فيها صوت ولا يتراءى في جوانبها شبح، ولا يلمع في أرجائها مصباح، فظننت أني أخطأت المنزل الذي أريده أو أنني بين يدي منزلٍ مهجورٍ حتى سمعت بكاء طفلٍ صغيرٍ، ولمحت في بعض النوافذ نوراً ضعيفاً،

فمشيت إلى الباب فطرقته فلم يجبني أحد فطرقته أخرى فلمحت من خصاصه نوراً مقبلاً، ثم لم يلبث أن انفرج لي عن وجه غلامٍ صغيرٍ في أسمالٍ باليةٍ يحمل في يده مصباحاً ضئيلاً فتأملته على ضوء المصباح فرأيت في وجهه صورة أبيه فعرفت أنه ذلك الطفل الجميل المدلل الذي كان بالأمس زهرة هذا المنزل وبدر سمائه، فسألته عن أبيه فأشار إلي بالدخول ومشى أمامي بمصباحه حتى وصل بي إلى قاعةٍ شعثاء مغبرةٍ باليةٍ المقاعد والأستار،

ولولا نقوش لاحت لي في بعض جدرانها كباقي الوشم في ظاهر اليد ـ ما عرفت أنها القاعة التي قضينا فيها ليالي السعادة والهناء اثني عشر هلالاً، ثم جرى بيني وبين الغلام حديث قصير عرف فيه من أنا وعرفت أن أباه لم يعد إلى المنزل حتى الساعة وأنه عائد عما قليل؛ ثم تركني ومضى وما لبث إلا قليلاً حتى عاد يقول لي: إن والدته تريد أن تحدثني حديثاً يتعلق بأبيه، فخفق قلبي خفقة الرعب والخوف وأحسست بشر لا أعرف مأتاه،

ثم التفت فإذا امرأة ملتفة بردءٍ أسود واقفةٍ على عتبة الباب فحيتني فحييتها.

ثم قالت لي: هل علمت ما صنع الدهر بفلان من بعدك؟

قلت: لا، فهذا أول يومٍ هبطت فيه هذا البلد بعد ما فارقته سبعة أعوام.

She said "If only you had stayed, you were his protection, you protected and shielded him from the evils and catastrophes of life. Ever since you left him, a group of people belonging to the party of Satan surrounded him. As you know, your friend was a straight forward person, a man of good conduct. The men of Satan kept on motivating and inclining him towards evil and would beautify for him evil the way the devil glorifies evil for people, until your friend landed right in it, and subsequently we all fell into that ditch of misfortune as well, as you can see."

I said "O my respectable lady, which evil are you talking about? And who are those surrounding people, causing his fall?"

She said "I will tell you everything, the whole story, listen to what I have to say. He was a man walking in good pathways until he joined connections with his superior manager and became linked with him. Your friend then became one of his closest associates, and never parted his company wherever he went. His associates followed him morning and evening. From that day, his state changed and his good conduct transformed also. He started becoming disconnected with his wife and children. He only used to see us a little from time to time, and would return home in the last portion of the night. Verily at the beginning, I was really happy that he had attained a promotion with his director and drawn closer to his heart. I hoped that good was to proceed this and so I pardoned him from his regular absences from home. Despite that, I would fear and was saddened over his disconnection with me and his refraining from the affairs of his wife and children. The matter continued until he returned home one night completely distressed, sighing and experiencing severe fatigue and bodily pain. I drew near him and smelled alcohol from his mouth. From then on, I understood everything.

I realised that certainly this high ranking official is the leader of his subordinates. If he were to walk the good path, he would be doing good with his juniors. If, however, he was to tread upon the evil path, then only bad would be obtained by his subservient workers. He took my poor young husband upon the bad path, and the worst way. He did not consider him as a friend the way my husband had assumed, but as a drinking partner. I requested, pleaded before him, for the sake of everything he loved, hoping these things would separate him from his wayward boss. I shed so many tears before him with all the power I had in my eyes. I was hoping that he would return to his former life where he had lived in prosperity with his wife and children. Alas, my tears were unsuccessful.

قالت: ليتك لم تفارقه، فقد كنت عصمته التي يعتصم بها وحماه من غوائل الدهر وشروره، فما هو إلا أن فارقته حتى أحاطت به زمرة من زمر الشيطان، وكان فتًى كما تعلمه غريراً ساذجاً، فما زالت تغريه بالشر وتزين له منه ما يزين الشيطان للإنسان حتى سقط فيه فسقطنا جميعاً في هذا الشقاء الذي تراه،

قلت: وأي شر تريدين يا سيدتي؟ ومن هم الذين أحاطوا به فأسقطوه؟

قالت: سأقص عليك كل شيءٍ فاستمع لما أقول: ما زال الرجل بخيرٍ حتى اتصل بفلان رئيس ديوانه وعلقت حباله بحباله وأصبح من خاصته الذين لا يفارقون مجلسه حيث كان ولا تزال نعالهم خافقة وراءه في غدواته وروحاته فاستحال من ذلك اليوم أمره وتنكرت صورة أخلاقه وأصبح منقطعاً عن أهله وأولاده لا يراهم إلا الفينة بعد الفينة وعن منزله لا يزوره إلا في أخريات الليالي؛ ولقد اغتبطت في مبدأ الأمر بتلك الحظوة التي نالها عند ذلك الرئيس والمنزلة التي نالها من نفسه ورجوت له من ورائها خيراً كثيراً مغتفرة في سبيل ذلك ما كنت أشعر به من الوحشة والألم لانقطاعه عني وإغفاله أمري وأمر أولاده حتى عاد في ليلةٍ من الليالي شاكياً متألماً يكابد غصصاً شديدة وآلاماً جساماً، فدنوت منه فشممت من فمه رائحة الخمر، فعلمت كل شيء.

علمت أن ذلك الرئيس العظيم هو قدوة مرؤوسيه في الخير إن سلك طريق الخير، والشر إن سلك طريق الشر، قاد زوجي الفتى المسكين إلى شر الطريقين، وسلك به أسوأ السبيلين، وأنه ما كان يتخذه صديقاً كما زعم، بل نديماً على الشراب، فتوسلت إليه بكل عزيزٍ عليه، وسكبت على يديه من الدموع كل ما تستطيع أن تسكبه عين، رجاء أن يعود إلى حياته الأولى التي كان يحياها سعيداً بين أهله وأولاده فما أجديت عليه شيئاً،

After a while it came to my attention that, that same hand which took him towards alcohol had also taken him towards gambling. This did not surprise me because I knew that certainly the path to evil is one. If one is standing on its starting point, it is inevitable for him to pass all the way through until he reaches its end.

Subsequently this noble and gallant young man whom yesterday used to refrain even from the medicine where he had smelled alcohol from, and was ashamed to sit down in the gathering of those who drank, became a drunkard, a gambler, a loafer and completely shameless himself. He did not care about his respect, neither was he bothered about any insult. He would not refrain from his shameful behaviour, nor would let go of his sins. My husband was once a kind father and merciful, noble husband, who never allowed even an ant bite to his children. Neither did he allow another man to look at his wife with lustful eyes. Now, he became a hard heartened father and a tyrant husband. Whenever his children would go to him he would start beating them up. If he looked at me, he would start swearing and abusing.

This once sentimental and devoted man, who used to safeguard his honour and his respect, simply did not care anymore and would come home some nights with some of his roguish and rascal friends. Thus, he used to bring them upon the upper floor of the house where me and my children were sleeping. Then they would sit in one of its rooms and would drink, gamble and make a lot of noise, until alcohol used to dominate their senses and they would lose control. Then they would start singing and dancing and would fill the atmosphere of the house with screams and cheering. Then they would run and chase each other in the passages of the house, entering different rooms until they would enter and take refuge in my room.

Most of the time, they would stare at my face, and try to pull my scarf off while my husband watched and heard, but he would not say anything or stop anything. Then I would run from one place to the other in front of them. Most of the time, I ran out of the house altogether without a coverlet neither a scarf. Only the coverlet and the scarf of the night would cover me at that point. Then I would go to the next door house of my neighbour and spend the remaining night there."

ثم علمت بعد ذلك أن اليد التي ساقته إلى الشراب قد ساقته إلى اللعب، فلم أعجب لذلك، لأني أعلم أن طريق الشر واحدة، فمن وقف على رأسها لا بد له أن ينحدر فيها حتى يصل إلى نهايتها،

فأصبح ذلك الفتى النبيل الشريف، الذي كان بالأمس يعف عن شرب الدواء إذا اشتم فيه رائحة النبيذ ويستحي أن يجلس في مجتمعٍ يجلس فيه قوم شاربون- سكيراً مقامراً مستهتراً لا يحتشم، ولا يتلوم، ولا يتقيِّ عاراً ولا مأثماً، وأصبح ذلك الأب الرحيم والزوج الكريم الذي كان يضن بأولاده أن يعلق بهم الذر، وبزوجه أن يتجهم لها وجه السماء، أباً قاسياً وزوجاً سليطاً، يضرب أولاده كلما دنوا منه، ويشتم زوجته وينتهرها كلما رآها،

وأصبح ذلك الرجل الغيور الضنين بعرضه وشرفه لا يبالي أن يعود إلي المنزل في بعض الليالي في جمعٍ من عشرائه الأشرار فيصعد بهم إلى الطبقة التي أنام فيها أنا وأولادي فيجلسون في بعض غرفها، ولا يزالون يشربون ويقصفون حتى يذهب بعقولهم الشراب فيهتاجوا ويرقصوا ويملأوا الجو صراخاً وهتافاً ثم يتعادوا بعضهم وراء بعض في الأبهاء والحجرات حتى يلجوا على باب غرفتي،

وربما حدق بعضهم في وجهي أو حاول نزع خماري على مرأئ من زوجي ومسمع فلا يقول شيئاً، ولا يستنكر أمراً فأفر بين أيديهم من مكانٍ إلى مكانٍ، وربما فررت من المنزل جميعه وخرجت بلا إزار، ولا خمار، غير إزار الظلام وخماره،، حتى أصل إلى بيت جارةٍ من جاراتي فأقضي عندهم بقية الليل.

Here, her tone of voice changed and she withheld her conversation and put her head down. I realised that she was crying. Internally, I started crying as well. Then she raised her head, and, returning to her conversation said "Not even a few years have passed since, that your friend has spent all that wealth which he had possessed. Then it became necessary for him to take out a loan, which he did. The load of the loan increased and he started pawning things. When he was unable to pay back, he sold his possessions, even this house we are living in. Now, nothing remains in his hand other than a meaningless monthly salary. In fact, it does not even remain in his hands anymore. Very soon after receiving his salary, it quickly become the ownership of his debtors or a win for his gambling companions.

This is what the hands of destiny have done to him. Myself and his children are also in great hardship, one complete year has passed since I have sold my last piece of jewellery. Now all my jewellery, clothes and household furniture are in the pawning shops, and in the shops of the debtors. My house and all its contents are deposited with pawn brokers. I have a close considerate relative, who, despite being in strained circumstances himself, has helped me occasionally with a little money saved by holding back on his own children. Without him, me and my children would have certainly died out of hunger.

O sir, maybe you have the power to help my husband, and save him from his problems and adversities. You hold a very sentimental and good opinion about him. I think that indeed you have the power to do this, because the station and the respect which he has in his heart for you, all mankind are deprived of it. Thus, if you were to help him, then you would be doing him, and all of us, a very big favour. It will be a huge act of kindness upon us, which we will never forget until death."

Thereafter she said goodbye to me and departed on her way. Then I asked the boy what time I would be able to see his father at home. He said "You can see him in the morning before he goes to his office." I walked out in my shocked state. I was concealing a burning restlessness in my heart, and the slumber of sleep had disappeared from my eyes. The night passed by, but it did not pass by easily.

I returned in the morning of the second day in order to see my old friend, who yesterday I used to consider being the best from all people. I did not know what would be the outcome after our meeting. My heart became anxious and petrified, like the heart of one who enters a racecourse as a competitor, spending on it all his wealth with no knowledge whether he shortly will win or lose, become the most fortunate or the most wretched.

***

وهنا تغيرت نغمة صوتها، فأمسكت عن الحديث، وأطرقت برأسها، فعلمت أنها تبكي فبكيت بيني وبين نفسي لبكائها، ثم رفعت رأسها، وعادت إلى حديثها تقول: وما هي إلا أعوام قلائل حتى أنفق جميع ما كان في يده من المال فكان لا بد له أن يستدين ففعل، فأثقله الدين فرهن، فعجز عن الوفاء فباع جميع ما يملك حتى هذا البيت الذي نسكنه، ولم يبق في يده غير راتبه الشهري الصغير، بل لم يبق في يده شيء حتى راتبه، لأنه لا يملكه إلا ساعة من نهار، ثم هو بعد ذلك ملك للدائنين، أو غنيمة للمقامرين.

هذا ما صنعت يد الدهر به، أما ما صنعت بي وبأولادي، فقد مر على آخر حليةٍ بعتها من حلاي عام كامل، وها هي حوانيت المرابين والمسترهنين ملأى بملابسي، وأدوات بيتي وأثاثه، ولولا رجل من ذوي قرباي رقيق الحال يعود علي من حينٍ إلى حينٍ بالنزر القليل مما يستله من أشداق عياله لهلكت وهلك أولادي جوعاً.

فلعلك تستطيع يا سيدي أن تكون عوناً لي على هذا الرجل المسكين فتنقذه من شقائه وبلائه بما ترى له في ذلك الرأي الصالح وأحسب أنك تقدر منه- للمنزلة التي تنزلها من نفسه- على ما عجز عنه الناس جميعاً، فإن فعلت أحسنت إليه وإلينا إحساناً لا ننسى يدك فيه حتى الموت.

ثم حيتني ومضت لسبيلها، فسألت الغلام عن الساعة التي أستطيع أن أرى أباه فيها في المنزل، فقال: إنك تراه في الصباح قبل ذهابه إلى الديوان، فانصرفت لشأني، وقد أضمرت بين جنبي لوعة ما زالت تقيمني وتقعدني وتذور عن عيني سنة الكرى حتى انقضى الليل، وما كاد ينقضي.

ثم عدت في صباح اليوم الثاني لأرى ذلك الصديق القديم الذي كنت بلأمس أسعد الناس به، ولا أعلم ما مصير أمري معه بعد ذلك، وفي نفسي من القلق والاضطراب ما يكون في نفس الذاهب إلى ميدان سباقٍ قد خاطر فيه بجميع ما يمتلك؛ فهو لا يعلم أيكون بعد ساعةٍ أسعد الناس أم أشقاهم؟

***

Now I have realised that certainly faces are the reflections of hearts. If the heart sparkles the face brightens up. If the heart becomes darkened, the face likewise becomes gloomy. I had parted from this man seven years ago, and, because of this long gap, I had forgotten his face. I only remembered in it a glowing bright light, the light of excellence and dignity, which shone like the glow of the sun upon his face. However, when I saw him now, I did not see that luminous white light which I had once known. I thought to myself that I was seeing a face which was not the face of the past, and the man who I am looking at is not the man who I knew from before.

I did not see in front of me that beautiful young man who was always in laughter and his face brightened with smiles. In his place, I saw a distressed and unfortunate man who wore the dress of old age before old age had struck him. It appeared that he had reached the age of sixty, despite not even being thirty. His eyebrows were droopy. His eyelids were heavy. His sight became motionless, and cheeks were dangling down. His forehead was fallen down between his shoulders like a hunchback. The first thing which I said to him was, "O my dearest friend, everything has changed about you, even your face has changed." It was like he knew what was in my heart, and had recognized that I knew everything about his affairs. Thus, he lowered his head like the one who acknowledges that the place under the earth is better than the earth above. He did not say anything. I drew nearer to him and I put my hand upon his shoulder and said,

"By Allah ﷻ, I do not know what can I say to you. Can I offer you advice? In the past, it was you who used to give me advice, you were the star of my guidance from which I used to brighten up my darkened life. Or, can I alert you towards what Allah ﷻ has ordained for you in respect of you and your wife? I do not recognize what you have become? I cannot advise you on the best way to withdraw from this life. Can I request you to be kind towards your weak children and be merciful towards your poor distressed wife? This is because none of them have any support save you, neither do they have any helper apart from you. You are a person with a merciful heart, a heart which beats for distant people. Without a shadow of doubt, your heart has more right to love and beat for your closest.

الآن عرفت أن الوجوه مرايا النفوس تضيء بضيائها وتظلم بظلامها، فقد فارقت الرجل منذ سبع سنواتٍ أنستني الأيام صورته، ولم يبق في ذاكرتي منها إلا ذلك الضياء اللامع، ضياء الفضيلة والشرف الذي كان يتلألأ فيها تلألؤ نور الشمس في صفحتها، فلما رأيته الآن، ولم أر أمام عيني تلك الغلالة البيضاء التي كنت أعرفها، خيل إلي أنني أرى صورةً غير الصورة الماضية، ورجلاً غير الذي كنت أعرفه من قبل.

لم أر أمامي ذلك الفتى الجميل الوضاح الذي كان كل منبت شعرةٍ في وجهه فماً ضاحكاً تموج فيه ابتسامة لامعة؛ بل رأيت مكانه رجلاً منكوباً شقياً قد لبس الهرم قبل أوانه وأوفى على الستين قبل أن يسلخ الثلاثين، فاسترخى حاجباه وثقلت أجفانه، وجمدت نظراته، وتهدل عارضاه، وتجعد جبينه، استشرف عاتقاه وهوى رأسه بينهما هوية بين عاتقي الأحدب ، فكان أول ما قلت له: لقد تغير فيك كل شيءٍ يا صديقي حتى صورتك! وكأنما ألم بما في نفسي، وعرف أني قد علمت من أمره كل شيء، فأطرق برأسه إطراق من يرى أن باطن الأرض خير له من ظهرها، ولم يقل شيئاً، فدنوت منه حتى وضعت يدي على عاتقه وقلت له:

والله ما أدري ماذا أقول لك؟ أأعظك، وقد كنت واعظي بالأمس، ونجم هداي الذي أستنير به في ظلمات حياتي؟ أم أرشدك إلى ما أوجب الله عليك في نفسك، وفي أهلك؟ ولا أعرف شيئاً أنت تجهله، ولا تصل يدي إلى عبرة تقصر يدك عن نيلها، أم أسترحمك لأطفالك الضعفاء وزوجتك البائسة المسكينة التي لا عضد لها في الحياة، ولا معين سواك؟ وأنت صاحب القلب الرحيم الذي طالما خفق بالبعداء، فأحرى أن يخفق رحمةً بالأقرباء!

O my dear, certainly the life which you are living is only for the useless and the jobless. These people do not have the capability, through any of their actions, to hide their shame and remorse from the eyes of mankind, until death comes to them. Thus, it is their death which then saves them from their misfortune, and from being exposed. Certainly you are not from them. O my dear, indeed you are walking the path to your grave. Despite that, you are not upset, neither are you distressed from life. So why are you facing the world like a person who is at despair from it, and wants to leave? If you do benefit from your second life and if your second life was going to restore all that which you had lost in your first life, then certainly I would have excused and pardoned you.

However, you know that indeed you were rich and now you became poor. You know that you were fit and well, and now you have become ill. You know that you were a nobleman and now you are humiliated. After all this, if you still consider yourself to be a fortunate man, then indeed this would mean that the earth is empty from unfortunate people.

Everything that you are labouring hard for in this life, only shows that you are in search of death. Why do you not gulp a drop of poison only once, and go straight to your death? This would be better for you than a slow agonising death during which you may forget your daily problems and difficulties, but your sins and crimes will increase. The punishment which Allah ﷻ is going to give in the hereafter is going to be far greater than any punishment He is giving you in this world.

O friend, sufficient is for us the calamities of this life, which destiny brings to us. So why do we need to import new catastrophes for ourselves in our lives? Please bring forth your hand and make a pledge with me that you will become for me the same person you were yesterday. We were prospering before we parted, but when we did part, we became very unfortunate. Nevertheless, because we have now met, let us live again under the shade of happiness, dignity and honour, as we did before."

Then I stretched forth my hand towards him, and was concerned that he did not make any movement with his hand. Hence, I said to him, "What is the matter with you? You did not bring out your hand for me?"

He burst into tears and said "I do not want to be a liar, nor a person who breaks promises."

I said "What hinders you from fulfilling your promise?"

He replied "I am an unfortunate person. I have no luck or fortune at all."

إن هذه الحياة التي تحياها يا سيدي أنما يلجأ إليها الهمل العاطلون الذين لا يصلحون لعملٍ من الأعمال ليتواروا فيها عن أعين الناس حياءً وخجلاً حتى يأتيهم الموت فينقذهم من عارهم وشقائهم، وما أنت بواحد منهم! إنك تمشي يا سيدي في طريق القبر، وما أنت بناقمٍ على الدنيا ولا بمتبرمٍ بها، فما رغبتك في الخروج منها خروج اليائس المنتحر! عذرتك لو أن ما ربحت في حياتك الثانية يقوم لك مقام ما خسرت من حياتك الأولى،

ولكنك تعلم أنك كنت غنياً فأصبحت فقيراً، وصحيحاً فأصبحت سقيماً، وشريفاً فأصبحت وضيعاً؛ فإن كنت ترى بعد ذلك أنك سعيد فقد خلت رقعة الأرض من الأشقياء.

إن كل ما يعنيك من حياتك هذه أن تطلب فيها الموت؛ فاطلبه في جرعة سم تشربها دفعةً واحدةً؛ فذلك خير لك من هذا الموت المتقطع الذي يكثر فيه عذابك وألمك، وتعظم فيه آثامك وجرائمك، وما يعاقبك الله على الأخرى بأكثر مما يعاقبك على الأولى.

حسبنا يا صديق من الشقاء في هذه الحياة ما يأتينا به القدر فلا نضم إليه شقاء جديداً نجلبه بأنفسنا لأنفسنا، فهات يدك وعاهدني على أن تكون لي منذ اليوم كما كنت لي بالأمس، فقد كنا سعداء قبل أن نفترق، ثم افترقنا فشقينا، وها نحن أولاء قد التقينا. فلنعش في ظلال الفضيلة والشرف سعداء كما كنا.

ثم مددت يدي إليه فراعني أنه لم يحرك يده فقلت له: مالك لا تمد يدك إلي؟

فاستعبر باكياً وقال: لأنني لا أحب أن أكون كاذباً ولا حانثاً.

قلت: وما يمنعك من الوفاء؟

قال: يمنعني منه أنني رجل شقي، لا حظ لي في سعادة السعداء،

I said "Indeed you had the power to become unfortunate, so why do you not have the power to become fortunate?"

He said "Because fortune is the sky and the misfortune is the earth. Descending to earth is easier than ascending to the sky. My foot has already slipped on the edge of a ditch. Now, I do not have the power to regain stability and I will continue to fall until I reach the bottom of that ditch. I have drunk the first gulp of life's bitterness. It is inevitable for me now to swallow the last remains of that bitterness. If I had never taken my first sip of this poison, then I would have a chance to change my wretched life. However, as I have done so, I have no choice but to accept my fate, and what Allah ﷻ has decreed."

I said "This is not true. You can still be saved from your wretched fate by making only one truthful pledge. If you were to make only one promise, then you will achieve salvation."

He replied "To have a conviction is the sign of a firm intention, whereas I have become a man who is dominated and overpowered by life. I have no power or firm intention. Therefore, my dear friend, leave me alone, let destiny do with me whatever it wants. Woe, do not cry over your old friend after today, there is no use in crying for fallen sinners."

He burst out crying loudly, and left me in my place without saying another word. I had no idea where he went. So I left as well, carrying the heavy burden of sorrow on my shoulders, only Allah ﷻ knew my pain.

***

As time progressed, the manager of the office could no longer bear his drinking partner, who's company he previously desired. Now he was a burden, he quickly took him out of his social circle. Following that, he started disliking his work, and discontinued his pay, having no sympathy for his desperate situation. My friend did not even shed a tear. Poverty meant he lost his house. The new owner did not give him enough notice, and threw him out after a few months. Thus he, his wife and two children took refuge in a vile room of an old house, nestled in an isolated alleyway.

After this, I used to see him either going to or coming back from the pub, and when he passed I would turn my face away from him. However, when I used to see him returning from the Pub in a poor state, I would draw closer to him, and wipe dust from his face, or clean off any blood which flowed upon his forehead. After that, I would take him to his house.

قلت: قد استطعت أن تكون شقياً، فلم لا تستطيع أن تكون سعيداً؟

قال: لأن السعادة سماء والشقاء أرض، والنزول إلى الأرض أسهل من الصعود إلى السماء، وقد زلت قدمي عن حافة الهوة فلا قدرة لي على الاستمساك حتى أبلغ قرارتها، وشربت أول جرعةٍ من جرعات الحياة المريرة، فلا بد لي أن أشربها حتى ثمالتها، ولا شيء من الأشياء يستطيع أن يقف في سبيلي إلا شيء واحد فقط، هو أن لا أكون قد شربت الكأس الأولى قبل اليوم، وما دمت قد فعلت فلا حيلة لي فيما قضى الله،

قلت: ليس بينك وبين النزوع إلا عزمة صادقة تعزمها فإذا أنت من الناجين،

قال: إن العزيمة أثر من آثار الإرادة، وقد أصبحت رجلاً مغلوباً على أمري، لا إرادة لي ولا اختيار، فدعني يا صديقي والقضاء يصنع بي ما يشاء، وابك صديقك القديم منذ اليوم إن كنت لا ترى بأساً في البكاء على الساقطين المذنبين.

ثم انفجر باكياً بصوتٍ عالٍ، وتركني مكاني دون أن يحييني بكلمةٍ، وخرج هائماً على وجهه لا أعلم أين ذهب، فانصرفت لشأني وبين جنبي من الهم والكمد ما الله به عليم.

***

لم يستطع رئيس الديوان أن يحمل نديمه بالأمس زمناً طويلاً، فأقصاه عن مجلسه استثقالاً له، ثم عزله عن وظيفته استنكاراً لعمله، ولم تذرف عينه دمعةً واحدةً على منظر صريعه الساقط بين يديه، ولم يستطع مالك البيت الجديد أن يمهل فيه المالك القديم أكثر من بضعة شهورٍ ثم طرده منه، فلجأ هو وزوجته وولداه إلى غرفةٍ حقيرةٍ في بيتٍ قديمٍ في زقاقٍ مهجورٍ،

فأصبحت لا أراه بعد ذلك إلا ذاهباً إلى الحانة أو عائداً منها، فإن رأيته ذاهباً زويت وجهي عنه، أو عائداً دنوت منه فمسحت عن وجهه ما لصق به من التراب أو عن جبينه ما سال منه من الدم ثم قدته إلى بيته.

Like this, the days and the years continued to weaken his body and his mind, until he appeared as a walking shadow or a dream passing by for anyone who looked at him. He would walk the streets like a lost, insane soul, hardly feeling or sensing his surroundings. He could not escape obstacles in his way, until he came completely close to them. He would stop from time to time and roll his eyes, as if he was searching for something which he had lost, despite there being nothing in his hand.

Sometimes, he would catch sight of his clothes, which were now nothing other than sewn patches and torn rags. He looked at every passing face with hatred and suspicion, as if he was seeing an abhorrent enemy, despite not having any enemy or friend. Sometimes children would cling onto his shoulder, and he would gently remove them with his hand. He did not have any care for the infants, he removed them like a deep sleeper removing the hand away from his shoulder which was trying to wake him up. This was his state until his stomach became empty from alcohol, and the intensity of its need would shackle his head. Then he would go to the pub. There, he would persistently and excessively drink until he would return to his former state.

He remained in this wretched condition for a few months, until the following incident occurred:

His poor wife became penniless, and unable to obtain any provisions. She would cry helplessly when she saw her son and daughter cry before her. Their tears would speak the sorrow which their tongues were silent about. Distressed and desperate, she had no alternative but to send both of her children to houses for some domestic labour. This way, they could feed themselves and give her some sustenance as well. However, now she saw them very little. Neither would she see her husband, other than on nights when the police were watching him and this was not often. Therefore, she became a lonely woman in her room and had no one to take care of her. Her only helper was her neighbour, an old woman who would come and see her from time to time. Whenever she parted from her she was left alone to remember those pleasant days in which she had lived her life, loving the merciful, compassionate and never ending bliss between her honourable husband and children, radiant stars in contentment beauty.

وهكذا، ما زالت الأيام والأعوام تأخذ من جسم الرجل ومن عقله حتى أصبح من يراه يرى ظلاً من الظلال المتنقلة، أو حلماً من الأحلام السارية، يمشي في طريقه مشية الذاهل المشدوه لا يكاد يشعر بشيءٍ مما حوله، ولا يتقي ما يعترض سبيله حتى يدانيه، ويقف حيناً بعد حينٍ فيدور بعينيه حول نفسه كأنما يفتش عن شيءٍ أضاعه وليس في يده شيء يضيع،

أو يقلب نظره في أثوابه وما في أثوابه غير الرقاع والخروق، وينظر إلى كل وجهٍ يقابله نظرةً شزراء كأنما يستقبل عدواً بغيضاً وليس له عدو ولا صديق، وربما تعلق بعض الصبيان بعاتقه فدفعهم عنه بيده دفعاً ليناً غير آبهٍ ولا محتفلٍ كما يدفع النائم المستغرق عن عاتقه يد موقظه، حتى إذا خلا جوفه من الخمر وهدأت سورتها في رأسه، انحدر إلى الحان، فلا يزال يشرب ويتزايد حتى يعود إلى ما كان عليه.

لم يزل هذا شأنه حتى حدثت منذ بضعة شهورٍ الحادثة الآتية:

عجزت تلك الزوجة المسكينة أن تجد سبيلاً إلى القوت، وأبكاها أن ترى ولدها وابنتها باكين بين يديها، تنطق دموعهما بما يصمت عنه لسانهما، فلم تر لها بداً من أن تركب تلك السبيل التي يركبها كل مضطر عديم، فأرسلتهما خادمين في بعض البيوت يقتاتان فيها ويقيتانها، فكانت لا تراهما إلا قليلاً، ولا ترى زوجها إلا في الليلة التي تغفل فيها عنه عيون الشرطة، وقلما تغفل عنه، فأصبحت وحيدةً في غرفتها لا مؤنس لها ولا معين إلا جارة عجوز تختلف إليها من حينٍ إلى حينٍ، فإذا فارقتها جارتها وخلت بنفسها ذكرت تلك الأيام السعيدة التي كانت تتقلب فيها في أعطاف العيش الناعم والنعمة السابغة بين زوجٍ كريمٍ وأولادٍ كالكواكب الزهر حسناً وبهاءً،

Then, she would remember how the master became the slave, how the employer became the employee and how the dignified become dishonoured and disgraced. She would recall how the diamond necklace, perfectly and marvellously sewn together upon the neck of time, had been broken and scattered. After, the scattered diamonds would appear as discarded pebbles upon the dusty land, trampled on by shoes, hooves and the feet of other animals. She would cry like a mad lover forsaken by his beloved, until it felt that she had drawn very close to death.

Nevertheless, she never fostered any hostility in her heart for the person who was responsible for her ruins and the misfortune of her children. Her heart never wished any day to become displeased with him or to abandon and leave him. This was because she was a highly dignified, gentle and virtuous woman. Such a woman never acts treacherously towards her husband, who has been afflicted with catastrophe, but she looks at him with kindness and affection like how a mother looks towards her small child.

If her husband was ill, she would spend the night besides him staying awake. If he returned injured, she would plaster and bandage his wounds. On some nights, when the bartender could not find any money with him to buy alcohol, he would simply throw him out. He would return to his house in distress and in need, and severely demand alcohol. His wife, unable to find any alternative solution, would give him money saved from the household rations, or she herself would buy him alcohol to calm him down and give peace to his soul. She did this to show kindness to him, trying her best to save and maintain his remaining intellect.

As if her burden was not enough, destiny made her bear a new heavy load. She felt some breath of life and some movement in her stomach. She realised she was pregnant, and would be bringing a new member to this house of misfortune. Upon realising, she screamed loudly saying, "O my Lord, have mercy on me, verily the tumbler has filled up, there is no more capacity in it for another drop." She continued to endure the pains of pregnancy like an ill woman, until the time came for her delivery. No one was with her, other than her old neighbour. Allah ﷻ helped her with her affair, and she gave birth. However, straight after she became severely ill with the fever of childbirth.

ثم تذكر كيف أصبح السيد مسوداً، والمخدوم خادماً، والعزيز الكريم ذليلاً مهيناً، وكيف انتثر ذلك العقد اللؤلئي المنظوم الذي كان حليةً بديعةً في جيد الدهر، ثم استحال بعد انتثاره إلى حصياتٍ منبوذاتٍ على سطح الغبراء، تطؤها النعال، وتدوسها الحوافر والأقدام. فتبكي بكاء الواله في إثر قومٍ ظاعنين حتى تتلف نفسها أو تكاد،

على أنها ما أضمرت قط في قلبها حقداً لذلك الإنسان الذي كان سبباً في شقائها وشقاء ولديها، لا حدثتها نفسها يوماً من الأيام بمغاضبته أو هجرانه، لأنها امرأة شريفة، والمرأة الشريفة لا تغدر بزوجها المنكوب، بل كانت تنظر إليه نظرة الأم الحنون إلى طفلها الصغير، فترحمه وتعطف عليه،

وتسهر بجانبه إن كان مريضاً، وتأسو جراحه إن عاد جريحاً، وربما طرده الخمار في بعض لياليه من حانه حينما لا يجد معه ثمن الشراب، فيعود إلى بيته ثائراً مهتاجاً يطلب الشراب طلباً شديداً فلا تجد بداً من أن تعطيه نفقة طعامها، أو تبتاع له من الخمر ما يسكن به نفسه رحمةً به وإبقاءً على تلك البقية الباقية من عقله.

وكأن الدهر لم يكفه ما وضع على عاتقها من الأثقال حتى أضاف إليها ثقلاً جديداً، فقد شعرت في يومٍ من أيامها بنسمةٍ تتحرك في أحشائها، فعلمت أنها حامل، وأنها ستأتي إلى دار الشقاء بشقي جديدٍ فهتفت صارخة: رحمتك اللهم فقد امتلأت الكأس حتى ما تسع قطرةً واحدة. وما زالت تكابد من آلام الحمل ما يجب أن تكابده امرأة مريضة منكوبة حتى جاءت ساعة وضعها فلم يحضرها أحد إلا جارتها العجوز، فأعانها الله على أمرها، فوضعت ثم مرضت بعد ذلك بحمى النفاس مرضاً شديداً.

Her poverty meant she could not find a doctor who would cure and treat her, as none were free. Hers was a town in which the doctors did not feel ashamed to ask the patient's family for their fee after the patient had died, even if it was their treatment which killed the patient. Thus, it would be impossible to find a charitable doctor here. Death started to slowly draw closer, until the mercy of Allah ﷻ reached her, and she died. At that time, she did not find besides her anyone other than her small baby who was attached to her breasts.

At the same time, her husband also entered in his mad state of addiction. He was in severe need of alcohol, finding his wife so that she could give it to him. He scanned his eyes around the room until he saw her lying down upon her straw mat. He saw the baby girl crying besides her, and presumed that she was a sleep. Drawing nearer to her, he pushed the child away and started shaking his wife aggressively. He felt and sensed no movement. Suddenly, he felt a fearful shudder slowly spread all over his joints until it reached his heart.

His senses returned and he slowly advanced towards her once again, staring at her intently until he saw the face of death staring at him with its gazing eyes.

Upon realising his loss, he recoiled in horror, and stepped back in fright and terror. However, worse was yet to come, as his ill thought steps landed unwillingly on his precious infant, crushing her chest and killing her instantly. She screamed one painful cry, after which she did not make a single movement ever again.

He ran out onto the streets like a rambling mad man, running frantically and screaming "Woe o misfortune! My daughter! My wife! Come back to me! Please take charge of me!" In despair, he hit his head on pillars and walls, pushing away all who came in his way, men and cattle.

Finally, he fell down exhausted on the floor, and started scraping the ground with his feet, sighing and screaming like a slaughtered animal. The people around him saw the agony and grief on his face, and rushed to console him even though he was a complete stranger to them.

For a brief moment, grief brought him back to his senses, showing him his terrible tragedy and loss. However, the shock was too great. Unable to face his dark reality, he quickly lost what remaining intellect he had left, and succumbed to madness.

Shortly after, he was locked away in a mental institution. May the Lord have mercy on him. May Allah ﷻ also shower mercy on his innocent infant, unfortunate children and martyred wife.

فلم تجد طبيباً يتصدق عليها بعلاجها، لأن البلد الذي لا يستحي أطباؤه أن يطالبوا أهل المريض بعد موته بأجرة علاجهم الذي قتله لا يمكن أن يوجد فيها طبيب محسن أو متصدق، فما زال الموت يدنو منها رويداً رويداً حتى أدركتها رحمة الله، فوافاها أجلها في ساعةٍ لا يوجد فيها بجانبها غير طفلتها الصغيرة عالقة بثديها.

في هذه الساعة دخل الرجل ثائراً مهتاجاً يطلب الشراب ويفتش عن زوجته لتأتي له منه بما يريد فدار بعينيه في أنحاء الغرفة حتى رآها ممددةً على حصيرها، ورأى ابنتها تبكي بجانبها فظنها نائمةً، فدنا منها ودفع الطفلة بعيداً عنها، وأخذ يحركها تحريكاً شديداً فلم يشعر بحركة، فرابه الأمر، وأحس برعدةٍ تتمشى في أعضائه حتى أصابت قلبه،

فبدأ صوابه يعود إليه شيئاً فشيئاً: فأكب عليها يحدق في وجهها تحديقاً شديداً، ويزحف نحوها رويداً رويداً حتى رأى شبح الموت يحدق إليه من عينيها الشاخصتين الجامدتين.

فتراجع خوفاً وذعراً، فوطىء في تراجعه صدر ابنته فأنت أنةً مؤلمةً لم تتحرك بعدها حركةً واحدةً،

فصرخ صرخةً شديدةً وقال: واشقاءاه واشقاءاه؟ وخرج هائماً على وجهه يعدو في الطرق ويضرب رأسه بالعمد والجدران، ويدفع كل ما يجد في طريقه من إنسانٍ أو حيوانٍ ويصيح: ابنتي! زوجتي، هلموا إليّ؟ أدركوني!

حتى أعيا فسقط على الأرض وأخذ يفحص التراب برجليه ويئن وأنين الذبيح، والناس من حوله آسفون عليه، لا لأنهم يعرفونه، بل لأنهم قرأوا في وجهه آيات شقائه.

فكانت تلك اللحظة القصيرة التي استفاق فيها من ذهوله الطويل سبباً في ضياع ما بقي من عقله.

وما هي إلا ساعة أو ساعتان حتى أصبح مقيداً مغلولاً في قاعةٍ من قاعات البيمارستان، فوارحمتاه له ولزوجته الشهيدة ولطفلته الصريعة ولأولاده المشردين البؤساء.

The Reward / Al-Jazā (Translation)

She was sitting at the corner of the lake so that she could fill up her water pot. The water was still and motionless, as if there was a layer of sparkling ice spread over its surface. She disliked to break this delicate and glossy mirror. To a woman, there is nothing more beloved to her than a mirror. She set her eyes upon it, and she saw upon its surface a handsome white face gazing back at her with a charming and entrancing look. She smiled back at him and he continued to smile at her. She speculated that certainly it was the face of her beautiful fiancé who was from the village. Her fiancé had always been infatuated with her.

She enjoyed this sight for a moment. Then, with fear, she realised that she was seeing another reflection in the water, a man who was not her fiancé. She became too frightened to look behind her, and drew her hand towards the water. She filled up her water pot and hastened to take it away.

The man who was standing advanced towards her and said to her, "O my respectable lady would you allow me to assist you with your water pot?" She turned back and discovered that he was both young and handsome. He was wearing good clothes, a stranger from the cities. She did not recognise him, and did not know that this land could give birth to the likes of him. She became doubtful about him and her face started to blush out of nervousness and shyness. Not saying anything, she picked up her pot and departed.

***

Susan and her paternal uncle's son Gilbert grew up together in one house, like two similar flowers grow and blossom together upon one twig. As a baby she drank milk with him, as a child she played with him and as a young lady she loved him. All times and eras had passed by them, filled with mutual happiness. Nevertheless, neither of them had ever obtained any castles, gardens, sofa sets, beds, horses, carriages, cups, casks, lutes, stringed musical instruments, flashing gold, sparkling diamonds, embroidered garments or decorated robes.

الجزاء

(مترجمة)

جلست على ضفة البحيرة لتملأ جرتها، وكان الماء ساكناً هادئاً كأنما قد امتدت فوق سطحه طبقة لامعة من الجليد؛ فعزّ عليها أن تكسر بيدها هذه المرآة الناعمة الصقيلة، ولا شيء أحب إلى المرأة من المرآة؛ فظلت تقلب نظرها فيها فلمحت في سفحتها وجهاً أبيض رائقاً ينظر إليها نظراً عذباً فاتراً، فابتسمت له، فابتسم لها، فعلمت أنه الوجه الذي افتتن به خطيبها القروري الجميل.

أنست بهذا المنظر ساعة، ثم راعها أن رأت بجانب خيالها في الماء خيالاً آخر فتبينته فإذا به خيال رجلٍ فذعرت، ولكنها لم تلتفت وراءها ومدت يدها إلى الماء فملأت جرتها، ثم نهضت لتحملها،

فتقدم إليها ذلك الواقف بجانبها وقال لها: هل تأذنين لي يا سيدتي أن أعينك على حمل جرتك؟ فالتفت فإذا فتىً حضري غريب، حسن الصورة والبزة، لا تعرفه، ولا تعرف أن هذه الأرض مما تنبت مثله، فرابها أمره، واتقد وجهها حياءً وخجلاً، ولم تقل شيئاً، واستلقت جرتها ومضت في سبيلها.

***

نشأت سوزان وابن عمها جلبرت في بيتٍ واحدٍ كما تنشأ الزهرتان المتعانقتان في مغرسٍ واحدٍ، فرضعت معه وليدةً، ولعبت معه طفلةً، وأحبته فتاةً، ومرت بهما في جميع تلك الأدوار سعادة لم يستمدها من القصور والبساتين والأرائك والأسرة، والجياد والمركبات، والأكواب والدنان، والمزاهر والعيدان، والذاهب اللامع واللؤلؤ الساطع، والأثواب المطرزة والغلائل المرصعة،

This was simply because both of them were two poor villagers. However, both obtained happiness and bliss from the rising and the setting of the sun, the coming and the going of the night, the sparkling stars in the bright sky, the greenery and the fresh vegetation of the earth, the long stays upon the distinguished rocky mountain above the motionless lake, the beautiful camping next to plants above soft grass under the shade of trees full of leaves, the rejuvenating humming of the birds, the songs of the shepherds, the noise of animals grazing at day and at night and from the crying of the waterwheel in the morning and in the evenings.

Their pure and noble love brightened up sad hearts and enlightened both of them. This love illuminated dark hearts and would become the feathers for broken wings. It would be the only comfort left when everything else in this world had come to pass, and the only satisfaction when everything else seemed to be lost. The woman of the lake was blessed with this love, until that fateful day at the lake.

***

A woman does not recognise her existence and her presence until she appears in the eyes and in the hearts of men. If, however, one area of the land had become empty from the faces that look and observe, or whether, from the corners of the ribs, the heart stopped throbbing and became desolate, then certainly her existence would be worthless in her eyes. However, if behind her a thousand eyes were looking, then certainly she would still glance at that star from amongst the stars of the sky which is adorning her with the sight of love. If, from any corner of the earth she hears a call of love, then she feels content over this new love and her heart fills up with happiness and prosperity.

Thus, this young woman returned to her house in a very happy state, her eyes were cold, she felt pride and a sense of self-importance. This was not because her new love had usurped her heart in place of her old love. Neither was this because her heart intended to attach her life with someone else other than of her fiancé, but because she had found in its way a new proof of her beauty which made her feel elevated.

لأنهما كانا قرويين فقيرين، بل استمداها من مطلع الشمس ومغربها، وإقبال الليل وإدباره، وتلألؤ السماء بنجومها الزاهرة والأرض بأعشابها الناضرة، ومن الوقفات الطوال فوق الصخور البارزة على ضفاف البحيرة الهادئة، والجلسات الحلوة الجميلة على الأعشاب الناعمة تحت ظلال الأشجار الوارفة، ومن سماع أناشيد الحياة وأغاني الرعاة وضوضاء السائمة في غدوها ورواحها وبكاء النواعير في مسائها وصباحها،

ومن الحب الطاهر الشريف الذي يشرق على القلوب الحزينة فيسعدها، والأفئدة المظلمة فينيرها، والأجنحة الكسيرة فيريشها، والذي هو العزاء الوحيد عن كل فائتٍ في هذه الحياة، والسلوى عن كل مفقود، ولم يزل هذا شأنها حتى كان يوم البحيرة.

***

لا تعرف المرأة لها وجوداً إلا في عيون الرجال وقلوبهم، فلو خلت رقعة الأرض من وجوه الناظرين، أو أقفرت حنايا الضلوع من خوافق القلوب، لأصبح الوجود والعدم في نظرها سواء، ولو أن وراءها ألف عينٍ تنظر إليها ثم لمحت في كوكبٍ من كواكب السماء نظرة حب، أو سمعت في زاويةٍ من زوايا الأرض أنة وجدٍ لأعجبها ذلك الغرام الجديد وملأ قلبها غبطةً وسروراً.

فقد عادت الفتاة إلى بيتها طيبة النفس قريرة العين مزهوةً مختالة، لا لأن حباً جديداً حل في قلبها محل الحب القديم، ولا لأن نفسها حدثتها أن تصل حياتها بحياة أحدٍ غير خطيبها، بل لأنها وجدت في طريقها برهاناً جديداً على جمالها فأعجبها،

She continued to visit the lake with her water pot, without any fear or doubt. She also saw that city gentleman mornings and evenings. He would greet her or he would smile at her. Either he would enquire directions from her or he would request her for drinking water. At times he would present her with a beautiful flower or occasionally whisper into her ear a gentle and sweet word. This continued until he finally managed to sit besides her for a little while beneath the shade of a lonely mountain. This moment marked the last pledge to her old life and the new pledge to her future life.

***

Sir Gustav Rostand had come to this village a few days ago in order to inspect his crops, as he did from time to time. He had built a beautiful palace two hours distance away from the lake, and enjoyed staying in it for a few days, before returning to Nice. However, this time, when he saw the young woman besides the lake in the mornings, he became attracted to her beauty. He nurtured his love in her heart and persistently whispered magical words in her ear. He adorned her neck and wrists with pearls and diamonds, and presented to her a beautiful sketch of city life, in its best and most beautiful form possible. He continued to give her very high hopes in respect to her present life and her future with him, eventually she submitted to him. She readily bowed down to his affections, how every woman kneels down when her guardians become careless of her. In reality, she had entrusted her destiny to the fangs of wolves.

***

A short distance away, Susan's fiancé Gilbert woke up at the same time he did every morning. As normal, he went to his cow and opened her rope. He then called Susan to take the cow with him towards the pasture and grazing land. She did not answer him, so he ascended to her room in the attic. He intended to wake her up, but did not find her there. He asked his mother about her whereabouts but she did not know anything more than him. He presumed that she had gone out to complete some jobs and would return later. He waited for her for a very long time but unfortunately she did not return. Now he had fallen into doubt and had returned the cow to its barn. He came out and started searching for her at every possible location, and asked her whereabouts from all people who were coming and going. He did not find anyone who could guide him to her. He stayed and inquired about her until the night shadowed him. Wearily, he returned upset and distressed, convinced that he was the most unfortunate person upon the face of the earth.

فكانت لا تزال تختلف بعد ذلك بجرتها إلى البحيرة غير خائفةٍ ولا مرتابة، فترى ذلك السيد الحضري في غدوها أو رواحها يحييها أو يبتسم لها، أو يسائلها عن طريق، أو يستسقيها شربة ماء، أو يقدم إليها زهرةً جميلةً، أو يلقي في أذنها كلمةً عذبة، حتى استطاع في يوم من الأيام أن يجلس بجانبها لحظةً قصيرةً في ظل صخرةٍ منفردةٍ فكانت هذه اللحظة آخر عهدها بحياتها القديمة، وأول عهدها بحياتها الجديدة.

***

هبط المركيز جوستاف روستان هذه الأرض منذ أيامٍ لتفقد مزارعه فيها، وكان لا يزال يختلف إليها من حينٍ إلى حينٍ فيقضي في قصره الجميل الذي بناه فيها على بعد ساعتين من البحيرة بضعة أيام، ثم يعود إلى بلدته (نيس)، حتى رأى هذه المرة هذه الفتاة في بعض غدواته إلى ضفاف البحيرة فاستلهاه حسنها، وما زال بها يفيض على قلبها من حبه، وعلى أذنها من سحره، وعلي جيدها ومعصميها من لآلئه وجواهره، ويصور لها جمال الحياة الحضرية في أجمل صورها وأبهاها، ويمنيها الأماني الكبار في حاضرها ومستقبلها، حتى أذعنت واستقادت وخضعت للتي تخضع لها كل أنثى نامت عنها عين راعيها، وأسلمها حظها إلى أنياب الذئاب.

***

استيقظ الفتى جلبرت في الساعة التي يستيقظ فيها من صباح كل يومٍ فعمد إلى بقرته فحل عقالها، ثم هتف باسم سوزان يدعوها إلى الذهاب معه إلى المرعى فلم تجبه، فصعد إلى غرفتها في سطح المنزل ليوقظها فلم يجدها، فسأل عنها أمه فلم تعلم من أمرها أكثر مما يعلم، فظن أنها خرجت لقضاء بعض الشؤون، ثم تعود، فلبث ينتظرها وقتاً طويلاً فلم تعد، فرابه الأمر وأعاد البقرة إلى معتلفها، وخرج يفتش عنها في كل مكانٍ، ويسائل عنها الناس جميعاً، غاديهم ورائحهم، فلم يجد من يدله عليها حتى أظله الليل، فعاد حزيناً مكتئباً لا يرى أن أحداً على وجه الأرض أعظم لوعةً منه، ولا أشقى،

Upon entering his humble home, he saw his mother, withdrawn, standing head down in a dilapidated room, scraping the soil with a wooden stick. He drew closer to her. She raised her head to him and asked "Where were you O Gilbert?"

He said "I was finding Susan in every location possible but I could not find her."

She cast upon him a sight full of pain and tears and she said "O son it is better for you not to wait for her anymore after this day."

Gilbert shuddered and said "For what reason should I not wait for her anymore?"

She replied "Recently our neighbour, has come and informed me that, for a few nights, she has been continuously witnessing that Susan has been coming and going to the corners of the lake, in order to meet a strange gentleman from the town who is not from here. I am presuming that it is Sir Gustav Rostand, the owner of the fields adjoining ours, and the red castle nearby. She also told me that she saw Susan last night, after midnight, mounted upon a grey horse behind Sir Gustav Rostand, riding towards his red castle. Clearly she has ran away with him."

Gilbert screamed out aloud, his spirit was close to departing from his body, and he fell down, unconscious.

His worried mother remained sitting beside him the whole night. At times she cried over him and at other times she would wipe his forehead with water, until he regained consciousness at sunrise. Perplexed, his tired eyes examined his surroundings. Then he saw his mother, she had her head down and was crying and sighing. Seeing her, he remembered everything, and lowered his head with grief.

After a while he raised his head, and put his hand on his mother's shoulder. He asked "O mother why are you crying?"

She replied "O my son, I am crying for you and for her."

He said "If you are crying then cry over someone else besides me, I am not upset neither am I the one who is going to cry." He continued "Verily I loved this young woman because she had loved me. Now, my heart has become hard as a rock. There is nothing which is going to incline me to her anymore. Neither is there any return for me to her after this day." Then, he wiped from his cheek the last tear flowing upon it. He stood up and advanced towards his cow, took its rope and went with it towards the grazing field all alone.

***

فرأى أمه قابعةً في كسر البيت، مطرقةً برأسها تفلي التراب بعودٍ في يدها، فدنا منها، فرفعت رأسها إليه وقالت له: أين كنت يا جلبرت؟

قال: فتشت عن سوزان في كل مكانٍ فلم أجدها،

فألقت عليه نظرةً مملوءةً حزناً ودموعاً وقالت: خير لك يا بني ألا تنتظرها بعد اليوم.

فانتفض انتفاضةً شديدةً وقال: لماذا؟

قالت: قد دخلت عليّ الساعة جارتنا فلانةٌ فحدثتني أنها ما زالت تراها منذ ليالي تختلف إلى البحيرة للاجتماع على ضفافها بفتًى حضريٍ غريبٍ عن هذه المدرة أحسبه المركيز (جوستاف روستان) صاحب هذه المزارع التي تلينا والقصر الأحمر الذي يليها، وقالت لي: إنها رأتها ليلة أمس، بعد منتصف الليل، راكبةً وراءه على فرسٍ أشهب يعدو بها في طريق القصر الأحمر، ولا بد أنها فرت معه،

فصرخ جلبرت صرخةً جادت لها نفسه أو كادت، وخر في مكانه صعقاً،

فلم تزل أمه جاثيةً بجانبه الليل كله تبكي عليه مرةً وتمسح جبينه بالماء أخرى حتى استفاق في مطلع الفجر، فنظر حوله نظرةً حائرةً فرأى أمه مكبةً على وجهها تبكي وتنتحب، فذكر كل ذلك فأطرق هنيهة،

ثم رفع رأسه ووضع يده على عاتقها وسألها: ما بكاؤك يا أماه؟

قالت: أبكي عليك يا بني وعليها،

قال: إن كنت باكيةً فابك على غيري، أما أنا فلست بحزينٍ، ولا باكٍ، فقد كنت أحببت هذه الفتاة لأنها كانت تحبني، وقد استحال قلبي الآن إلى صخرةٍ عاتيةٍ لا ينال منها شيء فلا رجعة لي إليها بعد اليوم، ثم مسح عن خده آخر دمعةٍ كانت تنحدر فيه، وقام إلى بقرته فأخذ بزمامها ومضى بها إلى المزرعة وحده.

***

Certainly that poor young soul had not been true to his heart. He did not forget Susan, neither had his heart forgotten the burning sensation of her love. However, his heart felt angry like a deserted lover, and he felt withdrawn from the extreme love which he had been clinging onto. When he reached the fields and sent his cow to graze in the pasture, he saw the sun slowly but gradually rising from its location, sending its scarlet sapphire rays all over the dark universe. This made the earth's layers brighter, flourishing its vegetation and soil. He liked the sight of this pure brightness upon the earth, and turned his eyes to examine its eastern and western hemisphere/ the horizon dazzling his eyes with its brightness. He felt that certainly the west had raised its own sun like the east had raised one. However, upon close scrutiny, he discovered that the sun was actually one big tablet, consisting of a round yellow mirror, playing the rays of the sun like how the rays play with the universe, this is why the light was extremely bright. He quickly moved his eyes back on himself and put his hand on his left ribs as if he was stopping his heart from escaping. This was because he had realised that this yellow mirrored tablet was flashing from one of the domes belonging to the domes of the red castle.

Now he realised that his heart had lied to him. Indeed, it was still glowing with love, lighting his forehead, and creating a raging blaze of fire which was tearing his heart into pieces. That raging fire penetrated into his heart the way death penetrates into life. Thus, his eyes began shedding countless tears, and he began crying and sighing very painfully. The winds in the air, the waves of the ocean, the vegetation in the fields and the cattle in the grazing land were all hearing and answering his cries. He cried until he heard the voices of the Shepard and the cattle, then he wiped away and withheld his tears. He lowered his head to his knees and in his imagination, with his pain and sadness, he went wherever Allah ﷻ wanted him to go.

He remained like this day after day, the poor man could not benefit his soul anymore. His sorrows took him very far in his beliefs, and severely tormented him, morning and night. For anyone who saw him in the street, he appeared as an upset and distressed individual who had lost his senses and lived in emotional isolation. He wandered like a madman at nightfall and all hours of the day, in between bushes, lake sides and under high mountains. He bonded with the wild cattle like an old friend, but if a human was to draw near to him, he would run away from them like they were wild beasts. He would descend to the water springs with the deer and gazelles, and when they had departed he would also leave with them.

لقد كذبت المسكين نفسه، فإنه ما سلا سوزان، ولا هدأت عن قلبه لوعة حبها، ولكنها الغضبة التي يغضبها المحب المهجور تخيل إليه أنه قد نفض يده من المحب أشد ما يكون به عالقاً، فإنه ما وصل إلى المزرعة وأرسل سائمته في مرعاها حتى رأى كوكب الشمس يتناهض من مطلعه قليلاً قليلاً، ويرسل أشعته الياقوتية الحمراء على هذه الكائنات فتنير ظلامها، وتجلو صفحتها وتترقرق ما بين خضرائها وغبرائها، فأعجبه منظر هذه الطبيعة المتلألئة بين يدي هذا الكواكب المنير، ودار بنظره في الفضاء من مشرقه إلى مغربه فلمح في الأفق الغربي بارقاً يخطف البصر بلألائه، فخيل إليه أن المغرب قد أطلع في أفقه شمساً كتلك التي أطلعها المشرق حتى تبينه فإذا هو لوح كبير من الزجاج أصفر مستديرٌ تعابثه أشعة الشمس فيما تعابث من الكائنات فيلتمع التماعاً شديداً، فاسترد بصره إليه سريعاً، ووضع يده على يسرى أضالعه كأنما يحول بين قلبه وبين الفرار، لأنه علم أن ذلك اللوح الزجاجي الأصفر إنما يلوح في برجٍ من أبراج القصر الأحمر.

هنا علم أن نفسه قد كذبته فيما حدثته، وأن تلك البارقة التي كانت تضيء ما بين جنبيه من الحب قد استحالت إلى جذوة نارٍ مشتعلةٍ تقضم فؤاده قضماً، وتمشي في نفسه مشي الموت في الحياة، فأطلق لعبرته سبيلها، وأنشأ يئن أنيناً محزناً تردده الرياح في جوها، والأمواج في بحرها، والأعشاب في مغارسها، والسائمة في مرابضها، حتى سمع أصوات الرعاة وضوضاء السائمة فكفكف عبراته، وأسلم رأسه إلى ركبتيه وذهب مع همومه وأحزانه إلى حيث شاء الله أن تذهب.

هكذا لم ينتفع المسكين بنفسه بعد اليوم فقد ذهب من الحزن إلى أبعد مذاهبه حتى نال منه ما لم ينل كر الغداة ومر العشي، فأصبح من يراه في طريقه يرى رجلاً بائساً منكوباً مشرد العقل، مشترك اللب، مذهوباً به كل مذهبٍ، يهيم على وجهه آناء الليل وأطراف النهار بين الغابات والحرجات، وفوق ضفاف الأنهار وتحت مشارف الجبال، يأنس بالوحوش أنس العشير بعشيره، ويفر من الناس إن دنوا منه فرار الإنسان من الوحش، ويرد المناهل مع الظباء واليعافير، ثم يصدر إذا صدرت معها،

At times, his walking took him very far, and he would reach the gardens of the red castle without even noticing. When he would see the domes in front of him, he would get extremely frightened and scream out aloud. Then, he would turn back and return to his village without any care. A lot of the time, Gilbert's mother used to spend complete days in search of him, carrying his food in her hand. She would search for him at every possible location until she would see him either sitting in between stones besides the river bank or in the ravine. Then she would put food in front of him, as Gilbert had no clue of her presence. Then she would raise her hands towards the sky, in humility and distress, she would beg Allah ﷻ through her tears and her sighs to return her only son. Then she would return to her village.

***

The night had not passed but only a little, as Susan was sitting down and looking at the lake from out of the window of her castle. She would glance at the bed of her daughter at one instance, and in the other instance she would look into the sky. It was the night of the full moon and she was saying,

"O the traveling moon in the midst of the sky, here I am seeing you complete for the twenty fourth time. So is my fiancé Gustav going to return to me? O moon, is he going to see you with me the way he had before?

O bright star, what an excellent helper were you for my frightful nights, for my sadness and for my grief. So do you have the power to tell me about Gustav? Do you know his station and when is he going to come back? Are we going to meet soon so that your favour upon me would become complete?

Tell me about him, does he remember me the way I remember him? Has he safeguarded my pledge the way I have safeguarded his? Does he sit down with you from time to time so that he could ask you about me the way I ask you about him? If he does, then say to him that his daughter is extremely beautiful. The beauty of her modest smiles is like the smiles of beautiful women. Her fairness is like that clear white drop which is upon the lily flower radiant from the rays of the sun which is spreading light. O star, say to him that she does not call any other name apart from yours. She does not smile at any other picture save yours. Certainly, if he saw her, he would not even require any mirror anymore to see his own reflection. This is because he will see his face in her face, their similarity is like two dolls which have been created with one mould."

وربما ترامى به السير أحياناً إلى أفنية القصر الأحمر من حيث لا يشعر فإذا رأى أبراجه بين يديه ذعر ذعراً شديداً وصاح صيحةً عظيمة، وانكفأ راجعاً إلى قريته لا يلوي على شيء،، وكثيراً ما قضت أمه النهار كله حاملةً على يدها الطعام تفتش عنه في كل مكانٍ حتى تراه ملقًى بين الأحجار على ضفة نهر أو في سفح جبل فتضع الطعام بين يديه من حيث لا يشعر بمكانها ثم ترفع يديها إلى السماء ضارعةً متخشعةً تسأل الله بدموعها وزفراتها أن يرد إليها وحيدها، ثم تعود أدراجها.

***

مضى الليل إلا أقله وسوزان جالسة إلى نافذة قصرها المشرفة على النهر، تلتفت إلى سرير ابنتها مرةً وتقلب وجهها في السماء أخرى، وكان القمر في ليلة تمه، فظلت تناجيه وتقول:

أيها القمر الساري في كبد السماء ها أنذا أراك في ليلة تمك وحدي للمرة الرابعة والعشرين، فهل يعود إلي خطيبي (جوستاف) فينظر إليك معي كما كان يفعل من قبل؟

لقد كنت لي أيها الكوكب المنير نعم المعين في ليالي الموحشة على همومي وأحزاني، فهل تستطيع أن تحدثني عن (جوستاف) أين مكانه ومتى يعود؟ وهل نلتقي قريباً فتتم بذلك يدك عندي؟

حدثني عنه.. هل يذكرني كما أذكره، وهل يحفظ عهدي كما أحفظ عهده؟ وهل يجلس إليك حيناً فيسائلك عني كما أسألك عنه؟ فإن فعل، فقل له: إن ابنته جميلةٌ جداً جمال الابتسامة الحائرة في فم الحسناء، وبيضاء بياض القطرة الصافية في الزنبقة الناصعة تحت الأشعة الساطعة، وقل له: إنها لا تهتف باسمٍ غير اسمه، ولا تبتسم لرسم غير رسمه، وإنه إن رآها أغنته رؤيتها عن المرآة المجلوة، لأنه يرى صورته في وجهها كما تتشابه الدميتان المصبوبتان في قالبٍ واحدٍ.

Susan used to keep on secretly talking to the moon like this until it descended towards the west. Then, she would bid her farewells to it, saying lovingly "O beautiful friend, I will see you tomorrow." She would advance to her daughter's bed, lean over and softly kiss her on her forehead with her evening kiss. Then she would go to her bed. The slumber of sleep would play upon her eyelids until her dreams would entrust her towards her hopes and happiness. Hence, in her dream she would see Gustav returned from his journey. She and her daughter would be waiting for him at the door of the castle, and Gustav would descend from his carriage to hug them both, pressing them to his chest very tightly. He would then continue to kiss them both, crying out of happiness and joy.

Whilst dreaming, she was shaken awake by an excited hand. Promptly she woke up to discover that it was noon and that the sun has ascended. She saw her maid standing next to her head laughing from happiness, declaring "O lady! Good news! My master is here!" Susan, in delight, said "Praise be upon you O Lord! Verily my dream has come true!" quickly, she ran towards her dressing room and changed her clothes.

She entered Gustav's room smiling and elated, holding their daughter in her hand. She saw him standing in the middle of the room, leaning behind his chair. She rushed towards him.

When she drew closer to him, her happiness to see him quickly became shadowed when she gazed upon his cold face. It contained no love or elation at her presence, and he was not even moved by her smiling before him. It certainly was him, yet she did not recognise his face, devoid of all affection, bleak and harsh. She stopped in her tracks, confused and disturbed, and nervously held out her hand to shake his.

Reluctantly, he shook her hand. Despite his daughter continuously smiling at him and stretching her arms towards him, he did not even look at her face. Then he coldly asked "Are you still living in my castle since that day?" It was his first word to her, filling her with terror, fright and confusion.

Perplexed, she asked "O master where would you like to see me?"

He replied "In this castle the way I had left you, however now I am thinking that you should not remain here after this day."

She asked "Why?"

ولم تزل تناجي القمر بمثل هذا النجاء حتى رأته ينحدر إلى مغربه فودعته وداعاً جميلاً، وقالت: إلى الغد يا صديقي العزيز... ثم قامت إلى سرير ابنتها فحنت عليها برفقٍ وقبلتها في جبينها قبلة المساء، وذهبت إلى مضجعها، وما هو إلا أن عبثت بجفنها السنة الأولى من النوم، حتى أسلمتها أحلامها إلى أمانيها وآمالها، فرأت كأن (جوستاف) قد عاد من سفره فاستقبلته هي وابنتها على باب القصر، فنزل من مركبته وضمهما معاً إلى صدره ضماً شديداً، وظل يقبلهما ويبكي فرحاً وسروراً.

فإنها لمستغرقة في حلمها هذا إذ شعرت بيدٍ تحركها فانتبهت فإذا صدر النهار قد علا، وإذا خادمتها واقفة على رأسها ضاحكة متطلقة تقول لها: بشراك يا سيدتي فقد حضر سيدي، فاستطيرت فرحاً وسروراً وقالت: أحمدك اللهم فقد صدقت أحلامي، وأسرعت إلى غرفة ملابسها فبدلت أثوابها،

ثم دخلت عليه في غرفته باسمةً متهللةً تحمل ابنتها على يدها، فرأته واقفاً في وسط الغرفة متكئاً على كرسي بين يديه، فهرعت إليه،

ولكنها ما دنت منه حتى تراجعت حائرةً مدهوشةً لأنها رأت أمامها رجلاً لا تعرفه ولا عهد لها به من قبل، لا بل هو بعينه، ولكنها رأت وجهاً صامتاً متحجراً لا تلمع فيه بارقة ابتسام ولا تجري فيه نظرة بشاشةٍ فأنكرته؛ إلا أنها تماسكت قليلاً ومدت إليه يدها تحييه،

فمد إليها يده بتثاقلٍ وفتورٍ كأنما ينقلها من مكانها نقلاً، ولم يلق على وجه الطفلة، وكانت تبتسم إليه وتمد نحوه ذراعيها، نظرةً واحدةً، وكانت أول كلمة قالها لها: أباقية أنت في القصر حتى اليوم؟

فازدادت دهشةً وحيرةً، ولم تفهم ماذا يريد وقالت له: وأين كنت تريد أن تراني يا سيدي؟

قال: في هذا القصر، كما تركتك ولكني أظن أنك لا تستطيعين البقاء فيه بعد اليوم.

قالت: لماذا؟

He answered "Because my wife is coming here today and she would not like to see in this castle anyone who would distress her."

She felt all her blood race to her beating heart in an instance. The rest of her body felt numb, not wanting to scream or sigh at the catastrophe before her, merely staring at him, dumbstruck and disturbed. Then she turned to her daughter and asked "And what do you consider about your daughter?"

He said "O lady, she is not my daughter, neither do I have a son. This is because I have only been married for three days. Therefore, take your daughter with you and live with her the way you please. I have left for you this bag on the desk, take it and seek help from its contents in terms of your livelihood." After saying this, he left her and departed.

Susan did not glance at the desk even once. She walked on enduring these harsh words until she reached her bedroom. It was here that she burst out crying and said, "O misfortune, verily he has paid me the price for my dignity and my respect." After this, she fell down unconscious, and did not regain consciousness until night. When she opened her eyes, she saw her daughter crying in the arms of her maid. The maid was also crying when she saw the infant crying. Susan hugged her baby girl and attached her to her chest for a brief moment. Then she stood up and went to her dressing room. She searched and took out her village clothes which she had worn three days before she entered into this castle. She had hidden these clothes from the eyes of people out of shame and embarrassment. She then took off her extravagant clothes and put her old clothes on. She did not leave any diamonds or any bangles around her wrists and neck, but took them off and threw them at her feet. She took hold of her child and left under the veil of the night. She was staggering in her walk as if she was walking upon uneven sand.

Susan had barely exited the castle when she stopped, still at that location where she and her daughter had been standing a couple of hours ago, waiting for her fiancé Gustav in her dream. At once from a distance, she saw a decorated carriage heading towards the castle, carrying Sir Gustav and his new wife. She closed her eyes and hid under the wall of the castle. After that she walked on her way.

***

قال: لأن زوجتي قادمة إليه اليوم وربما كانت لا تحب أن ترى فيه من يزعجه وجودها.

هنالك شعرت أن جميع ما كان ينبعث في عروقها من الدم قد تراجع كله دفعةً واحدةً إلى قلبها، فأصبح وحده الواجب الخفاق من دون أعضائها وأوصالها جميعاً، ولكن المصيبة إذا عظمت خلت عن البكاء والأنين، فلم تصح ولم تضطرب، بل نظرت إليه نظرةً طويلةً هادئة، ثم التفتت إلى ابنتها وقالت له: وما ترى في ابنتك هذه؟

قال ليس لي ابنة أيتها السيدة ولا ولد لي، لأني لم أتزوج إلا منذ ثلاثة أيام، فخذي ابنتك معك وعيشي معها حيث تشائين، وقد تركت لك هذا الكيس على المنضدة فخذيه واستعيني به على عيشك، وتركها ومضى.

لم تلق على المنضدة نظرةً واحدةً، ومشت تتحامل على نفسها حتى وصلت إلى غرفتها، وهنالك انفجرت باكية، وقالت: واسوأتاه! إنه يعطيني ثمن عرضي، وسقطت مغشياً عليها، فلم تستفق حتى أظلها الليل، ففتحت عينيها، فإذا ابنتها تبكي بين ذراعي الخادمة، وإذا الخادمة تبكي لبكائها، فضمتها إلى صدرها ساعة، ثم قامت إلى غرفة ملابسها وأخذت تفتش عن أثوابها القروية التي دخلت بها هذا القصر منذ ثلاثة أعوام، وكانت تخفيها عن أعين الناس حياءً وخجلاً، فخلعت أثوابها ولبستها، ولم تبق في معصميها ولا في جيدها لؤلؤةً ولا ماسةً إلا ألقت بها تحت قدميها. واحتملت طفلتها وخرجت تحت ستار الليل تترنح في مشيتها كأنما تمشي على رملةٍ ميثاء.

وما جاوزت عتبة الباب ووصلت إلى الموضع الذي كانت واقفة فيه في حلمها هي وابنتها منذ ساعات تنظر خطيبها حتى لمحت على البعد مركبةً فخمةً مقبلةً على القصر تحمل المركيز وامرأة بجانبه! فأغمضت عينيها وتسللت تحت جدار القصر، ومضت في سبيلها.

***

Only Allah ﷻ knew the weight of her grief and sadness. She had been hatefully thrown out from the castle, that castle of which she once thought herself queen. She was thrown out, cursed by that individual whom she believed had loved her dearly from all people and that she had given preference to. In that single second, this chaste young woman, a woman with a modest fiancé had changed into a prostitute with an illegitimate child. It became extremely difficult for her to return to her old house due to her shame and guilt. It was hard for her to face the two individuals who had done great favours upon her and loved her dearly. In return, she had been bad with them, and deceived them both. Every path was closed for her and everything between her and the entire world had darkened. There was no one who had mercy for her, in the world or in the heavens.

This is what she had been contemplating in her heart whilst anxiously walking under the walls of the castle, knowing no place or destination to go. As she was walking, she saw the head of her daughter swaying out of sleep. She ascended to a nearby hill top besides a flowing river, laid down her daughter on the grass, and placed her shawl on top of her. She then sat down besides her, and contemplated on what would be her outcome.

Certainly she was sitting in this location and verily the night was quiet. Every single thing was stationary other than the light of the moon, which was bursting into the atmosphere. The gusts of wind were creating waves upon the surface of the water. At once, she felt as if she heard near her, someone calling her name with a very low and a weak voice. When she looked, she saw a black thing lying down between two rocks nearby the lake, like a human being sleeping. She became frightened and scared. She then heard the same voice again. Considering the matter important, she rose and advanced closer towards the black shape.

There she saw a man dressed in poor clothing, lying down on his back and looking sharply towards the wall of the castle. When she scrutinized his gaze, she discovered that his eyes were glued to the window of her bedroom, where she used to sit every night in the castle. She trembled in amazement. She saw that he was holding a white thing on top of his heart very tightly. It was a piece of white paper. She kneeled over to see what thing he was pressing to his chest. She discovered that it was the sketch of her picture, and the being holding it was no other than her old love Gilbert, who was now very close to his death. He was persistently calling out her name with a low and dismayed voice, as if the voices of the deceased coming out from the depth of the graves due to being tortured. He was calling "Goodbye O Susan, goodbye O Susan."

لا يعلم إلا الله ما كانت تحمل هذه الفتاة المسكينة بين جنبيها في تلك الساعة من همومٍ وأحزانٍ، فقد خرجت مطرودةً من القصر التي كانت تظن منذ ساعات أنها صاحبته، وتولى طردها من كانت تزعم في نفسها أنها أحب الناس إليه، وآثرهم عنده، واستحالت في ساعةٍ واحدةٍ من فتاةٍ شريفةٍ ذات خطيبٍ شريفٍ إلى امرأةٍ عاهرةٍ ذات ولدٍ مريبٍ، وأصبح مستحيلاً عليها أن تعود إلى بيتها القديم بعارها فترى وجه ذينك الشخصين الذين أحسنا إليها كثيراً وأحباها حباً جماً فأساءت إليهما وغدرت بهما، فقد سدت دونها السبل، وأظلم ما بينها وبين العالم بأجمعه، فما من رحمةٍ لها في الأرض، ولا في السماء.

ذلك ما كانت تحدث نفسها به، وهي سائرة تحت سوار القصر سير الذاهل المشدوه لا تعرف لها مذهباً ولا مضطرباً، حتى رأت رأس ابنتها يميل به الكرى، فمشت إلى ربوةٍ عاليةٍ على ضفة النهر الجاري على مقربةٍ من القصر فأضجعتها فوق عشبها، وأسبلت عليها رداءها، وجلست بجانبها تفكر في مصيرها.

فإنها لجالسة مجلسها هذا، وقد سكن الليل، وسكن كل شيءٍ فيه إلا ضوء القمر المنبعث في أجواز الفضاء، ونسمات الهواء المترقرقة على صفحات الماء، إذ شعرت كأنها تسمع بالقرب منها هاتفاً يهتف باسمها بصوتٍ ضعيفٍ، فالتفتت حيث سمعت الصوت فإذا شبح أسود ممتد بين صخرتين على ضفة النهر، كأنه إنسان نائم فارتاعت وفزعت، ثم سمعت الصوت يتكرر بنغمةٍ واحدةٍ فأهمها الأمر ونهضت من مكانها وأخذت تدنو من الشبح رويداً رويداً حتى دانته،

فإذا هو إنسان في زي المساكين مستلقٍ على ظهره شاخص ببصره إلى جدار القصر، فذهبت بنظرها حيث يذهب فإذا عينه عالقة بنافذة غرفتها التي كانت تجلس إليها كل ليلة، فعجبت لذلك كل العجب، وخفق قلبها خفقاً متداركاً، ورأته يضم إلى صدره هنةً بيضاءَ، أشبه بالرقعة، ضماً شديداً، فأكبت عليه لتتبينه وترى ما يضم إلى صدره فإذا الرقعة رسمها، وإذا هو (جلبرت) يجود بنفسه، ويردد بصوتٍ خافتٍ متغلغلٍ كأنه أصوات المعذبين في أعماق القبور: الوداع يا سوزان! الوداع يا سوزان!

At once Susan understood everything, and screamed out aloud, such a great scream that it echoed in the atmosphere. She said "Woe, verily I have killed you O my uncle's son." Then she fell upon his hand, she kissed it and started soaking it with her tears. She said "O Gilbert look, I have come. I am sitting at your feet. Please show mercy to me and forgive me my sin. Indeed, I have become a very sinful and unfortunate woman. There is none upon the face of this earth who needs mercy more than me."

Gilbert sensed and felt the melody of her voice. He went into a brief shock, then turned his eyes until they rested upon her. Suddenly, a single warm tear drop fell from his eye lid and landed upon her hand. Sadly, this was his last pledge with life, as then he passed away.

Just as my soul was ready to depart, that is the time when she had come.

When she had come, I could not give her anytime.

She came at such a time that in between her and me there was the river of death.

She cherished me with her meeting at a time when that meeting was non-beneficial.

***

For a while Susan remained seated beside the corpse of Gilbert, fulfilling that obligation for her uncle's son, for her fiancé and for her friend who loved her like no one had ever loved her before, and had died remaining faithful to her. Then when she come back to her senses, she remembered her daughter, who she had left asleep alone on the hilltop. Returning to her haste, she had decided in her heart what to do next.

***

Susan said "I do not know from amongst the people who I could entrust you to O my daughter. This is because your father has denied you and also the only individual who had loved me in the entire world has also departed. However, I do know about the merciful Lord who knows the secrets of the hearts. He sees the wounds of pain in the hearts of the distressed and He sees the agony and troubles of the unfortunate. So I am entrusting your affairs to Him and I am leaving you in front of Him. He is the most merciful one. O my beloved daughter, I do not have the power to remain alive for you. This is because there is no one from amongst mankind who would pardon me the sin which I have committed. That person who encouraged me and was a partner in my crime, even he will not forgive me. Therefore, I am going towards that heavenly world which is filled with justice and mercy, so that perhaps I might find someone there who could forgive me my sin. However, if I am convicted, perhaps I might find someone there who would be merciful to me.

ففهمت كل شيء، فصرخت صرخةً عظمى، دوى بها الفضاء وقالت: آه.. لقد قتلتك يا ابن عمي، ثم سقطت على يده تقبلها وتبللها بدموعها وتقول: ها أنذا يا (جلبرت) جاثية تحت قدميك، فارحمني واغفر لي ذنبي، فقد أصبحت امرأةً شقيةً، ليس على وجه الأرض من هو أحق بالرحمة مني.

وكأنما أحس بنغمة صوتها فارتعد قليلاً، ثم مال بنظره نحوها حتى رآها، فسقطت من جفنه دمعة حارة على يدها كانت آخر عهده بالحياة وقضى.

ولما دنا مني السياق تعرضت

إلي ودوني من تعرضها شغل

أتت وحياض الموت بيني وبينها

وجادت بوصلٍ حين لا ينفع الوصل

***

جثت سوزان بجانب جثة جلبرت ساعةً، قضت فيها ما يجب عليها لابن عمها وخطيبها وعشيرها الذي أحبها حباً لم يحبه أحد من قبله أحداً حتى مات حسرةً عليها، ثم استفاقت فذكرت ابنتها، وأنها تركتها على تلك الربوة نائمةً وحدها، فعادت إليها مسرعة، وقد قررت في نفسها أمراً.

***

لا أعرف أحداً من الناس أوصيه بك يا بنيتي، لأن أباك أنكرك، ولأن الرجل الوحيد الذي كان يحبني في هذا العالم ذهب لسبيله، ولكني أعلم أن لهذا الكون إلهاً رحيماً يعلم دخائل القلوب وسرائر النفوس، ويرى لوعة الحزن في أفئدة المحزونين ولاعج الشقاء بين جوانح الأشقياء، فأنا أكل أمرك إليه، وأتركك بين يديه، فهو أرحم بك من جميع الرحماء. لا أستطيع أن أعيش لك يا بنيتي، فإن أحداً من الناس لا يغتفر لي الذنب الذي أذنبته حتى الذي أغراني به وشاركني فيه؛ فأنا ذاهبة إلى ذلك العالم العلوي المملوء عدلاً ورحمةً لعلي أجد فيه من يغفر لي ذنبي إن كنت بريئة، ويرحمني إن كنت مذنبة.

O my daughter, I would hate my life to bring shame to your life, every time they will see you they will remember me, and attack you because of my sin. Therefore, I am leaving you all alone in this location so that maybe some kind person from amongst the people may show you mercy when he passes by you. He will take you with him not knowing a thing of your affair. You will live in his house, happy and prosperous. You will not know your father so that his affairs can put you to shame, nor will you know your mother so that her remembrance could trouble you.

O Lord! This weak and deprived child requires a merciful carer for her, because it has become impossible for me to stay besides her anymore in order to raise her, please be kind and shower your mercy upon her. She is innocent, pure and has no hand in that sin which her father has committed. Therefore, please show her mercy and cover her with the cloth of your eminence and of your favour. Originate for her someone who has a loving heart, a good house and establish for her a cherishing livelihood."

Then she began to take her clothes off from her body and covered her daughter's body with it. She wanted to save her daughter from the coldness of the night, leaving only one shirt on her own body. She left this on in order to veil her floating corpse once she had jumped into the water. Then she kneeled over the child with compassion. She kissed her on her forehead with a farewell kiss, encompassing all the love, mercy, compassion and kindness which was in her heart. Then she called out "O Mary, goodbye. O Gilbert, we shall meet soon. O Catherine (the mother of Gilbert), forgive me." After that, she jumped into the water.

***

Sir Gustav Rostand spent the first night of his honeymoon with his wife upon the attic of the castle, admiring and talking to one another. Both their eyes travelled over the green lands. At times they looked at the blue sky or the flowing river. They were enjoying their present happiness, and looking forward to their future prosperity. They were drinking wine excessively from every glass, until they got drunk and both passed out. Both became completely senseless of their surroundings, and neither of them awoke from their slumber until they heard a gust of wind blowing upon the minaret of the castle, and shaking the branches of trees. Realising this was a storm, they got up and went towards their bedroom in the attic.

لا أحب أن تكون حياتي يا بنية شؤماً على حياتك، ولا أن يأخذك الناس بذنبي كلما رأوك بجانبي فأنا أتركك وحدك في هذا المكان لعل راحماً من الناس يمر بك فيعطف عليك ويضمك إليه من حيث لا يعلم شيئاً من أمرك فتعيشين في بيته سعيدةً هانئةً لا تعرفين أباك فيخجلك مرآه، ولا أمك فتؤلمك ذكراها.

اللهم إن كنت تعلم أن هذه الطفلة ضعيفة عاجزة تحتاج إلى من يرحمها ويكفل أمرها، وأنني قد أصبحت عاجزةً عن البقاء بجانبها أرعاها وأحنو عليها، وأنها بريئة طاهرة لا يد لها في الذي أذنبه أبواها، فارحمها وأسبل عليها ستر معروفك وإحسانك وهيء لها صدراً حنوناً، ومهداً ليناً، وعيشاً رغيداً.

ثم بدأت تسر ثيابها عن جسمها وتغطي بها جسم ابنتها وقايةً لها من برد الليل حتى لم يبق على جسدها إلا قميص واحد تركته ليكون ستراً لعورتها عند انتشال جثتها، ثم حنت على الطفلة برفق فلثمتها في جبينها لثمةً أودعتها كل ما في صدرها من حبٍ ورحمةٍ ورفقٍ وحنانٍ، ثم هتفت قائلةً: الوداع يا ماري، سنلتقي عما قليلٍ يا جلبرت، المغفرة يا كاترين. وألقت بنفسها في الماء.

***

قضى المركيز الليلة الأولى من ليالي شهر العسل مع عروسه في شرفة القصر يسمران ويتناجيان، ويذهبان بنظرهما حيث تذهب خضرة الأرض وتمتد زرقة السماء وتطرد مياه النهر، ويتقلبان بين سعادةٍ حاضرةٍ وأخرى مرجوةٍ، ويرشفان من كل كأسٍ من تلك الكؤوس رشفةً تكثراً بما عندهما منها حتى ثملا واستغرقا، وأصبحا لا يشعران بشيءٍ مما حولهما، فلم يستفيقا حتى سمعا دوي الريح في أبراج القصر، وفي ذوائب الأشجار، فعلما أنها الزوبعة، فنهضا من مكانهما ليذهبا إلى مضجعهما.

In their bedroom, Gustav's wife was worried by the anxiety on Gustav's face. She saw him looking around in distress, as if listening to a strange voice. She asked "What is the matter?" He did not reply. Silently, he looked at the river from the attic window. In the light of the moon, he saw a child standing at the river side screaming "O mother! O mother!" in a high pitched voice and pointing towards the water. At once, both looked in her direction, only to discover that a half-naked woman was being tossed about in the midst of waves, plunging and drowning.

Gustav left his wife and started running towards the river, sighing "What a misfortune it would be if it is her." He shouted out to his worker to follow him, and they ran quickly to the locality of the child. He recognised immediately that she was his daughter, and indeed the drowning woman was Susan. Hence, the atmosphere darkened in front of his eyes. He instructed one of his workers to return the child to the castle, and search out the drowning lady. Then Gustav collapsed, traumatised and distressed. Many farmers, men and women, had gathered at the riverside. Some of them swam behind the swimmers and the remaining stood around Gustav, awaiting the mercy of Allah ﷻ and His favour to be delivered.

The swimmers spread out at every angle of the river, the eyes and the hearts of people followed them. A giant war raged between them and the great waves. Sometimes, the swimmers would overpower, and at other times the waves would push them back. From a distance, they would catch sight of Susan's shirt, or feel her presence, and would advance forth in extreme haste, overpowering any great waves in their way. However, whenever they thought they had finally reached her, they would find nothing before them, apart from large waves pushing them back to their starting point at the riverside.

At times, the drowning lady became visible, but then disappeared. This continued until she completely disappeared from sight and was not visible at all. The swimmers followed her deep into the water searching and hunting. Then triumphantly, they resurfaced above the water, holding her between their hands. No one knew whether she was alive or dead, but they continued swimming with her. The people started praying for her and crying over her. The sky and both sides of the river started echoing with cries. Finally, the swimmers brought her to the riverside and placed her on the land, but she was already dead.

Very quickly after, the riverside become a place of mourning for the innocent dead. The women cried there over Susan's innocent death and the men cried over Gilbert's death.

***

فإنهما لواقفان موقفهما هذا إذا لمحت المركيزة في وجه المركيز دهشةً واضطراباً، ورأته يلتفت التفاتاً شديداً كأنما يتسمع لصوتٍ غريبٍ فسألته ما باله. فلم يجبها، وأطل من الشرفة على النهر فرأى كما رأت هي على نور القمر طفلةً واقفةً على الضفة تصيح وتعول وتشير بيدها نحو الماء وتقول: أماه! أماه! فنظرا حيث تشير فإذا امرأة عارية إلا قليلاً تتخبط في لجج الماء تخبط الغرقى؛

فترك المركيز مكانه ونزل يعدو إلى النهر، وهو يقول: والهفتاه إن كانت هي. وصاح بخدمه أن يتبعوه ففعلوا. حتى بلغ موقف الطفلة فعرف أنها ابنته، وأن الغريقة سوزان، فأظلم الفضاء في عينيه، وأشار إلى أحد خدمه أن يعود بالطفلة إلى القصر، وأمر الباقين أن يسبحوا وراء الغريقة، ثم سقط في مكانه واهناً متهالكاً، وكان قد اجتمع على الضفة خلقٌ كثيرٌ من الفلاحين رجالاً ونساء، فسبح بعضهم وراء السابحين ووقف الباقون حول المركيز ينتظرون رحمة الله وإحسانه.

انتشر السابحون في كل مكانٍ، ومشت وراءهم عيون الناظرين وقلوبهم، فقامت بينهم وبين الأمواج المتلاطمة معركة هائلة كانوا يظفرون فيها مرةً ويتراجعون أخرى، وكانوا إذا لاح لهم على البعد قميص الغريقة أو شعرها عظم عندهم الأمل فاندفعوا وراءها مستبسلين مستقتلين يغالبون جبال الأمواج المعترضة في طريقهم، حتى إذا دنوا من المكان الذي لمحوها فيه لا يجدون أمامهم شيئاً، ثم لا يلبث الموج أن يكر عليهم فيدفعهم إلى الضفة كما كانوا.

وما زالت الفترات بين ظهور الغريقة واختفائها تتسع شيئاً فشيئاً حتى غابت عن الأعين ولم تظهر، فهبط السابحون وراءها ولبثوا ساعةً يرسبون ويطفون، ثم ظهروا على وجه الماء يحملونها على أيديهم ولا يعلم الناس أحية أم ميتة؟ وما زالوا يسبحون بها، وأصواء الدعاء لها والبكاء عليها ترن في الضفتين فتردد رنينها آفاق السماء، حتى وصلوا بها إلى الضفة فألقوها على الأرض فإذا هي ميتة.

وما هي إلا ساعة أو بعض ساعةٍ حتى كانت الضفة مأتماً قائماً يبكي فيه النساء على الشهيدة والرجال على الشهيد.

***

After this day, Sir Gustav Rostand could not benefit himself anymore, and became helpless like Gilbert had been. His daughter became extremely ill due to the effects of this tragedy, and joined her dead mother after three nights. The love which his wife had in her heart for Gustav turned into enmity and hatred, she too left him and travelled back to Nice.

Gustav continued thinking about that sight which he had seen from the attic of the castle on the night of the drowning. The horrific memory of Susan did not part from him day nor night. Wherever he went, he would imagine that he was in front of the river and the waves were drowning Susan. He would see Mary screaming. At once, he would shout out "O Susan! I am here!" advancing forth in haste, as if he wanted to jump into the river to save her. When he was unsuccessful he would collapse with exhaustion, grief and regret.

At times, Gustav would wonder around, head down, until he would reach the outskirts of Leynes village. There he would see an old woman kneeling over a grave, crying and screaming. Realising this was the grave of Gilbert and the old woman was Catherine, he would recoil in fear and trauma, yelling "Mercy! Mercy! Forgiveness! Forgiveness!" A lot of the farming women would see Gustav collapsed in grief at places where they used to see Gilbert in. Accordingly, they would say "Verily, Allah ﷻ has taken revenge for that poor martyr and for the death of that victimised, innocent woman."

The sight of the water would scare him more than anything, and his emotions would flare up, causing unrest. He would try to jump into the river, intending to drown, but the people passing by him would hold him back when they saw him. One fateful morning, there were no passers-by, and the people saw his corpse floating upon the surface of the river, in the same place where Susan had drowned. Everyone knew he had paid the price for his disloyalty to Susan.

***

Many years have passed by since this tragedy took place. The old women of Leynes and its surroundings still remember and cry over this ill-fated love. They narrate the story to their daughters and granddaughters, in order for it to serve as a lesson for them, if, God forbid, they were ever to be surrounded by evil people.

لم ينتفع المركيز بنفسه بعد هذا اليوم كما لم ينتفع جلبرت بنفسه من قبل، فقد مرضت ابنته على أثر تلك الحادثة مرضاً شديداً، فلم تلبث أن لحقت بأمها بعد ثلاث ليال، واستحال الحب الذي كانت تضمره له زوجته إلى بغضٍ واحتقار، فهجرته وسافرت إلى (نيس).

ولزمه خيال ذلك المنظر الذي رآه من شرفة القصر ليلة الغرق لا يفارقه ليله ونهاره، فكان كلما مشى في طريقٍ توهم أن أمامه نهراً هائجاً تتخبط سوزان في لجته وتصيح ماري على ضفته، فيصرخ قائلاً: لبيك يا سوزان، ويندفع إلى الأمام كأنما يريد أن يلقي بنفسه في النهر الذي توهمه لينجي الغريقة التي تخيلها، فينأى عنه المنظر كلما دنا منه حتى ينال منه التعب، فيسقط حسيراً طريحاً.

وكان يهيم على وجهه أحياناً حتى يصل إلى ضاحية قرية (ليني) فيرى امرأةً عجوزاً مكبةً على قبرٍ بين يديها تبكي وتنتحب، فيعلم أنها كاترين، وأن القبر قبر قتلاه، فيتراجع خائفاً مذعوراً، ويصرخ قائلاً: الرحمة الرحمة! العفو العفو! وكثيراً ما كان يراه نساء الفالحين ساقطاً في بعض الأماكن التي كن يرين فيها جلبرت فيقلن: لقد انتقم الله للشهيد المسكين والشهيدة المظلومة،

وكان منظر الماء يهيجه أكثر من كل منظرٍ سواه، فإذا رآه ثار واضطرب وتهافت عليه يريد اقتحامه، لولا أن يتداركه من يراه من المارة. ولم يزل هذا شأنه حتى رأى الناس جثته في صباح يومٍ من الأيام طافيةً على وجه النهر في المكان الذي غرقت فيه سوزان؛ فعلموا أنها نهاية الجزاء.

***

مرت على هذه الحادثة أعوام طوال ولا يزال عجائز قرية (ليني) والقرى المحيطة بها يحفظنها حتى اليوم ويبكين كلما ذكرنها، ويروينها لبناتهن وحفيداتهن عبرةً يعتبرن بها كلما طاف بهن طائف من شرور الرجال.

The Punishment / Al-ʿIqāb (Composed)

One night from the nights of last summer, I had a dream. I descended upon a very big town, I did not recognise the town's name or locality, neither did I know in what era were its residents living in. Nevertheless, I walked along the streets for a few hours. I saw all kinds of different people in a large group, talking in many different languages which I could not understand. So, I speculated that certainly all the people of the world had gathered up in one town. I guessed that the people before me were all the people belonging to the past, the present and the future.

Thus, I continued to shift from one location to the other. At times I stopped and at times I carried on until I reached a very big building. I did not see any other building greater than this in terms of its prestige and its construction. A large crowd of people were standing all around the door of this huge building. There were soldiers coming and going there, walking in its courtyard and its veranda, holding their swords along with their sheaths. Accordingly, I asked some people who were standing, "What is this building and for what reason is this large crowd of people gathered upon its door?" They informed me that certainly this was the castle of the ruler and indeed today is the Day of Judgment, the day in which the ruler will issue his verdicts for people regarding their crimes. Not even a brief moment passed by, that a caller from amongst the people had called out saying, "Indeed the courthouse has opened, therefore all of you present yourself."

Consequently, the people entered and I also entered behind them. I sat down wherever I could find a place. Then I saw the ruler sitting upon a chair which was made out of gold. This chair was sparkling in the middle of the courthouse like how the sun shines in its horizon. Verily there was a man sitting on his right side wearing a sackcloth. Upon the ruler's left hand side was another man wearing a prestigious cloak. I questioned about them both. I recognised that certainly the one on his right is the priest of the church and the man on his left-hand side is the judge of this town.

I saw the ruler looking at a white piece of paper which was in front of him. He had his head down for a while, then he raised his head and said, "Let the criminals be brought."

العقاب

(موضوعة)

رأيت فيما يرى النائم في ليلةٍ من ليالي الصيف الماضي كأني هبطت مدينةً كبرى لا علم لي باسمها ولا بموقعها من البلاد ولا بالعصر الذي يعيش أهلها فيه، فمشيت في طرقها بعض ساعاتٍ فرأيت أجناساً من البشر لا عداد لهم، ينطقون بأنواعٍ من اللغات لا حصر لها، فخيل إلي أن الدنيا قد استحالت إلى مدينةٍ وأن الذي أراه بين يدي إنما هو العالم بأجمعه من أدناه إلى أقصاه،

فلم أزل أتنقل من مكانٍ إلى مكانٍ وأداول بين الحركة والسكون حتى انتهى بي المسير إلى بنيةٍ عظيمةٍ لم أر بين البنى أعظم منها شأناً ولا أهول منظراً، وقد ازدحم على بابها خلق كثير من الناس، ومشى في أفنيتها وأبهائها طوائف من الجند يخطرون بسيوفهم وحمائلهم جيئةً وذهوباً، فسألت بعض الواقفين: ما هذه البنية وما هذا الجمع المحتشد على بابها؟ فعلمت أنها قصر الأمير، وأن اليوم يوم القضاء بين الناس والفصل في خصوماتهم، وما هي إلا ساعة حتى نادى منادٍ في الناس: أن قد اجتمع مجلس القضاء فاشهدوه،

فدخل الناس ودخلت على أثرهم، وجلست حيث انتهى بي المجلس، فرأيت الأمير جالساً على كرسي من الذهب يتلألأ في وسط الفناء تلألؤ الشمس في دارتها، وقد جلس على يمينه رجل يلبس مسوحاً وعلى يساره آخر يلبس طيلساناً، فسألت عنهما، فعرفت أن الذي على يمينه كاهن الدير، وأن الذي على يساره قاضي المدينة،

ورأيته ينظر في ورقةٍ بيضاء بين يديه فأكب عليها ساعةً ثم رفع رأسه وقال: ليؤت بالمجرمين،

Thus, the door of the prison was opened. On the left hand side of the prison, there was the courtyard. It felt like a cage containing lions in it roaring was opened. They came out, police officers who were dragging a very old man. It appeared that his bones and joints had given up due to extreme old age and weakness.

The ruler asked, "What is his crime?

The priest replied, "Indeed he is a thief, he entered the church, and then he stole a sack of flour from the church, which was collected for the distribution to the poor and the destitute."

Upon hearing this, the people cried out loudly and yelled, "Woe upon the sinful criminal, has he stole Allah's ﷻ wealth from Allah's ﷻ house?"

Then, witnesses were brought forth. The panel of priests gave testimony against him. Then the ruler discussed this matter with the priest briefly. Thereafter, the ruler declared his verdict, "This criminal should be taken to the slaughter ground, his right hand should be cut off followed by his left hand, then the rest if his body parts should also be amputated, and at the end his head should be separated from his body. His segmented body should be fed to vultures and the wild animals."

At once, that old man bowed down in front of the ruler and stretched out his trembling and weak hands towards him and begged him for mercy. The police officers hit him on his mouth and dragged him into his cell.

Thereafter the police officers returned, holding a young man who was about eighteen years of age. He was extremely pale and slim. He was trembling and shaking out of extreme fear.

When the police officers had made him stand before the ruler, the ruler asked, "What is his crime?"

The judge replied, "He is a murderer, one of your representatives approached him in his village to collect tax and requested the money which was due upon him. Indeed, he refused to pay in a very harsh tone of voice. Therefore, your representative shouted at him. In response, this man became extremely angry and in his rage, drew out his sword from its sheath and struck your representative which led to his death."

ففتح باب السجن وكان على يسار الفناء فتكشف عن مثل خلق الليث منظراً وزئيراً، وخرج منه الأعوان يقتادون شيخاً هرماً تكاد تسلمه قوائمه ضعفاً ووهناً،

فسأل الأمير: ما جريمته؟

فقال الكاهن: إنه لص دخل الدير، فسرق منه غرارةً من غرائر الدقيق المحبوسة على الفقراء والمساكين.

فضج الناس ضجيجاً عالياً وصاحوا: ويل للمجرم الأثيم، أيسرق مال الله في بيت الله؟

ثم نودي بالشهود. فشهد عليه رهبان الدين، فتسار الأمير مع الكاهن هنيهةً ثم صاح: يقاد المجرم إلى ساحة الموت فتقطع يمناه ثم يسراه ثم بقية أطرافه، ثم يقطع رأسه، ويقطع طعاماً للطير الغادي والوحش الساغب،

فجثا الشيخ بين يدي الأمير ومد إليه يده الضعيفة المرتعشة يحاول أن يسترحمه، فضرب الأعوان على فمه واحتملوه إلى محبسه.

ثم عادوا وبين أيديهم فتىً في الثامنة عشرة من عمره، أصفر نحيل يضطرب بين أيديهم خوفاً وفرقاً،

حتى وقفوا به بين يدي الأمير. فسأل: ما جريمته؟

فقال: إنه قاتل، ذهب أحد قواد الأمير إلى قريته لجمع الضرائب، فطالبه بأداء ما عليه من المال فأبى وتوقح في إبائه، فانتهره القائد فاحتدم غيظاً وجرد سيفه من غمده وضربه بضربةٍ ذهبت بحياته.

The crowd began to scream again shouting, "O what outrageousness and what an atrocity, indeed the one killing the ruler's representative is like killing the ruler himself!"

The panel of representatives who were the victim's team where brought forth by the police and they testified against the young man. For a short moment, the ruler lowered his head. When he raised his head, he said, "Take the criminal to the place of crucifixion, and hang him upon a branch of a tree, cut all of his veins and leave him until not even one drop of blood remains in his body." That young man screamed loudly and before he could explain himself the police guards surrounded him and took him back to the prison.

The police constables returned with an extremely beautiful young woman. Her beauty was comparable to an illuminated star had it not been for the cloud of sadness upon her forehead. The ruler asked, "What is her crime?"

The judge replied, "Verily she is an adulteress woman, a man from her family had entered her house only to discover that she was alone in her house with a strange man whom she loves and has decided to marry him before this day."

The crowd again broke out with a loud noise and in anger yelled, "Kill her, kill her, stone her, stone her, indeed this is a big crime and a grave deception."

The ruler asked, "Where is the one who witnessed this?"

Her relative entered and testified against her. The judge started whispering something into the ear of the ruler. Then, the ruler decreed, "Take this young woman to the ground of death as well, stone her naked until there remains not even one bit of flesh on her body or bones.

The crowd starting cheering and declaring how just and wise the ruler was. In joy they were praising and hailing the ruler, the priest and the judge.

The judge rose from his seat and the crowd also stood up with him. They left happy and overjoyed.

I also left the court behind these people upset and distressed questioning how strange and unjust these verdicts were, the ruler did not hear anything in defence of the accused, nor were these punishments proportionate to the crimes. I was amazed at the people due to their weakness and their surrendering in front of a powerful kingdom. I was amazed that they considered this government honourable and prestigious. They had entrusted all their affairs to it; whether it be just or unjust; whether it be mercy or dictatorship; the people had accepted the verdict.

فصاح الناس: يا للفظاعة والهول، إن من يقتل نائب الأمير فكأنما قتل الأمير نفسه،

ثم جيء بأعوان القائد المقتول، فأدوا شهادتهم، فأطرق الأمير لحظة، ثم رفع رأسه وقال: يقاد المجرم إلى ساحة الموت فيصلب على أعواد شجرة، ثم تفصد عروقه كلها، حتى لا يبقى في جسمه قطرة واحدة من الدم، فصرخ الغلام صرخة، حال الأعوان بينه وبين إتمامها واحتملوه إلى السجن؛

وما لبثوا أن عادوا بفتاةٍ جميلةٍ كأنها الكوكب المشبوب حسناً وبهاءً لولا سحابة غبراء من الحزن تتدجى فوق جبينها، فقال الأمير: ما جريمتها؟

فقال القاضي: إنها امرأة زانية، دخل عليها رجل من أهلها فوجدها خاليةً بفتًى غريبٍ كان يحبها ويطمع في الزواج منها قبل اليوم،

فهاج الناس واحتدموا وهتفوا: القتل القتل. الرجم الرجم! إنها الجريمة العظمى والخيانة الكبرى.

فقال الأمير: أين شاهدها؟

فدخل قريبها الذي كشف أمرها فشهد عليها. فهمس القاضي في أذن الأمير ساعة، ثم قال الأمير: تؤخذ الفتاة إلى ساحة الموت فترجم عاريةً حتى لا يبقى على لحمها قطعة جلدٍ ولا على عظمها قطعة لحم،

فهلل الناس وكبروا إعجاباً بعدل الأمير وحزمه، وإكباراً لسطوته، وقوته، وهتفوا له ولكاهنه وقاضيه بالدعاء،

ثم نهض فنهض الناس بنهوضه ومضوا لسبيلهم فرحين مغتبطين،

وخرجت على أثرهم حزيناً مكتئباً أفكر في هذه المحاكمة الغريبة التي لم يسمع فيها دفاع المتهمين عن أنفسهم، ولم يشهد فيها على المتهمين غير خصومهم، ولم تقدر فيها العقوبات على مقدار الجرائم! واعجب للناس في ضعفهم واستخذائهم أمام القوة القاهرة وغلوهم في تقديسها وإعظامها وإغراقهم في الثقة بها والنزول على حكمها عدلاً كان أو ظلماً، رحمةً أو قسوة،

I thought to myself, is there no thief, murderer or fornicator in this crowd? Are they free from sins? Is not there anyone here who could understand the excuses and justifications of the crimes committed by these individuals and then show mercy to them? Is there no one in this circle, who could observe their crimes with the same sympathy they would want for their own crimes? Is there no one present who would wish mercy and forgiveness for those standing in the dock as they would wish mercy and forgiveness for themselves?

Can it not be that the accused adulterous woman may not be adulterous? Can it not be, that the murderer had only killed in self-defence to protect his honour and his wealth? Can it not be that the thief had stolen only to feed his starving family and self?

Has not the ruler ever been committed to kill anyone even once in his life so that he maybe merciful to the murderers when he is investigating their crimes? Has the priest himself never obtained a coin unlawfully? If he has, then he should be less angry and more remorseful towards the one who has stolen the sack of flour from the church. If the priest has attained a coin unlawfully then he should be able to pardon that thief's crime as well.

Has the judge never slipped? Even once in his life, so that because of it, his anger over the criminal men and women could extinguish?

Who are these people who are sitting on these chairs ruling over the souls and hearts of men the way they please? Are they distributing good alongside evil between people the way they want?

Indeed, these people are not innocent Prophets, nor are they pure angels; nor are they holding a pledge with Allah ﷻ from which they can investigate His people's affairs and decide their fate. With what right are they sitting in this gathering in a position of power? What jurisdictive authority do they have with which they have obtained this government and are ruling upon all people?

Who is this ruler? Is he not a very big tyrant or the son of a very big tyrant, who through his authority and power has taken the necks and the shoulders of people as a ladder to climb to the throne he is sitting upon?

Who is this priest? Is he not the shrewdest and the most expert in terms of robbing the weak and the faint hearted people?

وأردد في نفسي هذه الكلمات: ليت شعري ألا يوجد بين هذه الجماهير لصٌ أو قاتل أو زانٍ يعلم عذرهم فيرحمهم، وينظر إلى جرائمهم بالعين التي ينظر بها إلى جريمته، ويتمنى لهم من الرحمة والمغفرة ما يتمنى لنفسه إن قدر له أن يقف في موقفٍ مثل موقفهم، أمام قضاةٍ مثل قضاتهم؟

ألا يجوز أن تكون الزانية غير زانية، والقاتل إنما قتل دفاعاً عن عرضه أو ماله، واللص إنما سرق ما يسد به جوعته أو جوعة أهل بيته؟

ألم يرتكب الأمير جريمة القتل مرةً واحدةً في حياته فيرحم القاتلين عند النظر في جرائمهم؟ ألم يسقط إلى يد الكاهن يوماً من الأيام دينار من غير حله، فتخف لوعة أسفه على الغرارة المسروقة من ديره ويغتفر هذه لتلك؟

ألم تزل قدم القاضي مرةً واحدةً فيما مر به من أيام حياته فتهدأ ثورة غضبه على الساقطين والساقطات؟

من هم هؤلاء الجالسون على هذه المقاعد يتحكمون في أرواح العباد وأموالهم كما يشاؤون؟ ويقسمون السعود والنحوس بين البشر كما يريدون؟

إنهم ليسوا بأنبياء معصومين، ولا بأملاكٍ مطهرين، ولا يحملون في أيديهم عهداً من الله تعالى بالنظر في أمر عباده وتوزيع حظوظهم وأنصبتهم بينهم، فبأي حق يجلسون هذه الجلسة على هذه الصورة؟ ومن أي قوةٍ شرعيةٍ يستمدون هذه السلطة التي يستأثرون بها من دون الناس جميعاً؟

من هو الأمير؟ أليس هو المستبد الأعظم في الأمة أو سلالة المستبد الأعظم فيها الذي استطاع بقوته وقهره أن يتخذ من أعناق الناس وكواهلهم سلماً يصعد عليها إلى العرش الذي يجلس عليه؟

من هو الكاهن؟ أليس هو أبرع الناس وأمهرهم في استغلال النفوس الضعيفة والقلوب المريضة؟

Who is this judge? Does he not have the power to allow truth to prevail over falsehood? From where did the tyrants, the thieves and the unjust become the righteous, the pure and the good doers?

How strange is this, that a man has killed another man to save his wealth and dignity, and he is called a criminal? However, when the ruler decreed for the murderer to be killed he is called just. How amazing is this, that when a thief has stolen a morsel in order to fulfil his and his family's need, he is called a thief! However, when the judge ordered his hands to be cut off and his body to be mutilated, he is called a fair man! How strange is this, that a woman has slipped, perhaps due to the deception of men or through the influence of Satan, making people completely disliking her and not wanting to look at her anymore? But when they see her fastened upon some pillar naked, they pelt her with stones from every angle. Surprisingly, they are pleased with this sight and are happy at her location and at the retribution.

The way fire cannot extinguish fire, the second drop of poison cannot become the cure for the first drop of poison. Just like cutting off the right hand cannot become a remedy for the one who's left hand has already been cut off, evil cannot become the remedy for evil and a misfortune of this world cannot be wiped out by another misfortune. I kept on thinking about these things until evening.

I walked through a dark, frightful, open space until I reached the other end. There I saw a very scary scene which to this day haunts me. I saw the corpse of an old man drenched in soil. It had neither a head nor any other body parts attached to it. Then I saw his head and his body parts scattered all around him as if they were mourning and wailing over him in remorse. Then I saw that young man fastened upon a very dense tree as if he was one of its branches. All the blood drained from his body. After that I saw the young lady who had become a red lump of meat. Her head and her feet were not visible. There was a pile of stones which were drenched in her blood. I saw three dead bodies beside her in a deep ditch full of blood. I felt a black cloud descending over my eyes until everything turned black and I fell to the floor unconscious.

I did not regain consciousness until a great portion of the night had passed. I opened my eyes only to see a black thing slowly drawing closer to me. I became frightened at this sight. At once, I took refuge towards the trunk of a tree, I hid behind it. The dark figure kept on approaching me until it was right next to me. The dark figure, then lit a small candle he held in his hand. I discovered the figure was an old woman resembling a witch, dressed in tattered old clothes.

من هو القاضي؟ أليس هو أقدر الناس على إلباس الحق صورة الباطل والباطل صورة الحق؟ ومتى كان المستبدون واللصوص والظلمة أخياراً صالحين وأبراراً طاهرين؟

عجيب جداً أن يقتل الرجل الرجل لغضبةٍ يغضبها لعرضه أو شرفه فيسمى مجرماً، فإذا قتل الأمير القاتل سمي عادلاً، وأن يسرق السارق اللقمة يقتات بها أو يقيت بها عياله فيسمى لصاً. فإذا أمر القاضي بقطع أطرافه والتمثيل به سمي حازماً. وأن تسقط المرأة سقطةً ربما ساقتها إليها خدعة من خداع الرجال أو نزعة من نزعات الشيطان فيستنكر الناس أمرها، ويستبشعون منظرها، فإذا رأوها مشدودةً إلي بعض الأنصاب، عاريةً تتساقط عليها حجارة من كل صوب أنسوا بمشهدها وأعجبهم موقفها ومصيرها.

كما أن النار لا تطفىء النار، وشارب السم لا يعالج بشربه مرةً أخرى، وكما أن مقطوع اليد اليمنى لا يعالج بقطع اليد اليسرى؛ كذلك لا يعالج الشر باشر، ولا يمحى الشقاء في هذه الدنيا بشقاء. ولم أزل أحدث نفسي بمثل هذا الحديث حتى أقبل الليل.

فمررت بساحةٍ مظلمةٍ موحشةٍ تتطاير في جوها أسراب من الطير غادية رائحة، فاخترقتها حتى بلغت أبعد بقاعها؛ فرأيت منظراً هائلاً لا يزال أثره عالقاً بنفسي حتى الساعة. رأيت الشيخ جثةً معفرةً بالتراب لا رأس لها، ولا أطراف، ثم رأيت رأسه وأطرافه مبعثرة حواليه كأنها نوادب يندبنه حاسرات. ورأيت الفتى مشدوداً إلى شجرةٍ فرعاء كأنه بعض أغصانها، وقد سال جميع ما في عروقه من الدم حتى أصبح شبحاً ماثلاً، أو خيالاً سارياً. ورأيت الفتاة كتلةً حمراء من اللحم لا يستبين لها رأس، ولا قدم، وقد أحاطت بها أكوام من الحجارة المخضبة بدمائها، ثم رأيت بجانب هذه الجثث الثلاث حفرةً جوفاء تفهق بالدم، فعلمت أنها مجمع دماء هؤلاء المساكين، فشعرت كأن سحابةً سوداء تهبط على عيني قليلاً قليلاً حتى غاب عن نظري كل شيءٍ فسقطت في مكاني لا أشعر بشيءٍ مما حولي،

فلم أستفق حتى مضت دولة من الليل ففتحت عيني فإذا شبح أسود يدنو مني رويداً رويداً، فارتعت لمنظره، وفزعت إلى ساق الشجرة فاختبأت وراءه؛ فما زال يتقدم حتى صار بجانبي فأشعل مصباحاً صغيراً كان في يده فتبينته على نوره فإذا عجوز شمطاء في زي المساكين وسحنتهم،

She walked on and then started examining the faces of the dead until she reached at the place of the old man. She knelt beside him for a moment and cried and wailed over him. She then walked towards his head and other body parts gathering them up, she placed them next to his corpse. She proceeded to dig a ditch for him under the trunk of the tree and then she buried him in it. After that she stood up upon his grave and saying her farewells she said, "O wronged man, O martyr, in the way of Allah ﷻ you have died trying your best to save me and your troublesome grandchildren from catastrophe. Now you are in the guardianship of Allah ﷻ. Verily your soul had departed from your body and your body remains in your grave. Without a shadow of doubt, you were the best husband and the best father. Your speech and your conduct was the most excellent. As a person, you had the noblest heart and spirit. Therefore, go to your Lord so that only He may recompense you, and beg Him to shower his mercy upon all mankind including even your murderers and those who did injustice upon you. Also, request Him to join me with you very soon. Thus, after separating from you, there is nothing which remains which could give me satisfaction other than the hope of meeting you."

I became very deeply touched seeing all of this and her crying made me cry. I was convinced in my heart that whatever she was saying was the truth; certainly, this old man was a martyr. I became determined to find out more about their story. I came out from my hiding place and walked towards her. Upon seeing me she became startled and frightened. Then she became calm as if she remembered that after the catastrophe that had fallen upon her, there is no bigger calamity than this.

I began my conversation with her saying, "O honourable lady, do not fear me, verily I am a stranger in this town. I do not know anything from the affairs of this town, nor of its residents. Indeed, I saw you standing upon this grave at this moment crying over the person who is in it. Hence, I felt sorry for you and I cried because you had cried. I would like you to share the pain in your heart, perhaps, I may be able to help you ease your pain." Upon hearing me her tears began to flow and she began her story;

فمشت تتصفح وجوه القتلى حتى بلغت مصرع الشيخ فجثت بجانبه ساعةً تبكيه وتندبه، ثم مشت إلى رأسه وأطرافه فجمعتها وضمتها إلى جثته، ثم احتفرت له حفرةً تحت ساق الشجرة فدفنته فيها، وقامت على قبره تودعه وتقول: في سبيل الله ما لقيت في سبيلي وسبيل أحفادك البؤساء أيها الشهيد المظلوم، وفي ذمة الله وكنفه روح طار عن جسدك، وجسد ضمه قبرك، فقد كنت خير الناس زوجاً وأباً وأطهرهم لساناً ويداً وأشرفهم قلباً ونفساً؛ فاذهب إلى ربك لتلقى جزاءك عنده، واطلب إليه الرحمة لجميع الناس حتى لقاتليك وظالميك، واسأله أن يلحقني بك وشيكاً، فلا شيء يعزيني عنك بعد فراقك إلا الأمل في لقائك،

فأبكاني بكاؤها وأحزنني منظرها، ووقع في نفسي أنها صادقة فيما تقول، وأن شيخها شهيد من شهداء القضاء. وأحببت أن أقف على قصتها وقصته فبرزت من مخبئي ومشيت إليها فارتاعت لمرآي عند النظرة الأولى، ثم سكتت كأنما ذكرت أن لا قيمة لمصائب الحياة بعد مصابها الذي نزل بها،

فابتدرتها بقولي: لا تراعي يا سيدتي فإنني رجل غريب عن هذا البلد لا أعرف من شأنه ولا من شأن أهله شيئاً، وقد رأيت الساعة موقفك على هذا القبر وتفجعك على ساكنه فرثيت لك وبكيت لبكائك وتمنيت لو أفضيت إلي بذات نفسك علني أستطيع أن أكون لك عوناً على همك، فاستعبرت باكيةً وأنشأت تحدثني وتقول:

"Indeed, my husband was never a robber or a thief in any one day belonging to the days of his life. He passed his days of youth and of old age labouring very hard. He was never reluctant even for a single moment in terms of striving for the livelihood for himself and for his family until our son had grown up. This was our only child. When he grew up he took away his father's responsibilities, which he could bear no more due to old age. Then, we were blessed through our son's help and life was good for a long period until our son tragically passed away. He died at a time when we needed him more than ever. He left behind, five small children, the eldest not even being ten years of age.

Certainly, by this time his father had reached extreme old age and the trauma of his son passing away had combined and he was unable to work. Therefore, we all landed into great distress and hardship. There was no one who could understand the hardship which we were enduring other than the one who has been afflicted himself with this kind of tragedy in life. It came to a point where we had nothing to feed our young with. We were in a dilemma! We knew that if the mercy of Allah ﷻ does not reach us we would all indeed be destroyed. Thus, I did not see any other alternative but to resort to a scheme which all the troublesome and the poor take refuge towards. I started begging people for donations but I found no one kind enough to even give me a drop of water or a morsel of food. Neither did I find anyone who could guide me towards it. Due to this I found myself in tattered clothes and with a begging bowl in my hands. Then I returned home.

Only Allah ﷻ knew what pain I had in my heart. I saw the little children awake and crying out of hunger. Then I saw the old man, my husband sitting with them drenching the ground with his tears. He was rubbing his palms together not knowing what to do or how to overcome this problem. If death had approached me this moment, then certainly that would have been easier for me to endure than this scene that lay before my eyes. My grandchildren were staring at my face as I entered and started circulating around me to see what have I returned with which would get rid of their hunger. But I had returned empty handed so I went to my husband and said to him; 'Certainly in the city's church there will be some stock for donation purposes and the senior priest has the authority to spend it on the poor and the destitute. If you were to go there and explain your need to him and request him to give you a little bit which will aid your need, then hopefully you shall return to us with that, which will eliminate the hunger of these poor children.'

إن زوجي لم يكن في يوم من أيام حياته لصاً ولا سارقاً، بل قضى أيام شبابه وكهولته عاملاً مجداً لا يفتر ساعةً واحدةً عن السعي في طلب رزقه ورزق أهل بيته حتى كبر ولده، وكان واحده، فاشتد به ساعده واحتمل عنه بعد ما كان يستقل بحمله من الهم، وما هو إلا أن نعمنا به وبمعونته حقبةً من الدهر حتى نزلت به نازلة الموت فذهبت بحياته أحوج ما كنا إليه، وخلف وراءه خمسة أولادٍ صغارٍ لا يتجاوز أكبرهم العاشرة من عمره،

وكانت قد أدركت أباه الشيخوخة، فاجتمع عليه هم الكبر وهم الثكل فأصبح عاجزاً عن العمل لا يستطيعه إلا في الفينة بعد الفينة، وأصبحنا جميعاً في حالةٍ من الشقاء والبؤس لا يعرف مكانها من نفوسنا إلا من ألم به في حياته طرف منها حتى طلعت علينا شمس يومٍ من الأيام، وليس في يدنا ما نقوم به أصلاب صغارنا، ولا ما نعللهم به تعليلا، فأسقط في يدنا وعلمنا جميعاً إن لم يتداركنا الله برحمةٍ من عنده فلم أر بداً من أن ألجأ إلى الخطة التي يلجأ إليها كل مضطر عديم، فبرزت إلي الناس أتعرض لمعروفهم وأستندي ماء أكفهم فلم أجد بينهم من يحسن إلي بجرعةٍ أو مضغة، ولا من يدلني على سبيل ذلك، وكان أكبر ما حال بيني وبينهم وصرف وجوههم عني أني لا ألبس مرقعة الشحاذين، ولا أحمل ركوتهم فعدت إلى منزلي.

وبين جنبي من الهم ما الله به عليم، فرأيت الأطفال سهداً يتضاغون جوعاً، ورأيت الشيخ جالساً بينهم يبل تربة الأرض بدموعه ويقرع كفه بكفه لا يعلم ماذا يصنع، ولا كيف يحتال، ولو أن شخص الموت برز إلي في تلك الساعة لكان منظره أهون على نفسي من منظر هؤلاء الصبية، وهم يحدقون في وجهي عند دخولي ويدورون حولي ليروا هل عدت إليهم بما يسد جوعتهم؟ وما عدت إليهم إلا باليأس القاتل والكمد الشامل؟ فتقدمت نحو الشيخ، وقلت له: إن في دير المدينة كما يزعمون مالاً للصدقات يتولى الكاهن الأعظم إنفاقه على الفقراء والمساكين فلو ذهبت إليه وكشفت له خلتك وسألته أن يمنحك علالةً تستعين بها على أمرك لرجونا أن نطفىء لوعة هؤلاء الأطفال المساكين،

My husband's face lit up with hope. He stood up and went towards his walking stick, taking its support, he walked towards the church until he reached it. He went towards the priest's room and stood in front of him. My husband presented his dilemma before him and wept at the priest's feet. The priest was unmoved and told my husband;

'Certainly the church does not do favours upon those people who have not done any favours upon the church before. On any day from amongst the days of your happiness and prosperity, you had never given any charity to the church. Therefore, mind your way, the doors of livelihood are open in front of you. If, however, the doors of livelihood do become tight upon you, then the doors of crimes are more spacious in respect to it.'

Thereafter, my husband came out upset and distressed. The sadness and despair of his life could clearly be seen in his eyes.

He descended from there and came to the courtyard of the church. Then he saw in one of its corners a sack of flour. A sudden idea occurred to him, he thought to himself that he should take it. This thought however, only came because of need and starvation, but he felt covered in shame. He closed his eyes and carried on walking until he reached the place where the sack of flour was and the thought of taking the flour reoccurred to him! He tried to get rid of his thought but he could not. He sat down beside the sack and thought to himself, 'I do not know anyone within the boundaries of this city and upon its land, a needier person and a poorer person than me. If taking this flour sack is a crime, then verily the priest has granted me the permission to commit this crime to safeguard my livelihood.'

He then lifted the sack of flour on his back and walked struggling under its weight. He had not yet left the church building and could feel the extreme weight of the sack. He thought he would not be able to carry on. His heart whispered, 'Remove the sack from your back.' However, in that instant he saw his grandchildren starving and crying from hunger. This spurred him on to continue walking home, every so often stopping taking support on a wall or his walking stick. This continued until fatigue overtook him, he struggled to breathe. His vision extinguished as he started vomiting blood and fell unconscious.

فاستنار وجهه بنور الأمل وقام إلى عصاه فاعتمد عليها ومشى إلى الدير حتى بلغه فصعد إلى حجرة الكاهن حتى وقف بين يديه، فنفض له جملة حاله وسكب تحت قدميه جميع ما أبقت الأيام في جفنيه القريحين من دموع، فاستقبله الكاهن بأقبح ما يستقبل به مسؤول سائلاً، وقال له:

إن الدير لا يحسن إلا إلى الذين أسلفوه الإحسان من قبل، وما كنت في يومٍ من أيام رغدك ورخائك من المحسنين إليه فاذهب لشأنك فأبواب العيش واسعة بين يديك، فإن ضاقت بك فأبواب الجرائم أوسع منها،

فخرج من حضرته كئيباً محزوناً لا يرى فضاء الدنيا في نظره إلا ككفة الحابل أو أفحوص القطاة،

حتى نزل إلى ساحة الدير فلمح في إحدى زواياه غرارة دقيق فحدثته نفسه بها، وما كانت تحدثه لولا العوز والفاقة، ثم أدركه الحياء فأغضى عنها واستمر سائراً في طريقه حتى صار بجانبها فوقع نظره عليها مرةً أخرى فعاوده حديثه الأول فحاول دفعه فلم يستطع فجلس بجانبها يحدث نفسه ويقول: إن الطعام طعام الفقراء والمساكين، وأنا فقير مسكين، لا أعلم أن بين أسوار هذه المدينة، ولا في جميع أرباضها رجلاً أحوج، ولا أفقر مني، فإن كان الطمع في هذه الغرارة جريمة فقد أذن لي الكاهن بارتكاب الجرائم في سبيل العيش،

ثم مشى إليها فاحتملها على ظهره ومشى بها جاهداً مترجحاً، فما تجاوز عتبة الدير حتى أثقله الحمل وشعر أنه عاجز عن المسير فحدثته نفسه بإلقائه عن ظهره، ثم تمثل له منظر أحفاده الصغار، وهم ألقاء تحت جدران البيت يتضورون جوعاً، فحمل على نفسه ومشى يعتمد على عصاه مرةً، وعلى الجدار مرة أخرى حتى نال منه الجهد فأحس كأن أنفاسه قد جمدت في صدره لا تهبط، ولا تعلو، وأن ما كان باقياً في عينيه من نورٍ قد انطفأ دفعةً واحدةً فأصبح لا يرى شيئاً مما حوله، وإذا نفثة من دم قد دفقت من صدره فانحدرت على ردائه فسقط في مكانه مغشياً عليه،

He remained in his place until some watchmen had walked passed him and they saw the flour sack beside him. By this time the priests of the church had created havoc, shouting and screaming, saying, 'The flour sack, the flour stack.'

They had been searching for the missing flour sack in all corners of the church, in the end they had given up on finding it. Thereafter, the priests had come out still searching for it everywhere until they met the watchman and then spotted their missing item. Not even an hour had passed by and the flour sack had returned to the church and the old man was put into prison. Then after that you already know what happened. O what a misfortune, my husband has been slayed unjustly. May the Lord have mercy upon me and my poor destitute children after him."

The old woman got up from her place and wiping away her tears with the corner of her scarf she cast a long look at the grave and said, "O my childhood friend, O support for my old age, farewell to you. Good bye O best husband. Goodbye O the best friend of friends, may Allah ﷻ join me and you on the day of retribution." Then she turned back and left on the same path which she had come from.

In the depth of the darkness, her shadow had not yet disappeared, that I saw another shadow appearing exactly from the place I had seen the first. This second shadow was advancing towards me slowly and steadily. So, I hid behind the tree to see what this one would do. At this point the moon had become visible in the sky and it was sending its light upon this big ground. Thus, in the light of the moon I saw this shadow. It came apparent to me that it was a beautiful woman crying. In my entire life, I had never seen tears flowing upon such beautiful cheeks. For a moment, these eyes scanned all around until finally they landed upon the crucified corpse fastened upon a tree.

She walked towards the crucified corpse taking the rope in her hand. She then, untied its knot. She took the young man's body into her arms and placed him on the ground, standing beside it for a while observing it very quietly and peacefully as if she did not care. Then she burst out crying and wept, "O brother." She fell on him and started touching him. She began kissing him and stroked his hair and his forehead. She cried over him excessively in pain. She continued until tiredness had got the better of her. Her incessant crying stilled and she fell beside him like a twig falling to the ground. She did not move. The scene distressed me, so, I walked towards her until I reached her. I saw that she was struggling with her breathing but was alive. I sat at her head crying for her and praying to Allah ﷻ for her until she regained consciousness. Thereupon, she saw me besides her surprised and said,

ولم يزل على حاله تلك حتى مر به العسس فرأوه ورأوا الغرارة بجانبه فارتابوا به، وكان رهبان الدير قد أخذوا يتصايحون فيما بينهم: الغرارة! الغرارة!

وينشدونها في أنحاء الدير حتى يئسوا منها فخرجوا يطلبونها في كل مكانٍ حتى التقوا بالعسس حول مصرع الشيخ فعرفوا ضالتهم، وما هي إلا ساعة حتى كانت الغرارة في الدير وكان الشيخ في السجن، ثم كان بعد ذلك ما رأيت من أمره، فواأسفاه عليه لقد مات شهيداً مظلوماً، ووارحمتاه لي ولأطفالي البؤساء المساكين من بعده!

ثم نهضت من مكانها ومسحت عبرتها بطرف ردائها ونظرت إلى القبر نظرةً طويلةً وقالت: (الوداع يا رفيق صباي، وعماد شيخوختي! الوداع يا خير الأزواج وأبر العشراء! الوداع حتى يجمع الله بيني وبينك في دار جزائه) ثم انكفأت راجعةً في الطريق التي جاءت منها.

وما هو إلا أن تغلغل شخصها في أعماق الظلام حتى رأيت شبحاً آخر يتزاءى من حيث اختفى الشبح الأول وما زال يتقدم نحوي متسللاً يختلس خطواته اختلاساً، فاختبأت وراء الشجرة لأرى ما هو صانع، وكان القمر قد بدأ يشرف على الوجود من مطلعه، ويرسل الخيوط الأولى من أشعته على تلك الساحة الكبرى، فرأيت الشبح على نوره فإذا فتاة جميلة باكية لم أر في حياتي دمعةً على خدٍ أجمل من دمعتها على خدها، فدارت بعينيها لحظةً حتى وقع نظرها على جثة المصلوب بين أعواد الشجرة،

فمشت إليه، ومدت يدها إلى الحبل المشدود به، فعالجت عقدته حتى انحلت ثم احتملته على يدها وأضجعته على الأرض ووقفت بجانبه ساعةً تنظر إليه جامدةً، ساكنةً، كأنها غير آبهةٍ ولا حافلةٍ ثم هتفت صارخةً: واشقيقاه! وسقطت فوقه تضمه وتقبله وتلثم شعره وجبينه، وتزفر فيما بين ذلك زفيراً متداركاً كأنما تنفث أفلاذ كبدها نفثاً، حتى نال منها الجهد فترنحت قليلاً ثم هوت بجانبه هوي الجذع الساقط لا حراك بها، فأهمني أمرها، وخفت أن يكون قد لحق بها مكروه، فمشيت إليها حتى صرت بجانبها فشعرت بأنفاسها الضعيفة تتردد في صدرها؛ فعلمت أنها حية، فجلست فوق رأسها أندبها وأدعو الله لها حتى استفاقت بعد هنيهةٍ، فرأتني بجانبها، فنظرت إلي نظرةً حائرةً، ثم تقدمت نحوي وقالت:

"O strange man, upon who are you crying?"

I said, "I am crying over you and upon your poor unfortunate brother."

She said, "Yes he was an unfortunate and a poor man, therefore O sir, cry over him abundantly, indeed he was the pride of the youth, the flower of life, the fragrance of life and the tranquillity of hearts. Without a shadow of doubt, they did injustice upon him when they killed him. He was not a murderer nor was he a criminal, but he was a man who saw his self-respect and self-honour being compromised by the hands of those who wanted to tarnish it. Therefore, my brother cut off that hand which advanced towards it, and he took revenge for himself, for his honour and for his dignity. If people had done justice upon him, then certainly they would have let him go having mercy upon him and upon his youth. This is because the one who defends his self-respect and the one who kills the one who intends to murder him cannot be a criminal."

I said, "O respectable lady, can you narrate to me his story?"

She replied "Yes, one morning in our village, a delegate from amongst the delegation of the ruler had come who would roam around towns and villages to collect tax. Thus, that deputy had passed by each house in our village until he reached our house. I was standing upon the door of my house and he looked at me with a lustful and an evil look that cast terror and fright in my heart. He then asked me about my brother. I took him where my brother was. When the deputy met my brother, and demanded from him money, my brother requested him for a few days to sell his stock. The deputy refused and stipulated that my brother pay immediately at that moment or he would take me as a security until payment was made. He then gestured to some of his troopers who surrounded me. Indeed, I have heard before this day the stories of those unfortunate young ladies who enter the ruler's castle in terms of security and deposit and after the payment they leave the castle despised, exploited, raped and impregnated.

I ran towards my brother and clung to him. My brother stood in between me and that man and said,

'You have no business whatsoever with this young lady, verily I am the one responsible for the money, therefore I should be taken in and not any other person. If it is security and deposit that you require, then take me as a deposit for my money until the money reaches you.'

على من تبكي أيها الرجل الغريب؟

قلت: أبكي عليك يا سيدتي وعلى فقيدك البائس المسكين،

قالت: نعم إنه بائس مسكين فابك عليه يا سيدي كثيراً فقد كان زينة الشباب وزهرة الحياة وريحانة النفوس ومتعة الأفئدة والقلوب، ولقد ظلموه إذ قتلوه فما كان قاتلاً ولا مجرماً، ولكنه رجلٌ رأى عرضه فريسةً في يد من يريد تمزيقه فقطع اليد الممتدة إليه، وانتقم لنفسه وللشرف والفضيلة منها، ولو أنصفوه لاستبقوه رحمةً به وبشبابه، فما أجرم من ذاد عن عرضه، ولا أثم من قتل قاتله.

قلت: هل لك أن تقصي علي قصته يا سيدتي؟

قالت: نعم. نزل قريتنا صباح يوم من الأيام قائدٌ من قواد الأمير الذين يطوفون البلاد لجمع الضرائب، فمر بأبيات القرية بيتاً بيتاً حتى بلغ منزلنا، وكنت واقفةً على بابه فنظر إلي نظرةً مريبةً طار لها قلبي رعباً وفرقاً، ثم سألني عن أخي فأرشدته إلى مكانه، فسأله عن المال فأستنسأه إياه أياماً قلائل حتى يبيع غلته فأبى إلا أن ينقده الساعة أو يأخذني رهينةً عنده إلى يوم الوفاء. وغمز بي بعض أعوانه، فداروا حولي، وكنت أسمع قبل اليوم حديث أولئك الفتيات الشقيات اللواتي يدخلن رهائن في قصر الأمير فلا يخرجن منه إلا ساقطاتٍ أو محمولات،

ففزعت إلى أخي ولصقت به فوقف بيني وبين الرجل، وقال له:

لا شأن لك مع الفتاة إنما أنا صاحب المال وأنا المأخوذ به من دون الناس جميعاً؛ فإن كان لا بد لك من رهينةٍ فأنا رهينة مالي حتى يصل إليك،

The deputy said, 'It is inevitable upon me to collect the money or either take some security, and inevitably the security is going to be of my choosing. Therefore, if you refuse, then you would have to forfeit your life.'

My brother became enraged with anger and a stream of sweat poured down his forehead. I had never seen such anger within my brother before this day. Then my brother said to him,

'Then let my life be sacrificed for my pride, for my honour and for my values.' Saying this he withdrew his sword and struck it removing the deputy's head right off from his body with one swipe. My brother remained standing there and did not run. Drops of blood were dropping down from his sword until the soldiers had shackled him up, and taking him as a captive imprisoned him in the prison.

O dear, this was his life and this was his death. Thus, if I am crying, I am crying over a courageous young man. I am crying over a young man who had integrity and honour. He was the best of brothers in terms of mercy and decency."

Then she asked, "O sir, are you going to help me to bury him before day light comes between me and him? This is because verily I have become weak and helpless. I do not possess the power to do anything."

I stood up towards the tree and started digging up a ditch near the tree's trunk next to the grave of the old man. I buried him in it and hid him within the grave. The young lady advanced forth towards the grave and kneeled over besides it for a short while, having her head down, she sat quietly. I did not know whether she was crying or whether she had fallen unconscious until eventually she got up from that location. Thus, I saw the soil of the grave which was drenched with her tears. Then she spread out her hand towards me and said, "Thank you very much O respectable person. Indeed, you have helped me at a time when a very few people find any helpers." After that, she left and went on her way. My eyes followed her until she disappeared out of sight.

I returned to my thoughts and to myself. I realised that the corpse of that stoned woman was still at its location. Her sight was distressing and I thought to myself that indeed what could be a greater act of kindness which I could hope for reward from Allah ﷻ on the Day of Judgment, then to bury this poor woman in the ground. Therefore, I started digging up for her a ditch next to the graves of the other two martyrs. Then I put over her my garment and holding her in my arms, I laid her down in her ditch. While I was in the process of throwing soil over her, I felt some movement behind me.

فقال له لا بد لي من المال أو الرهينة، ولا بد أن تكون الرهينة كما أريد، فإن أبيت فحياتك فداء عنها،

فغضب أخي غضبةً انتفض لها جبينه عرقاً، ولم أره في ساعةٍ من ساعات غضبه قبل اليوم، وقال له:

(فلتكن حياتي فداءً لشرفي) ثم جرد سيفه وضربه به ضربةً طارت برأسه، ووقف في مكانه لا يبرحه، وسيفه يقطر دماً حتى غله الأعوان، واحتملوه إلى السجن.

فتلك حياته يا سيدي وذاك مماته، فلئن بكيته أنا أبكي فتى الفتيان همةً ونجدةً، ونادرة الرجال عزةً وإباءً، وأفضل الأخوة رحمةً وحناناً.

ثم قالت: هل لك أن تعينني يا سيدي على مواراته قبل أن يحول النهار بيني وبينه، فقد أصبحت واهيةً متضضعةً لا أقوى على شيء،

فقمت إلى الشجرة فاحتفرت حول ساقها حفرةً بجانب حفرة الشيخ فواريته فيها، فتقدمت الفتاة نحو القبر وجثت بجانبه ساعةً مطرقةً ساكنةً، لا أعلم هل هي باكية أو ذاهلة حتى فارقت مكانها؟ فرأيت تربة القبر مخضلةً بدموعها ثم مدت يدها إلي وقالت: شكراً لك يا سيدي فقد أعنتني على موقفٍ قلما يجد فيه مستعين معيناً، ومضت لسبيلها. فأتبعتها نظري حتى اختفت آخر طيةٍ من طيات ردائها،

فعدت إلى نفسي، فإذا جثة الفتاة المرجومة لا تزال مكانها، فهاجني منظرها وقلت في نفسي: إنني لا ادخر لنفسي عملاً أرجو فيه رحمة الله وإحسانه يوم جزائه، أفضل من مواراة هذه المسكينة التراب، فاحتفرت لها حفرةً بجانب حفرة الشهيدين ثم ألقيت عليها ردائي، واحتملتها علي يدي حتى أضجعتها في حفرتها، فإني لأجثو عليها التراب إذ شعرت بحركةٍ ورائي،

I turned back to find a young troubled man standing, enveloped in a black cloth. Only the whiteness of his face was visible. He was the first to start conversation with me, he said, "O good man, who is the person of the grave whom you are throwing soil over?"

I replied, "It is the young woman who was stoned. I saw her corpse being unattended to in this ground, therefore, out of compassion for her, I decided to dig a grave for her."

Then the man said, "O kind man, between me and this young woman, there is a bond, would you allow me to say my last farewells to her before this soil comes between us."

I said, "Yes certainly, it is your affair, you may do as you please."

I Moved aside. He drew closer to the grave and knelt on top of the grave. He started talking to the deceased lady. I felt as if the stars in the sky and the winds in the atmosphere were re-echoing his words. He continued with his discussion until his heart attained tranquillity. Then he stood up and started putting soil over her until he had buried her.

After that he turned towards me and said, "Most certainly Allah ﷻ has thanked you for this act of kindness which you did for this young lady who was wronged. You covered her up whereas people had completely disclosed her body. You safeguarded that which the people had disrespected. May Allah ﷻ reward you good over what you did, and may He also do a favour upon you the way you had done favour upon her."

He was about to leave but I promptly stopped him and asked him, "Did this young woman die unjustly the way you are saying?"

His lips moved generating a small smile and he looked at me with a peaceful and a content look and said, "O kind man, yes, if she was not then you would have not seen me here in this moment of time standing in the corner of her grave crying. I am the man whom they had slandered and accused her with. I am confident enough to declare to you the way I am going to declare to my Lord on the day when I am going to stand in front of Him, highlighting the injustice which was done upon her, certainly she is exempted from the sin which the people had accused her with. Without a shadow of doubt, she was purer than the dew which is upon a flower. She was cleaner than a clean drop of water. Verily I loved this young woman ever since we had been small, we played with each other. She likewise had loved me. Then we became adults and our love also blossomed. We pledged to be loyal and sincere. Then I sent the proposal of marriage to her father. He accepted my proposal with happiness and with prosperity.

فالتفت فإذا فتًى يافعٌ متلفعٌ ببردةٍ سوداء لا يستبين منها غير بياض وجهه، فابتدرني بقوله: من صاحب هذا القبر الذي تجثو ترابه يا سيدي؟

قلت: فتاة مرجومة رأيت جثتها الساعة منبوذةً في هذا العراء، فرحمت مصرعها، واحتفرت لها هذا القبر الذي تراه،

فقال: إن لي يا سيدي مع هذه الفتاة شأناً، فهل تأذن لي أن أودعها الوداع الأخير قبل أن يحول التراب بيني وبينها؟

قلت: نعم شأنك وما تريد؛

وتنحيت قليلاً، فدنا من القبر وجثا فوق تربته، وظل يناجي الدفينة نجاءً خلت أن الكواكب تردده في سمائها، والرياح ترجعه في أجوائها، حتى اشتفت نفسه، فقام إلى التراب يهيله عليها حتى واراها،

ثم التفت إلي وقال: لقد شكر الله لك يا سيدي هذه اليد التي أسديتها إلى هذه الفتاة المظلومة بستر ما كشف الناس عن عورتها، وحفظ ما أضاعوا من حرمتها، فجزاك الله خيراً بما فعلت، وأحسن إليك كما أحسنت إليها،

وأراد الرجوع فاستوقفته وقلت له: وهل ماتت هذه الفتاة مظلومةً كما تقول؟

فانفجرت شفتاه عن ابتسامةٍ مرةٍ ونظر إلي نظرةً هادئةً مطمئنةً وقال: نعم يا سيدي؟ ولولا ذلك ما رأيتني الساعة واقفاً على حافة قبرها أندبها. أنا الرجل الذي اتهموها به، وأستطيع أن أقول لك كما أقول لربي يوم أقف بين يديه رافعاً إليه ظلامتها: إنها بريئة مما رموها به، وإنها أطهر من الزهرة المطلولة، وأنقى من القطرة الصافية. لقد أحببت هذه الفتاة مذ كانت طفلةً لاعبة، وأحبتني كذلك، ثم شببنا وشب الحب معنا، فتعاقدنا على الوفاء والإخلاص، ثم خطبتها إلى أبيها فأخطبني راضياً مسروراً،

When there were only a few days remaining for our wedding night, her father tragically passed away. Thus, we realised that we inevitably would have to wait for one full year. When one year was almost over I had to go to the judge of the city regarding some issue relating to her inheritance. However, when the judge saw her, he fell in love with her and sent a message to her paternal uncle.

Her uncle had become her guardian in her affairs after her father's death. Her uncle was a very greedy man. He was amongst those people that if they saw a sparkling coin on the other side of an ocean full of blood, they would jump in it.

The judge had expressed his desire to marry her to her uncle. Her uncle overwhelmed with joy and excitement, not delaying a moment accepted his offer and went to the young woman to share the good news.

She was saddened and said to him,

'Verily I do not have the power to have two fiancés' in one time.'

Her uncle did not care about what she had said and told her, 'Soon you shall get married with him, whomever I choose, willingly or unwillingly. You do not have any authority over yourself, verily all the authority is mine in matters concerning you.'

Not even a few days passing by, all the preparations of her wedding were complete and the day of her departure was fixed. Before the sun could set on that day, she gathered all her belongings from her house, encompassing her clothes and her jewellery and then left under the stars of that night, not knowing where was she heading, where she was going and which path she should adapt. Verily her uncle raised the matter of her running away to the judge. The judge promptly sent his helpers and his guards in search of her at every possible location. Some of his guards had seen her sitting behind some walls and went towards her. She became scared when she saw them. She left her bag at that place and ran away from them as fast as she could.

At that moment, I was just returning to my house. At once, she saw me and then she threw herself upon me and said,

'Verily they are following me, if they find me they will kill me, have mercy on me so that Allah ﷻ may have mercy upon you.'

Her situation had completely stressed me out as I then took her to my house and I hid her in one of the rooms. Not even a moment passed by that her uncle entered. Behind his uncle there were the judge's guards. Her uncle was searching for her with extreme determination. I denied having seen her at all but he did not believe me.

حتى إذا لم يبق بيني وبين البناء بها إلا أيام معدودات إذ نزلت بأبيها نازلة الموت، فعلمنا أن لا بد لنا من الانتظار بأنفسنا عاماً كاملاً، ففعلنا، حتى إذا انقضى العام أو كاد، حدث أن ذهبت الفتاة إلى قاضي المدينة في أمرٍ يتعلق بميراثها، فرآها القاضي فتبعتها نفسه فأرسل وراء عمها،

وكان ولي أمرها بعد أبيها، وهو رجل من الطامعين المداهنين الذين لا يبالون أن يخوضوا بحراً من الدم إذا تراءى لهم على شاطئه الآخر دينار لامع،

فعرض عليه رغبته في الزواج مع ابنة أخيه، فطار بهذه المنحة فرحاً وسروراً، ولم يتردد في إجابة طلبه، وعاد إلى الفتاة يحمل إليها هذه البشرى،

فاستقبلته بوجهٍ باسرٍ وقالت له: إنني لا أستطيع أن أكون خطيبة رجلين في آنٍ واحدٍ،

فلم يبال بقولها وقال لها: ستتزوجين ممن أريد طائعةً أو كارهةً، فلا خيار لك في نفسك إنما الخيار لي في أمرك وحدي،

وما هي إلا أيام قلائل حتى أعدوا لها عدة زواجها وسموا يوماً لزفافها، فما غربت شمس ذلك اليوم حتى جمعت ما كان لها في بيتها من ثيابٍ وحليةٍ، وخرجت تحت ستار الليل هائمةً على وجهها لا تعلم أين تذهب، ولا أي طريقٍ تسلك، وكان عمها قد رفع إلى القاضي أمر فرارها، فبث عليها عيونه وأرصاده يطلبونها في كل مكان، حتى لمحها بعضهم جالسةً تحت بعض الجدران، فأقبل عليها فذعرت لمرآه، وتركت حقيبتها مكانها وفرت بين يديه تعدو عدواً سريعاً،

وكنت عائداً في تلك الساعة إلى منزلي، فرأتني فألقت نفسها علي وقالت:

إنهم يتبعونني، وإنهم إن ظفروا بي قتلوني، فارحمني يرحمك الله؛

فأهمني أمرها، وذهبت بها إلى منزلي، وأخفيتها في بعض حجراته. وما هي إلا ساعة حتى دخل عمها ووراءه أعوان القاضي يطلبها طلباً شديداً، فأنكرت رؤيتها فلم يصدقني،

He started slamming open all the doors until eventually he had found her and shouted, 'Here is the young adulterous woman and this is her companion.'

I swore to him every kind of oath belonging to the faith that indeed she is free from that slander which they were accusing her with. Regardless, they did not believe me. Her uncle ordered the guards to capture her, I got in between them and her. Then, one of them hit me over the head with a heavy blow due to which I fell down unconscious upon the floor.

I did not wake up from unconsciousness for an hour. When I did, I felt a very strong fever burning my body and became bed bound for a few days. Whenever, I had gained slight consciousness, I would picture that scene which I had seen. This would cause me to fit and I would fall unconscious. This continued until I attained the mercy of Allah ﷻ as I became and felt better. A few days after my recovery, I had the strength to come out of my house. I came to know all this innocent lady had gone through. So, I have come here to bid her my last farewells and to wrap up her dead body and bury it, I am not going to enjoy the taste of life after her until I meet with her."

Then after that, he casted a final look at her full of sorrow, sadness, burning passion and remorse. After that he went on his way.

Not even a little while passing by, I saw the moon disappearing. The entire atmosphere became quiet, and the ground became scary and gloomy. Then I climbed upon a hilltop, I could see the three graves from here. Then with my large scarf I covered myself up, and rested my head on some rocks and thought to myself,

Is there no just person or a compassionate man left upon the face of this earth anymore? If the earth does not contain neither, does that mean that within the heavens there is also no just or compassionate being?

That religious guide sinned because he became miserly towards that poor old man over one coin which was amongst his possessions. This one coin however could have got rid of his and his families hunger. Due to this, the man was forced to commit the crime of stealing. Then the thief was penalised for his stealing. However, the cruel man was not penalised for his harshness and his ruthlessness. If it was not for the cruelty of that cruel man, then they would have not been stealing from him.

وأخذ يضرب أبواب الحجرات باباً باباً حتى ظفر بها فصاح: ها هي الفتاة الزانية، وهذا صاحبها،

فأقسمت له بكل محرجةٍ من الأيمان أنها بريئة مما يرميها به فلم يصغ إلي، وأمر الأعوان فاحتملوها، وحاولت أن أحول بينهم وبينها فضربني أحدهم على رأسي ضربةً طارت بصوابي فسقطت مغشياً علي،

فلم أستفق إلا بعد ساعة، فوجدت الحمى قد أخذت مأخذها من جسمي، فلزمت فراشي بضعة أيام لا أفيق ساعةً حتى يتمثل لي ذلك المنظر الذي رأيته فأشعر بالرعدة تتمشى في أعضائي فأعود إلى ذهولي واستغراقي حتى أدركتني رحمة الله، فأبللت منذ الأمس بعض الإبلال واستطعت أن أخرج الليلة من منزلي، فعلمت ما تم من أمر تلك المسكينة، فجئت كما تراني أودعها الوداع الأخير وأواري جثتها التراب، وما أنا بالسالي عنها، ولا بالذائق حلاوة العيش من بعدها حتى ألحق بها.

ثم ألقى على قبرها نظرةً جمعت في طياتها جميع معاني النظرات البائسات من حزنٍ وبأسٍ ولوعةٍ وشقاءٍ، ومضى لسبيله.

فما أبعد إلا قليلاً حتى رأيت القمر ينحدر إلى مغربه، ثم ما لبث أن اختفى، فإذا الفضاء ظلمة وسكون، وإذا الساحة وحشة وانقباض، فصعدت على ربوةٍ عاليةٍ مشرفةٍ على القبور الثلاثة، ثم تلفعت بردائي، وألقيت رأسي على بعض الصخور، وأنشأت أحدث نفسي وأقول:

ليت شعري! ألا يوجد في هذه الدنيا عادل، ولا راحم، فإن خلت منهما رقعة الأرض فهل خلت منهما ساحة السماء؟

أجرم الزعيم الديني لأنه ضن على ذلك الشيخ المسكين بدرهمٍ من مال يسد به جوعته وجوعة أهل بيته، فاضطر الرجل إلى ارتكاب جريمة السرقة، فعوقب السارق على سرقته، ولم يعاقب القاسي على قسوته، ولولا قسوة القاسي ما كانت سرقة السارق.

Regarding the ruler, indeed he sinned because he sent his deputy to abduct a chaste woman who did not want to compromise her honour, because of this her brother was forced to confront the deputy which led him towards the crime of killing. Accordingly, the young man was punished for his crime. However, the one who caused this crime to be committed in the first place, has been exempted from punishment.

The judge had also sinned. This is because he intended to force a young lady who did not love him to marry him. Thus, because of this, she ran away and due to her fleeing she was penalised. Regardless, the judge was not punished for his tyranny or injustice. Like this, the criminal became exempted and the exempted became a criminal. Moreover, ironically, it is the culprit judge who has been given the authority to penalise the innocent.

So, after this day, is the sky going to fall upon the earth? Is the sky going to continue to brighten the earth through its stars ever again? Is the sky going to send rain again?

Then I turned towards the place of the slaughter where these inhabitants of the graves were killed, my sight landed upon the ditch which was filled with blood of these martyrs. I saw the reflection of the star lighting up the surface of the bloody trench. I raised my eyes towards that star only to discover that it was the planet Mars. It was blazing with fire and rage as if it was the hearts of these people demanding retribution. I stared at it for a while. Then I saw it descending from its height slowly and gradually. As it was descending, its body kept getting bigger and bigger. It continued to mount down until there remained between it and the earth what appeared like a mile or even less in distance. Then I saw it having a shivering fit and it suddenly turned into an angel of punishment, fire was blazing out of its eyes and from its nostrils. With its wings and other body parts it was gliding down. It kept on descending until it landed upon the head of the tree that was shading the graves of those martyrs. Then its wings triggered off a shake so severe that all corners of the earth had shook and lit up. It started speaking with a voice like a thunderbolt of lightning in the horizon. It said,

"Look, these people are repeating those acts which they used to do before. Look, this earth has filled up with evil and mischief once again. Look, there remains no vicinity or location which is pure and righteous where an angel from the angels belonging to the heavens can take refuge towards. Look, the powerful have become more powerful and the weak have become weaker. Look, the flesh of the weak is entering the bellies of the rich continuously and the ones at the forefront are not going to bear this anymore and the ones who are behind them are not going to suffice upon this anymore.

وأجرم الأمير لأنه أرسل قائده لاختطاف فتاةٍ حرةٍ لا تؤثر أن تجود بعرضها فاضطر أخوها إلى الذود عنها فارتكب جريمة القتل، فعوقب الفتى على جريمته وسلم من العقوبة من دفعه إلى الإجرام.

وأجرم القاضي لأنه أراد أن يكره فتاةً لا تحبه على الزواج منه، ففرت من وجهه فعاقبوها على فرارها، ولم يعاقبوا القاضي على ظلمه واستبداده. وهكذا أصبح المجرم بريئاً، والبريء مجرماً، بل أصبح المجرم قاضي البريء وصاحب الحق في معاقبته.

فهل تسقط السماء على الأرض بعد اليوم، أم لا تزال تنيرها بكواكبها ونجومها، وتمطرها غيثها ومزنها.

ثم التفت إلى مصرع المقبورين فوقع نظري على بركة الدم التي اجتمعت فيها دماء هؤلاء الشهداء. فرأيت خيال نجم في السماء يتلألأ فوق صفحتها، فرفعت نظري إلى النجم فإذاً هو المريخ يتلهب ويضطرم كأنه جمرة الغيظ في أفئدة الموتورين، فعلق نظري به ساعة، ثم رأيت كأنه يهبط من عليائه رويداً رويداً، فيعظم جرمه كلما ازداد هبوطه، حتى إذا لم يبق بينه وبين الأرض إلا ميل أو بعض ميل، إذا به ينتفض انتفاضاً شديداً، وإذا هو على صورة ملكٍ من ملائكة العذاب ينبعث الشرر من عينيه ومنخريه، ويتطاير من أجنحته وأطرافه، فلم يزل هابطاً حتى نزل على رأس الشجرة التي تظلل قبور الشهداء، ثم صفق بجناحيه تصفيقةً اهتزت لها جوانب الأرض، وأضاءت بها الأرجاء، ثم أخذ ينطق بصوتٍ كأنه جلجلة الرعد في آفاق السماء ويقول:

(ها هم الناس قد عادوا إلى ما كانوا عليه، وها هي الأرض قد ملئت شروراً وفساداً حتى لم يبق فيها بقعة طاهرة يستطيع أن يأوي إليها ملك من أملاك السماء. ها هم الأقوياء قد ازدادوا قوة، والضعفاء قد ازدادوا ضعفاً، وها هي لحوم الفقراء تنحدر في بطون الأغنياء انحداراً، فلا الأولون بمستمسكين، ولا الآخرون بقانعين.

Look, the poor are dying of starvation, they are not finding anyone who could be kind towards them. Look, the distressed are dying, they are not finding anyone who could help them with their problems and with their adversities.

Look these are the rulers, indeed they have breached the trust and the pledge of Allah ﷻ and have broken it. They have put away the swords which Allah ﷻ had given to them to establish justice and the truth. In place, they have drawn out other swords which are not used to establish the law of Allah ﷻ and neither to serve humanity. They are walking along with their own swords, in search for their own desires and lusts. They keep on going until they obtain it.

Look at these Judges, certainly they have become greedy and tyrant. They have made laws only to exercise their hunting and oppress the weak. They arrest whoever they want under their order, as there is no one to question them.

Look at these contractors of religion, verily they have become the contractors of the world. They have converted their places of worship into the houses of thieves. They collect for it, stealing wealth from people. Then they become stingy with it, not even giving a little to the poor and the destitute.

Look at these people, verily they have become the helpers for their rulers over their desires and fantasies. Indeed, these people have become the supporters for their judges over their injustices. Certainly, these people have become the assistance for the contractors of religion over their stealing.

Let the wrath and the punishment of Allah ﷻ fall upon them all, whether it be the rulers or the ruled, or whether it be the king or its subjects.

Let the thrones be overturned. Let the places of worship be destroyed. Let the courts be broken down. Let the towns, villages, the mountains, the elevated and lowered places all be destroyed. Let the earth be drowned in the ocean of blood drowning in it men, women, old people, the children, the good, the bad, the criminals and the innocent all. Allah ﷻ has not done injustice upon them but it is them who have done injustice upon themselves."

ها هم الفقراء يموتون جوعاً، فلا يجدون من يحسن إليهم، والمنكوبون يموتون كمداً، فلا يجدون من يعينهم على همومهم وأحزانهم.

ها هم الأمراء قد خانوا عهد الله وخفروا ذمامه؛ فأغمدوا السيوف التي وضعها الله في أيديهم لإقامة العدل والحق، وتقلدوا سيوفاً غيرها، لا هي إلى الشريعة، ولا إلى الطبيعة، ومشوا بها يفتتحون لأنفسهم طريق شهواتهم ولذائذهم حتى ينالوا منها ما يريدون.

ها هم القضاة قد طمعوا وظلموا، ووضعوا القانون ترساً أمام أعينهم يصيبون من ورائه، ولا يصابون، وينالون من يشاؤون تحت حمايته، ولا ينالون.

ها هم زعماء الدين قد أصبحوا زعماء الدنيا، فحولوا معابدهم إلى مغاور لصوصٍ يجمعون فيها ما يسرقون من أموال العباد، ثم يضنون بالقليل منه على الفقراء والمساكين.

ها هم الناس جميعاً قد أصبحوا أعواناً للأمراء على شهواتهم، والقضاة على ظلمهم، وزعماء الأديان على لصوصيتهم،

فلتسقط عليهم جميعاً نقمة الله ملوكاً ومملوكين ورؤساء ومرؤوسين.

لتسقط العروش، ولتهدم المعابد، ولتتقوض المحاكم، وليعم الخراب المدن والأمصار، والسهول والأوعار، والنجاد والأغوار، ولتغرق الأرض في بحرٍ من الدماء يهلك فيه الرجال والنساء، والشيوخ والأطفال، والأخيار والأشرار، والمجرمون والأبرياء، وما ظلمهم الله، ولكن كانوا أنفسهم يظلمون).

The angel of punishment did not complete his supplication yet, that the ditch of blood started to boil and heat up, like on the day of the supplication of Prophet Noah, how the stove boiled and heated up. Then the blood over flowed from the ditch and travelling with a fast current, it spread in the earth creating a fast-flowing flood of blood. At once, the earth appeared as an ocean of blood which was spreading and scattering fast. It was destroying everything which came in front of it, whether it was the green lands, the cattle, the castles, the cottages, the animals, the humans, those who spoke and those who did not, all were destroyed.

Then I felt the ocean of blood was gradually rising higher and higher until its waves had hit the top of the hill where I was sitting, I screamed out.

I woke up from my sleep and from my dream. It was the morning of the day, 28th of July 1914. At once I heard a caller screaming, "The War has begun." (The 1st World War)

وما انتهى من دعوته تلك، حتى رأيت بركة الدم تفور كما فار التنور يوم دعوة نوح، ثم فاضت الدماء منها ومشت تتدفق في الأرض تدفق السيل المنحدر، وإذا الأرض بحرٌ أحمر يزخر ويعج ويكتسح أمامه كل شيءٍ من زرعٍ وضرعٍ، وقصور وأكواخ، وحيوان وإنسان، وناطق وصامت،

ثم شعرت به يعلو شيئاً فشيئاً حتى ضرب بأمواجه رأس الربوة التي أنا جالس فوقها، فصرخت صرخةً عظمى.

فاستيقظت من نومي، وكان ذلك في صباح اليوم الثامن والعشرين من شهر يوليو سنة ١٩١٤ فإذا صائحٌ يصيح تحت نافذة غرفتي: إعلان الحرب!

The Victim / Ad-Dahiyyah (Translation)

(The Story)

Margaret Jowita became an adult. She was poor and had no money from which she could buy herself a husband. She did not find any man who could sell himself to her without any money, nor did she find anyone who could fulfil her needs and to safeguard her chastity. However, by all means, it was inevitable for her to live. She did not find any way of earning a livelihood other than by compromising her respect. Thus, she took her self-dignity to the markets of misfortunes and grief. Some dealers fixed a mean price for her. Despite disliking this occupation, she sold herself and became from amongst the bearers of loss.

Indeed, her beauty became a misfortune for her. If she had been ugly, perhaps she would have found someone from amongst the people who would have shown mercy to her but beauty is the merchandise of profitable trade. The possessor of beauty does not endure the power to obtain anything from the people if she is poor and deprived, other than to sell herself.

For this reason, the burdensome woman became hateful towards all men. She swore that she would beautify her appearance in order to take revenge from them as they have exploited her dignity and her chastity.

She fulfilled her promise, the way a loyal person fulfils his pledge. She starting living with men but she did not love them. She became extremely happy when she destroyed them and their wealth without any remorse. She used to see under her feet the tears of those who used to cry with extreme joy and pleasure and she used to say,

"Woe upon you O the assembly of men, I did not ask you but only one bread in the afternoon and one bread in the evening with respect and honour, but you refused to give them to me. However, when I asked you through indecency and through vile behaviour, you gave everything you possessed, all your wealth and all your properties, knowingly and with your free will in the state of happiness. How small are your hearts and how corrupt are your characters?

الضحية

(مترجمة)

نشأت (مرغريت جوتييه) فقيرةً لا تملك مالاً تشتري به زوجاً، ولا تجد بين الرجال من يبيعها نفسه بلا مالٍ أو يحسن إليها بما يسد خلتها، ويستر عورتها، وكان لا بد لها أن تعيش فلم تجد بين يديها سوى عرضها، فذهبت به إلى سوق الشقاء والآلام، فساومها فيه بعض المساومين بأبخس الأثمان، فباعته إياه كارهةً مرغمةً، وكانت من الخاسرين.

ولقد كان جمالها شؤماً عليها، فلو أنها كانت شوهاء لوجدت في الناس من يرحمها ويحنوا عليها، ولكن الجمال سلعة من السلع النافقة. لا يستطيع صاحبه أن ينال ما في أيدي الناس إن كان فقيراً معوزاً، إلا من طريق المساومة فيه.

لذلك نقمت تلك الفتاة المنكوبة على الرجال جميعاً، وأقسمت أن تتخذ من جمالها الذي هو مطمع أنظارهم وقبلة آمالهم: آلة انتقامٍ تنتقم بها منهم لعرضها وشرفها.

ولقد برت بيمينها بر الوفي بعهده، فعاشرت الرجال ولم تحبهم، ونكبتهم في أموالهم، وفي أنفسهم، ولم تأسف عليهم، ونظرت إلى دموع الباكين تحت قدميها نظرات الغبطة والسرور، وهي تقول:

ويحٌ لكم يا معشر الرجال، ما كنت أطلب منكم باسم الفضيلة والشرف إلا رغيفاً واحداً لغذائي وآخر لعشائي فأبيتموهما علي، فلما طلبت منكم باسم الرذيلة جميع ما تملك أيديكم من مال ونشب، بذلتموه لي طائعين مختارين، فما أصغر نفوسكم وأخس أقداركم!

Indeed, the most inferior within the society and the one considered the most humiliated in front of people had the power to marry me; he could have had my body, my heart, my life without any money in exchange of fulfilling my needs and safeguarding my respect. However, you did not do this! Now, all your respected and honourable people are bowing down upon my feet the way a despised, a humiliated dog bows down next to his master's dinner table. Though, they do attain from me more than what that dog receives.

You loved your wealth abundantly and you rejected to marry anyone other than a wealthy woman, so that you can mix your new wealth with your old wealth. However, today, spend all your money on a woman who is a prostitute, who will give you neither any money nor any love. Spend all of your silver and gold until remains neither for you any new wealth nor any old wealth."

***

Margaret appeared in the sky of Paris as a sparkling star which spread its light, dazzling the eyes and enveloping all corners of the atmosphere with brightness. The intellects started circulating around her like a honeybee hovers around a flower. Gold and silver started flowing in front of her rapidly like a fast river in the evening sun. Respected faces had kneeled in front of her and the elevated foreheads had stooped at her feet. The necks of all men together had appeared in her hand as if she had tied them in one rope. She would to shake one corner of the rope, causing the men to shake, and when she withheld the rope in a stationary position the men also became stationary. Her state with them became like a master dealing with their dog. She never quenched their thirst completely and neither did she satisfy them totally. However, she did not keep them hungry lest they become unresponsive towards her. She used to create hope and desire within her lovers until they assumed that now their luck had drawn them close to her and there was no distance remaining between him and his desire so much so that that if he was to stretch his hand towards her he would obtain it. Promptly she used to cast him away like a poor thirsty being is refused water at his mouth. However, when she would learn that now he has become hopeless, has had enough and that he intended to go away with full conviction of not returning, she would send him a ray from the rays of her sweet intoxicating smiles, there after he used to return to her willingly and being submissive.

ولقد كان في استطاعة أصغركم شأناً، وأهونكم على نفسه وعلى الناس جميعاً، أن يشتري مني جسمي وقلبي وحياتي بلا ثمنٍ سوى سد خلتي وصيانة عرضي فلم تفعلوا، فها هم أولاء اليوم عظماؤكم وأشرافكم يجثون تحت قدمي جثي الكلب الذليل تحت مائدة سيده، فلا ينالون مني أكثر مما ينال منها.

أحببتم المال حباً جماً فأبيتم إلا أن تتزوجوا ذات مال لتضموا طارفها إلى تليدكم فابذلوا اليوم لامرأةٍ مومسٍ، لا تمنحكم مالاً ولا حباً، جميع ما في أيديكم من فضةٍ وذهبٍ، حتى لا يبقى لكم طارف و لا تليد.

***

ظهرت مرغريت في سماء باريس كوكباً متلألئاً يبعث الأنوار ويبهر الأنظار، ويملأ اجواز الفضاء بهجةً وضياء، فطارت حولها العقول طيران النحل حول الزهر، وسال النضار بين يديها سيلان الجدول المتدفق تحت أشعة الأصيل، وعنت لها الوجوه الكريمة، وتعفرت تحت قدميها الجباه الرفيعة، وأصبحت أعناق الرجال في يدها كأنما قد سلكتهم جميعاً في سلكٍ واحدٍ، ثم أمسكت بطرف السلك تحركه فيتحركون، وتمسك عنه فيمسكون، وكان شأنها معهم شأن صاحب الكلب مع كلبه، لا يشبعه فيستغني عنه، ولا يجيعه فييأس منه، فكانت تملأ نفس عاشقها أملاً ورجاءً حتى إذا ظن أن قد دنا به حظه، وأن ليس بينه وبين أمله إلا أن يمد إليه يده فيناله، ذادته عنه ذود الظامىء الهيمان عن ورده أدنى ما يكون إلى فمه، فإذا علمت أن اليأس قد بلغ من نفسه، وأنه قد أزمع أن يركب رأسه إلى حيث لا مرد له؛ بعثت وراءه شعاعاً من أشعة ابتساماتها العذبة الخلابة فاستردته إليها صاغراً مستسلماً.

In this manner, this young naked hungry woman who needed a morsel yesterday and did not even have rags to cover herself with, became the Queen of Paris and the Sovereign of its throne. Like this, she became the possessor of the bridle connected to all the men and she became a pain for the women of Paris. She became that bright star that the eyes gaze upon. She became that hidden secret which even the intellects used to reflect upon.

This was what the people knew about her. However, what she knew about herself was that whatever the people had given to her in form of gold, silver wealth, money, houses, flats, properties, horses and carriages, were not even equal to, nor compensated for even one tear from amongst the tears she had shed on the day when she had sold herself. Certainly, these diamonds, these gems, these clothes, these crowns were given to her by men so that she could wear them so that she could please and satisfy their desires the way an owner of a dog enjoys seeing a beautiful collar around his dog's neck which the dog himself gains no personal benefit from. Nevertheless, she acknowledged that she had sold herself without a price and without any gain.

Whenever she was alone, she remembered that these hearts which were flying around her were flying only over her beauty and not for her. Her speculation was that if she was deprived from this beauty even for a second, then all people around her would flee inevitably and she would be left alone, abandoned in this world. As then no heart would show affection to her and neither would an eye cry over her. Thus, she used to cry, weeping in pain. She used to consider herself to be a troublesome lady like them because she lives with them and yet has no love for them. She was living between a nation who didn't have genuine love for her but fake and false love.

Whenever she passed by the servant quarter of her castle in the morning and evenings, she saw her servant sat besides his wife and children. She saw his show of a lot of love, affection and sincerity towards them and likewise they in return were showing the same compassion. She too wished, if only she too could have this love and compassion in the form of a husband and children. She wanted this more than anything in the whole world.

وكذلك أصبحت تلك الفتاة الجائعة العارية التي كانت تعوزها بالأمس اللقمة، وتعييها الخرقة؛ سيدة باريس وصاحبة عرشها، ومالكة أزمة رجالها، وفاجعة قلوب نسائها، والنجم الخالق الذي تبتهل إليه العيون، والسر الغامض الذي تحار فيه الظنون.

ذلك ما يعلمه الناس من أمرها؛ أما ما تعلمه من أمر نفسها فهي ترى أن جميع ما يبذله لها الناس من فضةٍ وذهبٍ، وأثاثٍ ورياشٍ، وقصورٍ ودورٍ، وجيادٍ ومركباتٍ، لا يساوي دمعةً واحدةً من تلك الدموع التي سكبتها على نفسها يوم باعت عرضها، وأن جميع هذه اللآلىء والجواهر والأردية والتيجان التي يهبونها إنما يهبونها أنفسهم ليتمتعوا بمنظرها فوق جسمها كما يتمتع صاحب الكلب بمنظر القلادة في عنق كلبه، وما له من ذلك شيء، فكأنما باعت عرضها بلا ثمنٍ ولا جزاءٍ.

وكانت تخلو بنفسها حيناً فتذكر أن جميع هذه القلوب الطائرة حولها إنما تطير على جمالها لا عليها، وأنها إن حرمت هذا الجمال ساعةً واحدةً انفض الناس جميعاً من حولها، وأصبحت وحيدة منقطعةً في هذا العالم لا يعطف عليها قلب ولا تبكي عليها عين، فتبكي بكاء الأشقياء على أنفسهم، بل ترى أنها شقية مثلهم، لأنها تعاشر من لا تحب، وتحيا بين قومٍ لا يحبونها إلا حباً كاذباً.

وربما مرت بعض غدواتها أو روحاتها بغرفة حارس قصرها، وهو جالس بين زوجه وأولاده، يمنحهم حبه وإخلاصه ويمنحونه من ذلك مثل ما يمنحهم؛ فتتمنى أن لو كان حظها من هذه الحياة غرفةً كهذه الغرفة وزوجاً وأولاداً كهذا الزوج وهؤلاء الأولاد. ثم لا تقترح على دهرها بعد ذلك شيئاً.

People saw Margaret never allowed a married or engaged man to enter her house. People assumed that this was due to her selfishness. They used to say that she is a greedy woman who does not love anyone other than him who is completely sincere to her. Only if the people had known her reality and the secret of her heart, then they would learn that she was an extremely hurt woman who was torn apart with sadness. Verily the world had deprived her with the blessing of marriage but she still safeguarded and acknowledged its value. She hated to give pain to another lady.

Indeed, some people had recognised her affairs of her private life, and stated that she has given money to poor young girls as a dowry two or three times and with its aid they got married to whom they wanted. However, people did not believe this news and said, "Indeed a thief can never become charitable and certainly the spring of good deeds can never gush out from the heart of an adulteress women." Nevertheless, the truth was that she did do this and she had done so numerous times.

This was the heart of Margaret and this was the secret of her heart. She herself was destroyed, despite that she was not pleased with her destruction. She was a fallen woman yet, she disliked to see other women falling in society like her. Only if it was within the power of a fallen lady to return, after repenting and re-establishing her state amongst the hearts of men again. Only if they could wipe out whatever they had committed before from amongst the indecency through reconciliation, then this would have been the most superior thing for women in terms of repentance and in terms of disposing their affairs. Nonetheless, it was the society which made her fall, and it was the society which stripped away her veil of honour which she used to wear. If now, she was to request her veil back, society would refuse to return it to her. Consequently, she had to now continue living in a fallen state whether she liked it or not!

A few years passed and Margaret became ill, so much so that she became bound to her house for quite some days. After that her illness increased. Therefore, the doctors suggested that she should go to the Pioneer in California to use their baths and spas so that through its water and air she recovers from illness. She travelled there alone with her maid. There was an old rich gentleman called Duke Mohan at Pioneer with his daughter. His daughter was also ill. She was suffering from a severe chest infection as her father wanted to cure her illness. However, he could not find any cure for her and tragically she died in his hands. He buried her there and remained there for a few days. He kept on going to her grave and kept on crying profusely.

وما رآها الناس في يومٍ من أيامٍ استقبلت في قصرها رجلاً متزوجاً أو خاطباً، فكانوا يحملون هذا الأمر منها على محمل الأثرة، ويقولون إنها امرأة طامعة لا تحب إلا أن يكون عاشقها خالصاً لها، ولو أنهم عرفوا حقيقة أمرها وألموا بسريرة نفسها، لعلموا أنها امرأة حزينة منكوبة، قد فجعها الدهر في سعادة الزوجية فعرفت قيمتها، فهي لا تحب أن تفجع فيها امرأةً غيرها.

لقد تحدث بعض الذين ألموا بشؤون حياتها الخاصة أنها وهبت مرتين أو ثلاثاً بعض الفتيات الفقيرات مهوراً يستعن بها على الزواج ممن يردن، فلم يصدق الناس هذا الخبر وقالوا: إن السالب لا يكون واهباً، وإن ينبوع الخير لا يمكن أن ينفجر في قلوب النساء الفاجرات؟ ولكن الحقيقة أنها فعلت ذلك، وربما فعلت أكثر منه.

هذا هو قلب (مرغريت)، وهذه هي سريرة نفسها: فهي فتاة فاسدة ولكنها غير راضيةٍ عن فسادها؛ وساقطة، ولكنها لا تحب أن ترى الفتيات ساقطاتٍ مثلها، ولو كان في استطاعة المرأة الساقطة أن تسترجع بتوبتها وإنابتها مكانتها في قلوب الناس، وأن تمحو بصلاحها ما سلف من فسادها لكانت هي أقرب النساء إلى التوبة والنزوع، ولكن المجتمع الذي أسقطها وسلبها ذلك الرداء من الشرف الذي كانت ترتديه، يأبى عليها أن يعيد إليها رداءه إن طلبته؛ فلا بد لها من الاستمرار في سقوطها راضيةٌ أو كارهةٌ، وكذلك كان شأنها.

ولم يمض على (مرغريت) في حياتها هذه أكثر من بضعة أعوام حتى نزل بها مرض حجبها في بيتها عدة أيامٍ، ثم اشتد عليها، فأشار عليها الأطباء أن تذهب إلى حمامات (البانيير) للاستشفاء بمائها وهوائها، فسافرت إليها وحدها لا تصحبها إلا خادمتها، وكان في ذلك المصطاف في هذا العام شيخ من الأثرياء اسمه (الدوق موهان) حضر إليها مع ابنته وكانت مريضةً بداء الصدر ليستشفي لها من دائها فلم يجدها العلاج، وماتت بين يديه، فدفنها هناك ولبث بعد موتها عدة أيامٍ يختلف إلى قبرها ويبكيها بكاء شديداً؛

One day he was returning from her grave and Margaret was walking ahead of him on the path, it was Margaret's second day in Pioneer. The old man was astonished and amazed when he saw her. He thought to himself that verily Allah ﷻ had sent his daughter back from her grave or that He ﷻ has sent him her duplicate, her identical so that he can give his heart contentment. This was because both of their faces looked the same. In a surprised and astounded manner, he approached her and held the corner of her scarf. Then he stared at her face for a long time. Margret was also surprised at this strange occurrence and she asked him, "What do you want?"

He said to her, "O lady do you grant me the permission that I may kiss your hand?"

Margaret extended her hand towards him, she did not know what he wanted and what pain he was enduring in his heart. Then that old wealthy man kissed her hand and then he apologized to her for his strange behaviour. That old man then walked besides her telling her his story and the story of his separation from his daughter, and the resemblance between his daughter and Margaret. She felt sorry for him and through his pain she also became upset. The old man saw her eye wet with tears. Thus, he fell upon her hands and starting kissing them and he thanked her for the generosity which she had given to him through this tear in his unfortunate time. They continued walking until both reached their destination. The old man bade his farewells and departed after seeking her permission to meet her from time to time. After granting this permission Margaret went to her room.

However, when she was alone in her room, she starting thinking about that young poor woman, and how death had taken her away from her father's hands, and that neither a doctor nor an herbalist could save her from dying. Then she feared over herself that she too was ill like the that young girl who had died. She thought to herself that verily, if she was to die like her, she would not find next to her, a father expressing pain and crying over her. This thought and this concern pained her heart severely. She cried over this for a long time locking herself to her room and not coming out.

فإنه لعائد من المقبرة ذات يومٍ إذ لمح في طريقه (مرغريت) سائرةً وحدها، وكان ذلك اليوم الثاني من وصولها إلى البانيير؛ فدهش لمنظرها دهشةً عظمى وخيل إليه أن الله قد بعث له ابنته من قبرها، أو أرسل إليه خيالها ليعزيه عنها لمكان الشبه بين صورة هذه الفتاة وصورتها، فتقدم نحوها ذاهلاً مشدوهاً، وأمسك بطرف ردائها، وظل يحدق في وجهها تحديقاً طويلاً، فعجبت لشأنه وسألته: ما باله؟

فقال لها: هل تأذنين لي يا سيدتي أن أقبل يدك؟

فمدت إليه يدها وهي لا تعلم ماذا يريد ولا ما الذي أصابه، فلثمها ثم اعتذر إليها عن جرأته، بذهوله ودهشته، ومشى معها يقص عليها قصته وقصة مصابه في ابنته، وما راعه من الشبه بين صورتها، وصورتها، فرثت له، وحزنت لحزنه واستهلت دمعةً رآها الشيخ من خلال أهداب عينيها المبتلة بالدموع، فسقط على يدها يقبلها ويشكر لها تلك الدمعة التي جادت بها عليه في ساعة شقائه، ولم يزل سائراً معها حتى وصلا إلى النزل، فودعها ومضى بعد ما استأذنها أن يختلف إليها من حينٍ إلى حين، فأذنته بذلك وصعدت إلى غرفتها.

فلما خلت بنفسها أنشأت تفكر في أمر تلك الفتاة المسكينة التي اختطفها الموت من يد أبيها في زهرة صباها من حيث لم يستطع طبيب ولا عائد رد دعاية القضاء عنها، ثم خطر لها أنها مريضة بمثل المرض الذي ماتت به، وأنها ربما ماتت موتتها فلا تجد بجانبها أباً كهذا الأب يندبها ويبكي عليها. فأثر في نفسها هذا الخاطر تأثيراً شديداً، وبكت له بكاءً طويلاً ولزمت غرفتها في ذلك اليوم لا تفارقها.

Duke Mohan kept on coming and going to Margaret's room after this and would sit there for a long time. He obtained love and comfort from her and became happy in her company. Whenever the flame of pain flared up in his heart, he would obtain peace and tranquillity just by sitting with her. He became so attached that he did not have the power to part from her. Margaret liked to see that an old distressed man who has lost his daughter found tranquillity and patience every time he looked at her face. In return, she also showed kindness to him and gave him love which he had never received before and that she also loved him like she had never loved anyone else before.

Not even a few days passed by, she gained recovery from her illness. Her splendour and beauty had returned upon her beautiful face. The stunning smile and laughter had reappeared on her lips. Her staying at Pioneer for a long period had been beneficial for her and she liked it until she felt the cold winds of the winter coming through so she decided to return to Paris. This decision was hard upon the Duke. He knew if she was to go back, he will not be able to meet her the way he had at Pioneer. This was because then she would be in large crowds and gatherings amongst her companions and friends. He stayed with her all night before her journey. He talked to her for a very long time in which she agreed to leave her former life, the life of deception and the life of living with other people and to live in a house which he will provide for her along with providing her provision and sustenance. In return he only asked for one thing, which was that she grants him the permission to come and meet her from time to time. They both travelled together to Paris.

From that day forward, her lifestyle changed. She started living in the castle which Duke had provided for her. She stopped meeting a lot of people like she did before. Sometimes days used to pass and people would not see her leaving her house. When she did come out, she used to embark in her carriage alone, without any companion male or female. When she walked her path, she read a book or a magazine. Whenever she walked past people whom she knew and recognised, she would not look at them. However, when her sight did land upon any one from amongst them, she smiled briefly, no one used to see this other than that person. Then she used to continue her journey until she reaches the Shanzelize Park. Then she would descend from her carriage and walk towards the forest where she remained for some time. Then after this she used to return to her mansion.

وظل (الدوق) يختلف إليها بعد ذلك فيجالسها طويلاً ويجد من الأنس بها، والاغتباط بعشرتها، ما تسكن به لوعة نفسها كلما شبها الوجد في صدره، حتى أصبح لا يستطيع مفارقتها ساعة واحدة، وكأنما لذ لها أن يرى ذلك الشيخ الثاكل المنكوب في وجهها سلوته وعزاءه، فمنحته من عطفها وحبها ما لم تمنحه أحداً من قبله، وأنست به أنساً لم تأنسه بإنسانٍ سواه.

وما هي إلا أيام قلائل حتى أبلت من مرضها بعض الإبلال، وعاد إلى وجهها الجميل رونقه وبهاؤه، وإلى ثغرها البديع ابتسامه وافتراره، فلذ لها المقام في البانيير أياماً طوالاً حتى شعرت بهبوب رياح الشتاء فأزمعت العودة إلى باريس، فشق ذلك على الدوق، وعلم أنها إن عادت إليها لا يظفر منها في ذلك المزدحم العظيم الحافل بخلانها وأصدقائها بمثل ما كان يظفر به منها في البانيير؛ فخلى بها ليلة السفر ساعةً، وحادثها حديثاً طويلاً انتهى بالإتفاق معها على أن تهجر حياتها الأولى، حياة المخالة والمعاشرة، وتعيش في منزلٍ يهيئه لها ويقوم بنفقاتها فيه، على أن تأذن له بالاختلاف إليها من حينٍ إلى حين، ثم سافرا في اليوم الثاني إلى باريس.

ومنذ ذلك اليوم تغيرت صورة حياتها عما كانت عليه من قبل، فأصبحت تعيش في قصرها الذي هيأه لها الدوق عيشاً بين العزلة والاختلاط، فلا تستقبل الناس فيه إلا قليلاً. ولا تمتزج مع الذين تستقبلهم الامتزاج كله. وربما مرت بها أيام لا يراها الناس خارج قصرها إلا قليلاً؛ فإذا خرجت ركبت عربتها وحدها دون رفيقٍ أو رفيقةٍ، ومشت في طريقها تقرأ في كتاب أو صحيفة؛ فربما مر بها كثير ممن تعرفهم فلا تراهم، فإذا وقع نظرها على واحد منهم ابتسمت له ابتسامةً قصيرةً موجزةً قلما يشعر بها أحد سواه، ثم استمرت أدراجها حتى تصل منتزه (الشانزلزيه) فتنزل من عربتها وتمشي في الغابة على قدميها ساعةً، ثم تعود إلى قصرها؛

When it was night time, she used to go to the theatre alone or she went with her bodyguard. Thus, she used to spend a lot of her time watching the entertainment on stage. The audience did not distract her when they and those who were obsessed with her, kept on staring at her. Also, when she was performing herself, she was not distracted by them as she used to continue with her story and with her act until the end.

Not many days had passed that the news spread amongst the people that Margaret's state had changed and her life had changed. She has attained contentment with her new life, the life of peace, quiet and living alone. She was pleased with herself. No one could dominate her anymore. The greed that the people had before for her had lessened and all their desires had also finished.

Then the people started to investigate about the reasons which led her to change her state. They speculated every possible reason for this other than the real reason behind her transformation. The actual reason was the tragedy of Duke Mohan's daughter's death who was the spitting image of Margaret and had suffered a similar illness. Indeed, this touched her heart very deeply which caused her to change her life in respect to what it was before. Thus, she became hateful towards men because they were the cause of her destruction. She hated her downfall more than she did ever before because this was what led her to her illness. She was not upset anymore over the fact that she was being deprived from other people's wealth. This was because she was living on the wealth which the Duke provided for her. She was living in such prosperity that not even a greedy person could ask for more. Sometimes she used to ponder that, indeed her life was connected to an extremely old man who does not want anything at all from her but only to see her. She used to consider her life like the virgin pure girls who are blessed under the honourable shade of their parents. She liked this and having this thought made her feel happy. This was because, it was this honourable life which she longed for and cried excessively over before this day. She had admired having this life before.

***

Now, the days of autumn had passed and the days of winter had approached. The icy cold and bitter winds had increased and Margaret's illness which was hidden had returned and her chesty coughs which contained blood in them also returned. She was in severe pain. When she was in pain, she stuck to her bed and did not part from it. However, when she felt better, she went outside for fresh air in the morning and evenings. Sometimes she used to go to the theatre at night to lessen her pain. She would remain there for an hour or two alone in her gallery box and then return to her abode.

فإذا جاء الليل ذهبت إلى ملعب التمثيل وحدها، أو مع الرجل القائم بشأنها؛ فتقضي فيه أكثر وقتها ناظرةً إلى المسرح، لا يشغلها كثرة الناظرين إليها أو المتهافتين على مقصورتها عن تتبع فصول الرواية والاهتمام بوقعها حتى تنتهي.

فلم تمض عليها أيام كثيرة حتى علم الناس جميعاً أن (مرغريت) قد استحالت حالها، وتغيرت صورة حياتها، وأنها قد قنعت بهذه الحياة الجديدة، حياة الهدوء والسكينة، والوحشة والانفراد، ورضيتها لنفسها، فلا سبيل إلى مغالبتها عليها فقصرت عنها أطماعهم، وانقطعت منها آمالهم،

وظلوا يتلمسون الأسباب لتلك الحالة الغريبة التي طرأت عليها، فذهبوا في شأنها المذاهب كلها إلا المذهب الصحيح منها، وهي أن تلك الحادثة المحزنة التي حدثت لابنة الدوق شبيهتها في صورتها ومرضها، قد أثرت في نفسها تأثيراً شديداً، وصورت لها الحياة بصورةٍ غير صورتها الأولى، فأصبحت تعاف الرجال لأنهم سبب سقوطها، وتستنكر سقوطها أكثر مما استنكرته من قبل لأنه سبب مرضها، ولا تأسف على ما فاتها مما في أيدي الناس لأنها تعيش من مال الدوق في نعمةٍ لا يطمع طامع في أكثر منها، وربما خطر لها أن حياتها مع هذا الشيخ الهرم الذي لا يطمع منها في أكثر من أن يراها تشبه حياة العذارى الطاهرات اللواتي ينعمن بنعمة الشرف في ظلال آبائهن؛ فأعجبها هذا الخيال ولذ لها؛ وكثيراً ما بكت ذلك الشرف قبل اليوم وحنت إليه.

***

انقضت أيام الخريف وأقبلت أيام الشتاء، وسالت الأجواء برداً وقراً، فثار ما كان كامناً من داء (مرغريت)؛ وعاد إليها نفثها وسعالها؛ فظلت تكابد من مرضها آلاماً جساماً؛ لا تفارقها يوماً حتى تعاودها أياماً، فإن ألمت بها لزمت سريرها لا تفارقه؛ وإن روحت عنها برزت إلى الخلاء في بكور الأيام وأصائلها تطلب الهواء الطلق والجو النقي؛ وربما ذهبت في بعض لياليها إلى ملعب التمثيل لتتفرج ما هي فيه فتخلو بنفسها في مقصورتها ساعة أو ساعتين؛ ثم تعود إلى منزلها.

Whenever she used to go to the theatre, she used to always look at the gallery box which was next to hers. There she used to see a young man who was dressed like a gentleman and had noble etiquettes. He used to look at her secretly too from time to time. Whenever she was looking down that's when he took a glance at her and whenever she looked at him he would look away. However, whenever their eyes met each other simultaneously, his face used to blush and his forehead used to sweat like he had sinned greatly which there is no expiation for. However, she never felt concerned over it because she did not see anything new in this other than that young man was extremely patient and silent, and that for a long time he would lower his head and his gaze. The cloud of distress was scattered over his face. The thing that astonished and amazed Margaret greatly was that from the whole audience, he was the only one who would cry when he saw a tragic and a heart-breaking scene on stage. This was because she knew that verily young happy men who are flourishing in their youth and health do not care if some real tragedy took place, let alone an imitation of this tragedy upon stage.

One night Margaret was alone in her gallery box. The night was extremely cold and at once she underwent a state of severe coughing. Then her symptoms increasing, so much so that she was going to fall off her chair due to her weakness and illness, that she felt a hand which was holding her hand. She took support from the hand and without paying attention to whose hand it was, she managed to reach her carriage and embarked on it. After a little while she felt better. Then she turned back to thank that gentleman for his favour but saw no one there but in the distance, she saw a person walking away. Nevertheless, she recognised him as his appearance was etched in her mind. She was astounded. When she reached her house, she felt a shivering fit of a fever which spread all over her body. Then for a few days, she remained in her bed and did not part from it until she felt better. Her maid came to her with the visiting cards which those young men had left when they had visited her during her illness but she did not read even one of them. Then her maid said, "There was one young man who used to come every day or twice a day to find out your well-being. He did not mention his name neither has he left a visiting card. Indeed, he became stressed out every time I told him that you were still in bed and in severe pain."

وكانت لا تزال ترى في المقصورة المجاورة لمقصورتها، كلما ذهبت إلى الملعب، فتًى في زي أبناء الأشراف وشمائلهم، لا يزال يخالسها النظر من حينٍ إلى حين؛ فينظر إليها إن غضت عنه، ويقضي عنها إن نظرت إليه؛ ولا يلتقي نظرها بنظره حتى يتلهب وجهه حمرةً، ويرفض جبينه عرقاً؛ كأنما جنى جنايةً لا مقيل له منها؛ فلم تحفل به كثيراً لأنها لم تر في أمره شيئاً جديداً، إلا أنها كانت تعجب لسكونه وجموده، وطول إغضائه وإطراقه، ولتلك العبرة من الحزن المنتشرة على وجهه، وكان أكثر ما يدهشها منه أو يعجبها أنه الفتى الوحيد الذي كان يبكي في ذلك المجتمع لمنظر المشاهد المحزنة التي تمثل على مسرح التمثيل، لأنها تعلم أن الفتيان الفرحين المغتبطين بشبابهم وصحتهم لا يحفلون بمناظر الشقاء الحقيقية فأحرى أن لا يحفلوا بتمثيلها.

فإنها لخالية بنفسها في مقصورتها ذات ليلة، وكان الجو بارداً مقشعراً إذ فاجأتها نوبة سعالٍ، اشتدت عليها كثيراً حتى كادت تسقط عن كرسيها ضعفاً وَوَهناً، فشعرت بيدٍ تمسك يدها، فاعتمدت عليها دون أن تستطيع الالتفات إلى صاحبها حتى بلغت عربتها فركبتها. فشعرت بالراحة قليلاً، فالتفتت لتشكر لصاحب تلك اليد يده، فلم تر أمامها أحداً، ورأت على بعد خطواتٍ منها إنساناً منصرفاً، فلم تتمكن من رؤيته، إلا أنها تخيلت صورته تخيلاً؛ فعجبت لأمره ومضت في طريقها؛ فما وصلت إلى منزلها حتى شعرت برعدة الحمى تتمشى في أعضائها، فلزمت سريرها بضعة أيامٍ لا تفارقه حتى أبلت قليلاً، فقدمت إليها خادمتها بطاقات الزيارة التي تركها الفتيان الذين زاروها في أثناء مرضها تجملاً وتلوماً، فلم تقرأ واحدةً منها، ثم حدثتها الخادمة أن فتًى كان يأتي للسؤال عنها في كل يومٍ مرةً أو مرتين، ولا يذكر اسمه، ولا يترك بطاقته، وأنه كان ينقبض انقباضاً شديداً كلما أخبرته أنها لا تزال طريحة فراشها تشكو وتتألم،

Margaret asked her to describe him. The maid described him but she did not recognise him. Margaret was completely amazed at this gentleman's actions and wished to see him, so that she could thank him for his exclusive sincerity which she did not see from any from amongst the people before. Then she instructed her maid to inform her whenever that man comes again to ask about her once more.

Not long had passed that the man returned. Margaret was sitting in the balcony facing the road and so, she saw him. She recognised that certainly he is that young emotional man whom she saw in her neighbouring gallery box in the theatre. Also, she discovered that it was his hand which had come out to help her on the night when she had undergone her illness. Promptly she instructed her maid to go to him and bring him to her.

The man became extremely nervous upon this invitation and he was very close to declining the offer. Then he realized that Margaret was sitting upstairs and became extremely shy. He walked behind the maid until she got to Margaret's room and leaving him there departed.

He entered her room and gave his greetings to her. He was sweating profusely and could not speak. Margaret stretched her hand towards him. He held her hand and gave it a very long kiss. Margaret came to know about that secret love he held in his heart for her. She was well-aware of the secrets found within kisses. Then she granted him permission to sit down. She began asking him about himself, which family was he from and the reason for looking after her. She kept on smiling at him to soften the tension between them and to get rid of the apprehension that he was feeling in his heart. Then he told her that verily he is a stranger in Paris. He had arrived with a delegation twenty days ago, from his town Nice so that he could spend three months here. His father had granted him the permission to do this to have a change in the air and water and to revitalise him. Then after that, his instruction was to return back to his town.

She asked him, "Did you find this place beautiful?" He remained silent for a little while. Then he looked at her hopelessly and said,

"No dear lady."

She asked, "Why?" He was unable to respond for a long time and put his head down. Margaret repeated her question to him.

فاستوصفتها إياه، فوصفته لها فلم تعرفه، وعجبت لأمره كل العجب، وتمنت لو رأته، فشكرت له هذا الإخلاص النادر الذي لا عهد لها به في أحدٍ من الناس، وأمرت خادمتها أن تخبره خبره إن جاء للسؤال عنها مرةً أخرى،

فلم يلبث أن جاء، وكانت مرغريت جالسةً في شرفة المنزل المطلة على الطريق، فرأته، فعرفت أنه ذلك الفتى الحزين الذي كانت تراه في المقصورة المجاورة لمقصورتها في ملعب التمثيل، وأنه صاحب تلك اليد التي امتدت لمعونتها ليلة النازلة التي نزلت بها هناك، فأشارت إلى خادمتها بالنزول إليه واستدعائه إليها ففعلت،

فاضطرب الفتى لهذه الدعوة اضطراباً شديداً حتى كاد يرفضها، ثم شعر بمكان مرغريت من الشرفة، فتلوم ومشى وراء الخادمة حتى صعدت به إلى غرفة سيدتها فتركته وانصرفت،

فدخل عليها فحياها ووجهه يرفض عرقاً ولسانه لا يكاد يبين، فمدت إليه يدها فتناولها وقبلها قبلةً طويلةً عرفت مرغريت سر ما أودعها من عواطف قلبه، وهي العالمة بأسرار القبلات، ثم أذنته بالجلوس، فجلس، فأنشأت تسائله عن نفسه وعن قومه وعن سبب اهتمامه بشأنها، وتبتسم له فيما بين ذلك ابتساماتٍ تلاطفه بها وتمسح عن فؤاده ما ألم به من الروع، فحدثها أنه غريب عن باريس، وأنه وفد إليها منذ عشرين يوماً من بلدته (نيس) ليقضي فيها ثلاثة أشهرٍ، أذن له أبوه بها، طلباً لتغيير الهواء وترويح النفس، ثم يعود في نهايتها إلى وطنه،

فسألته: هل وجد المقام حميداً هنا؟ فصمت هنيهةً، ثم نظر إليها نظرةً منكسرةً وقال:

لا يا سيدتي،

قالت: لماذا؟ فحارت بين شفتيه كلمة لم يستطع أن ينطق بها فعاد إلى صمته وإطراقه، فأعادت عليه سؤالها.

Then he said to her, "O my respectable lady, do you grant me the permission to say everything which is in my heart?" Before he said anything, Margaret had already sensed what was in his heart, and said to him,

"Say whatever you please, however do not express to me your love and the passion that you have for me. This is because verily I am an ill woman, I do not even have the power to endure this life which is free from problems, let alone enduring a life which is encompassed with love and pain."

His face turned pale and he stretched his hand towards his eyes where he wiped away a tear and said to her, "O my dear lady, this is what troubles me, this is what makes me cry and this is what has made my life unbearable ever since I have come to Paris! Ever since I have laid my eyes upon you, I fell in love with you at first sight. I started querying about you and I found out everything about you. I even found out that verily you are now living a life for a couple of months where no person of desire will be granted his yearning and no hopeful person would be able to fulfil his expectation. Thus, if I had any bad intention with you, that also perished other than that sincere love which I had for you did not extinguish. Then after that, I saw you at the theatre and I saw this yellow veil which was woven from the hands of illness upon your beautiful face, this turned my love that I had for you into mercy and kindness. Now I cry over your illness more than which I used to cry over your love. Now all that I wish for, from Allah ﷻ is that, in my lifetime I see you happy, in tranquillity and in a healthy state. May you receive your portion of happiness in your life in abundance. After this, I do not have any greed for anything anymore, unlike the avidity of those lovers and devotees. Thus, now I am standing in front of you, not to express my love and my emotions to you, but standing only to request your permission to come to your doorstep, so that whenever I come I may enquire about you from your maid. Then after that, I will be on my way. You will not see my face neither will you be aware of my coming or going."

Thus, a shivering fit penetrated through her body parts, this was a fit other than the fit she used to feel when she was feverish. She felt that verily she was listing to a song of love which she had never heard before this day from the mouths of men. Thus, she looked at him with a sight which other than Allah ﷻ no one knew. Then she said to him, "O dear I give you the permission and I am very thankful to you. In fact, I grant you the permission to visit me whenever you want upon the condition of coming as a helpful friend and not as a fornicating lover. This is because indeed I need a sincere friend and not an obsessed lover."

فقال لها: هل تأذنين لي يا سيدتي أن أقول لك كل ما في نفسي. فشعرت بما في نفسه قبل أن يقوله، وقالت له:

قل ما تشاء إلا أن تطارحني حبك وغرامك، فإنني امرأة مريضة لا أستطيع أن احتمل الحياة وحدها خالصةً لا مؤونة فيها، فأحرى أن لا احتملها مثقلةً بالحب والغرام،

فاصفر وجهه اصفراراً شديداً، ومد يده إلى دمعةٍ تترقرق في عينيه فمسحها ثم قال لها: ذلك ما يحزنني يا سيدتي ويبكيني وينغص علي عيشي منذ هبطت باريس حتى اليوم، فإنني رأيتك فأحببت للنظرة الأولى، ثم سألت عنك فعرفت من أمرك كل شيء، وعلمت أنك تعيشين منذ شهورٍ عيشةً لا مطمع فيها لطامع ولا أمل لآمل، فانقطع أملي منك، إلا أن حبي إياك لم ينقطع، ثم رأيتك بعد ذلك في ملعب التمثيل ورأيت هذا القناع الأصفر الذي نسجته يد المرض على وجهك الجميل فاستحال حبي إياك رحمةً وشفقة، وأصبحت أبكي لمرضك أكثر مما أبكي لحبك، وأصبح كل ما أتمنى على الله في حياتي أن أراك بارئةً ناعمة، موفوراً لك حظك من سعادة العيش وهنائه، ثم لا أطمع بعد ذلك في شيءٍ مما يطمع فيه المحبون المغرمون؛ فأنا أقف الساعة بين يديك لا لأطارحك الحب والغرام؛ بل لأسأل أن تأذني لي بالوقوف على بابك كلما جئته أسأل خادمتك عنك، ثم أمضي لسبيلي من حيث لا ترين وجهي، ولا تشعرين بمكاني،

فسرت في أعضائها رعدة غير الرعدة التي تعرفها من الحمى، وخيل إليها أنها تسمع نغمةً في الحب غير النغمة التي كانت تسمعها من قبل اليوم من أفواه الرجال، فنظرت إليه نظرةً لا تأويلها إلا الله تعالى. ثم قالت له: إني آذن لك بذلك يا سيدي، وأشكره لك شكراً جزيلاً، بل آذنك أن تزورني كلما شئت، على أن تفد إلي صديقاً مساعداً، لا محباً مغرماً، فإني إلى الأصدقاء المخلصين أحوج مني إلى المحبين المغرمين،

She drew out her hand towards him. From this he gathered that verily she has given him the permission to leave. Then he kissed her hand and left in a very happy state. Her eyes followed him until he disappeared. Hence, she fell upon her cushion which was next to her and cried, "O Lord please have mercy on me, verily I fear that will start loving him."

Certainly, she did start loving him in a state that she did not know. This was because the fear of falling into love itself is an indication of love. Nonetheless, she felt extreme happiness in his love, a feeling of which she had never felt before. Every day she welcomed him in her house. She became highly attached and friendly with him and became extremely excited with his conversations. She revealed to him all her secrets just like a friend discloses to a friend. She told him the story of her past life and her present life. She did not lie about a thing neither did she hide any matter from him. Then the matter accelerated to such a degree, that she started missing him if he got late to meet her even for a few seconds. Then, there came a time when he could not visit for three days because of some issue arising. She was traumatised with his absence greatly and her speculation and thoughts ran wildly in every direction. She came to realize that certainly this kind of pain and sadness of him not coming and this type of conjecturing of hers did not arise before. She became deeply saddened as her heart started worrying due to fear and terror. At this point she realized that she was standing upon the edge of a ditch and there was not option remaining for her other than to jump into it. She remained awake for a very long portion of the night and endured her heart's fear and its pain until the morning burst forth.

Arman came on the fourth morning. He found her lying down on her bed and because of her crying and being awake, her eyes were red. Arman became worried seeing her in this state and said to her, "Possibly you have been awake all night or maybe you have been crying my dear? I see in your eyes the effect of either one of them."

She said, "Both of them O Arman."

He said, "Why, has a new issue arisen?"

She replied, "O friend, sit beside me so that I may talk to you for a little while, as this maybe the last discussion between you and me. Then after this I might not see you and you may not see me." Thus, Arman became troubled and concerned. Terror and fright penetrated his mind and his tongue. He did not have the power to say anything as he fell next to her unnerved and powerless. He began looking at her face like how a criminal looks at the face of a judge waiting to hear the verdict. She leaned towards him and said,

ومدت إليه يدها، فعلم أنها قد أذنته بالانصراف، فقبلها وانصرف مسروراً مغتبطاً، فأتبعته نظرها حتى غاب عنها، فسقطت على وسادةٍ بجانبها وقالت: رحمتك اللهم فإني أخشى أن أحبه.

لقد أحبته من حيث لا تدري؛ فإن الخوف من الحب هو الحب نفسه، بل شعرت في حبه بسعادةٍ لم تشعر بمثلها من قبل، فأصبحت تستقبله كل يومٍ في منزلها، وتأنس به وبحديثه أنساً كثيراً، وتفضي إليه بذات نفسها إفضاء الصديق إلى صديقه، وتقص عليه قصة ماضيها وحاضرها لا تكذبه شيئاً ولا تكتم عنه أمراً، ثم ترامى بها الأمر حتى أصبحت تشعر بالوحشة إن تخلف عن ميعاد زيارته بضع دقائق. ثم حدث أن انقطع عن زيارتها ثلاثة أيامٍ لأمرٍ عرض له لم يتمكن من إخبارها به. فحزنت لانقطاعه حزناً عظيماً، وذهبت بها الوساوس والظنون كل مذهب، ثم ذكرت أن ذلك الحزن وهذا الوسواس ليس من شأنها قبل اليوم. فقلقت لذلك قلقاً شديداً، وخفق قلبها خفقة الرعب والخوف، وعلمت أنها قد وقفت على حافة الهوة، ولم يبق إلا أن تتردى فيها، فسهرت ليلةً طويلةً عالجت فيها من نوازع النفس وخوالجها ما عالجت حتى أصبح الصباح وقد أضمرت في نفسها أمراً.

جاء (أرمان) في صباح اليوم الرابع فوجدها طريحة فراشها، وفي عينيها حمرة البكاء والسهر. فارتاع لمنظرها وقال لها: لعلك سهرت بالأمس كثيراً يا سيدتي أو بكيت، فإني أرى في عينيك أثر واحدٍ منهما؟

قالت: هما معاً يا أرمان،

قال: وهل حدث شيء جديد؟

قالت: إجلس بجانبي قليلاً أيها الصديق أحدثك حديثاً قصيراً، وربما كان آخر حديثٍ بيني وبينك، ثم لا أراك بعد ذلك ولا تراني، فذعر ذعراً شديداً، وداخله من الرعب والهول ما ملك عليه عقله ولسانه، فلم يستطع أن يقول شيئاً وسقط بجانبها واهياً متضعضعاً، وظل ينظر إلى وجهها نظر المتهم إلى وجه قاضيه ساعة نطقه بالحكم، فأقبلت عليه تحدثه وتقول:

"I have recognized you O Arman. I have seen within you a generous man, who loves me more than he loves himself. You are a lawful friend in whose heart kindness and mercy have united with the sentiments of love. You have taken refuge towards me, towards an ill woman, at a time when people ran away from me due to my illness and you stayed with me without having any expectation at a time when people had boycotted me because their yearning has ended. In my heart, I have been hiding your love and your esteem which I have never had for anyone before. I became blessed with you with such a blessing that I have never felt anything like it in my life. However, Allah ﷻ had written for me misfortunes in the divine tablet, all the way from my mother's cradle till the final resting place in the grave. He ﷻ did not intend me to enjoy this blessing of having you for a long time. He ﷻ denied it and took it away from me very quickly. For a few days now I have felt that pure dignified sentiment of love which existed in the depths of my heart, which I used to seek solace in for my calamities and for my catastrophes. Now this sentiment has changed into another sentiment. This new sentiment I do not like as I can see this leading me towards my downfall and ruin. Indeed, my heart has deceived me from time to time. Sometimes I deny it and sometimes I grant it. When you had gone away from me for three days, I realized and felt the pain of your absence. This stressed me out a great deal and had me extremely worried. This stress has overshadowed all my sentiments and senses. If you want me to say this, then I will say that it is this stress which has caused me to cry a lot and it has kept me awake. Woe to me, I have found out that certainly I have fallen in love and verily this sentiment has woken up my heart. This feeling makes me stand up and makes me sit down. Indeed, this is love and devotion.

I spent all night yesterday thinking of a way of salvation from this great trial which has afflicted me. I did not find anyone who could save me from this other than you. Thereby, O Arman, I ask you in the name of friendship and love, over which we had made a pledge yesterday, but in fact, with the name of those merciful tears which you shed caring for me, that you stop coming to see me from this day onwards. If you can, please travel back to your family tonight and do not ever return to see me after this. I will establish patience within myself from you until Allah ﷻ favours me to become despaired of your love."

Then she looked towards him awaiting his reply. He became still and his face became pale. Becoming like a statue, his eyes were staring at her in a frozen state, the likes of which when the eyes are staring but cannot see. In a very difficult manner, he just about managed to move his lips and said in a very quiet manner as if it was the voice of his heart. "If it is love, then what is your fear O Margaret?"

عرفتك يا (أرمان) فعرفت فيك الرجل الكريم الذي أحبني لنفسي أكثر مما أحبني لنفسه، والصديق الوفي الذي امتزجت في قلبه عاطفة الحب بعاطفة الرحمة والحنان فآوى إلي مريضةً حينما جفاني الناس لمرضي، وعاش معي بلا أمل حينما انقطع الناس عني لانقطاع أملهم مني؛ فأضمرت لك في قلبي من الحب والاحترام ما لم أضمره لأحدٍ سواك، وسعدت بك سعادة لم أشعر بمثلها في يومٍ من أيام حياتي، ولكن الله الذي كتب لي الشقاء في لوح مقاديره من ضجعة المهد إلى رقدة اللحد، لم يشأ أن يمتعني طويلاً بهذه السعادة، وأبى إلا أن يسلبنيها وشيكاً، فقد أصبحت أشعر منذ أيامٍ أن تلك العاطفة الشريفة المقدسة التي كنت أستمد منها سعادتي وهنائي قد أخذت تستحيل في أعماق قلبي إلى عاطفةٍ أخرى غيرها لا أريدها لنفسي، ولا أرى إلا أنها ستكون سبب شقائي وبلائي؛ فخادعت نفسي عنها حيناً، أكذبها مرة وأصدقها أخرى، حتى كان ما كان من انقطاعك عني تلك الأيام الثلاثة، فشعرت لغيابك بحزنٍ أقلقني وأمضني، وملك علي جميع عواطفي ومشاعري، ولو شئت أن أقول لقلت إنه أبكاني كثيراً، وأسهرني طويلاً، فعلمت والأسفاه أنني قد أصبحت عاشقةً، وأن هذا الذي يختلج في قلبي ويقيمني ويقعدني، إنما هو الحب والغرام،

فقضيت ليلة الأمس كلها أفكر في طريق الخلاص من هذه النكبة العظمى التي نزلت بي، فلم أجد أحداً يخلصني منها سواك، فأنا أسألك يا (أرمان) باسم الصداقة والود الذي تعاقدنا عليه بالأمس، بل باسم الدموع التي طالما كنت تسكبها رحمةً بي وإشفاقاً علي، أن تنقطع عن زيارتي منذ اليوم، وأن تسافر إلى أهلك الليلة إن استطعت، ثم لا تعد إلي بعد ذلك، فأحمل نفسي على الصبر عنك حتى يمن الله علي براحة اليأس منك.

ثم نظرت إليه لترى ما يقول، فإذا هو جامد مصفر كأن وجهه وجه تمثالٍ منحوتٍ، وإذا عيناه شاخصتان إليها شخوص العين القائمة التي تنظر إلى الشيء ولا تراه، وبعد لأيٍ ما استطاع أن يحرك شفتيه ويقول لها بصوتٍ خافتٍ كصوت الضمير: وما يخيفك من الحب يا مرغريت؟

She said, "A great trial and punishment is scaring me, which I am expecting from Allah ﷻ, due to those sins and mistakes I committed in the earlier days of my life. Verily Allah ﷻ has written for our assembly of fallen women in his decree, that we play around with the hearts and minds of men, and that we put them through various problems and several punishments. We continue to do this until Allah ﷻ becomes enraged for the men and feel's a sense of honour for the men, and He retaliates by punishing us through love, and then we experience all that punishment ourselves which we had inflicted upon the men before us. We suffer harms and sorrows throughout our life and we die as unknown women whom no one cares about. There is no one who gives the news of our death and there is no one who cries over us. Thus, this is what I fear. Therefore, before I can see this I would like to die. O Arman Indeed I am not accusing you of cheating and deceiving, you are greater than that in my eyes. However, I do know that you are here in this town only for an appointed term. Then after your time lapses you will travel back to your family then you will not return to me after that and if you refuse to go back and decide to stay with me then your family will come between you and your decision. This is because your family are honoured and dignified people who are protective over you and will want to safeguard your respect. They will never allow a prostitute woman to stain you with shame and disgrace.

Thus, you will not find any way of redeeming yourself from them and you will have to give in to their verdict. Then you will see me standing staggered and in pain and I will be seeking you but I will not gain you and I will want to have patience over you but I will not be able to do so. I have even thought that if I return, after being rejected by your family towards the shelter of that honourable old man, who had done a very big favour for me, he will even reject me by punishing me for my breaching of his trust and being unthankful for his blessings. Thus, in that position I will not able to find another alternative but to return to my former life, the life of sins and immoralities, the life of sadness and pain, the life which I despise like the earth dislikes blood. I will become trapped in an everlasting punishment and in a long calamity.

Verily I know, O Arman, that you indeed love me a lot and I know that you will suffer a lot of pain parting from me. However, I do know that in the path of mercy, an honourable heart manages to endure pain. So, endure this punishment because of me, indeed you have more strength than me to withstand this pain and agony. I will supplicate to Allah ﷻ that He grants you, patience over my pain, and that He gives me patience and contentment of the soul after you. I pray that Allah ﷻ gives you, patience like the patience that He will give me. I hope that Allah ﷻ showers his mercy upon us both collectively."

قالت: يخيفني منه العقاب الأليم الذي أتوقع أن يعاقبني به الله على ما اقترفت من الذنوب والآثام في فاتحة حياتي، فقد كتب الله لنا معشر النساء الساقطات في لوح مقاديره أن لا نزال نعبث بقلوب الرجال وعقولهم، ونبتليهم بصنوف العذاب وأنواع الآلام، حتى يغضب الله لهم ويغار عليهم، فيبتلينا بحب نحمل فيه العذاب جميع ما حملناه من قبل، ونشقى فيه شقاءً لا ينتهي إلا بانتهاء حياتنا، فنموت بين يدي أنفسنا مهملاتٍ مغفلاتٍ لا ينعانا ناعٍ ولا يبكي علينا باكٍ، فهذا الذي أخافه وأخشاه، وأحب أن يسبق إلى أجلي قبل أن أراه. أنا لا أتهمك بالخيانة والغدر يا (أرمان)، فأنت أجل من ذلك عندي، ولكني أعلم أنك باقٍ في هذا البلد إلى أجل، فإذا انقضى الأجل سافرت إلى أهلك سفراً لا تملك بعده العودة إلي. فإن أبيت إلا البقاء بجانبي حال أهلك بينك وبين ذلك لأنهم قوم شرفاء يضنون بك وبشرفك أن تلوثهما امرأة مومس بعارها وشنارها،

فلا تجد لك بداً من الخضوع لهم والنزول على حكمهم، وهنالك أقف موقف الحيرة واللوعة أطلب السبيل إليك فلا أجدك، والسلو عنك فلا أستطيعه، وربما حاولت بعد ذلك العودة إلى كتف ذلك الشيخ الكريم الذي أحسن إلي إحساناً كبيراً فطردني من بين يديه عقاباً لي على خيانة عهده وكفر نعمته، فلا أجد لي بداً من الرجوع إلى حياتي الأولى - حياة الشرور والآثام، والهموم والآلام - التي أبغضها بغض الأرض للدم، وهنالك العذاب الدائم والشقاء الطويل.

أني أعلم يا (أرمان) أنك تحبني حباً جماً، وأنك ستكابد في ابتعادك عني عذاباً كثيراً، ولكني أعلم أن قلباً شريفاً يحتمل العذاب في سبيل الرحمة، فاحتمل هذا العذاب من أجلي فإنك أقدر مني على احتمال الآلام والأوجاع، وسأدعو الله تعالى ليلي ونهاري أن يمنحني الصبر عنك، ويرزقني راحة النفس وسكونها من بعدك، وأن يمنحك من ذلك مثل ما يمنحني؛ فلعله يرحمنا جميعاً.

Thus, he did not have any answer for her in respect to these words other than him getting up from his station trembling and unsteadily walking towards the door of the courtyard. He was forcing and dragging himself towards it until he finally reached the door. He stood upon the doorstep and turned towards Margaret and cast one last longing look at her, like a dying person who looks at his family in the last moments of his life. Then he said, "Goodbye O Margaret!" and walked away. He had not even disappeared that Margaret got up from her bed, crying and shaking she ran towards the door intending to join him. Then she came back. After a split second, she got up and ran again once more after him but, her integrity had brought her back. She returned to her bed and began to cry, began to scream and wailed loudly. Then she started pacing her room like an upset woman who just had a death in the household. She was screaming "Return him to me. I do not have the power to endure his separation. Soon after him I will die."

She was in this state and suddenly she heard a loud scream from the direction of the garden. She rushed out to the door of the house and saw it was Arman who has fallen down in front of the door step unconscious. Consequently, she raised her eyes towards the skies and said, "Let it be whatever Allah ﷻ intends." Then she placed herself over him and hugged him. Then she kissed his lips. That kiss was the first kiss in which she had felt the true taste of life within her. Arman felt the kiss and woke up. He hugged her to his chest. So much so, that, if he had died after this mere hug, he would not have cried over not having anything else from the blessings and the happiness of this world.

***

Winter had passed and Margaret's illness and sickness had also come to pass. She recovered from the virus and became blessed with his love. Now, her only task was to sanctify this relationship before Allah ﷻ. She proposed to Arman that they both leave Paris, its crowd and its fast lifestyle and go towards a summer residence of their choice in a quiet area. Thus, he accepted her decision and both travelled together in search of a suitable place until they reached a village called Bougival. This was a parish from the settlements of France which was two hours away from Paris. They found a small house built on a hill top and located behind a big green mountain, and a beautiful clean reservoir was flowing beneath it. As if the originator of it had made it for the two of them. They rented the house. Margaret had transferred all her luggage and all the necessary things from her house in Paris to their new residence.

فلم يكن له جواب على كلمتها هذه سوى أن نهض من مكانه متضعضعاً متهالكاً، ومشى إلى باب القاعة يسوق نفسه سوقاً حتى بلغه، فوقف على عتبته والتفت إلى مرغريت وألقى عليها تلك النظرة التي يلقيها المحتضر على أهله في آخر لحظات حياته وقال لها: الوداع يا مرغريت! ومضى، فما غاب شخصه عن عينيها حتى نهضت من فراشها هائمةً مختبلة، واندفعت إلى الباب تريد اللحاق به، ثم تراجعت ثم حاولت ذلك مرةً أخرى؛ فأدركها رشدها وأناتها، فعادت إلى فراشها تبكي وتنتحب وتعول إعوالاً شديداً، وتدور في أنحاء الغرفة دوران الثاكلة المفجوعة، وهي تصيح: أرجعوه إلي، لا أستطيع فراقه، سأموت من بعده.

وأنها لكذلك إذا سمعت صرخةً عظمى آتيةً من ناحية الحديقة، فخرجت تعدو إلى حيث سمعت الصوت حتى بلغت باب المنزل فرأت (أرمان) ساقطاً تحت عتبته مغشياً عليه، فرفعت طرفها إلى السماء وقالت: ليكن ما أراد الله، ثم ألقت نفسها عليه ولثمته في ثغره لثمةً هي أول لثمةٍ ذاقت فيها لذة العيش في حياتها، فشعر بها (أرمان) فاستفاق وضمها إلى صدره ضمةً لو مات على أثرها ما بكى على شيء من نعيم الدنيا وهنائها.

***

انقضى الشتاء فانقضى بانقضائه شقاء (مرغريت) وعناؤها، فقد أبلت من مرضها، وأصبحت سعيدةً بحبها، فلم يبق بين يديها إلا أن تبلغ من تلك السعادة نهايتها، فاقترحت على أرمان أن يتركا باريس وضوضاءها، ومزدحم الحياة فيها إلى مصيفٍ يختارانه لنفسهما في بعض الأماكن الخالية، فقبل مقترحها وسافرا معاً يفتشان عن المكان الذي يريدان حتى بلغا قرية (بوجيفال)، وهي ضاحية من ضواحي باريس على بعد ساعتين منها، فوجدا في بعض أرباضها منزلاً صغيراً منفرداً واقعاً على رأس هضبةٍ عاليةٍ في سفح جبلٍ مخضرٍ تجري من تحته بحيرة صافية بديعة كأنما بناه بانيه لهما، فاكترياه، ونقلت (مرغريت) إليه من منزلها في باريس بعض ما يحتاجان إليه من أثاثٍ ومتاعٍ،

They both started living a life which was full of contentment, pleasure and happiness. Never did the clouds of sadness spread over them. Never did any assumptions neither any dangerous thoughts ever distress them. They would begin their day climbing on top of the mountain or descending from it to the lower ground. Or they would come and go on a small boat and cruise upon the lake. Or they would sit under a thick tree which used to shade them from the noon's heat and seam them both together to itself. Or they would lie down upon the carpet of grass in the open space talking to one another. They used to enjoy the beautiful sight on the corner of the lake. They used to attain bliss from the beauty of the water, the sight of the vast lands; the valleys, the forests, the places of grazing, empty spaces, ravines, caves, the clouds and the illuminations in all its forms and colours. They would enjoy the alternating and moving shadows and enjoyed looking at the peaks of mountains which looked like they were connected to the sky. They would adore the pebbles and rocks which were scattered around the reservoir as if they were the waves in that pool. They would admire that battle which took place every day between the light of day and the darkness of night. The light would attain victory at the break of morning, then at the end of the day the night would prevail over light. At nightfall, both would return to their house happy and content with their life.

Both continued living in prosperity and happiness until a whole year had passed. They had the power to obtain from the hands of destiny anything they wanted. Then after that the world had woken up for them. Woe is upon the fortunate people who wake up after being asleep. The money which Arman had was nearly coming to an end. Therefore, he wrote to his father requesting that he sends him some money so that he could remain in Paris for another term, pretending to be ill, in need and unable to travel. He would do did this from time to time. However, he did not receive a reply to his last letter. This upset him a great deal. Every day he would go to town; to the Toren Hotel. This hotel was where he used to stay before he met Margaret. He used to come here to ask about any post that may have arrived for him, each day he returned disappointed and distressed.

However, when he would reach Bougival and see Margaret in front of him he would become happy and smiled like he did not have a problem in the world. However, Margaret could see beyond the empty smiles into the depths of his heart. She shared her concerns with him saying; "Do not worry O Arman concerning the money. Indeed, I have with me an amount which will suffice us both for another few years." However, what she said was not true. This was because the Duke had stopped sending her money and deprived her from his care ever since he found out about her story with Arman and that she had deceived him and had breached his trust.

ثم عاشا فيه بعد ذلك عيشاً ناعماً هنيئاً لا تضطرب في سمائه غيمة ولا تمر بصفحته غبرة، ولا يكدر عليهما مكدر من خواطر الشقاء ووساوسه، فكانا يقضيان نهارهما صاعدين إلى قمة الجبل أو منحدرين إلي سفحه، أو راكبين زورقاً صغيراً يسبح بهما على صفحة البحيرة جيئةً وذهوباً، أو جالسين تحت شجرةٍ فرعاء تظللهما من لفحات الهجير وتضمهما إليهما كما تضم ثمارها، أو مضطجعين على بساطٍ من العشب الممتد في تلك البطحاء الفسيحة يتناجيان ويلهوان بمنظر الجمال المائل في الشاطىء، والأمواء والأخاديد والوديان والغابات والحرجات، والكهوف والأغوار، والغيوم والسحب والأضواء في تشكلها وتلونها، والظلال في نحولها وانتقالها، وفي رؤوس الجبال اللاصقة بجلدة السماء كأنها بعض سحبها، وفي قطع الصخور المبعثرة على جوانب الغدران كأنها بعض أمواجها، وفي تلك المعركة التي تدور في كل يومٍ مرتين بين جيشى الأنوار والظلمات فينتصر في صدر النهار أولهما، ثم يدال في آخره لثانيهما، حتى إذا جاء الليل عادا إلى منزلهما فنعمتا فيه بألوان النعيم وضروبه ورشفا من كل ثغرٍ من ثغور السعادة رشفةً تسري حلاوتها في قلبهما حتى تصيب صميمه.

مر بهما على ذلك عام كامل هو كل ما استطاعا أن يختلساه من يد الدهر في غفلته، ثم انتبه لهما بعد ذلك ـ وويل للسعداء من انتباهه بعد إغفائه ـ فقد نضب أو أوشك أن ينضب ما كان في يد (أرمان) من المال، وكان في يده الكثير منه، فكتب إلى أبيه يطلب إليه أن يبعث إليه بما يستعين به على البقاء في باريس مدةً أخرى، زاعماً أنه لا يزال مريضاً متألماً لا يستطيع السفر، وكذلك كان يفعل من حينٍ إلى حين. فلم يأته الرد، فأقلقه ذلك قلقاً شديداً، وظل يختلف إلى المدينة في كل يومٍ يسأل في فندق (تورين) الذي كان ينزل به قبل اتصاله بمرغريت عن الكتاب الذي ينتظره فلا يجده، فيعود حزيناً منقبضاً،

حتى إذا وصل إلى بوجيفال ورأى مرغريت بين يديه تطلق وتبسم كأنه لا يضمر في نفسه هماً قاتلاً، ولكن عين مرغريت أقدر من أن يعجزها النفاذ إلى أعماق قلبه فاكتنهت سره فكاشفته به وقالت: لا يحزنك شأن المال يا أرمان، فإن عندي منه ما يكفينا العيش معاً سنين طوالا. ولم تكن صادقةً فيما تقول لأن الدوق قاطعها ومنع عنها رفده مذ عرف قصتها مع (أرمان)، وعلم أنها خانته وخانت بعهده،

She was in debt and owed a great sum of money to the clothes and jewellery merchants. Now the debtors had started to ask her for their money after finding out that Duke had abandoned her and had taken his hand back from her. She had not reflected on the consequences of what she had said to Arman!

Arman did not like her offer and disliked to live off her money. He refused to live with her with the wealth which is other than his own. He intended to travel to Nice, so that he could bring back money from there. His intention to travel had upset Margaret and had scared her. She knelt in front of him and started requesting mercy and compassion from him. She started to beg him not to go. In fact, she had pleaded with him greatly not to go. Thus, Arman agreed and cancelled his trip. He became content with that thing which he should not have become content with. If it was not for the yearning of love and the burning tears, he would have never agreed to her request. Secretly he had decided he would bequeath his share of inheritance to Margaret, to compensate for her sincere loyalty and love.

Margaret was left with no choice but to start selling the diamonds and expensive treasures she had. She began selling them bit by bit in order to pay off her debt and also to maintain the expenses of the house. However, Arman did not know all of this, and both continued living like this for a few months.

One day a worker from the Toren Hotel came to them announcing, "Verily your father has arrived in the Hotel, and he is eagerly waiting for you."

***

When Arman came face to face with his father (who was called Duval) he said to him, "O Arman certainly you have been lying to me a lot. You had never lied before this, neither have you ever deceived us before this. I was pleased with you and I wanted you to have the best life ever in respect of other people before you. You have torn up with your own hands that beautiful veil of honour and modesty which was always over your face. You have started living your life with a prostitute. The status which this woman has; all the people including this woman know and acknowledge that she is a discarded and fallen down woman who has no prestige whatsoever. She is the leftover and the remains of rambling and erratic people. She is that chewed up bone of that dinner which is open to all kinds of people in the mornings and in the evenings. I have had enough of you, now stand up this instance and get ready to travel back with me to Nice. I am not going to leave you here after this day for another moment."

بل كانت مدينةً بمالٍ كثيرٍ لبعض تجار الجواهر والثياب، بل أصبح دائنوها يتقاضونها ديونهم بعد ما علموا أن الدوق قاطعها ونفض يده منها، ولكنها خاطرت بكلمتها مخاطرةً لم تفكر في عاقبتها،

فأكبر (أرمان) ذلك وأعظمه، وأنف منه أنفةً شديدة، وأبى أن يعيش معها بمالٍ غير ماله، وعزم أن يسافر إلى (نيس) ليأتي منها بالمال الذي يريده، فأزعجها عزمه هذا إزعاجاً شديداً وخافت عاقبته، فجثت بين يديه تستعطفه وتسترحمه، وتبذل في ضراعتها، ورجائها في سبيل بقائه أكثر مما بذلت قبل اليوم في سبيل رحيله، حتى أذعن واستقاد، ورضي بالتي لم يكن يرضى بمثلها لولا لهفة الحب وضراعة الدموع، وقد أضمر في نفسه أن يتنازل لها عن نصيبه في الميراث الذي ورثه من أمه مكافأةً لها ووفاءً بحقها،

فلم يكن لمرغريت بعد ذلك بد من أن تمد يدها إلى جواهرها وذخائرها، فأنشأت تبيع القطعة بعد القطعة، لتسد بعض دينها، وتقوم بنفقة بيتها، من حيث لا يعلم (أرمان) واستمرا على ذلك بضعة أشهرٍ،

حتى دخل عليهما، في يوم من الأيام في ساعات أنسهما وصفائهما، خادم فندق (تورين) الذي كان ينزل به (أرمان) في باريس وقال له: إن والده قد وصل الساعة إلى الفندق، وإنه ينتظره هناك.

***

قال دوفال لولده: لقد كذبت علي كثيراً يا (أرمان)؛ وما كنت قبل اليوم كذاباً، ولا خادعاً، ورضيت لنفسك بحياةٍ كنت أضن الناس بنفسك على مثلها من قبل؛ ومزقت بيدك ذلك القناع الجميل من الحياء الذي لا يزال مسبلاً على وجهك، وأصبحت تتبذل في العيش مع امرأةٍ عاهرة، كل ما لها من الشأن عند نفسها، وعند الناس جميعاً أنها نفاية من نفايات الرجال، وفضلة من فضلات الفساق، وفتات المائدة العامة التي يجلس عليها الناس جميعاً صباحهم ومساءهم، فحسبك هذا وقم الساعة لتعد نفسك للسفر معي إلى (نيس)، فلست بتاركك بعد اليوم في هذا البلد ساعةً واحدةً.

Thus, Arman raised his head towards his father and said to him in a very confident and peaceful voice, "I do not have the power to do this O father!"

His dad stared at him and said, "This is the second sin which you are committing. Do you not care for me at all? Do you not have any shame that you are rejecting my decision over a fallen woman who has no respect? She is playing with your mind and she only wants to strip away from you your wealth and honour. She wants to destroy your past and your future."

He said, "No father, indeed she is not playing with me neither is she deceiving me. In fact, she loves me so much that she has never loved anyone like this ever before. I believe if I were to leave her she would die. If I were to leave her, I would be committing such a big sin that its regret would not part from my conscience till death."

His father replied, "Women like this deceive men like you, filthy women like this do not have the hearts to love with. But they have the tongues with which they trap men with and they put a curtain between men until everyone from amongst them considers himself to be the most loved one, the most fortunate one to her in respect of the others."

Arman said, "Before this day, it maybe she lived like that, however now she does not love anyone else other than myself. In fact, she does not know anyone else besides me. Now she lives a life of an honourable lady, rather a life which is purer than a lot of honourable women. This is because a sincere friend who has sincerity for a friend is purer than that wife who cheats on her husband. I fear that if I leave her, that fire of despair in her heart will reignite and return her to her former life of sin, wickedness, misfortunes and punishment, which I had saved her from."

Arman's father said, "What do you think, this is the only good deed left for good people? That they rectify and correct dirty women?"

Arman said, "This is a better thing to do, bringing back a woman from the life of sin and wickedness towards the life of purity. This is because the respectable people of this day and age boast about how they have ruined the lives of respectable women and how they slowly but gradually misled women towards destruction and immorality. To rectify a character of a bad woman is better than misleading a pious woman."

Duval said, "Certainly you have become really merciful O Arman."

فرفع (أرمان) رأسه إلى أبيه، وقال له بصوتٍ هادىءٍ مطمئن: لا أستطيع يا أبتاه!

فنظر إليه أبوه نظرةً شزراء وقال له: وتلك سيئة أخرى، فقد أصبحت لا تعبأ بي، ولا تبالي بمخالفة أمري من أجل امرأةٍ ساقطةٍ لا شأن لها معك إلا أن تعبث بعقلك؛ وتسلبك مالك وشرفك؛ وتفسد عليك حاضرك ومستقبلك.

قال: لا يا أبتاه، إنها ليست بعابثةٍ ولا خادعة، ولكنها تحبني حباً جماً لم يحبه أحد من قبلها أحداً، وأحسب أني إن فارقتها قتلتها، وجنيت عليها جنايةً لا يفارقني الندم عليها حتى الموت.

قال: ذلك ما يخدع به أمثالها أمثالك، فليس للنساء العاهرات قلوب يحببن بها، بل لهن ألسن يختلن بها الرجال ويسبلنها حجباً بين بعضهم وبعض! حتى يظن كل واحدٍ منهم أنه الأثير عندها، وصاحب الحظوة لديها، من دون أصحابه جميعاً.

قال: ربما كان ذلك شأنها قبل اليوم، أما اليوم فهي لا تحب أحداً غيري، بل لا تعرف أحداً سواي، فهي تعيش عيشةً تشبه عيشة النساء الشريفات، بل أشرف من عيشة الكثيرات منهن، لأن الخليلة التي تخلص لخليلها، أشرف من الزوجة التي تخون زوجها، وأخشى إن فارقتها أن تثور في نفسها ثورة من ثورات اليأس فتردها إلى تلك الحياة الأولى حياة الشر والفساد، والشقاء والعذاب، بعد ما استنقذت نفسها.

قال: وهل ترى أن وظيفة الرجل الشريف في هذه الحياة إصلاح النساء الفاسدات؟

قال: ذلك خير له من أن تكون وظيفته إفسادهن، فإن الأشراف في هذا العصر يفخرون بإفساد النساء الصالحات، واستدراجهن إلى مواطن الفسق والفجور، وإصلاح المرأة الفاسدة، أدنى إلى الشرف من إفساد المرأة الصالحة.

قال: لقد أصبحت كثير الرحمة يا أرمان.

Arman said, "Why should I not have mercy for a poor, ill, young woman who does not have any one in this world who could look after her from amongst her relations and friends? Her illness has moved into her chest which does not finish neither does it part from her. However, from time to time she does feel relief from it and sometimes it triggers off again and she undergoes severe pain at times, and sometimes she fears that pain returning. There is no relief for her in these two states other than pondering over this blessing of love as she sees herself recovering through this. If I was to lose her, she will lose everything in life, her sadness and calamities will increase and her illness would further escalate until her remaining life will also come to an end. O father, please leave me here with her for another year or two so that I can lessen for her, her misery and it may be that these are the last few days of her life, after that I will return to you with a contented heart, with a clear conscience and pleased with myself over my actions and I will only shed tears of sadness and not the tears of guilt and regret; I will feel happy and peaceful every time I will think that I had never broken my promise to her and that I had never deceived her."

Duval put his head down for a while as though he was coming to terms with grief, then he lifted his head and looked at his son with love and mercy and said, "O my son how can I travel without you? Is it not enough for me that before this day I have also been enduring the pain of your separation? I have left your sister behind also who is also very anxious over you, she cries night and day and is extremely eager to meet you. Everything which you have said in your defence, will not save me nor you on the day when people will talk about your absurd behaviour. Many people have already started talking. They have said 'Indeed Arman Duval, the descendant of the family of Talleyrand is living with a prostitute in one house.' So please return to your senses O son, and seek guidance from Allah ﷻ, He will guide you, do not let your emotion overpower your intellect and leave living this low life with this woman. The only people who live like this are the people who have no courage unlike you. The only people who live like this are those who have no honour and no house, whereas you have both, dignity and a house. I am leaving you now alone so that I can go to do some work. Use this time to think over this, perhaps your lost understanding may return. Then I will return to you after a while to hear from you those words which I expect will cure me and will quench my thirst."

Then his father left and walked towards a coffee shop which was near the hotel. Thereafter, he went to visit his friends whom he knew in Paris. He took a very long time visiting them. He did not return to the hotel until the night had come to pass.

قال: لم لا أرحم فتاةً مريضةً مسكينةً ليس لها في الناس من يعولها من ذي قرابةٍ أو ذي رحم؟ وقد نزل داؤها من صدرها منزلةً لا يبرحها ولا يتحلل عنها، إلا أن يهدأ عنها حيناً ويستيقظ أحياناً، فهي تكابد الألم مرةً، والخوف من الألم أخرى، ولا عزاء لها في حالتيها إلا هذه السعادة التي تتوهمها في الحب، وترى أنها ناعمة بها، فإن فقدتها فقدت كل شيءٍ في الحياة، وعظم حزنها وبؤسها، وثقلت وطأة الداء عليها حتى كادت تأتي على البقية الباقية من حياتها، فدعني معها يا أبتاه عاماً آخر أو عامين أهون عليهما فيهما شقاءها، فربما كان ذلك آخر ما قدر لها أن تقضيه من أيامها في هذا العالم، ثم أعود بعد ذلك إليك هادىء القلب ساكن الضمير، راضياً عن نفسي وعن عملي، أبكيها بدموع الحزن، لا بدموع الندم، ويهون وجدي عليها كلما ذكرتها أنني لم أخنها، ولم أغدر بعهدها.

فأطرق دوفال هنيهةً كأنما يعالج في نفسه هماً معتلجاً، ثم رفع رأسه ونظر إلى ولده نظرةً تشبه نظرة العطف والرحمة وقال له: لا أستطيع أن أسافر بدونك يا بني، فحسبي ما كابدت من الألم لفراقك قبل اليوم، وقد تركت أختك ورائي تندبك وتبكي عليك صباحها ومساءها، وتحن إلى لقائك حنين الظامىء إلى الورود، واعلم أن جميع ما تعتذر به عن نفسك في هذا الشأن لا يغني عنك ولا عني شيئاً يوم يقول الناس كلمتهم التي لا بد أن يقولها غداً، وربما قال كثير منهم قبل اليوم: إن أرمان دوفال، سلالة آل تاليراند، يعيش مع امرأةٍ مومسٍ في بيتٍ واحدٍ، فعد إلى نفسك يا بني واستلهم الله الرشد يلهمك، ولا تجعل لهواك سبيلاً على عقلك. ودع هذه الحياة الساقطة التي يحياها من ليست له همة مثل همتك، ولا مجد ولا بيت مثل مجدك وبيتك، وإني تاركك الآن وحدك، وذاهب عنك لبعض شأني لتخلو بنفسك ساعةً تسترد فيها ما عزب عنك من صوابك، ثم أعود إليك بعد قليلٍ لأسمع منك الكلمة التي أرجو أن تكون شفاء نفسي، ورواء غلتي.

ثم تركه ونزل، فمشى إلى قهوةٍ قريبةٍ من الفندق، فكتب فيها لبعض الناس كتاباً خاصاً. ثم طاف ببعض أصدقائه الذين يعرفهم في باريس فزارهم زيارةً طويلةً؛ فلم يعد إلى الفندق حتى أظل الليل،

He saw that Arman was still sat in his place. Then he asked him, "What have you decided?" His answer was within his tears which were flowing upon his cheeks. Arman knelt in front of him and started beseeching for mercy and kindness from him. He started sharing the secrets which he had been hiding before.

He was saying, "By Allah ﷻ O father, if I could see any way to live in this worldly life without her, then I would definitely leave her, listening and obeying your command. However unfortunately, I know that verily if I were to do this, then I will be placing myself in harm for I fear that I might go insane or lose my life. I do not know what my outcome would be? The misfortune of going mad or the adversity of losing my life will inevitably strike me. If there was anyone before me who had the power to eliminate his desires from his heart, or had the power to wipe out what destiny had written for him from the troubles and difficulties of love in the pages of decree, then I would certainly follow his way of how he did it. However, the calamity which has struck me requires my death. Therefore, I have no say in this, neither do I have a plan to overcome it. This lady has become a part of my soul, she is the life in my body. If you find it compelled to take me, then take my lifeless empty body with you."

His father placed his hand on his shoulder and said to him, "Stand up now O my son, and go back to your life but return back to me tomorrow morning, so that I may complete my conversation with you, and I hope that tomorrow you will be in better state than today." Thus, Arman left upset and worried.

He was walking like an insane madman. He could not see what was in front of him, neither did he have any sense of his surroundings. He continued in this state until he saw a Hackney carriage. He mounted it and travelled in it to Bougival. He reached his home late and did not see Margaret in the balcony of the house waiting for him the way she used to.

He entered the house and then entered her room. He saw her bowing down over a table which was in front of her, it felt that either she was sleeping or either she was extremely worried. She sensed him entering and stood up startled. Arman noticed the letter which she was pressing in her hand. Arman assumed it was a letter from Mr John Phillip which he used to send her time to time. Mr John Phillip was a young gentleman and the son of an elite wealthy dignified family. He used to love Margaret in her former life and would spend a lot of money on her. However, when she broke connections with him, this did not deter his hope. So, he kept on sending a lot of letters to her declaring and presenting his love in them alongside with money. He offered good hope and faith to her to return to him and a request to connect her life with his. However, if it ever came to her attention, that the letter was from him or she recognised the handwriting she would rip it up. Arman did not care about the letter and went to her and gave her a kiss.

فرأى أرمان لا يزال في مكانه. فسأله: ماذا رأى؟ فلم يجبه إلا بدموعه تنحدر على خديه تحدر القطر على أوراق الزهر، وجثا بين يديه يستعطفه ويسترحمه، ويكشف له من خبيئة نفسه ما كان يكتمه من قبل.

يقول: والله يا أبت لو علمت أني أستطيع الحياة بدونها لفارقتها براً بك وإيثاراً لطاعتك، ولكني أعلم أني إن فعلت فقد وضعت أمري في موضع الغرر، وخاطرت بعقلي أو بحياتي مخاطرةً لا أعلم ماذا يكون حظي فيها. ولا أحسبه إلا أسوأ الحظين، وأنحس النجمين، ولو أن أحداً من قبلي استطاع أن يدفع هواءً عن قلبه أو يمحو ما قدر له في صحيفة قضائه من شقاء الحب وبلائه لسلكت سبيله التي سلكها، ولكنه بلاء بليت به لحينٍ أريد لي، فلا رأي لي في رده، ولا حيلة لي في اتقائه، وقد نزلت هذه الفتاة من نفسي منزلةً هي منزلة الحياة من الجسم، والغيث من التربة الفاحلة، فإن كنت لا بد آخذي فخذ معك جسماً هامداً لا حراك به. ونبتة ذاويةً لا حياة فيها.

فوضع أبوه يده على عاتقه وقال له: قم الآن يا بني، واذهب لشأنك، وعد إلي صباح الغد لأتمم حديثي معك، وأرجو أن تكون في غدك خيراً منك في أمسك، فخرج محزوناً مكتئباً،

يمشي مشية الذاهل المشدوه لا يرى ما أمامه ولا يشعر بما حوله، حتى رأى عربةً فركبها إلى بوجيفال حتى بلغها بعد هدأةٍ من الليل، فلم ير مرغريت في شرفة البيت تنتظره كعادتها،

فدخل عليها غرفتها فرآها مكبةً على منضدةٍ بين يديها كأنما هي نائمة أو ذاهلة، فشعرت به عند دخوله، فنهضت مذعورةً متلهفة. فخيل إليه عند نهوضها أنه لمح في يدها رسالةً تضم عليها أصابعها، فظنها بعض الرسائل التي كان يرسلها إليها المركيز (جان فيليب) من حينٍ إلى حين، وهو فتىً من أبناء الأشراف الأثرياء كان يحبها في عهدها الأول حباً شديداً، وينفق عليها أموالاً طائلةً، فلما انقطعت عنه لم ينقطع منها أمله، فظل يرسل إليها رسائل كثيرة يعرض فيها حبه وماله، ويمنيها الأماني الحسان في عودتها إليه، واتصال حياتها بحياته، فكانت تمزقها عند اطلاعها عليها أو على عنوانها، فلم يحفل أرمان بذلك ومشى إليها فقبلها،

She said to him, "O Arman what happened?"

He said, "My father wants me to go back with him but I refused and in front of him I cried a lot, I did not move from my decision. Verily he has ordered me to come back to see him tomorrow, but I am not intending to do so. This is simply because the distress of tomorrow will not be any better than the misery of today. My heart is motivating me to rebel and to stay here rejecting his order because I know that certainly I have passed that age where sons are in need or dependent upon their father's advice. Also, because I do not know anyone from amongst the people who could write in my destiny a fortune better than the way I can write for myself." Then he began narrating his complete story; the account with his father to her until he finished. Then he looked at her and found her bowing down and standing in a quiet state. He discovered that her face was pale and withered as if the cloud of death was hovering upon her. He asked, "What is the matter O Margaret?"

She said, "I feel severe pain in my head. I want to go to my bedroom." Thus, Arman held her hand and took her towards the bedroom. Arman gave her some drops of her medicine and she felt a little bit better. Then she slept in her bedroom a sleep which was fitful and frightening. Long nightmares and distressing dreams were disturbing her. In the morning, she said to Arman, "O Arman, I think you should return to your father the way he has ordered you to do so and that you beg him for mercy and love, perhaps today you might attain that which you were unable to achieve yesterday. Verily I will not become satisfied with myself neither will I be content with my life until your father becomes happy with you." She kept on persisting until he listened to her. He got up and went towards his clothes and got dressed. Then he walked towards her and hugged her tightly, pressing his chest with hers as if he did not want anyone to take her out of his arms. Then he kissed her and said to her, "I will see you in the evening O Margaret." She did not respond to his farewell until he was far away from her. Then she said to herself, "If only you do come back the way you say." Then she fell on her chair crying and screaming.

Arman kept on walking on his way until he reached Paris. Then he went to the Toren Hotel. Thus, he did not find his father there. However, he found a letter which his father had left there for him. In it he had instructed him to wait there for him until his return. So, he stayed put and waited until he came. Half a day had passed.

فقالت له: ماذا جرى يا أرمان؟

قال: أرادني أبي على السفر معه فأبيت وبكيت بين يديه كثيراً فلم أنل منه منالا، وقد أمرني بالعودة إليه غداً ولا أريد أن أفعل لأني لا أحب حظي منه في الغد خيراً منه اليوم، وقد أصبحت نفسي تحدثني بعصيانه، والبقاء هنا على الرغم منه، لأني أعلم أني قد تجاوزت السن التي يحتاج فيها الأبناء إلى إرشاد الآباء، ولأني لا أعرف أحداً بين الناس يستطيع أن يرسم لي خطة سعادتي كما أرسمها لنفسي، ثم أنشأ يقص عليها قصته مع أبيه حتى أتمها، ونظر إليها فإذا هي مطرقة صامتة، وإذا وجهها أصفر مربد كأنما قد نفض الموت عليه غباره. فقال: ما بالك يا مرغريت؟

قالت: أشعر بألمٍ شديدٍ في رأسي، وأريد الذهاب إلى مخدعي. فأخذ بيدها إليه، وجرعها بضع قطراتٍ من الدواء فاستفاقت قليلاً، ثم نامت في مخدعها نوماً مشرداً مذعوراً، تتخلله أناتٌ طويلة وأحلام مزعجة، حتى أصبح الصباح فقالت له أرى لك يا أرمان أن تعود إلى أبيك كما أمرك، وأن تعاود استرحامه واستعطافه لعلك بالغ منه اليوم ما عجزت منه بالأمس، إني لا أكون راضيةً عن نفسي، ولا هانئةً بحياتي، إن لم يكن أبوك راضياً عنك... ولم تزل به حتى أذعن لها وقام إلى ثيابه فارتداها، ثم مشى إليها وضمها إلى صدره ضمةً شديدةً كأنما يضن بها أن ينتزعها من ذراعيه منتزع، ثم قبلها وقال لها: إلى المساء يا مرغريت. فلم ترد عليه تحيته حتى أبعد عنها، فقالت بينها وبين نفسها: أرجو أن يكون كذلك.. وتهافتت على كرسي بين يديها باكيةً منتحبة.

ولم يزل أرمان سائراً في سبيله حتى وصل إلى باريس، فذهب إلى فندق (تورين) فلم يجد أباه هناك، ووجد رسالةً تركها له قبل ذهابه يأمره فيها أن ينتظره حتى يعود، فلبث ينتظره وقتاً طويلاً حتى عاد بعد منتصف النهار،

Indeed, that black cloud which was veiling his father's face yesterday had lessened. Arman walked towards his father and greeted him. Then his father said to him, "O my son, indeed I have been thinking about you extensively all night and I feel that I have been very harsh on you and that I have upset you significantly. I pondered over your issue with a narrow mind, whereas it was crucial for me to contemplate over it with an open mind. Certainly, the circumstances of young people are unlike the situations of old men and women. Young people have specific circumstances whether they are honourable or disgraceful. There is no differentiation between a vulgar person and a king."

So, I grant you the permission to stay with her the way you please O my son and you can live with the woman whom you love, just the way you want. However, this would be upon your pledge and promise to me, to return to me on the day when the relationship comes to an end. Regardless of whether your relationship ends with her whilst she is living, or when she dies. Indeed, I am not worried for you in respect of her, but I will certainly be worried over you in respect of a woman other than her."

Consequently, Arman was overcome with happiness and joy. He bowed down upon his father's hand and started kissing it. Arman was soaking his father's hand with his tears and he was saying, "I promise you O father, that I will certainly do this, this is my pledge which I will never go against neither will I break it and with you will be the decision, if you see me after this day lying or the one breaking a promise."

Then Arman stood up intending to leave. Thus, his father asked him, "Where are you intending to go?" He replied, "I am intending to go towards Margaret, to inform her of this great news, and to relieve her heart from the terror which has gripped it since yesterday." His father shook but Arman did not notice. Then Arman's father turned his face away from Arman, to allow time for the tears which were hovering in his eyes to dry up. Then he turned back facing Arman and said, "O my son, please stay with me today, most likely I will be going back tomorrow, and I do not know when I am going to meet you again." So, Arman stayed with him one full day until night came. Then he sought his permission to leave and go to Bougival. Hence, his father gave him the permission. He said his farewells to him and came out. His father's eyes followed him until he disappeared from his sight. Then, he allowed the tear to run free which he had been withholding uttering, "May the mercy of Allah ﷻ encompass you O poor child."

***

وقد رقت قليلاً تلك الغمامة السوداء التي كانت تلبس وجهه بالأمس، فتقدم نحوه أرمان، فحياه، فقال له: لقد فكرت ليلة أمس في أمرك كثيراً يا بني، فرأيت أني قد قسوت عليك، وغلوت في أمرك غلواً كبيراً، ونظرت إلى مسألتك بعينٍ أقصر من التي كان يجب علي أن أنظر إليها، فإن للشباب شأناً غير شأن الكهولة والشيخوخة، وحالاً خاصة به، لا يخرج عن حكمها شريف ولا وضيع، ولا يختلف فيها سوقة عن ملك،

فلك أن تبقى يا بني كما تشاء، وأن تعاشر الفتاة التي تحبها كما تريد، على أن تعدني بالعودة إلي في اليوم الذي تنقطع فيه الصلة بينك وبينها انقطاع حياةٍ أو موت، فإني إن أمنت عليك شرها فلا آمن عليك شر غيرها من النساء.

فاستطير أرمان فرحاً وسروراً، وأهوى على يد أبيه يقبلها ويبللها بدموعه ويقول: أعدك بذلك يا أبتاه وعداً لا أخالفه، ولا أخيس به، ولك حكمك ما تشاء إن رأيتني بعد اليوم كاذباً أو حانثاً.

ثم نهض يريد الذهاب فقال له: أين تريد قال: أريد الذهاب إلى مرغريت لأبشرها بهذا النبأ، وأمسح عن فؤادها ما ألم به من الروع منذ الأمس، فانتفض أبوه انتفاضةً خفيفةً لم يشعر بها أرمان، ثم أدار وجهه ليغالب دمعةً كانت تترقرق في عينيه، ثم التفت إليه، وقال: ابق معي اليوم يا بني فربما سافرت غداً، ولا أعلم بعد ذلك متى أراك. فبقي معه اليوم كله حتى جاء الليل، فاستأذنه في الذهاب إلى بوجيفال فأذن له فحياه وخرج؛ فأتبعه نظره حتى غاب عن عينيه؛ فانحدرت من جفنه تلك الدمعة التي كان يحبسها من قبل، وقال: وارحمتاه لك أيها الولد المسكين!

***

Arman rushed home to share his excitement with Margaret, until he got close to Bougival. He became frightened to see that the house was extremely dark and quiet. There was no ray of light in it neither did he see any shadow in there. He walked towards the door only to discover that it was locked. Then he placed his ear upon a crack of the door but did not hear any movement. Then he started knocking the door hard. He was shouting out for Margaret at times, and at times he was shouting out the maid's name but no one replied to him. Then Arman thought to himself, 'perhaps, she has gone to her house in Paris for some matter and her maid has also gone with her and that inevitably they will be returning now.'

Thus, he sat down upon a rock which was facing the door of the house waiting for her until one portion of the night had passed and she did not return. Then he forced himself to also go to Paris, to find her in those places where she could be. But he became afraid that if he left for Paris she maybe on her way back and he would miss her. So, he remained sitting in his place at times and other times he would get up. At times, he stayed put and at times he started pacing. He thought of every possible danger of loss and tragedy that could have occurred, other than the thought of her deceiving him and showing disloyalty to him. He remained in this state of distress until the light of morning spread. He became distressed at the thought that, inevitably something has happened to Margaret, and it was crucial for him to get to her. It became absolutely vital for him to see which condition she was in. Due to being anxious and being awake all night, fatigue overtook his body and mind in such a way that he could not think straight anymore.

Subsequently, he set off way to Paris like a drunken person falling all over the place until he reached Margaret's dwelling place. He saw the watchman of the house who had woken up from his sleep and was standing next to a tree with an axe. He was cutting down its branches. Arman asked him about Margaret. He replied, "She had come here during night yesterday, her maid was also with her, she was holding a big bag, she went in the house and stayed there for an hour and then she came out. She was wearing a dress from amongst the wedding dresses and giving me a letter said, 'When monsieur Arman asks about me give him this letter.' Then she embarked upon her carriage with her maid and went."

Arman asked, "Do you know where she went?"

The watchman replied, "I think I heard her say to the driver when she was embarking on her ride, 'Go to the house of Mr John Phillip.'"

حمل أرمان بين جنبيه آماله وآمال مرغريت وسعادتهما التي يرجوانها في مستقبل حياتهما، وطار بها إليها ليقاسمها إياها حتى دنا من بوجيفال، فأدهشه أن رأى البيت مظلماً ساكناً لا يضطرب فيه شعاع، ولا يتراءى فيه ظل؛ فمشى إلى الباب فرآه مرتجاً، فوضع أذنه على خصاصه، فلم يسمع حركة، فأخذ يقرعه قرعاً شديداً، ويهتف باسم (مرغريت) مرةً وباسم (برودنس) أخرى، فلم يجبه أحد، فقال في نفسه: لعلها ذهبت إلى بيتها في باريس لبعض شأنها واستصحبت خادمتها، ولا بد أن تعود الآن،

فجلس على صخرةٍ أمام باب المنزل ينتظرها حتى مضت هدأة من الليل فلم تعد، فحدثته نفسه بالعودة إلى باريس للبحث عنها في مظان وجودها، ثم منعه من ذلك خوفه أن يسلك في ذهابه طريقاً غير الطريق التي تسلكها في عودتها، فاستمر في مكانه يقعد مرةً ويقوم أخرى، ويقف حيناً ويتمشى أحياناً، ويحدث نفسه بكل حديثٍ يمر بخاطر القلق المرتاع إلا حديث خيانتها وغدرها، ولم يزل في حيرته واضطرابه حتى رأى جذوة الفجر تدب في فحمة الظلام، فساء ظنه، وانتشرت عليه وساوسه وأوهامه، وقال في نفسه: ما لمرغريت بد من شأن، ولا بد لي من المصير إليها، والنظر في الشأن الذي شغلها! وكان القلق والسهر قد أخذا مأخذهما من جسمه ونفسه من حيث لا يشعر؛

فمشى في طريقه إلى باريس يترنح ترنح الشارب الثمل، حتى وصل إلى منزل مرغريت، وقد علا صدر النهار؛ فرأى حارس المنزل قد استيقظ من نومه ووقف بفأسه على شجرةٍ من أشجار الحديقة يشذب أغصانها، فسأله عن مرغريت، فقال: إنها حضرت هنا بالأمس في منصرف النهار ووراءها خادمتها تحمل حقيبةً كبيرةً فصعدت إلى المنزل فلبثت فيه ساعةً ثم نزلت، وقد لبست ثوباً من أثواب الولائم، فأعطتني كتاباً، وقالت لي إذا جاء هنا المسيو أرمان للسؤال عني فأعطه إياه، ثم ركبت عربتها هي وخادمتها وانصرفت،

قال: ألا تعلم أين ذهبت؟

قال: أحسب أني سمعتها تقول للحوذي عند ركوبها (إلى منزل المركيز جان فيليب)،

Thus, Arman froze like a statue and his colour changed to the colour of death. Like lightning, that letter which he saw in her hand the day he returned to her after meeting his father, started circulating around him. The watchman left Arman in his place and went to his room and returned with the letter. Arman took the letter off him with shaking hands and opened it. He swiftly glanced over the text and had understood everything which was in it in his first glance. Then Arman's body started to tremble severely and he started stepping back a step or two towards the door of the mansion. Then he rested his back upon the door and returned upon reading the letter which was composed of the following words,

'This is the last thing between me and you O Arman. Do not think in your heart to ever meet me again. Do not ever ask me the reason. I do not have any explanation with me other than this is what I have decided fit for myself. Goodbye.'

Thus, Arman's eyes were glued on to the letter for a while. He did not raise his eyes from it neither could he read a word from it. He stood like a statue. Then the watchman returned towards his tree and continued cutting its branches. The watchman was singing when he climbed up the tree, he was enjoying its tune despite of not understanding its meaning. Suddenly he heard a heavy object falling upon the ground.

He threw his axe and ran towards the sound. He saw that Arman had fallen and was covered in dust under the doorstep. The watchman became extremely frightened and presumed that he has undergone an epileptic fit. The watchman placed his ears upon Arman's chest, he could hear a heartbeat, so, he rushed to get some water, splashing it on Arman's face until he gained consciousness after a while.

Arman opened his eyes and saw the watchman sitting beside him and the letter which was still in his hand. He reflected on the intense love Margaret held for him in the past, this thought made him impatient and restless and he screamed, "How far has today changed from yesterday!" Arman started crying, seeing him in this state, the watchman also started crying. Then the watchman hugged Arman to give him reassurance until he felt a little bit better. Arman requested the watchman to call a Hackney carriage for him, when it arrived Arman stood up with support from the watchman until he reached the carriage. Arman ordered the driver towards the Toren Hotel.

فجمد أرمان في مكانه جمود الصنم، واستحال لونه إلى صفرة الموت، ومر بخاطره مرور البرق ذلك الكتاب الذي رآه في يدها بعد عودته إليها من مقابلة أبيه، فتركه الحارس مكانه وذهب إلى غرفته وعاد إليه بالكتاب، فتناوله منه بيدٍ مرتجفةٍ ونشره وأمر نظره عليه إمراراً فأحاط بما فيه للنظرة الأولى، فارتعد جسمه ارتعاداً شديداً، وتراجع خطوةً أو خطوتين إلى باب القصر، فأسند ظهره إليه وأعاد قراءته فإذا هو مشتمل على هذه الكلمات:

(هذا آخر ما بيني وبينك يا أرمان؛ فلا تحدث نفسك بمعاودة الاتصال بي، ولا تسألني عن السبب في ذلك، فلا سبب عندي إلا أني هكذا أردت لنفسي... والسلام).

فعلق نظره بالكتاب ساعةً لا يرفع طرفه عنه، ولا يقرأ منه حرفاً، كأنما هو تمثال من تماثيل الحديقة، وكان الحارس قد عاد إلى شجرته يشذب أغصانها ويتغنى في صعوده إليها وانحداره عنها بقطعةٍ من الشعر الغرامي يعجبه لحنها، وإن كان لا يفهم معناها، فإنه لكذلك إذ سمع صوت جسمٍ ثقيلٍ قد سقط على الأرض،

فرمى بفأسه وهرع إلى ناحية الصوت فرأى أرمان صريعاً معفراً تحت عتبة الباب، ففزع فزعاً شديداً وظنها الصرعة الكبرى، فأهوى بأذنه إلى صدره، فسمع ما بقي من دقات قلبه، فاطمأن قلباً وعمد إلى جرةٍ بين يديه فأخذ ينضح بمائها وجهه ويدلك براحة يده صدره وصدغيه حتى استفاق بعد قليل،

ففتح عينيه فرأى الحارس جالساً بجانبه ورأى الكتاب لا يزال في يده، فدار بعينيه حول نفسه فمرت بخاطره في الحال ذكرى مصرعه القديم في هذا المكان عينه منذ خمسة عشر شهراً يوم ألقت مرغريت بنفسها عليه ورسمت على ثغره أول قبلةٍ من قبلات الحب، فهاجته تلك الذكرى وصاح: ما أبعد اليوم من الأمس! وأنشأ يبكي بكاء الطفل الذي حيل بينه وبين ثدي أمه، حتى بكى الحارس لبكائه وأقبل عليه يعزيه عن مصابه، ويهونه عليه حتى هدأ قليلاً؛ فأمره أن يستدعي له عربةً ففعل. فقام يتوكأ على يد الحارس حتى بلغها فركب، وقال للسائق (إلى فندق تورين).

He had almost reached Toren Hotel when a beautiful carriage passed by like a thundering lightning with a man and woman in it. Arman did not recognize any of them at his first sight then realised it was John Phillip and Margaret. He reached the hotel and met his father in a worried and sad state. His father said to him, "What has happened to you O my son?"

He replied, "O my father Indeed she has deceived me!"

His father said, "This is what I used to warn you of O my son."

The day passed and the night fell. Arman spent the whole night in his bedroom awake. He thought about the chapter of his life which he had spent with Margaret. He pondered over all her behaviours until none of her love or sincerity remained rather he could only see her evil, wicked, deceptive and abhorrent behaviour from today. Her betrayal overshadowed everything. His mind went back to the final night he had seen her…

He remembered not seeing her not waiting at the balcony for him as she usually did when he returned after meeting his father. He recalled her hiding the letter of John Phillip which was in her hand when he had entered the room. She was clinging on to the letter very tightly whereas she had never done this before. He remembered her refraining engaging in conversation with him after he had narrated to her of the incident with his father. She was pretending that she was ill and upset and could not live without him. He remembered her insisting the next morning that he return to his father and beg him for mercy and love.

From all of this he concluded that when she had planned that when she had no money remaining, and his father would not provide provision, she would despise living with him and would think of a way to get rid of him. She waited until the letter of John Phillip's arrived and through it she finally found a way to free herself.

He remained upset and distressed until fatigue overtook his eyes and he fell asleep for a little while. When he awoke in the morning he went to his father in his bedroom and said to him, "O father, I have one last wish from you and I intend nothing else in exchange I will always obey you and will always for eternity listen to your orders whether I like it or dislike it. So, father, will you grant me my last wish?"

فسارت به العربة إليه: حتى إذا لم يبق بينه وبينه إلا منعطف واحد مرت بجانبه عربة فخمة مرور البرق الخاطف، تحمل رجلاً وامرأةً لم يتبينهما للنظرة الأولى: ثم راجع صورتهما في خياله فإذا هما: (جان فيليب ومرغريت)، وكانت مركبته قد وصلت به إلى الفندق، فدخل على أبيه هائماً مختبلاً، فقال: ما دهاك يا بني؟

قال: (قد خانتني يا أبتاه).

قال: ذلك ما أنذرتك به من قبل يا بني.

ثم انقضى النهار، وجاء الليل فقضاه أرمان ساهراً في مخدعه يراجع فهرس حياته مع مرغريت صفحةً صفحةً، ويستعرض في نفسه جميع أطوارها وشؤونها فلم تبق حركة من حركاتها، ولا كلمة من كلماتها، ولا صورة من صورِ أعمالها، كان يراها بالأمس حسنةً من حسنات الإخلاص والوفاء، إلا رآها اليوم سيئةً من سيئات الخديعة والمكر، حتى وصل في مراجعته إلى الأمس واليوم الذي قبله.

فذكر عدم انتظارها إياه في شرفة البيت كعادتها يوم عاد إليها من مقابلة أبيه، وشدة احتفاظها بكتاب المركيز في يدها عندما دخل عليها غرفتها وضنها به ضناً شديداً، ولم تكن تفعل ذلك من قبل، وإعراضها عن التبسط معه في الحديث بعد ما قص عليها قصته مع أبيه، وزعمها أنها مريضة خائرة لا تستطيع البقاء معه، وإلحاحها عليه في صباح اليوم الثاني إلحاحاً شديداً في العودة إلى مقابلة أبيه واستعطافه، وقولها إنها لا تكون راضيةً عن نفسها ولا هانئةً بعيشها إن لم يكن أبوه راضياً عنه،

فاستنتج من هذا كله: أنها مذ شعرت بفراغ يده من المال وأن أباه، إما أن يحول بينه وبينها، وإما أن يقتر عليه الرزق تقتيراً، ملته واجتوته، وفكرت في سبيل الخلاص منه، ولم تزل تنتظر ما يأتيها به القدر حتى أتاها بكتاب المركيز فكان هو طريق خلاصها.

ولم يزل هائماً ما شاء الله أن يهيم في تصوراته وأوهامه حتى غلبته عيناه فهجع قليلاً: ثم استيقظ في الصباح فدخل على أبيه في مخدعه وقال له: لي عندك أمنية يا أبتاه لا أريد غيرها، وأريد أن أبتاعها منك بخضوعي لك ونزولي على حكمك أبد الدهر فيما سرني أو ساءني: فهل لك أن تبلغنها؟

His father replied, "What is it?"

He said, "I would like you to give me fifteen thousand francs."

He replied, "What are you going to do with this?"

Arman said, "I would like to keep this a secret to myself and do not want to disclose it to anyone, even you." After a moment of hesitation his father gave him a cheque for the amount of money he had requested. Arman took it and sent it to Margaret along with a long letter which concluded with these words,

'Verily I have realised that I was living with a disrepute prostitute who could not keep a promise neither did she have any sense of responsibility. Thus, I am sending the payment for all the nights which I have spent with you in the past.'

Then he came out to prepare for his journey. He spent a whole day out of the hotel. Then he returned to the hotel in the last portion of the day. There he found a letter with his name on it. He tore open its seal. He discovered that those pages which he had sent to Margaret had returned to him just the way he had sent them. There was not even a word written in response. He intended to return the letter to her one more time but his father prevented him doing so saying, "You have promised that you will not go against my decision so you must listen." Thus, he listened. Then both travelled together that night back to Nice.

Like this, Allah ﷻ had decreed to separate these two loyal friends and two sincere lovers. That young man returned to his father's care and the young lady returned to her former life, the life which she had eliminated herself from and which she feared. Each one of them felt sorrow and remorse for their companion. Neither did the days, the months nor did the years lessen their sorrow and remorse for each other.

***

There are a lot of unfortunate people in the world. However, the most unfortunate one is that troublesome and patient individual who is forced through the circumstances of life to bury his sorrows and pains in the depth of his heart and leave them there. In front of people he appears with a happy, smiling face as if he is not holding upon his shoulders the burdens of grief and sorrow.

قال: وما هي؟

قال: أريد أن تعطيني الساعة خمسة عشر ألف فرنك.

قال وما تريد منها؟

قال: أحب أن أستأثر بهذا السر لنفسي من دون الناس جميعاً حتى من دونك؛ فنظر إليه أبوه نظرة الملم بما دار في نفسه ولم يعاوده، وأعطاه صكوكاً بالمال الذي أراد، فأخذها وأرسلها إلى مرغريت وأرسل معها كتاباً طويلاً ختمه بهذه الكلمة:

(أما وقد عرفت أنني كنت أعيش مع امرأةٍ عاهرٍ ساقطةٍ لا عهد لها ولا ذمام، فها هي ذي أجرة لياليك الماضية مرسلة إليك).

ثم خرج ليعد نفسه للسفر، فقضى اليوم كله خارج الفندق ثم عاد إليه دبر النهار، فوجد فيه كتاباً باسمه، ففض ختامه فإذا الأوراق التي أرسلها إلى مرغريت عائدة إليه كما هي وليس معها كلمة واحدة، فحاول أن يعيدها إليها مرةً أخرى، فمنعه أبوه من ذلك وقال له: قد وعدتني ألا تخالفني في أمرٍ، فلا بد لك من الإذعان... فأذعن ثم سافرا معاً تلك الليلة إلى نيس.

وكذلك قضى الله أن يفترق ذانك الصديقان الوفيان والعاشقان المخلصان، فعاد الفتى إلى أحضان أبيه، وعادت الفتاة إلى حياتها الأولى التي كانت تأباها الإباء كله، وتخافها الخوف الشديد، وفي نفس كل منهما من الوجد يصاحبه والحسرة عليه ما لا تليه الأيام، ولا تنتقص منه السنون والأعوام .

***

الأشقياء في الدنيا كثير، وأعظمهم شقاءً ذلك الحزين الصابر الذي قضت عليه ضرورة من ضروريات الحياة أن يهبط بآلامه وأحزانه إلى قرارة نفسه فيودعها هناك ، ثم يغلق دونها باباً من الصمت والكتمان، ثم يصعد إلى الناس باش الوجه باسم الثغر متطلقاً متهللاً، كأنه لا يحمل بين جنبيه هماً ولا كمداً!

This was the state which Margaret was encompassed with after she had returned to her former life. She was living with the people with an appearance other than her real appearance and in the state of sadness which she felt in isolation. When she was with people, she spent time with them laughing, playing, in a happy state and spent time with them peacefully. She used to glimmer in the crowds and gatherings, and she used to fill the eyes and the ears of people with sweet melodies. However, when she was alone in her bedroom and in the seclusion of night, her eyes would recall those honourable moments which she had spent in the company of Arman. Then she would remember that she ran away from his hands like a captured bird that flies away from the hands of its pursuer.

Indeed, she ended up living with people whom she did not know. She never found the joy of love with them. She had no alternative but to seduce and show love to them. She beautified herself for them the way they had wanted and the way they had desired. She used to kiss the faces of those whom she did not like. She used to hug those people who she did not even want to look at. She drank alcohol with every alcoholic whereas alcohol used to burn her insides. She used to dance with every dancer despite dancing used to cause pain in her joints. She used to laugh the laughter of happiness with a crying heart. She used to sing happy songs with a dead heart.

Thus, she used to get awfully upset when she remembered the past days of her life that had been filled with bliss. She used to leave the way clear for her sighs and her tears, she used to sigh as loud as she could and shed tears as much as she could until she felt a little better. Then she used to stand up and go to her wardrobe and take out a picture and place it on her chest. Then she would take refuge on her bed. It was the picture of Arman.

She continued to endure this adversity of living this fallen life, despite not having the strength to endure it. She lost weight and her colour changed. The beauty of her smiles vanished. She kept busy with herself and did not give time to John Phillip. Due to this he became fed up with her and separated from her and replaced her with another woman. After John Phillip, Margaret's other friends and associates started coming to her but not even one of them stayed other than recognising her symptoms and then leaving her. Hence, in the market of beauty her merchandise and stock had lost value. Now those individuals started desiring her, those who in the past, could not even dream to obtain the dust of the ground she had walked on.

ذلك كان شأن (مرغريت) بعد عودتها إلى حياتها الأولى، فقد أصبحت تعيش مع الناس بصورةٍ غير الصورة التي تعيش بها مع نفسها، أما حياتها مع الناس فحياة ضاحكة لاعبة مرحة وثابة، تضيء المجامع والمحافل، وتملأ الأنظار والأسماع، فإذا ضمها مخدعها وخلا لها وجه الليل مرت أمام عينيها صورة تلك الساعات السعيدة التي قضتها بجانب أرمان. ثم ذكرت أنها قد أفلتت من يدها إفلات الطائر من يد صائده، وصارت بعيدةً عنها بعد الشمس عن يد متناولها،

وأنها قد أصبحت تعيش بين أقوام لا تعرفهم، ولا تجد في نفسها لذة الأنس بهم، ثم لا تجد لها بداً من ممادقتهم والتحبب إليهم والتجمل لهم بما يريدون ويشتهون، فتقبل الأفواه التي لا تشتهيها، وتعتنق القامات التي لا تطيق رؤيتها، وتشرب مع كل شارب، والشراب يحرق أحشاءها، وترقص مع كل راقص، والرقص يمزق أوصالها، وتضحك ضحكات السرور من قلبٍ باكٍ، وتنشد أناشيد الهناء من فؤادٍ محترق، فكأنها في يد الناس والعود في يد المغني يقطع أوتاره ضرباً ليطرب لنغماته، أو الزهرة في يد المقتطف يعصر أوراقها عصراً لينعم بشذاها،

فتهيجها ذكرى ذلك الماضي السعيد، وهذا الحاضر الشقي، فتطلق السبيل لزفراتها وعبراتها يصعد منها ما يصعد، وينحدر ما ينحدر، حتى تشتفي نفسها، فتقوم إلى خزانة ملابسها فتستخرج منها صورةً تضعها بين سحرها ونحرها، ثم تأوي إلى مضجعها فتجد برد الراحة في صدرها لأنها صورة أرمان.

ولم تزل تكابد من الشقاء في تلك الحياة الساقطة وآلامها ما لا طاقة لمثلها باحتمال مثله، حتى استيقظ في صدرها داؤها القديم بعد ما نام عنها حيناً من الدهر، فهزل جسمها وشحب لونها وغاض ماء ابتساماتها وانطفأ شعاع نظراتها، وشغلها شأن نفسها عن شأن المركيز، فلم يلبث أن ملها وفارقها، واستبدل بها أخرى غيرها، ثم اختلف عليها من بعده الأخلاء الرفقاء، فكان شأنهم معها شأنه، لا يلبث أحدهم أن يعرفها حتى يهجرها فكسدت سلعتها في سوق الجمال، وطمع فيها من لم يكن يطمع قبل اليوم في لثم مواطىء أقدامها، وخلت منها المجامع والمحافل، ثم خلت من ذكرها وحديثها،

At this point she needed money greatly. So, she started selling the remaining of her diamonds and gems but even after this, her debt remained. She sought help from a lot of her past friends. But only a handful of friends had helped her and this did not benefit her at all. Summons and letters from the debtors had started arriving, demanding she clear the outstanding amount. The matter became so bad that she was unable to pay any further payments. Accordingly, they bankrupted her and took away her belongings, her treasures, the household furniture and her clothes. Their conduct was extremely cold and merciless which increased her grief and her illness. Also, the remaining hope that she had left of life and its happiness came to an end. Thus, she forgot the whole world, its good and its bad, its life, its fortunes and its misfortunes. However, there was only one thought which went through her mind night and day. This was the wish to see Arman one last time before she died and met her Lord.

She had never written Arman a single word ever since she had parted from him. Neither did he write to her. In a distressed state, she went to her desk and penned the following;

'Come to me O Arman, whether you are pleased or whether you are upset. I am ill and close to death. I would like to see you before I die and disclose to you the reason for my betrayal. Betrayal which hurt you immensely and still hurts to this day. I hope that you can forgive me in my last moments of my life. Then your pardoning and you being pleased with me becomes the complete lot of provisions which I will take with me to my grave. Remember O Arman, the first sentiment which joined us together, and because of it love was born in our hearts. That was an act of mercy and kindness. So, here is the poor, ill, young woman whom you showed mercy and kindness in the days gone by when you loved her. Today she is calling you to show mercy and kindness to her even though you have forgotten her.

Regarding the letter which you wrote to me before your journey, indeed I have forgiven everything your said, even your statement that verily I was insincere in my love, that I had greed for your money. This is because, certainly I know that a woman who has been lying all her life to men in terms of declaring her love, will not find anyone who would believe her when she tells the truth. Whatever has been done, the justice is with Allah ﷻ.'

وأعوزها المال إعوازاً شديداً فمدت يدها إلى ما كان باقياً عندها من جواهرها ولآلئها فباعته، فلم يف بدينها، فطلبت المعونة من كثيرٍ من أصدقائها الماضين فأرسل إليها قليل منهم القليل منها، فلم يغن عنها شيئاً، واختلفت إليها جرائد الحساب يطلب أصحابها سداد ما فيها، فدافعتهم عنها حيناً ثم عجزت، فحجزوا على جميع مقتنياتها وذخائرها، وأثاث بيتها ورياشه. ولؤموا في مقاضاتها لؤماً ضاعف حزنها ومرضها، وقضى على بقية ما كانت تضمره في نفسها من الأمل في الحياة والسعادة فيها، فنسيت العالم، خيره وشره، والحياة، سعادتها وشقاءها، وأصبحت لا تفكر إلا في أمرٍ واحدٍ تقوم وتقعد به ليلها ونهارها، وهو أن ترى أرمان ساعةً واحدةً قبل موتها، ثم تذهب إلى ربها.

ولم تكن قد كتبت إليه قبل اليوم كلمةً واحدةً مذ فارقها ولا كتب إليها؛ فنهضت تتحامل على نفسها حتى وصلت إلى منضدتها فكتبت إليه هذا الكتاب:

(تعال إلي يا أرمان راضياً كنت أو غاضباً، فإنني مريضة مشرفة، وأحب أن أراك قبل موتي، لأفضي لك بسر الذنب الذي أذنبته إليك فيما مضى، والذي لا تزال واجداً علي بسببه حتى اليوم؛ فلعلك تعفو عني في ساعتي الأخيرة، فيكون عفوك ورضاك هو كل ما أتزوده من هذه الحياة لقبري. واذكر يا أرمان أن أول عاطفةٍ جمعت بيني وبينك وألفت بين قلبي وقلبك، كانت عاطفة الرحمة والشفقة، فها هي الفتاة المريضة المسكينة التي رحمتها بالأمس وعطفت عليها قبل أن تحبها تدعوك اليوم أن ترحمها وتعطف عليها. وإن تكن قد سلوتها.

أما كتابك الذي كتبته إلي قبل سفرك فقد اغتفرت لك كل ما فيه حتى قولك إنني كنت كاذبةً في حبك، طامعةً في مالك؛ لأني أعلم أن المرأة التي تكذب الناس في حبها طول حياتها لا يمكن أن تجد من يصدقها إذا صدقت فيه، وعدل من الله كل ما صنع).

Then she waited for his coming for a very long time. Thus, he never came, this increased her pain and sadness. She started thinking badly of him. A thought had appeared in her heart that verily he has forgotten her and has discarded her from his memories. She presumed that he did not care about her and he was not bothered with her life or either with her death. She speculated that he was not concerned about her wellbeing.

This presumption, however, was untrue. This was because Arman was never informed of the letter which she had sent him. Although he travelled to Nice he did not have power to stay there except for a few days. This was because he started becoming restless and his heart became constrained, failing to obtain any peace. Thus, he sought permission from his father to travel towards some western countries to please his heart and to lessen his pain. His father gave him the permission, and then he travelled to Alexandria, Egypt. He stayed there for a few months. He wrote to his father from there a few times. Then he left Alexandria and started roaming to other towns. He never stayed in one town except that his restlessness took him to another town. Now he had stopped writing to his father and his father was unaware of his location.

Whenever Margaret had sent him her letter to Nice, Arman's father had read it and treasured it with him. His farther had no means of sending it to him. Margaret on the other hand, had no knowledge of this. Thus, Margaret became extremely sad over her failing hope.

Eventually, despair had penetrated her heart like the shadow of death. Now, she knew that she would leave this world deprived of everything, her condition deteriorated further and she took refuge towards silence. Whenever her doctor came, when she was in severe pain, she never complained of her pain to the doctor. She used to hear the noise of the debtors and their pleas in the courtyard of her house. She never asked them what they wanted.

ثم لبثت تنتظر حضوره أياماً طوالاً فلم يأت، فأحزنها ذلك حزناً شديداً، وساء ظنها به، ووقع في نفسها أنه قد سلاها واطرحها، وأصبح لا يعبأ بها، ولا يبالي بحياتها أو موتها، وسعادتها أو شقائها،

وكانت مخطئةً فيما ظنت، فإن أرمان لم يطلع على الكتاب الذي أرسلته إليه مذ فارقها في العام الماضي، وسافر إلى نيس ولم يستطع البقاء فيها إلا أياماً قلائل، ثم ملكه الضجر وأحاطت به الوحشة، وضاقت في وجهه مذاهب السلوى فاستأذن من أبيه أن يسافر إلى بعض بلاد المشرق ترويحاً عن نفسه وتفريجاً من كربته، فأذن له فسافر إلى الإسكندرية فأقام بها بضعة أشهرٍ كاتب أباه فيها قليلاً، ثم تركها وأخذ يتنقل في أنحاء البلاد لم ينزل ببلدٍ حتى يطير به الضجر إلى غيره، فانقطعت رسائله عن أبيه، فأصبح لا يعلم مكان وجوده،

فلما أرسلت مرغريت إليه كتابها في نيس قرأه أبوه وحفظه عنده ولم يستطع أن يرسله إليه، ومرغريت لا تعلم بشيءٍ من ذلك؛ فحزنت لخيبة أملها حزناً شديداً، ودب اليأس في قلبها دبيب الموت في الحياة،

ووقع في نفسها أنها ستخرج من الدنيا فارغة اليد من كل شيءٍ حتى من هذه الأمنية التي بقيت في يدها من بين جميع آمالها الضائعة، فتنكر شأنها، واستحالت حالها، ولجأت إلى صمتٍ طويلٍ لا تقول فيه خيراً ولا شراً، وأصبحت تنظر إلى نفسها وإلى ما يحيط بها من الأشياء كأنها تنظر إلى شيءٍ تنكره ولا تعرفه؛ فربما دخل عليها طبيبها وهي في أشد حالات ألمها فلا تشكو له ألماً، أو سمعت ضوضاء الدائنين وصخبهم في فناء المنزل فلا تسأل ماذا يريدون!

However, when she felt a little bit better in terms of having relief from her pain, she embarking on a hackney carriage, travelled to Bougival, visiting the house where she had been living in happiness. The house was still maintained well. She passed by its rooms and its courtyards. She would sit in every place Arman had sat. She would look through all those windows which Arman used to look out of with her. She would kiss every sign and remaining mark affiliated with Arman. She would kiss the glass which Arman used to drink from. She kissed the flower which he used to like. She kissed the pen which he used to write with. She kissed the book which he used to read from. When she felt tired, she would sit down and take a rest. Whenever her thoughts hovered towards old times, her imagination used to make her believe that Arman was sitting in front of her and telling her his childhood stories in Nice, or that he was disclosing his love to her from the depths of his heart. She would smile contemplating over these things. She used to feel such a joy in her heart, a joy which the pious would feel in the highest gardens of Paradise. Then she would open her eyes, only to discover the seclusion, the quietness and the loneliness. She would cry as much as Allah ﷻ would allow her to do so.

Then she would return to her house in Paris where she would sit in her chair and would pretend Arman was there and would talk to him about all the things bothering her heart.

(The upcoming accounts of Diaries contribute towards the missing elements of this story. Through these accounts the readers can understand the reasons why Margaret had left Arman. Hence, the following accounts of the diaries are a part of this story.)

وكانت إذا شعرت بقليلٍ من الراحة والسكون ركبت عربتها إلى بوجيفال فزارت البيت الذي قضت فيه أيام سعادتها الذاهبة، وكان لا يزال باقياً على الصورة التي تركتها عليها يوم فارقته ومرت بغرفه وقاعاته، وجلست في كل مكانٍ كانت تجلس فيه مع أرمان، وأشرفت من كل نافذةٍ كان يشرف منها معها، وقبلت جميع آثاره وبقاياه، ولثمت الكأس التي كان يشرب بها، والزهرة التي كان يحبها، والقلم الذي كان يكتب به، والكتاب الذي كان يقرأ فيه، فإذا نال منها التعب جلست على بعض المقاعد لتأخذ لنفسها راحتها. فربما طار بها خيالها إلى ذلك العهد القديم، فتمثل لها أن أرمان جالس تحت قدميها يسرد عليها حادثةً من حوادث طفولته في نيس، أو يبثها ما يضمره لها في نفسه من الوجد والغرام، فتبتسم لحديثه ابتسام السعيد الهانيء، وتستشعر في نفسها لذةً لا يشعر بمثلها إلا المتقون في جنات النعيم، ثم تفتح عينيها فلا ترى أمامها غير الوحشة والسكون، والوحدة والانفراد، فتبكي ما شاء الله أن تفعل،

ثم تعود إلي بيتها في باريس، فتجلس على كرسيها بجانب منضدتها وتناجي أرمان في مذكراتها بجميع ما تحدثها به نفسه كأنه حاضر بين يديها يراها ويسمعها!

The Victim / A<u>d</u>-<u>D</u>ahiyyah – Diaries

Margaret's Diary

Memories of Margaret
Accounts from Margaret's Diary

15th December 1850

Dear Arman:

You did not write to me nor did you come to see me, as if, you fear that I intend to return to our past life. How can I return that time? If you saw me now, you would see an upset woman who is leaving this world, incapable of doing anything. All I want from you is, is to see you at my bedside in the final moments of my life, so that I can apologise to you regarding the crime I committed against you, bid you farewell and go to my grave.

O Arman, I did not deceive you neither was I disloyal to you. Certainly, the letter you saw in my hand, was not the letter of Mr John Phillip the way you had assumed, but it was the letter of your father which I had received an hour before you arrived to Bougival. This is what the letter said;

Dear Madame,

I intend to meet you tomorrow in your house at ten o'clock in the morning regarding an exclusive matter between me and you. I do not want Arman present nor do I want him to have any knowledge of it. Adding to that, he must not know that I have sent this letter to you. Indeed, I do have a very good opinion about you which gives me hope that whatever I have asked you, will remain secret between us until we meet. Goodbye.

Duval

الضحية - مذكرات

مذكرات مرغريت

١٥ ديسمبر سنة ١٨٥٠

أرمان:

لم تكتب إلي ولم تأتني، كأنما ظننت أني أريد أن أستعيد معك عهد الماضي، وأين أنا من ذلك العهد؟ فلو رأيتني لرأيت امرأةً مدبرةً ذاهبةً لا تصلح لشأنٍ من شؤون الحياة، ولم يبق فيها من صورتها الماضية إلا كما بقي من الزهرة الساقطة عن غصنها بعد ما عصفت الريح بأوراقها، وكل ما كنت أريدهَ منك: أن أراك بجانب فراشي في ساعتي الأخيرة لأعتذر لك عن ذنبي الذي أذنبته إليك، ثم أنظر إليك نظرة وداعٍ أغمض عليها جفني وأذهب بها إلى قبري!

ما أنا بخائنةٍ يا (أرمان) ولا خادعة، فإن الرسالة التي رأيتها في يدي يوم عدت إلي من مقابلة أبيك ليست رسالة المركيز كما ظننت، بل رسالة أبيك نفسه وصلت منه قبل وصولك إلى بوجيفال بساعةٍ واحدة. وهذا نصها الذي لا يزال عالقاً بذهني حتى الساعة:

سيدتي:

أريد أن أقابلك غداً في منزلك في الساعة العاشرة صباحاً في شأنٍ خاص بي وبك، وأريد ألا يكون أرمان حاضراً تلك المقابلة ولا عالماً بها، ولا بأني أرسلت هذه الرسالة إليك، ولي من حسن الرأي فيك ما يطمعني في أن يكون ما سألتك إياه سراً بيني وبينك حتى نلتقي.. والسلام.

دوفال

However, when I read the letter, I knew what he wanted from this meeting. I realised what was coming in this meeting. In fact, I had guessed the discussion that took place between you and him and that certainly you had rejected his proposal and he had fallen into despair. My heart urged me to decline this meeting and to disclose everything to you. Then I felt ashamed and embarrassed, that such an honourable man; the likes of your father was entrusting me with such a big secret that he does not deem me a fallen woman as he had presumed me to be. I hoped that in our meeting, I would obtain from him what he was hoping to obtain from me. So, I hid the matter of the letter from you. I hid all that which was in my heart from you. I was not lying regarding the illness and the pain which I was complaining about. The night which I spent in my bed after I had parted from you, was one of the most traumatic of my life.

I stayed in bed until morning broke, then I forced you to go and meet your father. I knew that when you go to him you will be unable to meet him. I also knew that if you were to meet him, the meeting will not give you any benefit. However, I feared that if your father came to visit and found you here with me he would see it as my breaching his trust!

Only a few moments after you left, your father arrived at Bougival as stated in his letter. He sought my permission to enter, as he entered I saw his eyes full of anger blazing like fire. However, I did not care and invited him to sit down. He did not. He did not greet me. The first thing with which he addressed me was, "What do you intend to do with my son O lady?" He was staring at me intently. I felt really disheartened and wanted to say to him,

"Sir, do you know that you are in my house, and I never invited you to come and see me, but it was you who invited yourself." Then I remembered his position as your father and did not respond.

He walked, hitting his stick and stamping his feet on the ground until he was near me and with a look of disgust uttered, "Verily my son has spent all the wealth which was in his hand upon you. There is no doubt that he had a lot of wealth in his hand. He spent all that wealth which I had sent him upon you as well, and indeed I have sent him wealth beyond my capacity. He does not have the power to give you more than that which he has given you. Neither is it in my power to bring down from the heavens gold which could be rained over you.

فلما قرأتها علمت ماذا يريد من تلك المقابلة، وشعرت بما وراءها، بل علمت بما دار بينك وبينه من الحديث، وأنك امتنعت عليه حتى يئس منك، فحاول أن يدخل عليك من بابي، فحدثتني نفسي، أن أرفض مقابلته، وأن أكاشفك بكل شيء، ثم استحييت من نفسي وأكبرت أن يعتمد علي رجل شريف كأبيك في كتمان سر بسيطٍ كهذا السر فلا يجدني عند ظنه، وطمعت في أن أنال منه عند المقابلة ما يطمع أن يناله مني، فكتمتك أمر الرسالة، وكتمتك ما في نفسي منها، ولم أكن كاذبةً في شكاتي وألمي حينما قلت لك في تلك الليلة: إنني لا أستطيع البقاء بجانبك، وسألتك أن تقوديني إلى مخدعي، فقد قضيت في فراشي بعدما فارقتك ليلةً لم أقض مثلها في جميع ما مر بي من ليالي الهموم والأحزان،

حتى أصبح الصباح فألححت عليك أن تذهب لمقابلة أبيك، وأنا أعلم أنك إن ذهبت إليه لا تراه، ولا تنتفع بمقابلته إن رأيته، ولكني خفت أن يزورني فيراك عندي فأصغر في عينيه، ولا أشد علي من ذلك،

وما هي إلا لحظات قليلة حتى وصل إلى بوجيفال في الموعد الذي ضربه في كتابه، فاستأذن علي فأذنت له فدخل فرأيت في عينيه جمرةً من الغضب تلتهب التهاباً فلم أحفل بها، ودعوته للجلوس فلم يفعل، ولم يحييني بيده، ولا بلسانه. وكان أول ما استقبلني به قوله: (ماذا تريدين أن تصنعي بولدي أيتها السيدة)؟ وظل ناظراً إلي نظراً جامداً ساكناً لا يطرف، ولا يختلج. فعجبت لمدخله الغريب، ونظراته المترفعة، ولهجته الجافة الخشنة، وامتعضت في نفسي امتعاضاً شديداً حتى كدت أقول له، ولا أكتمك ذلك:

تذكر يا سيدي أنك في منزلي، وأنني لم أدعك إلى زيارتي، بل أنت الذي دعوت نفسك بنفسك. ثم ذكرت مكانه منك فأمسكت عن كل شيءٍ حتى عن الجواب على سؤاله،

فمشى يضرب الأرض بعصاه وبقدمه حتى دنا مني وألقى علي تلك النظرة التي اعتاد الأشراف المترفعون أن يلقوها في طريقهم علي وجوه النساء العاهرات، وقال: لقد أنفق ولدي عليك جميع ما كان بيده من المال، وكان في يده الكثير منه، ثم جميع ما أرسلته إليه بعد ذلك، وقد أرسلت إليه فوق طاقتي، فلم يبق في استطاعته أن يمدك بأكثر مما أمدك، ولا في استطاعتي أن أستنزل له من السماء ذهباً يمطره عليك،

So, leave him and let him be alone. The towns are filled with boys whom their parents do not need, Indeed I need my son because he is my only son. I have not been given sustenance for other than him. Whereas, a lady who possesses the wealth of beauty like you, can never be disadvantaged in life. All her requirements and the necessities of life can be fulfilled."

Thus, his words penetrated in my heart the way fever penetrates to the bones. I felt that certainly this statue which is in front of me is not talking to me but is poisoning me severely with his words. I felt a sense of inferiority which I had never felt ever! However, despite this, I remained calm, remaining patient and controlling myself and in a very low, steady voice which contained neither any anger nor any indications of being upset, I replied,

"O sir, yes without a shadow of doubt I do love your son, but I am not greedy over his money, however, if I was greedy for his money, then certainly I would have parted from him three months ago, this was when all the money that he had finished. Nay, but I would have left him before this. This is because the elite and the wealthy people from amongst this town were bargaining a price in concerns of me even till today. These people were more in wealth than Arman and live life to the maximum. Adding to that, indeed your son has not spent on me that wealth which you are talking about other than only a little, most has been spent on himself. Despite that, I had the power to reject and refuse that small amount even if I wanted to but I did not want him to doubt me or feel any pain. That is why I used to accept his small and meagre gifts which he would give me from time to time. If, what you say is correct, that whatever was in his hand had transferred into my hands then unquestionably I would have become extremely rich. I have never struggled neither have I endured the problems and adversities which I am bearing and enduring today. Had you had queried about me, you would have come to realize that I am a poor woman in strained circumstances. I am not the owner of any worldly assets other than my jewellery, my carriage and the furniture of my house, if only these had remained mine, most of these things have become the property of the usurers and the loan sharks. I do not know what is coming towards my direction tomorrow. Adding to that, if you do want to know then let me inform you of the thing which I have hid from all people including your son."

فدعيه وشأنه، فالبلد مملوء بالأبناء الذين لا يحتاج آباؤهم إليهم والذين لا يحتاجون إلى أنفسهم، أما أنا فإني في حاجةٍ إلى ولدي، لأني لم أرزق ولداً سواه، ومن كانت بيده هذه الثروة من الجمال التي تملكينها لا يضيق به مذهب من مذاهب العيش، ولا يتلوى عليه مأرب من مآرب الحياة.

فسرت كلماته في نفسي سريان الحمى في عظام المحموم وخيل إلي أن هذا الماثل أمامي لا يحدثني، وإنما يجرعني السم بيده تجريعاً، وشعرت بذلةٍ لم أشعر بمثلها في يومٍ من أيام حياتي، إلا أنني تجلدت واستمسكت ورددت نفسي على مكروهها، وقلت له بصوتٍ هادىءٍ ساكنٍ لا يمازجه غضب، ولا نزق:

يا سيدي، نعم إنني أحب ولدك، ولكني لا أطمع فيه، ولو كان الذي يعنيني منه الطمع في ماله لفارقته منذ ثلاثة شهور أي منذ خلت يده من المال وأصبح لا يجد السبيل إليه بحالٍ من الأحوال، بل لفارقته قبل ذلك لأن الذين لا يزالون يساومونني في نفسي من أشراف هذا البلد ونبلائه منذ اتصلت به حتى اليوم أفضل منه وأكثر رغداً، على أن ولدك لم ينفق علي من هذا المال الذي تذكره إلا النزر القليل، وربما أنفق باقيه على نفسه؛ ولو استطعت أن أرفض ذلك القليل وآباه لفعلت، ولكني كنت أضن به أن يداخل نفسه ما يريبها أو يؤلمها فقبلت منه هداياه الصغيرة الصغيرة التي كان يقدمها إلي من حينٍ إلى حين إرعاءً عليه، وإبقاءً على عزة نفسه وكرامتها، ولو أن ما كان بيده من المال انتقل إلى يدي كما تقول لأصبحت غنيةً موفورة، لا أحمل هماً من هموم العيش، ولا أعاني من بأساء الحياة وضرائها ما أعانيه اليوم، فإنني ـ لو تبينت أمري ـ امرأة فقيرة معوزة لا أملك من متاع الدنيا إلا حلاي ومركبتي وأثاث بيتي، وليتها كانت خالصةً لي، فقد امتدت يد الضرورة إليها منذ عهدٍ قريبٍ فأصبح الكثير منها سلعةً في يد المرابين، ولا أعلم ما يأتي به الغد، وإن أبيت إلا أن تعرف ذلك بنفسك فسأطلعك على ما كتمته عن الناس جميعاً حتى عن ولدك،

Then I went to my drawer where I kept my official documentation. Thus, from there I brought the receipts and the documents which were inclusive upon the sale of my jewellery, my horses and the furniture of my house. In addition to that, I had even brought the deeds of those things which through pawning I had taken out on mortgage.

Duval continued turning over the pages for a while, and contemplated upon the dates for a long time. Then he folded up the documents and returned them to me. He put his head down and remained silent, not saying a word. He took the chair in front of him and dragging it sat down resting his head upon his stick. By this point, his anger had cooled down. The black cloud which was shadowing his face before had disappeared. I continued with my conversation;

"Other than that, O sir, verily I am not complaining nor am I seeking revenge from you. Indeed, I have lived days entailing extreme hardships and difficulties which have killed all my desires for life in my heart. These calamities have caused me to forget the colours of life along with its pride. Thus, I have become a woman who does not care of what the future will bring. Being wealthy or being poor, both are equal to me. Whether I wear jewellery and be scented with fragrance, whether I live in a castle or whether I live in a cottage I do not care. I am not bothered anymore if I ride on a carriage or walk upon my feet. However, all that I request from my life, from Allah ﷻ and from you is that, I would like to have Arman, so that he can share with me the pains and sorrows of life. Having him will then help me to overcome the troubles and problems of life until Allah ﷻ decrees for me a verdict the way He chooses. If, however, life is extended for me, then I would spend it thanking you and praising you, showing sincerity to you in secrecy and in the open. Alternatively, if I was to die, then the last words which I shall utter, would be the supplication to Allah ﷻ, begging and crying to Him to bless you and your family abundantly and that He bestows over you a beautiful veil in your present and in your future."

I inclined in front of him and held the cloth from the corner of his clothes. Thus, at this point I lost control of withholding my tears and said,

ثم قمت إلى خزانة أوراقي فجئته منها بالصكوك والوثائق المشتملة على بيع ما بعت من جواهري وخيولي وأثاث بيتي ورهن ما رهنت منها،

فظل يقلبها بين يديه ساعة ويتأمل في تاريخها طويلاً، ثم طواها وأعادها إلي مطرقاً صامتاً لا يقول شيئاً، ومد يده إلى كرسي بين يديه فاجتذبه إليه وجلس عليه معتمداً برأسه على عصاه، وقد هدأت في نفسه تلك الثورة التي كانت تضطرم وتعتلج منذ دخوله، وطارت عن وجهه تلك الغيرة السوداء التي كانت تظلله من قبل، فعدت إلى حديثي معه أقول:

على أنني يا سيدي غير شاكيةٍ ولا ناقمة، فقد مر بي من نوب الأيام وأرزائها ما محا من نفسي كل شهوةٍ من شهوات الحياة، وأنساني جميع مظاهر الدنيا ومفاخرها، فأصبحت لا أبالي بما تأتي به الأيام، وسواء لدي الفقر والغنى، والحلى والعطر، وسكنى القصر وسكنى الكوخ، وركوب المركبة، وركوب النعل، وكل ما أرجوه من حياتي وأضرع إلى الله، وإليك فيه، أن أرى أرمان يقاسمني هم الحياة وبؤسها، ويعينني على شدتها ولأوائها حتى يقضي الله في أمري بما هو قاضٍ، فإن كان في الأجل فسحة قضيتها في شكرك وحمدك، والإخلاص لك في سري وعلني، وإن كانت الأخرى كان آخر ما أنطق به في ساعتي الأخيرة أن أدعو لك الله تعالى ضارعةً مبتهلةً أن يبارك لك في نفسك، وفي أهلك، وأن يسبل ستره الضافي عليك في حاضرك ومستقبلك.

ثم جثوت بين يديه وتعلقت بأهداب ثوبه، وقد عجزت في تلك الساعة عن أن أملك من دموعي ما كنت مالكةً من قبل، فظللت أبكي وأقول:

"O master, have mercy on me. Verily I am a troubled, poor woman. Certainly, the necessities of life had forced me in the beginning of my life to stand upon the edge of a ditch, that ditch whose corner a prostitute stands. Thus, I fell into that ditch unwillingly and hatefully. The life which destiny had ordained for me to live in, I had accepted. Nevertheless, I struggled to live like this. I became a woman standing in two ways. Nor was I chaste so that I could be blessed with living a life like honourable women. Neither did my heart die which prevented me to live like a characterless and fallen women. In your son, I found an individual who loved me sincerely solely for myself. He cherished me with his love and with his sincerity which no one from the mankind had ever done before. Thus, I fell in love with him causing me to forget my falling down and my prostitution related affairs. Accordingly, I started loving life, which I had hated and felt disgusted over before. Now I have begun living my life with sincerity. O master do not deprive me of this gem. O master do not cause a separation between me and him. If, however you were still to do this, then you will make me a very unfortunate and an extremely distressed woman. You will fill my life with grief and sorrows. Whereas I see and consider you beyond and above one who builds their foundations of happiness and comfort upon the misfortunes of a poor woman the likes of myself.

What is going to be my outcome tomorrow if I were to become alone, boycotted from this world, and not find for myself a friend nor a helper? Am I going to return to my former life, the life which I hated and the life which I am frightened of? In that case, I would be returning to my sins and my crimes. Alternatively, I could commit suicide to escape the tortures and the ordeals of life. I do not have the power to carry out either of these actions. Therefore, please advance forth your beautiful hand and save me from this deep ditch which no one has the power to save me other than yourself.

I know that certainly you need your son, and without question you have more right over him from the entire creation from the earth. However, I do know that indeed you are extremely kind and merciful. Verily in these blessed moments, you are not going to refuse being charitable to an ill, troubled lady, like myself who's illness has worn her out. O honourable gentleman, I do not ask you for money, neither a connection nor any utilities of life, but I ask you to allow Arman to remain with me. This is because his staying with me would be the salvation for my life and for my fortune. Please be charitable to me, verily you are amongst the good doers."

رحماك يا مولاي، إنني امرأة بائسة مسكينة قد قضت علي بعض ضرورات العيش في فاتحة حياتي أن أقف على حافة تلك الهوة التي يقف على رأسها النساء الجائعات، فسقطت فيها كارهةً مرغمة، ثم أردت نفسي على الرضا بتلك الحياة التي قدرها الله لي فلم أستطع، فأصبحت في منزلةٍ بين المنزلتين، لا أنا شريفة أنعم بعيش النساء الشريفات، ولا ميتة القلب أسعد سعادة الفتيات الساقطات، وقد وجدت في ولدك الرجل الوحيد الذي أحبني لنفسي، ومنحني من وده وإخلاصه ما ضن به علي الناس جميعاً، فأنست به أنساني سقوطي وعاري، وحبب إلي الحياة بعد ما أبغضتها وبرمت بها، وكدت أقضي على نفسي بالخلاص منها، فلا تحرمني جواره، ولا تفرق بيني وبينه؛ فإنك إن فعلت أشقيتني وبرحت بي، وملأت حياتي همداً وكمداً، وأنت أجل من أن ترضى لنفسك بأن تبني سعادتك وهناءك على شقاء امرأةٍ مسكينةٍ مثلي.

ماذا يكون مصيري غداً إذا أصبحت وحيدةً منقطعةً في هذا العالم لا صديق لي، ولا معين؟ أأعود إلى حياتي التي أبغضها وأخشاها فأعود إلى جرائمي وآثامي؟ أم أقتل نفسي بيدي فراراً من شقاء الدنيا وبلائها، فأختم حياتي بأقبح ما ختم امرؤ به حياته؟ لا أستطيع واحدةً من هاتين، فأمدد إلي يدك البيضاء وأنقذني من هذه الهوة العميقة التي لا يستطيع أحد أن ينقذني منها سواك.

أنا أعلم أنك في حاجةٍ إلى ولدك، وأنك أولى به من كل مخلوقٍ على وجه الأرض، ولكني أعلم أنك شفوق رحيم، لا تأبى أن تتصدق على امرأةٍ مريضةٍ بائسةٍ مثلي بساعاتٍ من السعادة تتعلل بها في مرضها الذي تكابده حتى يوافيها أجلها، لا أسألك يا سيدي مالاً، ولا نسباً، ولا عرضاً من أعراض الحياة؛ بل أسألك أن تأذن لأرمان بالبقاء معي فإن بقائه بقاء حياتي وسعادتي. فتصدق بهما علي إنك من المحسنين.

After I had said all this, I felt and sensed that he was moving on his chair. He raised his head and looked at me with a glance which was less in anger and rage than his first sight and said, "And how are you both going to live?"

I replied, "I have remaining with me my gems and my jewellery which soon I shall sell and then with its money, I will live in some corner from the corners of Paris with Arman as poor straitened people. No one will see us nor sense our existence. It will be sufficient for us - our blessing of love which will replace all other blessings and happiness of the world."

Duval said, "In fact this is the misfortune itself. This is because love is like vegetation; a plant which requires shade, otherwise the hot sun of misfortune would exterminate it. In respect to all the blessings contained within this world which have not been obtained through money nor without any asset are inevitably false. These are nothing but the illusions of the mind which have no place.

Today, both of you are happy and prosperous because in your hands you have money from which you can live with. Also, it is because of this money, you both are living in this beautiful house which is located on top of this high mountain besides this astonishing lake. The instance your hands will be deprived from this money and from this blessing, both of you will become troubled and then your states will automatically deprive you from love and its pleasures. At that point, both of you will become burdened and tired. Most likely that feeling which both of you will feel of being burdened at that time will inevitably take you towards the opposite spectrum of love.

Without doubt, love entails an art of madness, and the craziest ideology is that love makes two lovers believe that their love will remain forever and that the days of catastrophes will not change their love. They believe that the interchanging and alternating days will not affect their love at all. However, when both lovers come back to their senses, they realize that certainly love is a colour from the colours of the heart. It is desire and longing which brings love and it is something else which takes it away. Certainly, hunger and straitened circumstances exterminate love. This is especially when hunger increases and its knots become tighter. Without a doubt, a person requires to live and to maintain his life before he could desire love, its pleasures and satisfy its yeaning.

وهنا شعرت كأنه يتحرك في كرسيه، فخفق قلبي خفقاناً شديداً، ثم رفع رأسه ونظر إلي نظرةً أهدأ ناراً وأقصر شعاعاً من نظرته الأولى وقال: ومن أين تعيشان؟

قلت: عندي بقية من جواهري وحلاي سأبيعها وأعيش بثمنها معه في زاوية من زوايا باريس عيش الفقراء المقلين، لا يرانا أحد، ولا يشعر بوجودنا شاعر، وحسبنا الحب سعادةً نغنى بها عن كل سعادةٍ في هذا العالم وهناءه.

قال: ذلك هو الشقاء بعينه، فإن الحب نباتٌ ظليٌ تقتله شمس الشقاء الحارة، وكل سعادة في العالم غير مستمدةٍ من سعادة المال أو لاجئةٍ إلى ظلاله فهي كاذبة لا وجود لها إلا في سوانح الخيال.

أنتما اليوم سعيدان لأن في يدكما مالاً تعيشان به، ولأنكما تسكنان هذا المنزل البديع، فوق هذه الهضبة العالية، بجانب هذه البحيرة الجميلة، فإذا خلت يدكما من المال، وحرمتما هذا النعيم الذي تنعمان به شقيتما وشغلكما شأن نفسيكما عن شأن الحب ولذائذه، وسرى إلى نفسيكما الضجر والملل، وربما امتدت تلك السآمة بينكما إلى أبعد غايتها.

إن للحب فنوناً من الجنون، وأقبح فنونه أن يعتقد المتحابان أن حبهما دائم لا تغيره حوادث الأيام، ولا تنال منه الصروف والغير، ولو عقلا لعلما أن الحب لون من ألوان النفس، وعرض من أعراضها الطائرة، تأتي به شهوة وتذهب به أخرى، ولا يذهب به المثل مثل الفاقة إذا اشتدت واستحكمت حلقاتها فإن النفس تطالب حياتها وبقاءها، قبل أن تطلب لذائذها وشهواتها!

Indeed, I know my son's circumstances which you do not know O lady. I know without question, he does not have the power to live this poor life the way you are expecting him to do. Now he has become a poor young man who is not the owner of anything in this world except for a small piece of land which he has inherited from his mother. This small piece of land however will not enrich him neither it would enrich you. I am not a person with a lot of money from which I have the power to protect and provide for him living this long life in Paris anymore the way he has been living here. Therefore, there remains for him no other option except to live of your money. This however, is a thing which I am not pleased with neither would Arman be pleased with. O my lady, excuse me for saying this to you, certainly all the problems and the worries of life, I and Arman can bear, other than to listen to the people saying, 'Indeed Arman Duval's girlfriend has sold all her diamonds and her jewellery which were gifted to her from her previous lovers so that she can spend that money on Arman.'

O my daughter, please forgive me for my conduct and pardon my harshness and my anger. This is because it is extremely difficult for an old father, the likes of me, to see his only son whom he had expected to fulfil all the hopes of his household; to fall in this deep ditch which has no end to it. Hence, his father's heart would therefore only inflame with fear and sorrow.

Certainly, ever since Arman got to know you, he has forgotten me and has forgotten his sister. Neither has he remembered me nor has he remembered her. Verily his sister has been critically ill for the past few months. I had written to Arman telling him to come so that he could help and assist me, but he never came nor did he reply to my letter. I was in a state that if I had died, I would have not seen him. At that point I would have been taking remorse and sorrow to my grave which no one had ever taken with them before.

O respectable lady, you are true in what you said that, Arman did not spend all that wealth which he had in his hand on you. This is because only yesterday I found out that he has been gambling for quite some time and he has lost a lot of money through gambling. I am aware that you do not know anything about this. Thus, my heart will not be at peace if I were to leave him in this town. This is because then he will indulge himself in this new problematic way of life completely where he has already stepped in to. In this path at some point, he will be afflicted with some big loss. It may at that point become crucial for me to hold his hand in that situation and give him all my life earnings which I have reserved for my old age and for the wedding arrangements for my daughter. Thus, all three of us, me, Arman and my daughter will then die on one day.

أنا أعلم من شأن ولدي يا سيدتي ما لا تعلمين، وأعلم أنه لا يستطيع أن يعيش هذه العيشة النكداء التي تظنين، وهو فتًى فقير لا يملك من الدنيا إلا قطعةً صغيرةً من الأرض ورثها عن أمه لا تغني عنه ولا عنك شيئاً، وما أنا بذي ثروةٍ طائلةٍ أستطيع أن أحفظ له بها زمناً طويلاً هذا العيش السعيد الرغد الذي يعيشه اليوم في باريس، فلم يبق بين يديه إلا أن يعيش بمالك، وهو ما لا أرضاه له ولا يرضاه لنفسه، واسمحي لي يا سيدتي أن أقول لك: إن جميع مصائب الدنيا وأرزائها أهون علي وعليه أن يقول الناس إن خليلة أرمان دوفال قد باعت جواهرها وحلاها التي أهداها إليها عشاقها الماضون لتنفق ثمنها عليه.

سامحيني يا بنيتي، واغتفري لي حدتي وخشونتي، فإن شديداً جداً على والدٍ شيخٍ مثلي أن يرى ولده الذي وضع فيه كل آمال بيته يهوي أمام عينيه في هذه الهوة السحيقة التي لا قرار لها دون أن يطير قلبه خوفاً وهلعاً.

إنه مذ عرفك نسيني ونسي أخته، فلا يذكرني ولا يذكرها، وقد مرضت منذ شهور مرضاً مشرفاً فكتبت إليه أن يأتي ليعودني فلم يفعل، ولم يرد على كتابي، أي أنني كنت على وشك أن أموت ولا أراه، ولو تم ذلك لذهبت إلى قبري بحسرةٍ لم يحمل مثلها في صدره راحل عن الدنيا من قبلي.

أنت صادقة يا سيدتي في قولك إنه لم ينفق عليك جميع ما كان بيده من المال لأنني علمت بالأمس أنه قامر منذ عهدٍ قريبٍ، وخسر في مقامرته كثيراً، كما علمت أنك لا تعلمين شيئاً من ذلك فما يؤمنني، إن أنا تركته في هذا البلد، ألا يستمر في هذه الغواية الجديدة التي خطا الخطوات الأولى في طريقها ولا يخسر في بعض مواقفه خسارةً عظمى لا أجد لي بداً من أن آخذ بيده فيها، فأقدم إليه ذخر شيخوختي، ومهر ابنتي فنهلك نحن الثلاثة في يومٍ واحدٍ؟

O my daughter, what would be your outcome if after staying with you for a long time, Arman becomes disheartened from you and his sight hovers upon another woman other than you? At that point your pain and grief of tomorrow would be more severe and greater than of today. What would be your state when you will become completely tight upon your money one day belonging to your frightful and lonely days of life? Then by all means, you would prefer returning to your former life which encompasses a delight, a gathering, some noise and the spotlight. You must not forget that Arman is a young ardent and a pessimistic man. If you were to go back to your first life, then Arman would reject you because of this. It may be that he might retaliate with his rivalry because of you. Through this, troubles will descend upon him. Hence, from his opposition he might get hurt and may forfeit his life in the process and at that point you will be responsible for giving me pain.

O my dear, what would be your answer tomorrow if Arman gets struck by an arrow from the decree of destiny in front of this poor crying father and that when his father comes to you and demands from you the blood retribution for his son? Adding to that what would be the state of your pain and grief in front of a crying and a troublesome father?"

Then after this, your father started shaking and his eyes started rolling in distress, as if he was watching the account which he had just narrated right before his eyes. Then he went quiet for a while and then he looked at me with a look which contained softness and was full of love and kindness. Then he started speaking,

"O Margaret, you have ranked higher in my eyes than I had expected. You are an honourable soul from amongst women. Verily, I have found in you such qualities and such attributes that I have not found but only in a few men before. Also, I have rarely seen this honour in women. If, however, honour was to be divided between mankind per their dignity and their attributes, then certainly your portion from it would be greater and most substantial.

O Margaret until I am alive, I will never forget your favour that you did upon me in terms of hiding the affair of that letter which I had sent to you, and that you safeguarded its secret at a time when most people would have revealed it. I will not forget your patience and you lowering your gaze in front of me despite having the power to say and do as you pleased to me in your house. You remained quiet in front of me during my harshness, my anger and my insane behaviour. Also, I will never forget what you spent on my son from your heart and from your wealth, despite him not knowing where you were spending it from. You did this only because of loyalty and to maintain his self-respect and honour.

من أين لك يا بنيتي أنه إن طال عهده بك لا يملك، ولا تمتد عينه إلى امرأةٍ سواك، فتكون فجيعتك فيه غداً شراً من فجيعتك فيه اليوم؟ ومن أين له أنك لا تضيقين ذرعاً يوماً من الأيام بعيشة الوحشة والوحدة فتحنين إلى حياتك الأولى حياة الأنس والاجتماع، والضوضاء واللجب، وهو فتًى غيور مستطار! فربما أنفت نفسه أن يزاحمه فيك مزاحم، وربما امتدت يده بشرٍ إلى ذلك الذي يزاحمه، فتنازلا، فأصابته من يد منازله ضربة تقضي على حياته وتفجعني فيه؟

كيف يكون موقفك يا سيدتي غداً إن نفذ فيه هذا السهم من القضاء أمام هذا الأب الثاكل المسكين إذا جاءك يسألك عن دم ولده؟ وكيف تكون آلام نفسك ولواعجها أمام مشهد بكائه وتفجعه؟

ثم ارتعش ارتعاشاً شديداً، وظل نظره حائراً مضطرباً، كأنما يخيل إليه أنه يرى أمام عينيه ذلك المنظر الذي يتحدث عنه، ثم سكن قليلاً ونظر إلي نظرةً هادئةً مملوءةً عطفاً وحناناً وأنشأ يقول:

مرغريت؟ أنت أعظم في عيني مما كنت أظن، وأكرم نفساً من أولئك النساء اللواتي يزعمن أنك واحدة منهن، وقد وجدت فيك من فضائل النفس ومزاياها ما لم أجده إلا قليلاً في أفذاذ الرجال، وأقل من القليل في فضليات النساء، ولو قسم الشرف بين الناس على مقدار فضائلهم وصفاتهم لكان نصيبك منه أوفر الأنصبة وأوفاها.

لا أنسى لك يا مرغريت ما دمت حياً كتمانك أمر الكتاب الذي أرسلته إليك واحتفاظك بسره في ساعةٍ تنفرج فيها الصدور عن مكنوناتها، ولا سكوتك وإغضاءك وأنت في منزلك، وموضع أمرك ونهيك، أمام حدتي وخشونتي وجنون غضبي، ولا بذلك ما بذلت من ذات نفسك وذات يدك لولدي ـ من حيث لا يعلم ـ وفاءً له وإبقاءً على عزة نفسه وكرامتها.

Without question, the sacrifice which you made for my son yesterday was very big. However, today I have come to beg you for another sacrifice, which is a greater sacrifice then yesterdays. This sacrifice is for my daughter. There is no ground upon which I can intercede to you to fulfil my request other than expecting you to listen to me through your kind and noble heart.

Indeed, I have left Susan, Arman's sister behind who is struggling in her bed with her illness. She was enduring more pain than she could bear and is extremely weak in body. This is because her fiancé who she loved to bits left her two months ago, he has not come to visit her nor has she seen him. Indeed, I was unaware of the reason to her illness before this day, as I was only speculating and assuming its causes until I stayed awake sitting at her bedside one night. When I did this, I discovered that her feverish symptoms had reached their peak and that she had reached such a point that now she was talking gibberish and nonsense. I heard her saying aloud the name of her fiancé many times. She cried every time she uttered his name. That is when I realized what the cause of her illness was. Upon the second day, I went to the father of her fiancé to ask him what thing had created doubt for his son regarding my daughter and the reason for him not meeting his daughter anymore. His father mentioned a reason to me which had some of your affairs included within it O respectable lady. Do you permit me to narrate to you his reason?"

My heart trembled severely and I felt that bad was drawing near to me slowly but surely. However, I kept calm and said to him, "Yes I grant you permission O sir."

He said, "Verily her fiancé's father answered my question by saying, 'Indeed my family is a very honourable and a well dignified family who do not tie the bond of matrimony with another family except if it is likewise a noble and a well-respected family from all angles. Certainly, it has come to my attention the despicable low lifestyle of your son and how he lives in Paris. Without question, your son has been living with a very well-known and a very notorious prostitute for a very long time. People are testifying to this cursed lifestyle that he is living with a woman who has been used and abused. My heart will never allow such a person like your son who has a bad character, living an immoral and roguish lifestyle, to become the brother in-law for my son. Adding to that, I do not want to bring shame upon my daughter in respect of this.' Then her fiancé's father stopped. I endured his hard, sharp words with patience and tolerance. This is because I was fearful for my daughter.

لقد كانت ضحيتك التي قدمتها لولدي بالأمس عظيمة جداً، واليوم جئتك أطلب إليك أن تقدمي ضحيةً أعظم منها لابنتي ولا معتمد لي أعتمد عليه في تلبية رجائي عندك إلا شرف نفسك وفضيلتها.

لقد تركت (سوسان) ورائي تتقلب على فراش المرض، وتكابد منه فوق ما يحتمل جسمها النائس الغض لأن خطيبها الذي تحبه حباً جماً قد هجرها منذ شهرين فلا يزورها ولا تراه، وقد كنت أجهل قبل اليوم سبب مرضها إلا الظن والتقدير حتى سهرت بجانب فراشها ليلةً كانت الحمى فيها قد نالت منها منالاً عظيماً، ووصلت بها إلى درجة الخبل والهذيان، فسمعتها تهتف باسم خطيبها مراتٍ كثيرة، وتبكي كلما جرى ذكره على لسانها كأنها حاضرة مستفيقة، فعلمت موضع دائها، وذهبت في اليوم الثاني إلى والد ذلك الخطيب أسأله عما راب ولده من أمر ابنتي، وقطعه عن زيارتها، فذكر لي سبباً غريباً لك فيه يا سيدتي بعض الشأن، فإن أذنت لي حدثتك حديثه.

فخفق قلبي خفقاناً شديداً، وأحسست بالشر يدنو مني رويداً رويداً، إلا أنني تماسكت وقلت له: نعم آذن لك يا سيدي؛

قال: لقد أجابني الرجل على سؤالي بقوله: (إن أسرتي أسرة شريفة لا تصاهر إلا أسرةً شريفةً مثلها من جميع وجوهها، وقد عرفت أسلوب المعيشة السافلة التي يعيشها ولدك في باريس، إنه يعاشر منذ عهدٍ طويلٍ امرأةً مومساً معروفةً هناك معاشرة تهتك وتبذل يشهدها الناس جميعاً، ولا أسمح لنفسي أن يكون مثل ولدك في تبذله واستهتاره، وصغر نفسه وفسولتها: صهراً لولدي ولا عاراً على ابنتي). فاستقبلت خشونته وجفاءه بصبرٍ واحتمال، لأن الخوف على ابنتي شغلني عن الغضب لنفسي،

I then said to him, 'Are you true in what you are saying?' He presented to me such evidence that I realized what he was saying was true. I did not see any other alternative but to accept whatever he was saying. I then requested him not to make any prompt decisions regarding the marriage until I go to Paris and return from there. This is what I am burdened with and that is why I have come to Paris. This is my story which I have come to narrate to you. I await your decision regarding this matter. Indeed, I have hidden the matter of our meeting from all mankind including my son Arman. Therefore, please contemplate over this matter and tell me what your decision is?"

Then he lowered his head for quite some time. When he raised his head, he had tears filling his eyes. When he commenced his discussion, he did not have the ability to talk. Thus, I felt sorry for the state he was in and I considered his calamity big, which led me to forget my calamity irrespective of his. Silence stretched between as I did not know what to say to him. There came a point where his distressed state calmed. He took my hand and held it between his arms. Returning to his conversation he began saying,

"O Margaret, certainly the life of my daughter is in front of you. Please Margaret save me from this trial. Margaret, bestow upon me a favour which I will never forget till death. Indeed, I do not have the power to see her dying in front of me. If, however she was to die then certainly I would also die with her grief, pain and sadness. In one day, both of us would be put into one grave. Indeed, I am still grieving the death of her mother for five years, the symptoms of which are still upon my heart even today. Now I do not have the power to witness this incident regarding my daughter. Indeed, I love my daughter dearly, I do not have the power to see her enduring distress and calamity at any time, so how am I going to see her enduring the pains of death?

O Margaret, indeed you do not know my daughter. Hand on heart, I am certain that if you were to see her, you also would love her the way I love her and you would also be merciful to her the way I show her mercy and you too would sacrifice for her whatever is in your power showing kindness and mercy to her.

Verily she is extremely beautiful and her fairness is like that of a star. She is pure like the purity of an Angel and her innocence is like the innocence of a child. Thus, for her soft and tender life please show kindness to her so that happiness remains for her. This is because she is not deserving of a misfortune. Indeed, today she is living upon a hope which I have entrusted in her heart the day I embarked my journey. If now I return to her with failure, I would be returning to her like a despaired murderer descending upon her death.

وقلت له: أواثق أنت مما تقول؟ فأدلى لي بما أقنعني، فلم أر بداً من أن أسلم له بصواب ما فعل، وسألته أن لا يبت في أمر الخطبة شيئاً حتى أسافر إلى باريس وأعود منها. ذلك ما حملني على المجيء إلى باريس. وهذه هي قصتي التي جئت أعرضها عليك، وأنتظر حكمك فيها، وقد كتمتها عن الناس جميعاً حتى عن ولدي أرمان، فانظري ماذا تأمرين؟

وهنا أطرق برأسه طويلاً، ثم رفعها، فإذا عبرة تترقرق في عينيه، وإذا هو يحاول الكلام فلا يستطيعه، فرحمته مما به، وأعظمت مصابه حتى نسيت مصابي بجانبه، وساد السكون بيننا ساعةً لا يقول لي شيئاً، ولا أدري ماذا أقول له: حتى هدأ ثائره قليلاً، فمد يده إلى يدي فأخذها بين ذراعيه، وعاد إلى حديثه يقول:

مرغريت: إن حياة ابنتي بين يديك، فامنحيني إياها تتخذي عندي يداً لا أنساها لك حتى الموت. إنني لا أستطيع أن أراها تموت بين يدي. ولو تم ذلك لمت على أثرها حزناً وكمداً، وضمنا في يومٍ واحدٍ قبر واحد؛ لقد رأيت مصرع أمها منذ خمس سنين، ولا يزال أثره باقياً في نفسي حتى اليوم، ولا أستطيع أن أرى هذا المشهد مرةً أخرى في ابنتها وصورتها الباقية عندي من بعدها. إنني أحبها حباً جماً، ولا أستطيع أن أراها في ساعةٍ من ساعاتها حزينةً أو مكتئبةً، فكيف أن أراها تعالج سكرات الموت!

إنك لا تعرفينها يا مرغريت، وأعتقد أنك لو رأيتها لأحببتها كما أحبها ولرحمتها كما أرحمها، ولفديتها بما تستطيعين رأفةً بها وإشفاقاً عليها.

إنها جميلة جداً، وبيضاء مثل الكوكب، وطاهرة طهارة الملك، وغريرة غرارة الطفل، فاسمحي لهذه الحياة الغضة الزاهرة بالبقاء والسعادة فإنها لا تستحق الشقاء. إنها اليوم تعيش بالأمل الذي أودعته قلبها يوم سفري، فإن عدت إليها بالخيبة عدت إليها باليأس القاتل، والقضاء النازل.

O Margaret, certainly you do love Arman and certainly I truly believe that you are completely devoted in his love sincerely. Therefore, preform an act which only devoted lovers can perform. Sacrifice your love for him and for his future. If, however you cannot do this for him, then do it for me.

Verily it is you who has said to me that certainly Arman is the only individual who has loved you sincerely for yourself, more than he has loved you for himself. Give him expiation for this love. In fact, give him a better requital then he has given to you in this love and let your comfort and satisfaction become a virtue which you will obtain after parting from him through pain and adversities, knowing that certainly he has become prosperous after you, knowing that indeed you have saved a young poor girl from the hands of death and knowing that you have saved an extremely old man from grief."

It was at this point when his voice shook as he sobbed and fell on his chair in front of me and said in a dying person's voice,

"O Margaret, show me mercy! O Margaret, show kindness upon my weakness and upon my old age. O Margaret, please bestow upon me the future of my son and the life of my daughter."

Then after this, he did not have the power to speak another word. He put his head down upon the chair where he was sitting and burst out crying.

O Arman, only if you had seen me in this situation, and only if you had seen the pain and the agony which I was enduring, and only if you had seen my tears which were flowing upon my cheeks feeling sorry for your father. Verily he was talking but my tears were flowing with cach word.

Verily the most supreme and prestigious person is whom who is great in everything including being big in his sorrows and in his hardships. Indeed, I thought to myself when your father was crying and beseeching in front of me, that verily every tear from his tears will descend the wrath of Allah ﷻ upon the earth, and that every sigh from amongst his sighs will burn the horizon and the atmosphere of the sky.

Verily I felt extremely guilty over this matter in my heart that such an old, pure, respectable man was kneeling in front of a fallen woman like myself. I felt such shame that I wished that the earth would tear open under my feet and I could bury myself in there eternally.

إنك تحبين أرمان يا مرغريت، وقد أصبحت أعتقد أنك مخلصة في حبه إخلاصاً عظيماً، فاصنعي ما يصنع المحبون المخلصون، وضحي حبك من أجله، ومن أجل مستقبله، فإلا تفعلي ذلك من أجله، فافعليه من أجلي.

لقد قلت لي أنه الرجل الوحيد الذي أحبك لنفسك أكثر مما أحبك لنفسه. فباديله هذا الحب، بل كوني خيراً منه فيه، وليكن عزاؤك تلاقيه عملاً بعد فراقه من حزنٍ وألم أنه قد أصبح سعيداً من بعدك، وأنك قد أنقذت من يد الموت فتاةً مسكينةً، ومن يد الشقاء شيخاً حزيناً.

وهنا اختنق صوته بالبكاء فهبط على كرسيه بين يدي، وقال بنغمة المشرف المحتضر:

ارحميني يا مرغريت، واشفقي على ضعفي وشيخوختي، وتصدقي علي بمستقبل ولدي، وحياة ابنتي.

ثم لم يستطع أن يقول بعد ذلك شيئاً، فألقى رأسه على كرسيه الذي كان جالساً عليه وانفجر باكياً.

آهٍ لو رأيتني يا أرمان في موقفي هذا ورأيت لوعتي وتفجعي ودموعي المنهمرة في خدي انهمار الديمة الوطفاء رحمةً بأبيك وإشفاقاً عليه! لقد كان يتكلم فتسيل مدامعي مع حروفه وكلماته، كأنما هو ينشد مرثيةً محزنة، أنا المبكية عليها فيها!

إن العظيم عظيم في كل شيءٍ حتى في أحزانه وآلامه، فلقد كان يخيل إلي وأبوك يبكي بين يدي وينتحب أن كل دمعةٍ من دموعه تستنزل غضب الله على الأرض، وكل زفرةٍ من زفراته تلتهب بها آفاق السماء.

لقد أكبرت في نفسي جداً أن يجثو مثل هذا الشيخ الشريف الطاهر بين يدي فتاةٍ ساقطةٍ مثلي، واستحييت من ذلك حياءً تمنيت معه أن لو انشقت الأرض تحت قدمي فسخت فيها أبد الدهر.

I started pondering over his problem, about his story which he had narrated to me and regarding the predicament he was in. Thus, I concluded that verily I am the one responsible for giving misfortunes to this respectable and honourable family, to this father, to his son and to his daughter. I found this thought very heavy upon my chest and upon my conscience. This situation became loathsome for me. I thought to myself that if my spirit had appeared in front of me verily I would throw it down from such a height that no place after this would combine my body and soul together. I thought to myself that verily my past life which I spent in crimes and in sins has indeed cut off from me the path of modesty and chastity. Now I do not even have the right to desire the life of chastity nor do I have the right to even quarrel with life for its fortunes and its happiness. Certainly, the crime which I have committed myself in the past verily I had committed on my own accord myself. Thus, it is only right now that only I bear its burden lest that I put it on anyone else's shoulder besides me. If it is destined for me to die a death of an inferior woman, then that is inevitable because I am a fallen woman. If it is decreed for my future to entail misfortunes and hardships, then that is also inevitable. This is certainly because the future is the outcome and the result of the past and encountering this outcome is inevitable.

O Arman, at this point I remembered you a lot. I thought to myself how am I going to separate from you and how am I going to have the power to live without you. I gathered that it will be me who is going to end my life with my own hands. This was because there was no other way of pleasing your father nor was there a way to give him his ultimate satisfaction other than to break ties with you, showing resentment towards you and appearing in front of you as a cheating and disloyal woman. I was forced to connect with someone else other than you to make sure that you see me and that you hear me. I did this only for you to leave me the way a despaired person would, in such a state that you are unaware that your father had any share in this whatsoever. Thus, in one split second, I made a firm decision to part from you and portray resentment towards you. I knew that when I left you, it would be inevitable for me to return to my former life, the life which I hated and disliked. This was because till this day, Duke Mohan had not forgiven or forgotten my betrayal towards him. So how can I go back to him? My former life was inevitable because I needed sustenance in life from which I could treat my illness and pay for my debts. For one hour, these thoughts circulated my head. Then, these thoughts prolonged until it was near that I go against my decision as then I casted my sight upon your father's face drenched in tears. At once, I became strong and collected myself, I went towards him leaving everything behind me.

وبينما هو مطرق صامت أخذت أفكر فيه، وفي مصابه، وفي قصته التي قصها علي، وفي الشأن الذي لي فيه؛ فعلمت أني قد أصبحت شؤماً على هذه الأسرة السعيدة جميعها، أبيها وابنها وابنتها، فثقلت نفسي علي، وسمج منظرها في عيني حتى خيل إلي أنها لو كانت حاضرةً بين يدي لرميت بها من حالقٍ إلى حيث لا يجمعني وإياها مكان بعد اليوم. ثم قلت في نفسي: إن حياتي الماضية التي قضيتها في الشرور والآثام قد قطعت علي طريق الشرف، فلا حق لي في أن أطمع في حياة الشرفاء، ولا أن أنازعهم سعادتهم وهناءهم، وإن الإثم الذي اقترفته في ماضي وحدي فلا بد لي أن أستقل بعبثه دون أن ألقيه على عاتق أحدٍ غيري، فإن كان مقدراً علي أن أموت موت النساء الساقطات، فذلك لأنني امرأة ساقطة، أو ألاقي في مستقبل حياتي شقاءً وآلاماً، فذلك لأن المستقبل نتيجة الماضي وثمرته الطبيعية.

هنا ذكرتك يا أرمان، وذكرت فراقك وكيف أستطيعه، وذكرت أنا التي سأتولى قتل نفسي بيدي؛ لأن الطريق التي لا طريق غيرها إلى بلوغ رضا أبيك وموافاة رغبته، أن أقاطعك، وأغاضبك، وأظهر أمامك بمظهر الخائنة الغادرة، وربما اضطررت إلى الاتصال بغيرك على مرأى منك ومسمع، حتى تنصرف عني انصراف يائسٍ مغلوبٍ على أمره من حيث لا يكون لأبيك مدخل في ذلك، فأكون قد جمعت على نفسي بين فراقك وغضبك في آنٍ واحدٍ، وذكرت أن لا بد لي متى فارقتك أن أعود إلى حياتي الأولى التي أبغضها وأمقتها، لأن الدوق موهان لم يستطع أن ينسى ذنبي الذي أذنبته إليه حتى اليوم، ولأني في حاجةٍ إلى بسطةٍ من العيش أستعين بها على معالجة مرضي ووفاء ديني، فدارت هذه الخواطر في رأسي ساعةً، وطالت دورتها حتى كادت تغلبني على أمري، ثم وقع نظري على وجه أبيك المخضل بدموعه فتجلدت وجمعت أمري ومضيت قدماً لا ألوي على شيء مما ورائي .

O Arman to leave you was extremely difficult for me. However, to see your father crying in front of me was more difficult. It was difficult for me to endure that I was going to become the reason for the death of your sister and for her loss.

Without question O Arman I love you. I recognize the pain of love and its heat which generates in hearts. Indeed, when your father was talking to me about your sister and about her devastation, I was picturing her lying down on her bed. I was seeing her hands pleading with me, crying and beseeching me saying, 'Save me O lady, have mercy upon my weakness and upon my youth.' I felt her words penetrating my heart in a way that only one in a similar situation could feel.

Indeed, I was deprived from the virtue of marriage and its happiness in the beginning of my life which caused great calamities to befall me that make me cry even today. Thus, my pain does not increase nor reignite except when a woman in similar circumstances is in hardship.

This is because verily I am in love and likewise she is also in love. Therefore, it is inevitable for one of us to sacrifice our love for the other. Thus, I give preference to sacrifice my love for her, only because she is your sister and only because she has not sinned in her life nor is she entitled for this misfortune.

Whenever I imagined that indeed soon your sister will become prosperous and content after me, and that she will appear in front of me wearing a white beautiful wedding dress and walking to the church having her fiancé besides her, my heart became filled with joy and happiness.

Yes, certainly this strike is extremely painful and I shall feel it in the future. My heart will not be able to endure this pain. However, I will try my utmost best to endure this pain through patience and serenity. This is because your father will soon become pleased with me and soon you will come to know and learn about the secret of my sacrifice. Then you will love me more than you had loved me ever before. Indeed, at that point, your sister will also become happy and will be indulged in a prosperous life. Perhaps my name might be included amongst those names which your sister will supplicate for in her prayers beseeching for mercy and for gratification.

Nevertheless, the time came where I could say my last words to your father. Verily it was a very distressing moment for me. I asked Allah ﷻ to forgive me for my past and future sins. I supplicated to Allah ﷻ that He never allows another woman taste the bitterness of this pain and torture after me.

لقد كان شديداً علي جداً أن أفارقك يا أرمان! ولكن كان أشد علي منه أن أرى أباك يبكي بين يدي، وأن أكون سبباً في موت أختك أو شقائها.

إنني أحب يا أرمان، وأعرف آلام الحب ولوعته في النفوس، ولقد كان يخيل إلي وأبوك يحدثني عن أختك وشقائها أنني أراها من خلال دموعي طريحة فراشها، وهي تمد يدها إلي ضارعة متوسلةً وتقول: أنقذيني يا سيدتي وارحمي ضعفي وشبابي.. فأجد لكلماتها من الأثر في نفسي ما لا يستطيع أن يشعر به إلا من كان له شأن مثل شأني.

إنني حرمت في مبدإ حياتي سعادة الزوجية وهناءها، ولقيت بسبب ذلك من الشقاء ما لا أزال أبكيه حتى اليوم، فلا يهيج حزني، ولا يستثير كامن لوعتي مثل أن أرى بين الناس فتاةً محرومة السعادة مثلي.

إنني أحب وهي تحب، ولا بد لواحدةٍ منا أن تموت فداءً عن الأخرى؛ فلأمت أنا فداءً عنها، لأنها أختك، ولأنها لم تقترف في حياتها ذنباً تستحق بسببه الشقاء.

وكنت كلما ذكرت أنها ستصبح سعيدةً هانئةً من بعدي وتراءى لي شبحها، وهي لابسة ثوب عرسها الأبيض الجميل، وسائرة إلى الكنيسة بجانب خطيبها، طار قلبي فرحاً وسروراً وهان علي كل شيءٍ في سبيل غبطتها وهنائها.

نعم إن الضربة التي سأستقبلها شديدة جداً، لا يقوى عليها قلبي. ولكني سأحتملها بصبرٍ وسكون، لأن أباك سيصبح راضياً عني. ولأنك ستعلم في مستقبل الأيام سر تضحيتي، فتحبني فوق ما أحببتني! ولأن أختك ستصبح سعيدةً مغتبطةً بعيشها وحبها؛ وسيكون اسمي بين الأسماء التي تدعو لها الله في صلواتها بالرحمة والرضوان.

جاءت الساعة التي أقول فيها لأبيك كلمتي الأخيرة، ولقد كانت شديدةً هائلةً أسأل الله أن يغفر لي بما لقيت فيها من الآلام ماضي ذنوبي وآتيها، كما أسأله ألا يذيق مرارتها قلب امرأةٍ على وجه الأرض من بعدي.

I hauled myself off the chair and dragged my feet towards your father like a dead person walks towards their grave. I knelt in front of him and took hold of his hand, he looked at me restlessly so, I said to him, "O my respected sir, do you believe that I love your son?"

He replied, "Yes."

I said, "I love him with an ardent love with all my being, do you believe that?"

He again replied, "Yes."

I then said, "Certainly this was the love which completed all my hopes and all my fortunes. It was the only thing I possessed in this world, do you acknowledge this too?"

Again, he replied, "Yes my daughter."

I then said, "Indeed because of your daughter I have sacrificed my love. Return to her and give her the good news of her bright future and tell her that, indeed there is a woman who does not know you, neither has she ever seen you, but she loves you and is very kind to you. She will die very soon because of you. Beg Allah ﷻ to shower His mercy and forgiveness over her."

His face glittered up with joy and happiness. He left no word of praise neither a word of gratitude, except that he showered them upon me. His happiness and his joy made me forget the severe pain and trauma which engulfed my heart. My pain and my sorrows changed into peace and harmony at that time. I praised Allah ﷻ for this, as your father did not see anything upon my face which would lessen his excitement and his happiness.

At that point I felt some movement next to the door of the room, when I looked I saw my maid Prudence who was gesturing at me with her hand. I went to her and then she gave me a letter which the postman had delivered. I read the address only to learn that it was a letter from Mr John Phillip therefore, I already knew what the letter contained before I had read it. It occurred to me that Allah ﷻ had sent this as a sign for me. I went running to my desk and read the letter. Then I wrote a reply in the following words, 'Indeed, soon I will be having the evening dinner with you.' Then I gave that piece of paper to Prudence for her to put into the post box.

قمت من مكاني كأنني أنتزع نفسي من الأرض انتزاعاً، ومشيت إلى أبيك كما يمشي الحائن إلى مصرعه حتى جثوت بين يديه، وأخذت بيده، فاستفاق من غشيته ونظر إليّ ذاهلاً مشدوهاً. فقلت له: أتعتقد يا سيدي أنني أحب ولدك؟

قال: نعم،

قلت: حباً هو منتهى ما تستطيع امرأة أن تحتمل؟

قال: نعم.

قلت: وأن هذا الحب هو كل آمالي وسعادتي، وما أملك في الحياة؟

قال: نعم يا بنيتي،

قلت: قد ضحيته من أجل ابنتك فعد إليها وبشرها بسعادة المستقبل وهنائه وقل لها: إن امرأةً لا تعرفك، ولم تترك في يوم من أيام حياتها، ولكنها تحبك وتشفق عليك.. تموت الآن من أجلك، فاسألي الله لها الرحمة والغفران.

فتهلل وجهه بشراً وسروراً، ولم يدع كلمةً من كلمات الشكر والثناء إلا أفضى بها إليّ، فأنساني سروره واغتباطه ألم الضربة التي أصابت كبدي، واستحال حزني واكتئابي إلى راحةٍ وسكونٍ، فحمدت الله على أن لم يرَ في وجهي في تلك الساعة ما ينغص عليه سروره واغتباطه.

وهنا شعرت بحركةٍ عند باب الغرفة فالتفت فإذا (برودنس) تشير إليّ بيدها. فذهبت إليها فأعطتني كتاباً جاء به البريد، فقرأت عنوانه، فإذا هو بخط المركيز (جان فيليب)، فعلمت ما يتضمنه قبل أن أراه، ووقع في نفسي أن الله قد أوحى إليّ بما أفعل، فذهبت مسرعةً إلى غرفة مكتبي كأنني أخاف أن يعرض لي في طريقي ما يزعزع عزيمتي، وهناك قرأت الكتاب، وكتبت لصاحبه في بطاقةٍ صغيرةٍ هذه الكلمة (سأتعشى عندك الليلة) ثم أعطيتها برودنس لتلقيها في صندوق البريد،

I then returned to your father and said to him, "Indeed Arman does not know anything about this meeting of yours with me. So, do not tell him about it when you meet him. I shall write to him soon, telling him of our separation. In this letter, he will not doubt anyone except me, he will know that certainly you were not involved in what happened. Arman will come to know today or tomorrow that verily I have joined connections with another man other than him and have broken my promise with him. Then he will inevitably find no other alternative but to travel back with you breaking all hopes and ties with me. This tragedy will cause him distress for a couple of weeks. Then after that he will not care about this anymore. My love in his heart will deteriorate, besides this, I only have one request from you, will you bestow this upon me?"

He replied, "Yes, I will bestow upon you anything you want."

I said, "Indeed I am an ill woman who is close to her death. Certainly, the illness which has afflicted me, a lot of people talk about it that verily it does not detach from a person, whether that illness is prolonged or whether it is short until it takes that person to his or her grave. All that I ask from you is that, on the day when you find out that indeed I have reached my deathbed, you grant Arman permission to come to see me so that I could see him, give him my last farewells and apologize to him regarding my betrayal because of you. This is because I am not going to bear loss in his love and in his dignity whether I am alive or whether I am dead."

He looked at me with the eyes which were drenched in tears and said, "O my daughter, may the Lord shower his mercy upon you, indeed I promise you whatever you want and I will pray to Allah ﷻ to grant you forgiveness and patience." Then after that he intended to give me something as a help, thus I strongly refused it and said to him, "O my respected gentleman, I have not sold myself, I have gifted myself." Accordingly, he took hold of my head in his hands and kissed me on my forehead. This kiss was an excellent compensation for the sacrifice which I had given. Then he said his farewells to me and departed.

After this, I stood up and went towards my wardrobe. I gathered my clothes and what was remaining from my jewellery. I travelled with my maid Prudence to Paris. I went to my house. It is then I wrote to you the letter which you received. Only Allah ﷻ knows how many tears I shed and only He knows how many times my heart stopped upon each word and what I went through. I gave that letter to the watchman of the house, entrusting him to give it to you upon your arrival. I went to Mr John Phillip to fulfil the promise of dinner.

وعدت إلى أبيك فوجدته حيث تركته، فقلت له: إن أرمان لا يعلم شيئاً من أمر زيارتك هذه فاكتمها عنه حين تلقاه، وسأكتب إليه كتاب مقاطعةٍ لا يشك في أني صاحبة الرأي فيه، وأن لا يد لك فيما كان، وسيعلم اليوم أو غداً أنني قد اتصلت برجلٍ غيره فيرى أنني قد خنته وغدرت بعهده، فلا يجد له بداً من أن يسافر معك قاطعاً رجاءه مني، وربما تألم لهذه الصدمة بضعة أيامٍ أو بضعة أسابيع فلا تحفل بذلك، فسيبلى حبي في قلبه، كما يبلى كل حبٍ في كل قلب، غير أن لي عندك طلبةً واحدةً لا أريد منك سواها، فهل تسمح لي بها؟

قال: نعم أسمح لك بكل شيء،

قلت: إني مريضة مشرفة، وإن العلة التي أكابدها كثيراً ما يتحدث الناس عنها أنها لا تترك صاحبها، طالت أم قصرت، حتى تذهب به إلى قبره، فكل ما أسألك إياه أن تأذن لأرمان في اليوم الذي تعلم فيه أنني قد أصبحت على حافة قبري أن يأتيني لأراه وأودعه الوداع الأخير، وأعتذر له عن ذنبي الذي أذنبته إليه حتى لا أخسر حبه واحترامه حية وميتة...

فنظر إليَّ نظرةً دامعةً وقال: وارحمتاه لك يا بنيتي، أنني أعدك بما أردت، وأسأل الله لك الشفاء والعزاء... ثم حاول أن يعرض عليَّ شيئاً من المعونة فأبيت ذلك إباءً شديداً، وقلت له: إنني لم أبع نفسي يا سيدي بيعاً، بل وهبتها هبة، فأخذ رأسي بين يديه وقبلني في جبيني قبلةً كانت خير جزاءٍ لي على تضحيتي التي ضحيت بها وودعني ومضى.

فما أبعد إلا قليلاً حتى قمت إلى خزانتي فجمعت ثيابي، وما بقي لي من حلاي ووضعتها في حقيبتي، وسافرت مع برودنس إلى باريس، وذهبت إلى منزلي هناك فكتبت إليك فيه ذلك الكتاب الذي تعلمه، والله يعلم كم سكبت من الدموع، وكم وقف قلبي بين كل كلمةٍ، وما يليها أثناء كتابته حتى أتممته، فأعطيته حارس المنزل، وأوصيته أن يسلمه إليك عند مجيئك. ثم ذهبت للوفاء بعهد المركيز.

Indeed, in terms of my life with that man, I do not have the power to narrate to you anything from his affair other than just to say to you, that indeed, he did not find in me the woman he was expecting nor did he find a woman of his desires. Neither did I see in him a man who could love me and mix in with me. Thus, we stayed separate. I became a woman who had lost the ability to distinguish an honest person from a liar.

This is my story O Arman the way it went and this is the betrayal which I committed with you. So, do you still consider me to be a cheat and a fraud after this?

My heart desires that verily I die before I could see you. I believe that whatever is in your heart of animosity and hatred towards me will perish after I die. Certainly, you will return to Paris the moment someone will inform you of my death for you to visit the grave of the woman who was the joy of your heart and belonged to the best days of your life. She will leave this world empty handed of everything, including your love and kindness. However, whenever you become curious about what happened to her after you left and that what led her to her death, you are welcome to find out.

Therefore, I am writing everything in my diary which I am going to leave with Prudence, hoping that perhaps you will read it someday in the future. Then you will look at these pages as you would look at a holy book, which will verify all that I went through and you will forgive me. Thus, your forgiveness and your pardoning will then enlighten the darkness in my grave and the fear clutching my soul will vanish.

***

3rd January 1851

O my Arman where are you? You have gone far away from me. Indeed, your body and your soul both, have become distant from me. This is because you have not replied to my letter which I wrote to you, in which, I invited you to come to see me in order to hear my last confession. I believe you have not come because the anger and hostility that you hold in your heart towards me has led you to forget and neglect me. You have become a person who does not remember me like a lover remembers his beloved. Neither are you showing kindness to me the way a friend shows mercy to a friend. Whatever Allah ﷻ intends let it be, and may that blessing always stay with you and your family and your people. Indeed, I am not hostile against you, neither am I wanting any revenge from you. I do not hold anything other than love in my heart and sincerity for you. I am pleased with everything which you came with and whatever you have left.

أما حياتي مع ذلك الرجل فلا أستطيع أن أقص عليك منها شيئاً سوى أن أقول لك: إنه لم ير في المرأة التي كان يتخيلها، ويمني نفسه بها، ولم أر فيه الرجل الذي يؤنسني ويخلط نفسه بنفسي، فافترقنا فأصبحت لا أعرف لي في العالم صديقاً صادقاً، ولا كاذباً.

هذه قصتي يا أرمان كما هي، وهذا ذنبي الذي أذنبته إليك.. فهل ترى بعد ذلك أني خائنة أو خادعة؟

قلبي يحدثني أنني سأموت قبل أن أراك، وأملي يخيل إلي أن ما في نفسك من الموجدة علي لا يستمر إلى ما بعد الموت، وأنك ستعود إلى باريس في الساعة التي ينعاني لك فيها الناعي؛ لتزور قبر تلك المرأة المسكينة التي تولت سعادة قلبك وهناءه حقبةً من أيام حياتك، ثم خرجت من الدنيا فارغة اليد من كل شيءٍ حتى من حبك وعطفك، وربما بلغ بك الاهتمام بشأنها أن تحاول معرفة ما تم لها من بعدك إلى أن ذهب بها الموت إلى قبرها.

فهأنذا أكتب هذه المذكرات، وأتركها لك عند برودنس لعلك تقرأها في مستقبل الأيام فتنظر إليها كما تنظر إلى كتاب اعتراف مقدس قد ألبسه الموت ثوب الطهارة والبراءة فتصدق ما فيها وتعفو عني، فينير عفوك ظلمات قبري، ويؤنس وحشة نفسي.

***

٣ يناير سنة ١٨٥١

أين أنت يا أرمان؟ أنت بعيد عني جداً، بعيد بجسمك وبقلبك، لأنك لم تهمل كتابي الذي كتبته لك ودعوتك فيه لزيارتي وسماع اعترافي الأخير إلا لأن ما كان في نفسك من العتب والموجدة علي قد استحال إلى نسيانٍ وإغفالٍ، فأصبحت لا تذكرني كما يذكر المحب حبيبه، ولا تعطف علي كما يعطف الصديق على صديقه، فليكن ما أراد الله، ولتدم لك تلك السعادة التي تنعم بها بين أهلك، وقومك، فإني غير واجدةٍ عليك، ولا ناقمة منك شيئاً، ولا حاملة لك في نفسي إلا الحب والإخلاص والرضا بكل ما تأتي، وما تدع.

A few days have passed and I have not seen anyone from amongst the people. This is because my doctor has prevented me from going out. Also, indeed my friends who know me from the past have verily sufficed upon sending me 'get well' cards only thorough my maid instead of coming themselves to see me. After they drop off their cards, they run away like people who are afraid of something. Certainly, they are the same people who before today, would wait hours on end to deliver cards in person to me, waiting for hours until I used to grant them the permission for a meeting. However, when they were granted the permission of a meeting they would rush inside with happiness. If, however, they were deprived from the meeting, they used to go back upset.

I do not understand; why do not they stop giving the greeting cards the way they have stopped meeting me? Indeed, they are hoping to see me in between them soon. They are hoping that I will start living with them and mixing in with them the way they used to live with me in the past. However, they are wrong.

Whatever they have done, they have done good. However now, I can only feel content and at ease through myself and not through anyone else. The only reason I feel content with myself is because when I am alone I have the power to ask my heart about you. Thus, my heart reminds me about you and about those days of happiness which I had spent with you at Bougival. I remember those days as this is all I have left of you.

O Arman, I never thought that a human body could endure the tragedies which I am enduring. Indeed, moments have passed which I truly believed was the pain and struggles of the soul at the time of death and verily these are the last moments of my life. Whenever I do come out of that state, I ask myself, if I cannot bear this pain of illness, how am I possibly going to bear the pain of death?

Has destiny written that I will see you besides me in my lifetime? Only if my heart can convince me of this. Then that would inevitably cure my illness and my soul will return, restoring my peace and my happiness. Is Allah ﷻ going to decree this for me?

I do not know. Thus, the future is in the hands of Allah ﷻ. He decrees whatever He wants and He does whatever He pleases.

***

لي عدة أيام لم أر فيها أحداً من الناس؛ لأن الطبيب منعني من الخروج، ولأن أصدقائي الذين كانوا يعرفونني فيما مضى قد أصبحوا يقنعون من زيارتي بإرسال بطاقاتهم إليّ مع خادمتي، ثم ينصرفون مسرعين كأنما يفرون من أمرٍ يخيفهم، ولقد كانوا قبل اليوم إذا أرسلوها لبثوا ينتظرون الساعات الطوال حتى آذن لهم بالمقابلة، فإذا ظفروا بها طاروا بها فرحاً وسروراً، وإن حرموها عادوا آسفين محزونين.

ولا أدري لم لا يقطعون بطاقاتهم كما قطعوا زياراتهم؟ فقد كانوا يظنون أنهم سيروني بينهم في مستقبل الأيام صحيحة الجسم طيبة النفس، أصلح للمعاشرة والمخادنة كما كانوا يعهدونني من قبل، فهم في ظنهم مخطئون.

لقد أحسنوا فيما عملوا، فإنني أصبحت لا آنس بأحدٍ في العالم سوى نفسي، ولا آنس بنفسي إلا لأني أستطيع متى خلوت بها أن أسائلها عنك فتذكرني بك وبتلك الأيام السعيدة التي قضيتها معك في بوجيفال، وذكرى تلك الأيام هي العزاء الباقي لي عن جميع ما خسرت يدي.

ما كنت أظن يا أرمان أن جسم الإنسان يحتمل كل هذه الآلام التي أكابدها، فلقد تمر بي ساعات أعتقد فيها أن الألم الذي أكابده إنما هو ألم النزع، وأنني في الساعة الأخيرة من ساعات حياتي، فإذا استفقت قلت في نفسي: هذا ألم المرض، وقد عجزت عنه، فمن لي باحتمال ألم الموت؟

على أن نفسي تحدثني أحياناً أنه إن قدر لي أن أراك بجانبي في يومٍ من الأيام برئت من مرضي، وتراجعت نفسي وعدت إلى راحتي وسكوني، فهل يقدر لي الله ذلك؟

لا أعلم: فالمستقبل بيد الله فليقدر الله ما يشاء وليفعل ما يريد.

***

24th January 1851

I did not part from my bed for many days until today. I sat down at the window for a little while looking out to observe ordinary life. My sight landed upon many people whom I recognised. They were walking very happily on their ways. Nevertheless, I did not see anyone from amongst them who looked up even once at my window. It was, as if, they were walking past a house which they did not recognize and that they had no connection with ever before.

How unfortunate is my loneliness? How tight has my chest become? How heavy has this wall become which surrounds me?

I do not have the power to look at my bed because my heart is telling me that soon my bed will become the ladder to my grave. Neither can I stand in front of my mirror because the mirror tells me the worst things and bad omens about me. Nor do I have the power to look out of my window because this reminds me of my past blissful life which has become forbidden for me. So now where shall I go? And how shall I live?

I do not eat but one type of food. I do not see but only the same scene every day. I do not hear but only the voice of my doctor and the voice of my maid whenever they enquire about me, every morning and every evening. I give them one reply every time. This has continued as now I have become tired and fallen into despair. I feel as if my heart is imprisoned in my chest and that my body is imprisoned in my room. Sometimes I encounter such moments that my mind stops working and my heart stops beating. I feel that I have become cut off from yesterday, today and tomorrow, in fact from everything in my life as now I am standing alone.

The severe coughing has shackled the insides of my chest. Only sometimes my eyes catch sleep. The doctor continues to punish me severely through his injections and his medication. Every day I am feeling that my heart is becoming tighter and my eyes have increased in darkness. I feel that my life is slowly but surely going far away from me. Now I presume that I have become a distant shadow. So, when is my torture going to finish?

***

٢٤ يناير سنة ١٨٥١

لم أفارق سريري منذ أيام طوال إلا صباح هذا اليوم، فجلست قليلاً بجانب نافذتي، وأشرفت منها على الحياة العامة، فوقع نظري على كثيرٍ ممن كنت أعرفهم من قبل سائرين في طريقهم لاهين مغتبطين، ولم أر بينهم من وقع نظره إلى نوافذ غرفتي مرةً واحدةً كأنما يمرون ببيتٍ لا يعرفونه، ولا عهد لهم به من قبل.

ما أشد وحشتي! وما أضيق صدري! وما أثقل هذا الجدار الذي يدور حولي؟

لا أطيق النظر إلى سريري؛ لأن نفسي تحدثني أنه سيكون عما قليلٍ سلم قبري، ولا الوقوف أمام مرآتي، لأنها تحدثني عن نفسي أسوأ الأحاديث وأشأمها، ولا الإشراف من نافذتي لأنها تذكرني بحياتي الماضية السعيدة التي حيل بيني وبينها، فأين أذهب وكيف أعيش؟

لا آكل إلا طعاماً واحداً، ولا أرى إلا منظراً متكرراً، ولا أسمع إلا صوت طبيبي وخادمتي حينما يسألها عني صباح كل يومٍ ومساءه فتجيبه بجوابٍ واحدٍ، حتى مللت وسئمت وأصبحت أشعر أن نفسي سجينة في صدري، سجن جسمي في غرفتي، وربما مرت بي ساعات يقف فيها ذهني عن التفكير وخاطري عن الحركة، وينقطع ما بيني وبين يومي وأمسي وغدي وكل شيءٍ في الحياة حتى نفسي.

السعال يهدم أركان صدري هدماً، والنوم لا يلم بعيني إلا قليلاً، والطبيب يعذبني بمشارطه وضماداته عذاباً أليماً، وكل يومٍ أشعر أن نفسي يزداد ضيقاً، وبصري يزداد ظلمة، وأن الحياة تبعد عن ناظري شيئاً فشيئاً، حتى أكاد أحسبها شبحاً من الأشباح النائية فمتى ينقضي عذابي؟

***

30th January 1851

Today I heard some noise in the courtyard. I enquired from Prudence about it. Thus, she went, then she came back informing me, "O my beloved lady, verily the bailiffs are seizing the furniture of our house."

Thus, I replied, "Leave them, let them do whatever they want to do." Not even a little while had passed by that the legal officers entered my room creating havoc. Not even one of them bothered to take off their hat for the lady of the house out of respect. Neither did anyone lower their voice to show kindness to a troubled ill lady. They started walking and registering an account of everything which their sight had landed upon. I became frightened lest that they make a note in their register about my diary. Accordingly, I gestured and gave a sign to Prudence to go and hide it away from them and she did. I thanked Allah ﷻ for this.

They advanced forth towards my bed. Then one of the debtors requested that the bed should also be seized saying that it is very expensive. Then he said, "Soon on the day of the auction, this bed would prove highly beneficial." The evictor explained to the debtor that certainly the law does not permit this, and exempts beds and carpets from being seized. The bailiff drew near to the debtor and whispered in his ear. I am guessing that he said this, "Indeed you will have the power to do this after her death." They departed after leaving a guard standing at the doorstep of my house. The guard never left his place, guarding my house day and night.

I wrote a letter to Duke Mohan. This was the first time I had written to him since I had left him. I wrote to him asking him for forgiveness for my sin which I had committed with him. I then complained to him about all the calamities which the hands of destiny had given to me. I gave him an oath and the medium of the remembrance of his respected daughter, begging him to come to me and to meet me. Thus, he did this and came. The moment he was next to me, he saw me and started crying. I did not know whether he was crying over me, or whether he was observing my circumstances which then made him remember the circumstances of his daughter in the last moments of her life, which then led him to cry. Then Duke Mohan remained with me for a while, standing head bowed in silence. He did not talk to me but only a little. He did not mention even a word of what had taken place in the past. Then he went and left in the hands of Prudence a bundle of money which Prudence spent on buying some provisions and sustenance. In addition to that, with the aid of that money Prudence delayed the eviction of household furniture for a couple of months.

I do not have the power to write to you more than that which I have written. This is because certainly the doctor is constantly taking blood from my body. This has weakened my body. Thus, now I do not feel anything other than devastating pain.

***

۳۰ يناير سنة ۱۸۵۱

سمعت صباح اليوم لجباً كثيراً في فناء المنزل، فسألت برودنس: ما الخبر؟ فذهبت وعادت إلي تبكي وتقول: إنهم يحجزون أثاث المنزل يا سيدتي،

فقلت: دعيهم يفعلوا ما يشاؤون، وما هي إلا لحظات قليلة حتى دخلوا غرفتي مندفعين متصايحين، ولم يمر بخاطرِ واحدٍ منهم أن يرفع قبعته عن رأسه احتراماً لصاحبة المنزل، أو يخفض صوته إشفاقاً على المريضة المعذبة، فمشوا يسجلون كل ما وقع نظرهم عليه، وخفت أن يسجلوا دفتر مذكراتي فأشرت إلى برودنس أن تخفيه عنهم ففعلت، فحمدت الله على ذلك،

ثم وصلوا إلى سريري فطلب أحد الدائنين حجزه، وقال إنه ثمين، سيكون له يوم البيع شأن عظيم، فأفهمه الحاجز أن القانون يستثني الأسرة وفرشها، وألقى في أذنه كلمة أحسب أني سمعته يقول فيها: إنك تستطيع أن تفعل ذلك بعد موتها، ثم انصرفوا بعد ما تركوا على باب بيتي حارساً لا يفارقه ليله ونهاره،

فكتبت إلى (الدوق موهان)، وهي أول مرة - كتبت إليه فيها أستغفره ذنبي الذي أذنبته إليه. وأشكو له ما نالته يد الأيام مني وأستحلفه بذكرى ابنته الكريمة عليه أن يأتي لزيارتي، ففعل، فبكى عندما رآني، ولا أدري هل بكاني أو ذكر عند رؤيته مصرعي مصرع ابنته الأخير فبكاها، ثم قضى بجانب فراشي ساعةً مطرقاً صامتاً لا يحدثني إلا قليلاً ولا يذكر الماضي بكلمةٍ واحدةٍ، ثم ذهب وترك في يد برودنس ضمة أوراق استبقت بعضها للنفقة واستعانت بباقيها على تأجيل بيع الأثاث بضعة أشهر.

لا أستطيع أن أكتب إليك اليوم أكثر مما كتبت فإن الطبيب ما زال يلح على جسمي بالفصد حتى أوهاه واستنزف دمه، فأصبحت لا أتحرك حركةً إلا شعرت بألمٍ عظيمٍ.

***

2nd February 1851

Certainly, this day was the happiest and the most soothing day from my days. This is because indeed today, a letter from your father arrived which stated;

O my Dear,

Indeed, I am enormously upset and extremely distressed for you. Indeed, I found out yesterday through some people who came to Nice, that you have been extremely ill for two months. It has also been brought to my attention that you hardly come out of your house. I pray to Allah ﷻ that He grants you recovery and patience. I will beg Him to recompense you with the best reward for the pain and calamities which you have endured because of me and my daughter. Also, let me give you the glad tiding that indeed Allah ﷻ has accepted your sacrifice which you sent forth for my daughter. Verily Susan got married to her fiancé twenty days ago, and she is content with her life. Even though she does not know about our secret, I have still told her as I did not mention your name, that certainly there are some people that have sacrificed their life and happiness for you to prosper. Therefore, do not ever leave supplicating for that person in your prayers so that the Lord can reward that person abundantly and give that person an excellent station. So, now my daughter is constantly praying for you that Allah ﷻ does well with you the way you did good with her.

In regards to the letter which you had sent to Arman in the beginning of last month, indeed he did not get it until today. This is because ever since he had parted from you and travelled to Nice, he did not have the power to stay here but only for a few days. Then he departed to the west agonised and drowned in sorrow because of you. I did not know of his whereabouts or where he was staying. Thus, I was unable to post your letter to him until I learnt about his location only a few days earlier. I posted your letter to him along with a letter explaining your story. Indeed, in that letter I told him that certainly I did not see any reason preventing me giving him permission to travel to Paris and stay there for as long as you want him to. This is because now his sister is married. I am hoping that he will reach you very soon.

٢ فبراير سنة ١٨٥١

إن هذا اليوم أسعد أيامي وأهنؤها، فقد وصل إليّ من أبيك كتاب هذا نصه:

سيدتي:

إني أتوجع لك توجعاً شديداً، فقد علمت بالأمس من بعض الوافدين إلى نيس أنك مريضة مرضاً شديداً منذ شهرين، وأنك لا تخرجين من منزلك إلا قليلاً، فأسأل الله لك الشفاء والعزاء، وأضرع إليه أن يجزيك خيراً بما قاسيت من الآلام والأوجاع في سبيلي وسبيل ابنتي، وأبشرك أن الله قد تقبل قربانك الذي قدمته إليه، فإن سوسان قد تزوجت من خطيبها منذ عشرين يوماً، وأصبحت هانئةً بحبه وعيشها كما أردت لها، وأنها وإن لم تكن تعلم من أمر تلك القصة التي نعلمها شيئاً فقد قلت لها: إن بعض الناس ـ ولم أسمه لها ـ قد ضحى بنفسه وبسعادته في سبيل سعادتك وهنائك، فلا تتركي الدعاء له في جميع صلواتك بجزيل الأجر وحسن المثوبة، فهي لا تزال تدعو لك صباحها ومساءها أن يحسن الله إليك كما أحسنت إليها.

أما الكتاب الذي أرسلته إلى أرمان في أوائل الشهر الماضي فلم يصل إليه إلا اليوم لأنه منذ فارقك وسافر إلى (نيس) لم يستطع البقاء فيها إلا بضعة أيام، ثم رحل عنها إلى الشرق حزيناً مهموماً من أجلك، وكنت لا أعرف الجهة التي يقيم فيها فلم أستطع أن أرسله إليه حتى عرفتها منذ أيامٍ قلائل، فأرسلته وأرسلت معه كتاباً أطلعه فيه على قصتك وأقول له إنني لا أرى مانعاً يمنعني بعد زواج أخته من أن آذن له بالسفر إلى باريس والبقاء فيها ما شاء أن يبقى، وأحسب أنه يصل إليك في عهدٍ قريبٍ.

Today I am sending you this letter in conjunction with fifteen thousand Francs, hoping that you will accept them from me. I am hoping that you will look at this money like a daughter looks at a gift from her father who loves her and honours her. Thus, if you were to accept this gift you would be doing a very big favour upon me.

I am hoping that I will soon hear the news of your recovery. Also, I am hoping that I will see your health blossoming and your heart relishing in happiness.

Duval.

The moment I read that letter, I felt a wave of happiness running through me, which I only felt when I was with you. Certainly, I know now that Susan is married and this is what I had been hoping for. Indeed, you have always loved me. Verily I feared you forgetting me more than I feared your anger. Indeed, soon I shall see you and this is the only desire of my life.

Verily that gift which your father had sent me, certainly I did look at it with the eye that he had expected me to look with. Thus, I had accepted it thanking and praising him. May Allah ﷻ favour him the way he has favoured me.

***

3rd February 1851

I could sleep last night unlike other nights. This is because the happiness which your father's letter left in my heart has indeed made me carefree of everything including my pain. In the morning, my doctor told me that I was much better than I had been in the recent past. He further added that indeed the sun is shining and the atmosphere is moderate, so mount upon your carriage and go out to the parks for a short while, then come back.

Thus, I went to the Shanzelize Park. Hence, I saw the park which was blossoming with life and with beauty. I saw the people in the park laughing, happy and enjoying themselves with a blessing whose value they did not recognise the way a deprived woman like me could recognise. I did get extremely upset when I saw a lot of people whom I knew walk passed me and not recognise me. Although I did see one of them looking at me, indeed he passed by the side of my carriage looking at me with a surprised and a suspicious look.

أرسلت إليك مع كتابي هذا عشرة آلاف فرنك أرجو أن تقبليها مني، وأن تنظري إليها بالعين التي تنظر بها الفتاة إلى هدية أبيها الذي يحبها ويجلها، فإن فعلت أحسنت إلي بذلك إحساناً عظيماً.

لي الأمل أن أسمع عما قليلٍ خبر شفائك، وأرجو أن أراك في مستقبل الأيام ناعمةً بصحتك وسعادتك.

(دوفال)

فما قرأته حتى شعرت بهزةٍ من السرور في قلبي لم أشعر بمثلها مذ فارقتك حتى اليوم، فقد علمت أن سوسان قد تزوجت، وذلك ما كنت أرجو لها، وأنك لا تزال تحبني، وقد أخاف نسيانك أكثر مما أخاف عتبك، وأنني سأراك عما قليل، وتلك آمالي في الحياة.

أما الهدية التي أرسلها إلي أبوك فقد نظرت إليها بالعين التي أرادها فقبلتها شاكرةً له حامدة، أحسن الله إليه كما أحسن إلي.

***

٣ فبراير سنة ١٨٥١

إستطعت أن أنام ليلة أمس أكثر من كل ليلة؛ لأن السرور الذي تركه كتاب أبيك في نفسي شغلني عن كل شيءٍ حتى عن ألمي، وفي الصباح قال لي طبيبي إنك اليوم خير منك في كل يوم. وإن الشمس مشرقة، والهواء فاتر عليل، فاخرجي في مركبتك إلى بعض المتنزهات ساعة، ثم عودي،

فخرجت إلى غابات (الشانزلزيه) فرأيتها زاهرةً بالحياة والجمال، ورأيت الناس فيها ضاحكين متهللين مغتبطين بسعادةٍ لا يعرفون قيمتها كما تعرفها امرأة محرومة منها مثلي، فلم أحسدهم على نعمتهم التي آتاهم الله، بل دعوت لهم لبقائها ودوامها، إلا أنني حزنت على نفسي حزناً شديداً حينما رأيت أن كثيراً من معارفي الماضين قد مروا على مقربة مني، ولم يعرفوني، ورأيت أحدهم ينظر إلي، وقد مر بجانب مركبتي نظر المتخيل المتوهم، ثم لم يلبث أن لوى وجهه عني ومضى لسبيله، وقد استقر في نفسه أنه يرى امرأةً غير المرأة التي يعرفها.

Thus, I have found out that I have certainly changed a great deal. Indeed, my mirror does not lie to me whenever it tells me about my weakness, about my pale colour and about my disfigured face. Verily my mirror tells me the truth the way the people tell the truth.

Then I saw the sun, indeed it was hiding behind its veil and I returned home. Certainly that fear which was in my heart, causing me to be upset, had perished. In place of it, a new thought which was better than it was born. This was the thought of meeting you very soon. Soon after meeting you, my days of misfortunes will be over.

***

7th February 1851

I do not think that you will meet me O Arman. Verily my illness has reached its last stages. I have become a lady who does not find any peace either in standing, sitting, sleeping or being awake. The pains have spread through my entire body and into my joints. I feel like a heavy stone from amongst the stones is resting upon my chest which is preventing me from breathing and moving. Today I am unable to get out of bed and go to my desk. So, I instructed Prudence to bring the ink pot and my diary to my bed and I am now writing to you while I am in my bed. O Arman when am I going to see you so that I can say my farewells to you before I die?

***

10th February 1851

My hopes and my desires in life have become extremely weak. This is because death is drawing closer to me slowly but surely. O Arman you have not come to me until now. I am presuming that I shall die before seeing you. Indeed, the thought of death is scaring me a great deal. It is filling up my heart with terror and fright. I do not know how I am going to have the power to live alone in that dark frightening ditch where I will have no helper, neither will I have anyone to speak with. I did not enjoy life for long. My dreams and my hopes were all I was left with and I am now dying before I could see any of my hopes and dreams turn to reality. How sweet is life and how bitter is the separation from it? I did not obtain much from life. However, I still would not like to leave this world. Verily lucky are those people who live a very long life and then die leaving behind pious offspring or righteous deeds. Then these pious offspring or righteous deeds remain living for a very long time after that person's death. Whereas me, soon I will be dying in the youth of my life. My memory will also die the moment I die. It will be like I had never lived a life.

فعلمت أني قد تغيرت تغيراً عظيماً، وأن مرآتي ما كانت تكذبني حينما تحدثني عن نحولي واصفراري، واستحالة صورتي، بل صدقتني كما صدقني الناس.

ثم رأيت الشمس قد توارت وراء حجابها فعدت إلى منزلي، وقد زال من نفسي ذلك الخاطر الذي أحزنني، وحل محله خاطر آخر خير منه، وهو أنني سأراك عما قليل . وسينقضي بلقائك عهد بؤسي وشقائي..

***

٧ فبراير سنة ١٨٥١

ما أحسب أنك مدركي يا أرمان، فقد بلغت بي العلة منتهاها، وأصبحت لا أجد الراحة في قيامٍ ولا قعودٍ، ولا نومٍ ولا يقظةٍ، وانتشرت الآلام والأوجاع في جميع أعضائي ومفاصلي، وكأن حجراً من الأحجار العاتية ممتد على صدري يمنعني التنفس والحركة، وقد عجزت اليوم عن أن أنتقل من سريري إلى مكتبي، فأمرت برودنس أن تأتيني بمحبرتي ودفتري حيث أنا، فجاءت بهما إلي، فأنا الآن أكتب إليك وأنا في فراشي؛ فمتى أراك يا أرمان لأحيا برؤيتك أو أودعك قبل أن أموت؟

***

١٠ فبراير سنة ١٨٥١

أملي في الحياة ضعيف جداً، ها هو الموت يدنو مني رويداً رويداً، لم تأت إلي حتى الساعة يا أرمان، وأظن أني سأموت قبل أن أراك، إن الموت مخيف جداً يملأ قلبي رعباً وهولاً، لا أعلم كيف أستطيع أن أسكن وحدي تلك الحفرة الموحشة المظلمة التي لا أنيس لي فيها ولا سمير، لم أتمتع بالحياة طويلاً، وكانت كل سعادتي فيها آمالاً وأحلاماً، وهأنذا أموت قبل أن أرى شيئاً من آمالي وأحلامي، ما أحلى الحياة وأمر فراقها، لم أنل منها طائلاً، ولكني لا أحب أن أتركها، لقد سعد الذين يعمرون في الحياة طويلاً، ثم يموتون فيتركون من بعدهم ذريةً صالحةً أو عملاً طيباً يعيشون به بعد موتهم زمناً أطول مما عاشوا، أما أنا فإني سأموت في ربيع حياتي، وسيموت ذكري في الساعة التي أموت فيها، وكأني لم أعش في الحياة يوماً واحداً،

Woe be upon me over the sins I committed in my past life. Today I am paying the price for my sins and for my mistakes. Indeed, I had the power to be content with one morsel and one gulp of water. I did not require anything else besides this. Nevertheless, I was not content. Thus, here I am now, I cannot even chew one morsel of food. Neither can I swallow one gulp of water. I cannot find anyway to continue living regardless of which form life takes. So, am I going to leave this world as a stranger the way I had come into this world? At my death, will not even my closest be present? Is there not going to be even a friend to cry over me? Will my life come to an end just like that? Are my dreams and my hopes going to reach fruition before they perish? Woe, only if death gave me a little respite. Only if when death approaches me I could see you one last time and then die.

After this I, do not have any desire. Only this morning, I saw my doctor whispering something in the ear of my maid when he was leaving me. I asked Prudence what he had said but she changed the topic and did not say anything about it. I am only presuming that it was a dangerous word which he had whispered to her. I cannot see things clearly around me anymore. I am struggling to see the whiteness of the paper which is in my hand. Before today I was only vomiting blood, but now I am also vomiting small chunks of my lungs. Only if there was a glass of poison which I could drink which then would relieve me from this torment. Death is approaching me faster than this poison. O Lord show mercy and show your favour. You are the only one who knows the proportion of my pain and my suffering. Be merciful to me and make easy for me my affair. O my Lord, grant me one ease out of the two. I do not see anything. Neither can I recognise what I am saying. Perhaps these might be the last words which I am writing with my hands.

***

14th February 1851

Do not grieve over me too much after my death O Arman. It is sufficient for me that you remember me and do not forget me. Let me give you good news, verily Allah ﷻ has accepted my prayer as He has put in my heart the seed of tranquillity and hope since yesterday. This has wiped out all terrors and whispers from my heart. I am now certain that He is pleased with me and has forgiven for me my sins. Now I do not fear death, neither do I fear its aftermath. I am not agonizing over my pain anymore. Thus, you will not grieve over the affair of my death when you will come to know about it. May you live in happiness between your people and between your family. May you always honour your father. Verily he is from amongst the best fathers. May you also always love your sister. Indeed, she is from amongst the pure ladies. I am entrusting you to do good with Prudence. Verily she is a lady with a pure heart. She has great sincerity for me and you. I fear that after I am gone, the world might destroy her.

والأسفاه على ما فرطت في حياتي الماضية، إنني أدفع اليوم ثمن ذنوبي وآثامي أضعافاً مضاعفة، لقد كنت أستطيع أن أقنع بالمضغة والجرعة ولا أمد عيني إلى ما تقصر عنه يدي فلم أفعل، فهأنذا لا أسيغ المضغة ولا الجرعة، ولا أجد السبيل إلى العيش على أية صورةٍ كانت؛ أهكذا أخرج من الدنيا غريبةً عنها كما دخلت فيها لا يحضر موتي قريب.. ولا يبكي علي صديق.. أهكذا تنتهي حياتي في الساعة التي أحببتها فيها وأصبحت على مرحلةٍ واحدةٍ من أحلامي، وآمالي؟ آه لو يمهلني الموت قليلاً فربما كنت على مقربةٍ مني فأنظر إليك نظرةً واحدةً... ثم أموت..

لا أمل لي في ذلك. فقد رأيت طبيبي صباح اليوم يلقي في أذن خادمتي، وهو خارج من عندي، كلمةً فسألتها عنها فدارت حولها.. ولم تقلها.. وما أحسبها إلا تلك الكلمة الهائلة: لا أكاد أبصر شيئاً مما حولي حتى بياض الصحيفة التي في يدي.. كنت قبل اليوم أنفث الدم وحده، والآن أنفث أفلاذ رئتي مصبوغةً بالدم، من لي بكأسٍ من السم أشربها جرعةً واحدةً فأستريح من هذا العذاب الذي يساورني، ولكن أي فائدةٍ لي من ذلك، وها ذا الموت يمشي إلي بأسرع مما أمشي إليه؟ رحمتك اللهم وإحسانك فأنت وحدك العالم بمقدار ألمي وعذابي، فارحمني وهون علي أمري، وامنحني إحدى الراحتين. لا أرى شيئاً، ولا أعرف ماذا أقول، وربما كانت هذه الكلمات آخر ما تخطه يدي!

***

١٤ فبراير سنة ١٨٥١

لا تحزن علي كثيراً بعد موتي يا أرمان، فحسبي منك أن تذكرني ولا تنساني، وأبشرك أن الله قد استجاب لدعائي فألقى في نفسي منذ الأمس برد الراحة واليقين، ومحا من قلبي جميع مخاوفة ووساوسه، فعلمت أنه قد رضي عني، وغفر لي ذنبي، وأصبحت لا أخشى الموت ولا أجزع من الألم، ولا أبكي أسفاً على الحياة، فلا يحزنك أمري حين تعلمه، وعش سعيداً بين قومك، وأهلك، وأكرم أباك فهو خير الآباء، وأحبب أختك فهي أطهر الفتيات، وأوصيك خيراً ببرودنس فهي فتاة طيبة القلب، عظيمة الإخلاص لي ولك، وأخاف أن يتنكر لها الدهر من بعدي.

Most certainly Allah ﷻ has created for a spirit another spirit from amongst the spirits which are similar to it and it meets it. It gets happy when it meets it and it becomes upset when it parts from it. However, Allah ﷻ has decreed that every spirit stays away from its counterpart spirit in the first life. Thus, this is the misfortune of this world. Nevertheless, the spirits join its counterpart spirit in the second life. Thus, this is the fortune of the hereafter.

So, if my happiness with you upon this earth has finished, then soon I will be waiting for that happiness, waiting for you upon the highest heavens.

(Here some words which were written in the state of commotion have been wiped out through Margaret's tears and nothing is legible except for the word, 'Goodbye.')

إن الله قد خلق لكل روح من الأرواح روحاً أخرى تماثلها وتقابلها.. وتسعد بلقائها.. وتشقى بفراقها.. ولكنه قدر أن تضل كل روح عن أختها في الحياة الأولى فذلك شقاء الدنيا.. وأن تهتدي إليها في الحياة الثانية.. وتلك سعادة الآخرة.

فإن فاتتني سعادتي بك في الأرض.. فسأنتظرها في علياء السماء.

وهنا كتبت بعض كلماتٍ مضطربةٍ قد محا الدمع أكثرها فلم يبق منها واضحاً بعض الوضوح إلا كلمة (الوداع).

The Victim / Ad-Dahiyyah – Remaining Diaries
Prudence's Diary

Remaining diary accounts through the pen of Prudence.

13th February 1851

O sir, Margaret did not have the power to write to you more than what she has already written because the doctor has prevented her from moving around. Even if she wanted to write she was unable to do so.

O sir, do you remember that fragile and tender body? Indeed, today that soft and glittering body has become a pile of bones. It has become a statue.

May mercy descend upon you, verily everything has collapsed in Margaret's body other than her heart and her brain. If only they had stopped functioning as well with the other organs. This is because your memories and your thoughts are punishing her.

Whenever someone enters through the door of her room, she raises her head thinking that you had come. However, when that person draws near her and she sees then she closes her eyes to hide her tears which will flow regardless.

Certainly, now she does not even talk a lot. Thus, if she was to speak, her first words would be, 'Has not Arman come?' When I reply with, 'No,' she starts questioning about some other affair shifting her attention towards it, or she simply returns to her state of silence again.

Indeed, her doctor not visiting today has placed doubt and suspicion in her mind. Nevertheless, when I presented her with an excuse, she did not believe me. She said, "Now I have understood that word which the doctor had whispered to you yesterday." I became silent and I did not know what I could say.

***

الضحية ـ بقية المذكرات

بقلم الخادمة برودنس

١٣ فبراير سنة ١٨٥١

لم تستطع مرغريت يا سيدي أن تكتب لك أكثر مما كتبت.. لأن الطبيب منعها الحركة.. ولو أرادتها لعجزت عنها.

أتذكر يا سيدي ذلك الجسم الغض الناعم الذي كان يموج بالنور موجاً، ويشرق وراء بشرته إشراق الخمر في كأسها؟ لقد أصبح اليوم عظماً مجلداً وهيكلاً قائماً لا يساوي ثمن النظر إليه!

وارحمتاه لك.. لقد مات كل شيءٍ فيها إلا قلبها وشعورها وليتهما ماتا معها.. فإنها لا يعذبها شيء مثل خواطرها وأفكارها.

لا يدخل من باب غرفتها داخل حتى ترفع نظرها إليه تظن أنك قد جئتها.. فإذا دنا منها ورأته أطبقت جفنيها على دمعةٍ تنحدر من بينهما بالرغم منها.

إنها لا تتكلم كثيراً فإذا تكلمت كان أول حديثها (ألم يأت أرمان)؟ فإذا أجبتها أن لا... سألت عن أمرٍ آخر تتلهى به.. أو عادت إلى صمتها مرةً أخرى.

لقد رابها اليوم أن طبيبها لم يأتها، فلما أردت أن أعتذر لها عنه لم تصدقني، وقالت (الآن عرفت كلمته التي ألقاها إليك بالأمس) فسكت.. ولم أعرف ماذا أقول.

***

14th February 1851

Today Margaret's voice became extremely weak and I could not understand her. Her eyesight also became very weak; she was looking at me but she could not see me. Verily she gestured to me many times to open the windows of her room, so she could breathe easily. The windows of her room were already open and fresh air was passing through but it did not reach her.

O sir, woe, only if I had the power to sell my life so that I could buy for her some breathes which she could then comfortably take in and out of her lungs, or if I could buy for her some moments of sleep which she could then comfortably take refuge in. This is because her breathing was hurting and punishing me very severely. Verily three days have passed and she has not slept even for a little while.

***

15th February 1851

After a long silence in which she had not spoken even one word, she opened her eyes and called me in a weak voice and said to me, "I would like a priest, bring him to me." I realized that verily she has become firm in knowing that soon she will die. I started crying. I cried as much as Allah ﷻ wanted me to cry. Then I went to the priest. He hesitated when I mentioned the name of the lady whom I wanted him to go to. Then I begged and pleaded to him to come. I said to him, "O my dear father, certainly the sinners and the transgressors are the ones who are entitled to the mercy of Allah ﷻ." Then after some persuasion he agreed to come with me.

When he came, he spent some time alone in isolation with Margaret. After that he came out. I asked him, "Is Allah ﷻ going to show mercy upon her O father?"

He said, "Indeed she has lived a very sinful life, however when she dies, she will die the death of the righteous." Thus, I thanked Allah ﷻ for that.

Since that moment, I have not heard a single word from Margaret. Neither did I see any of her body parts moving. However, I did see that she was breathing in and out.

***

١٤ فبراير سنة ١٨٥١

أصبح اليوم صوتها ضعيفاً جداً لا أكاد أسمعه وأظلم بصرها، فهي تنظر إلي ولا تراني، وقد أشارت إلي في الصباح مراراً أن أفتح لها نوافذ الغرفة لتستنشق الهواء وتروح عن نفسها، ونوافذ الغرفة مفتوحة يجري منها الهواء متدفقاً، ولكنه لا يصل إلى صدرها.

آهٍ لو أستطيع يا سيدي أن أبيع حياتي لأشتري لها بضعة أنفاسٍ تتردد في صدرها، أو بعض سناتٍ من النوم تأوي إلى جفنها، فإن تنفسها يؤلمني ويعذبني عذاباً شديداً، وقد مرت بها ثلاث ليالٍ لم تنم فيها لحظةً واحدةً.

***

١٥ فبراير سنة ١٨٥١

بعد صمتٍ طويلٍ لم تنطق فيه بحرفٍ واحدٍ فتحت عينيها ونادتني بصوتها الخافت الضعيف، فدنوت منها، فقالت لي: أريد الكاهن فأتيني به؛ فعلمت أنها قد أصبحت على يقينٍ من أمرها؛ فغالبت عبراتي حتى خرجت من الغرفة فبكيت ما شاء الله أن أفعل، ثم ذهبت إلى الكاهن فتردد عندما ذكرت له اسم المرأة التي يريد الذهاب إليها، فضرعت إليه، وقلت له: إن رحمة الله يا سيدي لا يستحقها أحد مثل الآثمين المسرفين؛ فأذعن بعد لأيٍ.

وجاء معي فخلا بها ساعةً، ثم خرج، فسألته: أيرحمها الله يا سيدي؟

قال: إنها عاشت عيش الآثمين، ولكنها ستموت موت المؤمنين؛ فحمدت الله على ذلك.

ومنذ تلك الساعة لم أعد أسمع منها كلمةً واحدةً، ولا أرى عضواً من أعضائها يتحرك، إلا ما كان في صدرها يترجح بين الصعود والهبوط.

***

15th February 1851, evening time

Certainly, Margaret is in a lot of agony O master. I am presuming that she is undergoing the agony of death.

I believe no person has endured this kind of torment in their lives which she is enduring at present.

Now she is suffering so much pain. From time to time she screams so aggressively that her screams melt down the hearts.

Verily there came a moment in which her pain increased, she stood up screaming. She was standing on her bed. Then she opened her eyes and two big tears left her eyes. She sensed my presence and hugged me. She pressed herself against me tightly. She continued to hug me until her arms became tired and she returned to her state of agony.

***

15th February 1851, midnight

The matter passed and Margaret died. There was nothing remaining on her bed other than her corpse which would be taken to its grave tomorrow. This was her end consequence and the end of every living being. One can only be patient upon life's tribulations and on the decree of Allah ﷻ.

Indeed, in the last moments of life, she yelled out your name many times O master. Her last action in her worldly life was that she looked at me for a very long time full of sorrows. Then she pointed with her finger towards her diary next to her and she said, "Arman." I understood that indeed she was entrusting me with it; that I ensure the diary reaches you. Then she entrusted her soul to Allah the Almighty.

O my dear lady Margaret, the punishment which you received before your death, has been very severe upon me. Your death has been very hard upon me. I did not find next to you anyone who could close your eyes and put a sheet of blanket over you other than myself. This pure and honourable soul has departed in the way of Allah ﷻ that never troubled anyone, friend or foe. That spacious chest which could encompass the entire world including the earth and the heavens never became tight nor felt straitened for anyone. That clean and pure heart contained nothing other than good and hospitality. Nothing came out from her heart other than mercy and kindness.

***

١٥ فبراير ـ ساعة الغروب

إن مرغريت تتعذب كثيراً يا سيدي، وأحسب أنها تعالج سكرات الموت.

لم يقاس إنسان في حياته مثل ما تقاسيه الآن من آلامها وأوجاعها.

إنها تصرخ من حينٍ إلى حينٍ صرخاتٍ تذوب لها حبات القلوب.

ولقد اشتد بها الألم الساعة فهبت من مكانها صارخة، وانتصبت على قدميها في سريرها حتى كادت تسقط عنه، فأدركتها وأضجعتها في مكانها، ففتحت عينيها فسقطت منهما دمعتان كبيرتان، وكأنما أحست بي فاعتنقتني وضمتني إليها ضماً شديداً، ثم ما لبثت أن تراخت يداها وعادت إلى نزاعها وجهادها.

***

١٥ فبراير ـ نصف الليل

قضي الأمر وماتت مرغريت، ولم يبق منها على سريرها إلا جثتها التي ستذهب غداً إلى قبرها، تلك غايتها وغاية كل حي؛ فصبراً على قضاء الله وبلائه.

لقد هتفت باسمك كثيراً يا سيدي في ساعتها الأخيرة.. وكان آخر عهدها بالحياة أن نظرت إلي نظرةً طويلةً مملوءةً حزناً ودموعاً.. ثم حركت أصبعها حركةً خفيفةً وأشارت إلى دفتر مذكراتها الذي كان ملقًى بجانبها وقالت: (أرمان) ففهمت أنها توصيني أن أبلغه إليك.. ثم أسلمت روحها.

عزيز علي يا سيدتي ما لقيت من العذاب قبل موتك، وعزيز علي أن تموتي، ولا تجدي بجانبك من يغمض عينيك، ويلقي رداءك عليك سواي، وفي سبيل الله تلك النفس الطاهرة الكريمة التي ما حملت في حياتها شراً لمحسن، ولا لمسيء، وذلك الصدر الرحب الذي كان يسع الدنيا بأرضها وسمائها.. فلا يضيق عنها، وذلك القلب النقي الأبيض الذي ما أضمر في حياته غير الخير أو الإحسان، ولا فاض إلا بالرحمة والحنان.

***

Prudence cried next to the dead body of her lady as much as she could cry. Then she lit up candles besides her and called for the priest. The priest came, bowing down near Margaret's head, he started reciting something from his book. During this, Prudence walked towards the desk where she sat down and wrote the last account in her dairy. She continued to write until she was finished. Then she got up from her place frightened as she saw a shadow hovering upon the door of the room. Thus, she walked towards it only to discover that it was Arman dressed in white.

Indeed, when Arman walked in and cast his sight upon the location of the bed where the deceased was, he had a fit. Arman rolled his eyes back and accordingly he started staring at her again and asked, "Who is this person who is bowing down over her bed?" Thus, Prudence cried and did not say anything. Thus, Arman's bag fell from his hand, he became still neither talking nor moving.

Then, Arman rushed quickly towards the bed screaming. He wanted to throw himself upon the bed as well but Prudence held him and the priest stood in front of him. The priest said to him, "O young man, have some respect for the dead." Arman's tears remained buried within his chest and he was completely traumatised. In this state, he fell, unconscious. He did not regain consciousness until the sun had risen. That was the time when he realised that some people had come to take away the corpse. He stood up and collecting himself together, drew closer to the bed.

Arman said, "O people have mercy upon me, verily I lost the opportunity to say goodbye to her when she was alive, give me some respite now so that I can say my farewells to her in her death." The people felt mercy for him and created some space for him as Arman then drew closer to her. Arman lifted the veil from her face and kissed her forehead. Arman then said, "Goodbye O most honourable lady to me, goodbye O best lady on the earth and the most dignified soul of the heavens." Then he covered her face with that veil and moved back granting them the permission to take her away.

Arman walked behind her dead body crying and wailing. There were only three people walking behind the dead body, Arman, her maid Prudence and Duke Mohan. Duke Mohan was walking and reclining upon his walking stick and saying while crying and sobbing, "Today, I can see that my daughter has died in front of me once again and I am still living in the prison of life." Some women were also present at the funeral.

بكت برودنس بجانب جثة سيدتها ما بكت، ثم أنارت حولها الشموع وبعثت إلى الكاهن فجاء وجثا عند رأسها يقرأ في كتابه، ومشت هي إلى المكتب فجلست إليه تكتب آخر مذكراتها حتى فرغت منها، ثم قامت من مكانها فراعها أن رأت شبحاً ماثلاً على باب الغرفة. فمشت إليه فإذا هو أرمان في لباس السفر،

وقد ألقى من مكانه على سرير الميتة نظرةً غريبةً هائلةً كتلك النظرة التي تسبق صرعات الجنون، ثم استردها وألقاها عليها وسألها: من هذا المسجى على هذا السرير؟ فبكت برودنس، ولم تقل شيئاً، فسقطت حقيبته من يده، وجمد في مكانه لحظةً لا ينطق ولا يتحرك.

ثم اندفع إلى سرير الميتة صارخاً يريد أن يلقي بنفسه عليه، فأدركته برودنس ووقف الكاهن في وجهه، وقال له: احترم الموت أيها الفتى، فاختنقت عبراته في صدره وارتعد ارتعاداً شديداً وسقط مغشياً عليه، فلم يستفق إلا مطلع الفجر حينما شعر أنهم قد أقبلوا يحملون الجثة، فقام يتحامل على نفسه حتى دنا من السرير،

وقال: (رحمةً بي أيها الناس؛ فقد فاتني أن أودعها، وهي حية، فأذنوا لي أن أودعها ميتةً، فرحموه وأفرجوا له عنها حتى داناها، ورفع الغطاء عن وجهها وقبلها في جبينها، وقال: الوداع يا أعز الناس عندي، الوداع يا خير فتاةٍ في الأرض وأشرف روحٍ في السماء) ثم أعاد الغطاء على وجهها، وتراجع عنها وأذنهم بحملها.

ثم مشى وراء نعشها يبكي وينتحب، ولم يمش وراء النعش غيره وغير الخادمة برودنس، والدوق موهان، وهو يتوكأ على عصاه ويقول في ندبه وبكائه: هأنذا أرى ابنتي تموت أمامي مرةً أخرى، ولا أزال حتى الساعة على قيد الحياة، وبعض نسوةٍ بائساتٍ من ضحايا تلك المقادير.

The day had not passed completely but everything else came to an end. Margaret was placed in her grave and Arman became ill and bed bound. He was reading Margaret's diary and crying incessantly, like one cries when he loses his beloved.

Then after this, Arman's illness increased. Thus, Prudence did not see any other alternative but to write to his father explaining the state of his son. Accordingly, his father, his sister Susan and Susan's husband came. They stayed with Arman for a month counselling him and treating his illness until he recovered and was completely out of danger.

Then all of them went together to the grave of Margaret to bid her farewell before travelling back. They all cried besides her grave. However, Susan's sobbing was the most painful, she did not know that the lady she was crying over was the one who has sacrificed her life for her.

Then Mr Duval approached his son and said to him, "O my son, do you forgive me my sin?"

Arman replied, "Yes I do O dear father because Margaret had already forgiven you." Then they all departed.

***

Many days and many years had passed. Mr Duval had passed away and his son had succeeded in his life just the way his father had wanted. However, their remained a wound in Arman's heart which never allowed him to be at peace whenever it inflamed. So, to attain some contentment he would read Margaret's diary, he would talk and hear about Margaret from Prudence, and he would visit Margaret's grave from time to time.

The End

وما انقضى النهار حتى انقضى كل شيء، وأصبحت مرغريت رهينة قبرها، وأرمان طريح فراشه، يقرأ في مذكراتها ويبكي بكاء الثاكل المفجوع.

ثم اشتد به المرض بعد ذلك فلم تر برودنس بداً من أن تكتب إلى أبيه تشرح له سوء حاله، فحضر وحضرت معه ابنته وزوجها ولبثوا بجانبه شهراً يعللونه ويستشفون له حتى أبل ونجا من خطره.

ثم ذهبوا جميعاً إلى قبر مرغريت ليودعوها قبل سفرهم فبكوا حوله بكاءً شديداً، وكانت سوسان أشدهم بكاءً عليها، وإن كانت لا تعلم أنها تبكي المرأة التي ضحت بنفسها في سبيلها.

ثم تقدم المسيو دوفال إلى ولده وقال له: أتغفر لي ذنبي يا بني؟

قال: نعم يا أبتاه لأنها غفرت لك ذنبك إليها، ثم انصرفوا.

***

مرت الأيام وانقضت الأعوام، ومات المسيو دوفال، وسعد ولده كما أراد له أبوه؛ ولكن بقيت بين جنبيه لوعة معتلجة لا يروحها عنه كلما ساورته إلا قراءة مذكرات مرغريت ومحادثة برودنس عنها وزيارة قبرها من حينٍ إلى حين.

تمت

Completed,

(with the Grace of Allah the Most Exalted the Most Wise)

All praises to Allah ﷻ and countless Peace and abundance of Blessings upon our most beloved Master, the seal of the Prophets, most honoured and the most loved Prophet, the Messenger of Allah Mohammad, upon his blessed wives which are the mothers of the believers, upon his family, upon the rightly guided Caliphs and upon all his companions.

O Allah (the Ever Forgiver) please forgive our sins and accept this book in your Royal Courts from this worthless, despicable and most useless servant through the medium of our most beloved and most respected Shaykh ʿAllāmah Pīr Alāudīn Siddīqī Sāhib (Rh).

O Allah ﷻ please become Sufficient for us who is the most excellent in terms of Guardianship, the most Wonderful Lord and the most Remarkable Patron as you have addressed yourself to be for my teachers, my parents, my loved ones, my siblings, my wife, my children, my friends, my family and relatives, for the clan which I belong to, for all the Muslims from the time of Prophet Adam (Peace of Allah be upon him) till the very last Muslim to come, in particular for the entire nation of our most beloved Master Prophet Mohammad ﷺ. Āmīn.

ربنا تقبل منا انك أنت السميع العليم

O our Lord accept (this) from us, verily you are the All-Hearing, the All-Knowing

وتب علينا انك أنت التواب الرحيم

and forgive us verily you are the Most Relenting the Ever Merciful.

Crediting of the Merits
(Īsāle-thawāb)

As a reader or student, if you have benefitted from this book, then all praise is for Allah Almighty, who has provided guidance and strength to his humble servant.

First and foremost, we dedicate the **Īsāl-e-thawāb** of this book to our beloved Rasūl ﷺ, his family, companions and followers. Secondly, we pray for all 124,000 (approx.) Prophets (Peace of Allah be upon them all) before him ﷺ, as well as all his ﷺ cherished ummah.

We also pray that the rewards of this book continually reach all people mentioned in its Dedication and Acknowledgements, their families and their loved ones. May Allah ﷻ continually bless all of them, both dead and alive, Āmīn.

Special dedication

Qiblah Hadrat Shaykh ʿAllāmah Pīr Alāudīn Siddīqī Sāhib (Rh) (1936-2017)

Adding to that, Qibla Pir Sahib's late wife Shezadi Shamsu-n-Nisa Sahibah, the daughter of Pir Qasim Mohrvi (Rh) and his sister dear Mia Sahiba from Keighley, the wife of late Pir Abdul Ghaffar Ghaznavi Sahib (Rh).

Additionally, the reward of this book is also dedicated to my great ancestors Allah Baksh, Khuda Baksh and Kareem Baksh, along with their progeny.

May the blessings of this book also touch every Muslim, male and female, living or deceased. Finally, may Allah grant all Muslims forgiveness, from the time of Prophet Adam (Peace of Allah be upon them all) till the very last believer, Āmīn.

From Bradford, UK: -

My Grandparents Haji Noor Alam and Hajan Karam Noor, my Beloved uncle Abdul Khaliq and my beloved cousin Haji Qurban Hussain. Grandfather Faiz Alam, Molana Fardosi Ashraf Shah, Abbas Bahadur, Noman Khan, Mohammad Adalat, Haji Matloob,

Haji Abdul Ghani and his wife. Sarwal Ahmad Din, Sakina Bi, the Grandmother of my childhood friend Imran Iqbal and his uncle Abdu-r-Rahman Mughal. Haji Sharif (Shekhupur PK), Uzram Bi and her father Haji Allah Ditta (Kandor PK), Haji Allah Ditta (Mirpur), Haji Abdul Khaliq and Karamat Jaan (Mirpur). Sai Rangeela (Mirpur) and Sai Ashraf. Mohammad Pinnu, Khalid Hussain, Molana Gulnawaz Chisti, Hajan Sugra Bi, Sobea Tabassum Khan and Haji M. Bashir (sweet centre).

From Reading UK: -

My maternal Grandfather Haji Mohammad Yaqub. Great Grandparents Haji Mohammad Jee and Hajan Zara Begum. Grandma Fatima Bi. Haji Mohammad Bashir and his wife Maqsood Begum.

From Birmingham UK: -

Allamah Saeed Ahmad Bandyalvi (Rh), Haji Abdur-Rahman along with his wife Saidh Bi and their beloved son Mohammad Hanif (Kalghar PK). Mohammad Alam and his son Mohammad Sultan (Kandor PK).

From Nottingham UK: -

Mohammad Bashir and his sons Mohammad Jangir and Mohammad Zameer, Hamida Bi the mother of Nasir Pasha, Mohammad Rafi and his wife Farzand Begum. Khalifa Qamar and Khalid Masood.

From Keighley UK: -

Respected scholar and saint of Islam Pir Abdul Ghaffar Ghaznavi (Rh), Haji Sufi Mahboob, Mohammad Sarwal (Batly,PK), Haji Fazal, Nazira Begum and Mohammad Aurangzeb.

From Leeds UK: -

Mohammad Abdal, Khurshed Begum, Haji Mohammad Anwar and Haji Mohammad Gulfaraz.

From Blackburn UK: -

Grandma Fazal Begum, Mohammad Aziz and Mohammad Meherban.

From Dewsbury UK: -

Haji Faiz Alam and Haji Mohammad Bashir.

Additionally, from **Oldham UK,** Molana Bashir Ahmad Siyalvi (Rh), from **Peterborough UK,** Haji Fazal Din, from **Nelson UK,** Haji Mohammad Bashir, from **Brighton UK,** Stich Master Waheed Hussain.

From Pakistan: -

From Kandor:- (My home village) My beloved uncle and father in law, Haji Mohammad Bostan. Great ancestors, Allah Ditta, Mohammad Mishri, Pola Khan, Biya Bi, Ismaeel and Fazal begum. Mohammad Ladda, Fathe Alam, Karam Jaan and Mohammad Fazal Kandor (Sufi Allah Ditta Naqshbandi's parents). Khadim Hussain, Maitab Bi and Ashraf Bi. Mohammad Sawar and Fazal Begum (Mohammad Jamil's Parents). Sai Ashraf, Zeb Khan, Hayaat Bi, Fazal Ilahi and Maqbul Jaan. Farzand Bi (wife of Pinnu Khan). Jee Seda and Begum Jaan (Parents of Abdul Latif), and also Mohammad Hussain.

From Jabba:- Great Grandparents Haji Sayd Mohammad and Sarwal Jaan. Great Grandma Fazal Begum, also Aisha Bi and Zaiban.

From Kangar:- Farzand Begum (Haji Qurban Hussain's mother), Mohammad Yunus, Mohammad Ghafur, Mohammad Hussain, Akhtar Jaan, Mohammad Yusaf and Aziza Bi.

From Bewal:- Captain Pakistan Army Abdul Rashid, Master Anwar, Nazeera Begum and Zarda Bi.

From Dhir Kot, AK:- Sufi Mohammad Latif Hashmi the father of Molana Shawal Hashmi and Taskeen Hussain Showq Hashmi the brother of Molana Shawwal Hashmi.

From Sirai Alamgir:- Gulzar Begum and from **Ranja Dheri:-** Abdul Khaliq and Abdul Malik.

Final Thought

This book is a humble effort from a sinful servant of Allah ﷻ, who begs for your supplications for his world and hereafter. We pray that Allah ﷻ bestows His countless blessings and mercies upon all of us, through the tawassul of the Messenger of Allah ﷺ. May Allah ﷻ reunite us all in the next life under the flag of our most beloved master Prophet Mohammad ﷺ. Āmīn.

References

Books

- Mustafa, L (2006). *Al-Abarat (Arabic)*. Beirut, Lebanon: Ad-Daru-n-Namudhijiyyah. Pages 7-197.

- Kokar, A & Akhyarullah, M (Date of Publication unknown). *Al-Abarat (Arabic - Urdu)*. Lahore, Pakistan: Maktaba Daniyal. Pages 4-381.

- Rohi, B Dr. (2002). *Al-Mawrid - A Modern Arabic -English Dictionary*. 16th ed. Beirut, Lebanon: Dar El-Elm Lilmalayin. Pages 7-1255.

- Ahmad Qureshi, B Prof. (1994). *Practical Twentieth Century Dictionary Urdu into English*. Delhi, India: Farid Book Depot (PVT) Ltd. Pages 1-688.

- Hafeez Biyalvi, A (Translator) (2002). *Al-Munjad Arabic - Urdu*. Lahore, Pakistan: Maktaba Kadussiyah. Pages 29-1123.

- Thackston, W.M (1994). *An Introduction to Koranic and Classical Arabic*. U.S.A: IBEX Publishers, Inc. Pages 14-22 (Roman numerals).

Websites

- Luebering, J.E. (2007). *Mustafa Lutfi al-Manfaluti Egyptian Author*. Available: https://www.britannica.com/biography/Mustafa-Lutfi-al-Manfaluti. Last accessed 3th April 2016.

- Joynal, A - Research Scholar, Department of Arabic, Assam University. (2013). *Contribution of Mustafa Lutfi al-Manfaluti to Arabic Short Story: A Brief Study*. Available: http://www.iosrjournals.org/iosr-jhss/papers/Vol10-issue3/G01033437.pdf. Last accessed 12th April 2016.

- Zaman, A. (2006). *Every Act of Goodness is charity*. Available: http://mohiuddintrust.com. Last accessed 14th March 2016.

TV

- Documentaries aired on **Noor TV, Sky Channel 812**; information regarding Dhera Ghazi Khan (DG-Khan PK).

Glossary

جلّ جلاله: *Arabic text stating **Jalla jalāla-hu** denoting '**May His glory be glorified**.' This is one of the phrases spoken every time the name of Allah is spoken or written. Besides these phrases, it's two other counterparts are; (a) **Subhana-hū ta'āla** denoting '**Glorified is He and His Majesty**,' (b) **Azza wa Jalla** denoting '**The Mighty and Sublime**.'*

صلى الله عليه وسلم: *Arabic Salutation specifically used after the name of the Messenger of Allah Prophet Mohammad ﷺ specifying **Peace and Blessings of Allah be upon him**.*

(Dba):   *Abbreviation for the Arabic text stating; **Dāmat barakātu-humu-l-'āliyah**. This is a supplication meaning **May his/their sublime blessing ever endure**. This phrase is used for respected scholars and authorities in Islam who are still living with us.*

(Rd):   *Abbreviation for the Arabic text stating; **Radiya-L-lā-hu ta'āla 'an-hū**. This is a supplication meaning **May Allah ﷻ be pleased with him**. Or it could be an abbreviation to denote the phrase; **Radiya-L-lā-hu ta'āla 'an-hā**. This is a supplication meaning **May Allah ﷻ be pleased with her**. Either it could be the abbreviated Arabic text meaning **Radiya-L-lā-hu ta'āla 'an-hum**. In this case, it would mean; **May Allah ﷻ be pleased with them all**. These Arabic phrases are exclusively used for the companions of the Messenger of Allah ﷺ.*

(Rh):   *Abbreviation for the Arabic text stating; **Rahmatu-L-lāhi 'alay**. This is a supplication meaning **May Allah ﷻ shower His mercy upon him**. This phrase is used for respected scholars and authorities in Islam who have departed away from this world.*

'Allāmah: *Noun of exaggeration: Title given to a Most learned scholar.*

Āmin: *It is a word meaning **'so be it'** or it is the abbreviation of the Arabic text **Al-lā-hummā istajib la-nā** meaning **'O Allah Accept***

	our invocation.' This word is commonly spoken in congregations and in supplications in terms of acceptance and gaining virtues.
Dars-e-Niẓāmī:	Literal meaning; **Studies of Niẓām**. This is a traditional Islamic course; upon its completion a person attains the title of a Mowlānā/ Islamic Scholar. They are taught to analyse Arabic books and all the relevant sciences. Subject to course duration, relevant Quranic and Aḥadīth material is studied. This course is called Dars-e-Niẓāmī simply because its criteria was laid out by ʿAllāmah Niẓāmu-d-Dīn Sehālwī (Rh). Hence the word **Niẓāmī** references his name.
Hadīth:	The narration of Prophet Mohammad ﷺ. Aḥadīth is the Plural of Hadīth.
Haḍrat:	A respect worthy title given to a person with authority.
Ḥāfiẓ:	Title given to the one who has memorized the Quran.
Īsāl-e-thawāb:	Crediting of Merits.
Mathnawī:	Works of Mowlānā Jalālu-d-Dīn Rūmī (Rh), in the form of Persian Poetry.
Milādu-n-Nabī:	Birthday of Prophet Mohammad ﷺ.
Mowlānā:	Literal meaning; our leader, spoken for an Islamic Scholar.
Naqshbandī:	Follower of a specific Sufi code of Naqshband; the major spiritual order of Sunni Islam, working towards cleansing the heart from evil desires and temptations and to ultimately achieve, maintain and embed the constant remembrance of Allah ﷻ at all times. The word Naqshband is the compound of two words Naqsh and band. **Naqsh** meaning to mark, print, draw or to engrave (engraving the name Allah ﷻ) and **band** meaning to bound, close, knot or to fasten. Thus, a Naqshbandī would therefore mean a person who has engraved the name of Allah ﷻ upon his heart and upon his soul, and has bound it. So, when we say Naqshbandī we intend a person following a specific code in which his goal is to embed the name of Allah ﷻ upon his heart and

upon his soul. If a person has not attained that level as of yet we could metaphorically still address him as a Naqshbandī. The origin of the Naqshbandī Sufi order can be traced back to the 1st Caliph of the Muslims Hadrat Abū Bakr Siddīd (Rd).

Pīr: Persian word meaning **old man**. However, in Islamic society this word is spoken for a very learned old man, who is a guide for his people. Sometimes the meaning of old is eliminated and thus the word Pīr would indicate to a learned man who is a guide. The word Pīr is also spoken for a Sufi teacher and a Sufi spiritual leader.

Qārī: A reciter of the holy Quran who recites with the correct pronunciation.

Qiblah: Literal meaning; **direction**; often associated with the Kabah, to indicate the direction for prayer. Also, this word is used as a special title given to a very respectable person.

Qurān: The divine book which was revealed upon Prophet Mohammad ﷺ gradually over a span of twenty-three years. The Quran was sent by Allah ﷻ and was brought to the Messenger of Allah ﷺ through Ark Angel Gabriel. The Qurān consists of 30 chapters, which are made up of 114 Sūrāhs.

Sūfi/Sūfism: A Sufi is a practitioner of Tasawwuf/Sufism, a religious science belonging to Sunni Islam. This is a religious science, an art belonging to Sunni Islam in which a Sufi's goal is to maintain the constant remembrance of Allah ﷻ, elevating his spiritual rank to cleanse the heart and soul. It is a science to reform one's inner character, to make it like the inner character of the Messenger of Allah ﷺ. It is a science which has been derived from the Quran and Sunnah and has been acknowledged by many prominent scholars. There are many branches of Sufism, which in Arabic are referred to as turuq (plural) and tarīqah (singular). These include Naqshbandiyyah, Suhrawardiyyah, Chistiyyah, Uwaysiyyah, Qādiriyyah, and so forth. Tasawwuf/Sufism is a code which enables a Sufi to carry out his inwardly worship. The origin of the Naqshbandī Sufi order can be traced back to the 1st Caliph of the Muslims Hadrat Abū Bakr Siddīq (Rd). The origin of the Suhrawardī Sufi order could be traced back to Ḥaḍrat ʿAlī (Rḍ) through Ḥaḍrat Junayd Baghdādī (Rh) and Imām Al-Ghazālī (Rh). The origin of the Qādirī Sufi order could be traced back to Ḥaḍrat Pīr Sayyed ʿAbdu-l-Qādir Gilānī (Rh). Despite the fact, the Wahhābī/Salafī/Ahle-ḥadīth movement are against Sufism, their leading scholars Ibn-e-Taymiyyah and Muḥammad Bin ʿAbdul Wahhāb, have also acknowledged taṣawwuf/Sufism in their works.

Sunni/Sunnī: The original, largest and orthodox Muslims in the whole world. The followers of this movement are called the Ahle-Sunnah wa-l-jamʿāt. The Sunnis' follow the Quran, the Sihah-Sittāh books and binding consensus of the four schools of thought, (Ḥanafī, Shafaʿī, Mālikī and the Ḥanbalī). Laws are derived from the Quran, Sunnah, Consensus/Ijmaʿ and through analogical deduction/reasoning by the Jurist schools in order to derive verdicts for the welfare of the community.

The Sunnis' believe that the best man after all the Prophets was Abū Bakr Ṣiddīq (Rḍ) the first Caliph of the Muslim nation. Following him, the remaining three caliphs, ʿUmar bin Khattāb (Rḍ) second Caliph, ʿUthmān bin ʿAffān (Rḍ) third Caliph and ʿAli bin Abī Ṭālib (Rḍ) fourth Caliph. Subject to the order of their succession they hold their degrees of excellence accordingly. Sunnis' accept all the companions to be sound and that Allah ﷻ was pleased with them all, although they may have had disputes with each other. Although other movements and sects claim to be Sunni Muslims, the traditional and mainstream Sunnis are those Muslims who share all these qualities, beliefs and methods discussed. They also believe that the Messenger of Allah ﷺ has two states, human form and nūr/light. Through the power of observation given to Prophet Mohammad ﷺ by Allah ﷻ, he ﷺ can observe the entire mankind even after his departure from the world. Sunni Muslims consider the shrines of the Prophets, companions and the pious people to be sacred. They do not object to the celebration of the Milādu-n-Nabī ﷺ.

Taṣawwuf: A synonym of Sufism. (Read Sufism)

Tawassul: Intercession/Medium.